The Classical Music Industry

This volume brings together academics, executives and practitioners to provide readers with an extensive and authoritative overview of the classical music industry. The central practices, theories and debates that empower and regulate the industry are explored through the lens of classical music-making, business and associated spheres such as politics, education, media and copyright.

The Classical Music Industry maps the industry's key networks, principles and practices across such sectors as recording, live, management and marketing: essentially, how the cultural and economic practice of classical music is kept mobile and alive. The book examines pathways to professionalism, traditional and new forms of engagement, and the consequences of related issues—ethics, prestige, gender and class—for anyone aspiring to "make it" in the industry today.

This book examines a diverse and fast-changing sector that animates deep feelings. *The Classical Music Industry* acknowledges debates that have long encircled the sector but today have a fresh face, as the industry adjusts to the new economics of funding, policy-making and retail.

The first volume of its kind, *The Classical Music Industry* is a significant point of reference and piece of critical scholarship, written for the benefit of practitioners, music-lovers, students and scholars alike. It offers a balanced and rigorous account of the manifold ways in which the industry operates.

Chris Dromey is Associate Professor in Music at Middlesex University, UK.

Julia Haferkorn is Senior Lecturer in Music Business and Arts Management at Middlesex University, UK, and Director of Third Ear Music, a production company.

Routledge Research in Creative and Cultural Industries Management

Edited by Ruth Rentschler, University of South Australia Business School, Australia

Routledge Research in Creative and Cultural Industries Management provides a forum for the publication of original research in cultural and creative industries, from a management perspective. It reflects the multiple and inter-disciplinary forms of cultural and creative industries and the expanding roles which they perform in an increasing number of countries.

As the discipline expands, there is a pressing a need to disseminate academic research, and this series provides a platform to publish this research, setting the agenda of cultural and creative industries from a managerial perspective, as an academic discipline.

The aim is to chart developments in contemporary cultural and creative industries thinking around the world, with a view to shaping future agendas reflecting the expanding significance of the cultural and creative industries in a globalized world.

Published titles in this series include:

Arts Governance
People, Passion, Performance
Ruth Rentschler

Building Better Arts Facilities
Lessons from a U.S. National Study
Joanna Woronkowicz, D. Carroll Joynes, and Norman M. Bradburn

Artistic Interventions in Organizations
Research, Theory and Practice
Edited by Ulla Johannson Sköldberg, Jill Woodilla and Ariane Berthoin Antal

Rethinking Strategy for Creative Industries
Innovation and Interaction
Milan Todorovic with Ali Bakir

Arts and Business
Building a Common Ground for Understanding Society
Edited by Elena Raviola and Peter Zackariasson

Performing Arts Center Management
Edited by Patricia Dewey Lambert and Robyn Williams

The Classical Music Industry
Edited by Chris Dromey and Julia Haferkorn

The Classical Music Industry

Edited by Chris Dromey
and Julia Haferkorn

NEW YORK AND LONDON

First published 2018
by Routledge
711 Third Avenue, New York, NY 10017

and by Routledge
2 Park Square, Milton Park, Abingdon, Oxon, OX14 4RN

Routledge is an imprint of the Taylor & Francis Group, an informa business

Library of Congress Cataloging-in-Publication Data
A catalog record for this book has been requested

ISBN: 9781138203693 (hbk)
ISBN: 9781315471099 (ebk)

Typeset in Sabon
by Apex CoVantage, LLC

C.D.—to Helen, Millicent, and George
J.H.—to Ben, Emily, Lillian, and Dave

Contents

Figures

Contributors

Dawn Bennett is John Curtin Distinguished Professor of Higher Education and Director of the Creative Workforce Initiative with Curtin University in Australia. With a discipline background in music education and performance, her research focuses on the development of employability, including identity and graduate work. Dawn is a National Senior Australian Learning and Teaching Fellow and Principal Fellow with the Higher Education Academy in the UK. Through her current Australian Fellowship, which features a student employABILITY starter kit (http://student.developingemployability.edu.au/), she is rolling out a metacognitive model for employability with faculty and students in Australia, the UK, Europe, and the US. Dawn is Vice-Chair Australia for the International Federation of National Teaching Fellows.

Dr Anna Bull is Senior Lecturer in Sociology at the University of Portsmouth. Her research interests include social class, education, gender, music, embodiment, young people, and sexual harassment and abuse. She has published in *The Sociological Review*, *Cultural Sociology*, and *Action, Criticism and Theory for Music Education*. Her monograph *Class, Control, and Classical Music*, an ethnography examining classed and gendered identities of young people playing classical music in England, is forthcoming with Oxford University Press. Anna is also co-founder of The 1752 Group, a research and lobby organisation addressing staff sexual misconduct in Higher Education. Anna previously worked as a pianist, cellist, and educator with such groups as Scottish Opera, Royal Scottish Academy of Music and Drama, New Zealand Symphony Orchestra, New Zealand Chamber Orchestra, and Live Music Now.

Dr Marius Carboni is Senior Lecturer in Music Business at the University of Hertfordshire. He also lectures at City, University of London. He was formerly Head of Press and Promotion at EMI and Press Officer at Decca Records. Since 1995, he has run his own PR and music marketing consultancy, Carboni Media. Over the years he has worked with the BBC Symphony and Royal Philharmonic Orchestras, BBC Proms, BBC Radio

3, Bernard Haitink, and the Royal Philharmonic Society, among other organisations and ensembles. Marius has published on the classical music business (Routledge, 2011/16), having gained his PhD in 2010 at the University of Hertfordshire, where he now specialises in the music business and the creative industries.

Dr Chris Dromey is the author of *The Pierrot Ensembles: Chronicle and Catalogue, 1912–2012* (Plumbago, 2013) and has contributed essays and chapters to the volumes *Music in the Social and Behavioral Sciences* (SAGE, 2014), *British Music and Modernism, 1895–1960* (Ashgate, 2010), *New Makers of Modern Culture* (Routledge, 2007), and *Zemlinsky Studies* (Middlesex University Press, 2007). His articles have also appeared in *Tempo*, *International Journal for Contemporary Composition*, *Proceedings of the Third International Meeting for Chamber Music*, and *New Grove Dictionary of Music and Musicians*. He is currently completing an article remembering the achievements of Grupo Novo Horizonte de São Paulo (1988–99). Formerly of PRS for Music, he is now Associate Professor in Music at Middlesex University, where he teaches music analysis and applied musicology and leads BA Music Business and Arts Management.

Susanna Eastburn is Chief Executive of Sound and Music. She was previously Director (Music) at Arts Council England, Executive Director of the London International Festival of Theatre, International Promotions Manager at Music Sales Ltd (working with composers such as Judith Weir, Kaija Saariaho, and Esa-Pekka Salonen), and Artistic Director/Chief Executive of the Huddersfield Contemporary Music Festival. Susanna's particular interest is in supporting composers at different stages of their careers. In 2013, she was elected President of the International Association of Music Information Centres. Susanne is also on the Board of Birmingham Contemporary Music Group, Trustee of Trinity College London, and a member of The Queen's Medal for Music Committee. In 2017, she was awarded a Gold Badge Award by the British Academy of Songwriters, Composers and Authors in recognition of her support for the songwriting and composing community. Susanna is a keen chamber musician and plays the viola.

Julia Haferkorn is Senior Lecturer in Music Business and Arts Management and Programme Leader of MA Classical Music Business at Middlesex University as well as Director of Third Ear Music, the production company she co-founded to specialise in contemporary music and arts events. She has worked in the classical music sector for over 20 years, starting at Peters Edition, where she promoted the music of John Cage and Brian Ferneyhough, among others. In 1998, Julia founded the artist agency Haferkorn Associates, which she ran for 18 years. She has worked with such artists as the Arditti Quartet, Apartment House, Icebreaker, Matthew Herbert, Loré Lixenberg, and Ian Pace, setting up concerts and tours across the UK and worldwide. Julia carried out the Arts Council England–funded research project *Mapping Contemporary Music Activity in Great Britain*, and authored *The Composer's Toolkit* and *The Producer's Toolkit* for Sound and Music. Julia has also served as Co-Artistic Director of the British Composer Awards (2014–16).

Dr Sophie Hennekam is Associate Professor in Human Resource Management at Audencia School of Management in Nantes, France, with a specific focus on employability, identity, diversity, and the creative industries. She has a Master's degree in Psychology from the University of Utrecht in the Netherlands, an MSc in Diversity Management from Rennes Business School, and a PhD from the Open University in the UK. Sophie's most recent academic articles have appeared in *Human Relations, Journal of Vocational Behaviour, Gender Work and Organization, and Human Resource Management Journal*.

Dr Brian Inglis is Senior Lecturer and BA Music Programme Leader at Middlesex University, having taught previously at Trinity Laban Conservatoire of Music and Dance and the Royal College of Music. A composer and musicologist, Brian first studied at Durham University then completed his MA and PhD at City University London. His music has featured at international festivals ranging from the Huddersfield Contemporary Music Festival to I Kärlekens Namn, been broadcast on media ranging from BBC Radio 3 to Bayern 2, and has been released on Nonclassical and Sargasso, including his debut solo album, *Living Stones* (2017). As a musicologist, Brian works on twentieth- and twenty-first-century British classical and popular music, from Kaikhosru Sorabji to The Feeling, and focussing particularly on identity and genre. He is co-editing Sorabji's letters to Peter Warlock (Routledge, forthcoming), having previously published on solo/unaccompanied opera for *Music on Stage, Vol. 2* (Cambridge Scholars, 2016) and for *Tempo* and PRS members' magazine, *M*. Brian has also held positions with PRS for Music and Boosey & Hawkes.

Dr Brian Kavanagh is a Teaching Fellow in Digital Humanities at King's College, London. He holds degrees in Classical Music Performance (Trinity College, Dublin), Music Technology (University of Limerick), and Interactive Media (Goldsmiths, London), and has won several awards as a guitarist, including the Bach Gold Medal at the Dublin Conservatory of Music. He recently completed his PhD at Imperial College Business School, where he investigated how classical music performing organisations in the United States and Europe are responding to industry crises, specifically declining audiences for classical music, reduced funding opportunities, and technological change. Brian has worked closely with such organisations as the London Symphony Orchestra, Royal Opera House, New York Philharmonic, London Sinfonietta, Concertgebouw Orchestra, Detroit Symphony, and the Liverpool Philharmonic.

Glen Kwok has been Executive Director of the International Violin Competition of Indianapolis since 2000. He was previously Director of the D'Angelo School of Music at Mercyhurst College in Erie, Pennsylvania, where he was also Executive Director of the D'Angelo Young Artists Competition, which rotated annually between strings, piano, and voice. In 2010–15, Glen was privileged to serve as the first American President of the Board of the World Federation of International Music Competitions, based in Geneva. The federation is the international governing body of the world's foremost competitions in all disciplines. As a violinist, Glen received his Bachelor and Master of Music degrees from Indiana University.

Sarah Osborn is Director of West Lanvale Creative, a creative industries consultancy and project management company she founded in 2015. She was previously Chief Executive of the Music Publishers Association, where she was instrumental in establishing the first reprographic licensing scheme for schools in the UK, permitting the photocopying of sheet music. Following studies at Goldsmiths, University of London, Sarah spent the early part of her career as a music publisher, first at Faber Music, assisting Thomas Adès, Julian Anderson, and George Benjamin, then at Schott, where she managed the catalogues of Richard Ayres, Gavin Bryars, Gerald Barry, and Huw Watkins, among others. Sarah has been a Trustee of the National Music Council since 2013 and co-founded Music Network UK in 2016.

Dr Christina Scharff is Senior Lecturer in Culture, Media and Creative Industries at King's College London. Her research explores gender, media, and culture, and focuses on two areas: engagements with feminism and the politics of cultural work. Christina has published widely in a range of journals, including *Culture & Society*, *Gender, Work & Organization*, and *Cultural Sociology*. She is co-editor of the edited collections *New Femininities: Postfeminism, Neoliberalism and Subjectivity* (with Rosalind Gill; Palgrave Macmillan, 2011) and *Aesthetic Labour: Rethinking Beauty Politics in Neoliberalism* (with Ana Sofia Elias and Rosalind Gill; Palgrave Macmillan, 2017). Christina has also written the monographs *Repudiating Feminism: Young Women in a Neoliberal World* (Ashgate, 2012) and *Gender, Subjectivity, and Cultural Work: The Classical Music Profession* (Routledge, 2018).

Masa Spaan is a Concert Programmer/Curator and Artistic Advisor. Her priorities are to revitalise concert practices and to collaborate with festivals, orchestras, venues, and other organisations to create innovative, high-quality music programmes for contemporary audiences. To that end, she has worked in recent years with the Wonderfeel Classical Music Festival, Rotterdam Philharmonic Orchestra, South Netherlands Philharmonic Orchestra, Netherlands Chamber Choir, Classical:NEXT, Concertgebouw de Vereeniging (Nijmegen), and Huddersfield Contemporary Music Festival, among others. Masa gained two Masters awards: in Musicology and Philosophy of Art (Amsterdam, 2008) and in Music Programming (ArtEZ Institute of the Arts, 2013). She has also given talks and lectures at Classical:NEXT, ArtEZ Institute of the Arts, Splendor Summer Academy (Amsterdam), and Fontys School of Fine and Performing Arts (Tilburg).

Atholl Swainston-Harrison is Chief Executive of the International Artist Managers' Association. He studied music in South Africa before managing the Pro Music Orchestras and becoming Assistant Director of the Roodepoort City Theatre and Opera (Johannesburg). Atholl took on the role of Chief Executive of International Artist Managers' Association (IAMA) from 2000 after further study in London. He serves on several charities in his spare time and is a council member of the Royal Philharmonic Society. Atholl's duty as Chief Executive of IAMA is to implement board policy and to broaden the effective reach of the association in the interests of artists and the profession of artist management.

Foreword

Music, as a living art form, will always be subject to change and development that in any one moment could be experienced as "turmoil". For those of us involved in classical music there is a lot of change about: the habits of audiences in terms of ticket-buying and the way they listen to recorded music; how new audiences discover classical music and in what settings; the constant promises and opportunities offered by new technology that can be interpreted as threats to the status quo or whose possibilities may simply not be understood; the fact that those involved in classical music have themselves to convince younger audiences that there is something there of interest—audiences no longer necessarily come armed with knowledge and deep love gleaned from schooldays. All this and more, with business models being turned upside down for those who present, perform, or compose classical music. These interesting times could be seen as *so* interesting as to be debilitating, or they could be seen as exhilarating.

I prefer the latter. The fact that knowledge of classical music is no longer "mainstream" in terms of the public gives us an opportunity to glory in a new countercultural appeal and, in engaging younger audiences, to celebrate the heritage of classical music and explore the new. That's why this book is timely and important. In the midst of this sea of change we should observe what is going on amongst the eddies and see the opportunities to keep the art form alive and growing. This book explores many angles in this living debate, from the business of presenting, producing, and even talking about classical music, to the places in which it is experienced and the new life of the composer and the musician. In taking a snapshot of where we are, it allows those of us involved in the industry better to consider where we might go—and how.

There are many challenges here but much from which to take heart. I regularly hear new classical music in a pub in East London, with an attentive, young, and respectful audience and much discussion afterwards and between the music—as discussed here in Chapter 10. There is hunger and curiosity for music that demands attentive listening, and that is what classical music is. There are actual, and potential, audiences, but we may need to work harder and in different ways to get them. This book, then, is a timely opportunity to draw breath and look to the future—in an optimistic and hopeful way, but with knowledge that there is much for all of us to do.

—Alan Davey (Controller, BBC Radio 3, BBC Proms, BBC Orchestras and Choirs)

Introduction

Chris Dromey and Julia Haferkorn

In recent years, discussion of classical music practices has flourished in areas as diverse as business studies, sociology, philosophy, information and communications technology (ICT), cultural studies, law, and education. From Dawn Bennett's landmark study of the classical music profession, through assorted publications on the genre's economic and social situation, to organisations reflecting on their own identity and impact, the classical music industry is being studied from strikingly new and different angles.[1] Our motivation for producing this volume was the realisation that these perspectives deserved to be recognised for what they comprise: a vibrant field of enquiry with the potential to effect change, in both academia and the industry itself. We decided to take a deliberately inclusive approach, bringing together scholars, industry professionals, and practitioners to survey and scrutinise the classical music industry in a comprehensive but critical way.

The past decade has witnessed an outpouring of articles and monographs on the wider music industry, prompted by a parallel growth in its study in universities and recognition of its importance to the creative economy. Although classical music merits few if any pages in today's key texts—a shortcoming this volume looks to address—it is heartening that a new generation of researchers are adding to scholarship in the area and doing so in ways comparable to Bennett et al., for example, by investigating changing concert cultures, diversity, e-marketing, economics, and the cultural implications of orchestral programming.[2] Musicology at large can sometimes appear resistant to such changes in direction; nevertheless, we took inspiration from the ideas of authors such as Nicholas Cook, Julian Johnson, and Adam Krims on the place, purpose, and definition of classical music at the turn of the twenty-first century.[3] Thinkers who look to defend classical music or to modernise how it is perceived occupy a similar space to those who work each day to market and promote classical music. In other words, the line between philosophical and aesthetic discourses on classical music, and the impulses behind its marketing and promotion, is thinner than many imagine.

From this starting point it followed that to bring academia and industry closer together, to recognise a nascent musicology *of* industry, and to produce a volume with theoretical and empirical import were logical, optimistic, and related aims. Indeed, we do not accept the argument embraced by some commentators that classical music or its industry are in terminal decline. Nor do we indulge a common failure to distinguish between industries, wherein the classical record industry, and fatalistic views that sometimes encircle it, is allowed to speak for classical music's other sectors. Rather, by mapping the genre's myriad practices, *The Classical Music Industry* intends not only to raise awareness of the industry's mechanisms and dynamics, but also to voice and advance significant themes and debates. The volume therefore examines the central practices and theories that empower and regulate the classical music industry, drawing together different strands of enquiry in the contexts of music-making, business, musicology, and associated spheres such as education, media, and copyright.

The volume falls into three parts to articulate these themes. Part I, "Principles and Practices", takes a broadly practical perspective to explore some of the classical music industry's most important sectors and to assess how the cultural and economic practices of classical music are kept mobile and alive. Musicologist, composer, and former PRS for Music employee Brian Inglis draws on his experiences to evaluate the historical and present-day relationship between classical music, copyright, and collecting societies. Sarah Osborn's recent leadership of the Music Publishers Association informs her examination of that sector, outlining a similar debate to Inglis's to consider how political, technological, and economic realities have altered the publisher's role, their relationship with composers and retailers, and their attitude to risk. Scholar and former Decca Records manager Marius Carboni confronts two fields often perceived to be beleaguered—the recording industry and classical music itself—but rejects talk of crisis as he scrutinises how business models are responding to new formats, subgenres, and marketing techniques. Evolving responsibilities also underpin Atholl Swainston-Harrison's contemporary focus on artist management in a wide-ranging chapter that explains how different types of management agreements are negotiated and how they affect their signatories. Just as Swainston-Harrison's leadership of the International Artist Managers' Association offers a unique and authoritative outlook in his chapter, so Glen Kwok's presidency of the World Federation of International Music Competitions informs the next. Musicologist Chris Dromey joins Kwok for a chapter of theoretical and empirical import, chronicling competitive music-making historically and topically, and appraising competitions' efforts to innovate in light of thorny controversies, such as bias and musical judgement, that such events can provoke.

The focus of Part II is "Identity and Diversity" in classical music-making. Sociologist Anna Bull conducts an ethnographic study of several youth music ensembles to assess how extracurricular education can serve to reproduce the classical music industry's generally high levels of class and gender inequality. Studying female musicians based in London and Berlin, Christina Scharff also examines these and other inequalities as she addresses some of their less visible factors, for example, networking, parenting, and the subjective construction of "ideal" classical musicians. Dawn Bennett and Sophie Hennekam survey classically trained musicians in the Netherlands and Australia and critique employability in the profession, whereby various stages in a musician's career can force priorities and, indeed, identities to change, often abruptly. Brian Kavanagh addresses these same themes—engagement, adaptability, identity—from the perspective of classical music performing organisations; his chapter charts how digital innovation has disturbed the industry's fundamental logics, encouraging orchestras to reimagine themselves and to modernise access to classical music, for example, through video-streaming, media partnerships, and orchestra-owned record labels.

Part III, "Challenges and Debates", takes up related challenges in a series of chapters dedicated to debates that have long encircled the sector but today have a fresh face, as the classical music industry adjusts to the new realities of funding, policy-making, and retail. Describing a Composer-Curator initiative she spearheaded at Sound and Music, Susanna Eastburn considers composer-led enterprises and argues that for classical music to be a living (not merely "heritage") art form, decision-making and control should be shared more often with artists. Musicologist and artist manager Julia Haferkorn delves further into a similar topic, recognising the twenty-first-century trend of presenting classical music in nightclubs and other non-traditional settings and assessing its consequences for audience engagement, the classical concert experience, and perceptions of classical music more generally. In comparable ways, the concept of classical music's "curation" common to Osborn, Eastburn, Haferkorn, and Masa Spaan, whose chapter draws on her experiences as a concert programmer to define a mode of curation she calls "synergetic concert dramaturgy". Spaan exemplifies its principles in the context of her interviews with international festival organisers and artistic directors and such pioneering events as Rundfunkchor Berlin's *Human Requiem* and Dutch outdoor classical music festival Wonderfeel. Chris Dromey's closing chapter examines how BBC Radio 3 and Classic FM speak about the music they broadcast, evaluates three of classical music's contemporary debates (defence of its intrinsic values, critique of its contemporary practices, and its relationship with radio), and concludes by making the case for the rejuvenating potential of *public* musicology.

The order of chapters should not obscure the connections that can be drawn between them: that working in classical music can be hugely rewarding but also highly precarious (Bennett/Hennekam, Eastburn, Scharff); that the task of defining classical music itself is either inspiring or obliging scholars, musicians, promoters, and audiences to adapt (Carboni, Dromey, Inglis, etc.); that the industry is truly international (Kavanagh, Kwok/Dromey, Spaan, Swainston-Harrison, etc.); and that decisions about which platforms and formats are best for classical music and its consumers are no longer straightforward (Carboni, Kavanagh, Haferkorn). In these ways, we hope the volume will demonstrate that the potential for scholars and industry professionals to share and develop knowledge about the classical music industry is both exciting and, most significantly, achievable.

We are indebted to Dave Varley, Mary Del Plato, and Brianna Ascher at Routledge for the steadfast and patient support they have given us. Special thanks are due to Dawn Bennett, Natalie Bleicher, Anna Bull, Francesca Carpos, and Christina Scharff for generously reading and commenting on various sections of the volume as it developed. We owe a similar debt to Ananay Aguilar, Naomi Barrettara, Alan Davey, Tim Davy, Antony Feeny, Sally Groves, Annabelle Lee, Allison Portnow Lathrop, Mark Pemberton, Yvette Pusey, and Christopher Wintle. We are deeply grateful to all of the authors for agreeing to contribute to the volume and for tolerating our editorial nitpicking. Thanks are also due to our colleagues at Middlesex University, particularly Zuleika Beaven, Paul Cobley, François Evans, Peter Fribbins, Sareata Ginda, Brian Inglis, and Fiorenzo Palermo—their advice and understanding was crucial.

Notes

1 See, for example: Dawn Bennett, *Understanding the Classical Music Profession: The Past, the Present and Strategies for the Future* (Abingdon: Ashgate, 2008); Anastasia Belina-Johnson and Derek B. Scott (eds). *The Business of Opera* (Farnham: Ashgate, 2015); Fiona Harvey, *Youth Ensembles Survey Report* (Association of British Orchestras, 2014), www.abo.org.uk/media/33505/ABO-Youth-Ensemble-Survey-Report-App.pdf; and Natalie Bleicher, *New Music Commissioning in the UK: Equality and Diversity in New Music Commissioning* (British Academy of Songwriters, Composers & Authors, 2016), https://basca.org.uk/newsletter/BASCA_Music-Commissioning.pdf (both accessed 21 December 2016).

2 See, respectively: Sarah May Robinson, *Chamber Music in Alternative Venues in the 21st Century U.S.: Investigating the Effect of New Venues on Concert Culture, Programming and the Business of Classical Music* (DMus diss.; University of South Carolina, 2013); Sarah M. Price, *Risk and Reward in Classical Music Concert Attendance: Investigating the Engagement of 'Art' and 'Entertainment' Audiences with a Regional Symphony Orchestra in the UK* (Ph.D. diss.; University of Sheffield, 2017); Anna Bull, *The Musical Body: How Gender and Class Are Reproduced among Young People Playing Classical Music in England* (Ph.D. diss.; Goldsmiths, University of London, 2015); Annabelle Lee, *#Classical: An Analysis of Social Media Marketing in the Classical Music Industry* (Ph.D diss., Royal Holloway, University of London, 2017); Antony Feeny, *Notes and Coins: The Financial Sustainability of Opera and Orchestral Music* (Ph.D diss.; Royal Holloway, University of London, 2018); and Ingrid Bols, *Programming Choices and National Culture: The Case of French and British Symphony Orchestras* (Ph.D diss.; University of Glasgow, forthcoming).

3 See Nicholas Cook, *Music: A Very Short Introduction* (Oxford: Oxford University Press, 1998), especially Chapter 3; Julian Johnson, *Who Needs Classical Music? Cultural Choice and Musical Value* (Oxford: Oxford University Press, 2002); and Adam Krims, 'Marxism, Urban Geography and Classical Recording: An Alternative to Cultural Studies', *Music Analysis*, 20/3 (October 2001), 347–63.

Part I
Principles and Practices

1 Classical Music, Copyright, and Collecting Societies

Brian Inglis

Introduction: Copyright and the (Classical Music) Work-Concept[1]

Copyright and classical music have a symbiotic relationship.[2] Although copyright once simply denoted the legal right to copy specific documents, it achieves its fullest potential when it defines fixed, bounded, and original abstract entities manifested in one or more physical modalities. The description readily applies to (implicitly classical) musical works, which Lydia Goehr calls 'ontological mutants': a piece's identity lies neither in its score, for music is an aural medium, nor in any single performance or recording, for the same score gives rise to different interpretations; it is instead abstracted from the sum of *all* potential realisations.[3] These conceptions, then, rely on abstraction but also containment and association with a single individual: musically, the composer. Goehr coined the term 'work-concept' to encapsulate her idea, defining musical works as 'complete and discrete, original and fixed, personally owned units.'[4]

This theoretical framework is important because it corresponds perfectly with how modern copyright professionals routinely use the term 'work' to denote discrete units under copyright protection, be they musical, artistic, or literary. As Anne Barron has observed:

> Copyright law not unlike musicology operates with a conception of the musical artefact as a bounded expressive form originating in the compositional efforts of some individual: a fixed, reified work of authorship.[5]

Friedemann Sallis has identified a 'weak' work concept informing music composition before the French Revolution: composer-performers were seen as enacting a craft, and music was about events rather than ideas; process rather than product. This was overtaken by 'the era of the strong work concept' from the late 1700s to the present day, in which 'music conceived as "works" consigned to paper . . . emerged as a new concept that had a major impact in Western culture.'[6] Significantly, the newer concept acquired a regulative role, not only in terms of aesthetic ideology but also by influencing copyright legislation:

> In the early eighteenth century, publishing houses acquired copyright . . . insofar as sheets of music were produced. For most of the eighteenth century copyright remained so defined. In 1793, however, copyright laws were passed in France to transfer ownership away from publishers to composers . . . [reflecting] the basic idea that composers are the first owners of their works, for it is they who put the works in permanent form [by notating them].[7]

Goehr and others have traced the rise of this strong work-concept, which spread from France across Europe in the late eighteenth and early nineteenth centuries—a period in which the enduring productions of copyright legislation and Viennese musical life also flourished. The pivotal figurehead, of course, was Ludwig van Beethoven, who effectively elevated the musical score from being 'a more or less detailed map to being a full and complete representation of a work.'[8] Similarly, a composition was no longer mere craftsmanship but an autonomous work of transcendent art.[9] An emerging Romantic aesthetic accordingly emphasised, and valorised, originality.

This cultural *zeitgeist* engendered changes in copyright legislation that enhanced abstraction. New laws were enacted to extend protection to performances of musical works (the "performing right") in Prussia (1837) and the United Kingdom (Thomas Talfourd's Act of 1842).[10] The ideology of Romanticism *continues* to inform the regulative function of the work-concept: both modernist classical music and the rock concept of "authenticity" inherit elements of it, as qualities such as rebellion, shock, alienation, the transcendent power of the original, and the aspiration to art attest. The incorporation of popular musics into the ambit of the work-concept is particularly interesting—and, as we shall see, relevant to classical music. In nineteenth-century France, such styles were originally excluded from legislation, being considered insufficiently "original" or worthy of artistic or commercial status.[11] Because certain popular forms, such as Victorian ballads and Tin Pan Alley standards, divide labour between writer(s) and performers—a mode still evident in modern pop icons reliant on "hit factories" or shows such as *The X Factor*—they more obviously fit the work-concept template than, say, the group dynamic of later blues-based rock music, where the functions and boundaries of composers, performers, and indeed of the work itself, are more blurred.[12]

For popular music productions in oral traditions to acquire copyright protection, the tangible trace (in copyright law, the "fixed form") became the original recording. This required some abstract thinking on the part of lawyers and administrators to conceptualise the "work" underlying and separate from the sounds (a case of strengthening a weak work-concept). In the UK, copying the underlying works in musical recordings ("mechanical copyright") was first controlled by the 1911 Copyright Act, which led to the establishment of what became the Mechanical-Copyright Protection Society (MCPS, allied with the Performing Right Society (PRS) since 1998). Protection of copyright in sound recordings themselves was established by a court case that led to the founding of the "neighbouring rights" (i.e. non-authorial copyright) society Phonographic Performance Limited (PPL) in 1934.

As Ron Moy has argued, the evolution chronicled here has much to do with a general desire to identify popular music-based products with individuals, and the consequent necessity to construct singular authorial subjects.[13] More recent popular music forms, such as electronic dance music with its reliance on sampling and remixing, have posed stronger ontological challenges to the work-concept. Such issues will be revisited later in the chapter, which focuses primarily on the copyrights of classical composers.[14] It scrutinises how and why the PRS instituted a Classical Music Subsidy and removed it at the end of the twentieth century. The episode illuminates the roles of collecting societies, how the performing right is mediated in practice, and how socio-political shifts reframe copyright societies in general and classical music in particular. Finally, we zoom out to examine contemporary copyright challenges and debates, again nuanced by a classical music perspective. As in academia, the worlds of copyright and collecting societies are replete with acronyms and specialist terminology. Figure 1.1 therefore offers a glossary of some of this chapter's key terms.

Black box revenue or income—Sums received by collecting societies and publishers that are deemed unattributable to specific works or creators, and which are therefore distributed on an *ex gratia* basis.

Blanket licensing—A form of licensing used by collecting societies to offer licensees access to the entire repertoire of a society and its affiliates in other countries. In return, an annual fee is paid, often in accordance with a specific usage *tariff*.

General revenue—A term used by performing right organisations (PROs) to encompass licence fees paid by all their live and recorded public performance licensees.

Multiplier—A royalty enhancement system whereby specific factors determine a higher royalty amount. The simplest and most common factor is performance duration, but in certain contexts multipliers may result in a higher royalty rate e.g. for longer works (*bonus for length*), performances in certain locations, and broadcasts at certain times of day.

Point(s); point value—The mechanism by which royalties for specific performance usages are periodically calculated for distribution from a *revenue pool*. NB the term "points" as used here in the context of collecting societies should be differentiated from its wider use in the music industry to signify *percentage* points in contract negotiations.

Figure 1.1 Glossary of Specialist Terms Used by Collecting Societies and Musicologists

Public reception—When recorded and broadcast music is heard in public places, typically as "background" music, for example, via radio, TV, jukebox etc. in bars, restaurants, cafes, and shops.

Revenue pool (colloquially, **"pot"**)—An internal society account in which all licence revenue from a particular source or sources is held, pending distribution according to set criteria, for example, by dividing the revenue into *points* with specific *point values*. The pool therefore represents a totality of usages in a specific revenue section, rather than being divided into specific events or productions, in contrast with *straight-lining*.

Sampling—A common term with two discrete meanings: (*artistic*) digitally extracting a recording for use in another; (*statistical*) distributing royalties across only a selection of performances in a certain category, in contrast to paying 100% of reported performances (*census*).

Straight-lining—A system of distributing licence revenue whereby the fee paid for a specific event or production equates (after an administration charge) to the total royalty payable.

Subsidy—A boost to a specific *revenue pool* drawn from outside that pool; in contrast to a *multiplier*, where the enhancement comes from within the same revenue section.

Tariff—A set rate or formula for determining licence payments, for example, a percentage of box office receipts. Examples pertinent to this chapter are the "LC" (Live Classical) and "LP" (Live Pop) tariffs, as administered by the Performing Right Society (PRS for Music).

Work-concept—A term coined by philosopher Lydia Goehr to denote a regulative concept of musical composition, identified as emerging in the early nineteenth century. Its main predicates are the fixing through notation of those parameters of a composition considered most important, allowing it to exist as an "ideal" concept independent of specific performances. Intertwined with the development of (music) copyright law historically and internationally, the concept is ideologically linked with copyright protection, not least through common use of the term "musical work". Musicologist Friedemann Sallis differentiated Goehr's *strong work concept* from a *weak work concept*, identifying the latter as a more traditional paradigm that focuses on music as a performance event.

Figure 1.1 (Continued)

Collective Licensing: The Performing Right Society (PRS)

To administer copyrights, composers and their publishers rely on collecting societies to license music "users" on their behalf, from live and recorded performance premises and cinemas, to record labels, broadcasters, and, more recently, online entities.[15] Also known as authors' societies, or Performing Right Organisations (PROs) when performing rights are involved, collecting societies are typically national monopolies, linked by reciprocal agreements with affiliated societies across the world. The PRS ("PRS for Music" since 2009) was formed in 1914 with a committee of composers, authors, and publishers.[16] Composers were largely drawn from the popular and light music sphere, but classical publishers were well represented, including William Boosey and Charles Volkert (of German publisher Schott, among other publishers). Tracing the society's history three-quarters of a century later, Cyril Ehrlich argued that

> [The PRS], as it approached a seventy-fifth birthday, continued to serve the general public no less than its members. The former were provided with access to the world's music, easily and cheaply, while giving due reward to its producers . . . Among the members there was general satisfaction with the Society: an efficient alliance of interests, maintaining a reasonable balance between writers and publishers, [and between] serious and popular music.[17]

This Panglossian conclusion may not have been entirely inappropriate at the time of the book's publication, but, a mere decade later, members, management, the Board, and even promoters, would be at loggerheads—a situation that threatened to pull the PRS apart and, according to some, to decimate the composing profession in the UK. Let us now explore the primary catalyst for this explosive reaction.

§

To the Arts Council, it had been an 'enlightened example of musical patronage.'[18] To British Academy of Songwriters, Composers and Authors (BASCA) chief executive Chris Green its removal was 'the most terrible tragedy.'[19] To Terri Anderson (PRS's then Communications Director), its abolition was part of the 'slaughtering of a number of sacred cows' by a 'determined and unsentimental' chief executive, John Hutchinson.[20] To composer George Benjamin, its disappearance was 'the worst thing that has happened to classical music in my lifetime.'[21] One of many changes PRS made to its distribution policy at the end of the twentieth century, the withdrawal of its subsidy for live classical concert royalties was a high drama of cultural politics, bitter wrangling, unresolved resentments, and long-term relationship disruption. The voluminous textual trace left by the episode allows us to recount the facts of the matter and to examine some of the contexts and ideologies underlying participants' actions, responses, and debates.

What was the Classical Music Subsidy (CMS)? The origins of the mechanism that had acquired this label by the 1990s are hard to pinpoint, but its contexts are clear. The first is the enormity of the task facing all PROs in identifying all public performances of copyright music by any means within their given territory of jurisdiction; that is, licensing them *and* acquiring data to inform distributions of this "general" revenue. Recorded public performances—to the smallest shop or bar with a radio, TV, or stereo playing in the background—are arguably the hardest to identify. The impossibility of negotiating separate licenses for every work that might be used leads to "blanket" licensing solutions. In return for access to the repertoire of the licensing society and its international affiliates (that is, virtually all copyrighted music), users are charged according to tariffs for different types of use, creating revenue "pools". Likewise, the impracticality of having a direct royalty distribution from every licence fee paid to every work performed (sometimes called a "straight line") means that distributions of general revenue have always depended to an extent on ideological decisions. And while broadcasters are easier to manage in licensing and reporting terms, the issue of how to allocate, or subdivide, into multiple usage subcategories those large blanket licence lump sums paid annually by public broadcasters such as the BBC is inevitably a matter of collecting society policy.

This practical reality leads to a second, more specific context, which Ehrlich outlines:

> Methods of redistributing income within the Society had been discussed at least since the 1920s, when there was talk about compensating "serious work" as against "commercial music". It was also a policy long established by CISAC [Confédération Internationale de Sociétés d'Auteurs et Compositeurs, the umbrella organisation representing collecting societies worldwide] that societies should give preferential treatment to serious works when distributing royalties, usually by means of paying more per minute for longer works.[22]

As the end of Ehrlich's last sentence implies—although this has not always been appreciated—"serious work" is not inherently identified with classical music in this context. Nor is the "serious" intent necessarily located in the music itself. A PRS bulletin from the early 1970s that refined "general" distributions explicitly invokes an underlying principle to distribute according to the type of usage rather than the nature of the music used.[23] This implies less an appraisal of musical worth and more a value judgement about modes of engaging with music: rapt, undivided attention in the concert hall was deemed more serious than performances at dances, for example, and was rewarded with higher royalty payments, whether the composers were Benjamin Britten or The Beatles. Other factors influencing live royalties also tended to objective phenomena: number of performed lines adduced from notified instrumentation, duration, and concert hall capacity. Such an approach is echoed by international PROs today (see Figure 1.2 for comparisons), where the music's *scale and ambition* ('symphonic', 'complex', with more 'voices', longer duration) as much as its style is invoked to justify enhanced royalty payments. Indeed, the stylistic marker 'classical' is rarely used explicitly.

Framed in largely utilitarian terms, a 1978 article in the *PRS Yearbook* defines the Classical (serious) Music Subsidy and its rationale:

> Performing Right Societies across the world generally accept that, as the production of works of serious music involves a far greater investment of time and labour on the part of their creators than most of the more popular forms of music, and that as performances of such works are relatively few and far between, it is appropriate that the societies should adopt *preferential forms of treatment* for these works in their distribution of royalties, both in order adequately to remunerate the actual performances and also to encourage the continued creation of such works.[24]

SOCIETY	COUNTRY	Concert weighting? (Y/N)	Broadcast weighting? (Y/N)
APRA	Australia/New Zealand	N	Y (for broadcast works over 6 minutes)
JASRAC	Japan	N	Y (for broadcast works over 10 minutes)
APDAYC	Peru	N (but the government applies a lower rate of VAT for 'cultural' live events; believed to be equated with classical concerts)	N
ASCAP	USA	Y (events at 'concert and symphony halls')	N
BMI	USA	Y ('serious music concerts')	Y (minimum guarantee for classical music radio broadcasts)
PRS	UK	N (but higher licensing tariff for classical music)	N
GEMA	Germany	Y (dependent on instrumentation)	
TONO	Norway	Y (for 'symphonic/other large' works). A September 2016 update suggests weighting is focussed more on live performance	

Figure 1.2 Performing Right Societies' Distribution Weightings Benefitting Classical Music: Selective International Comparison[1]

SOCIETY	COUNTRY	Concert weighting? (Y/N)	Broadcast weighting? (Y/N)
BUMA	Netherlands	Y (complex weighting system which also depends on duration)	
AKM	Austria	Y (for 'serious music', dependent on number of 'voices' and duration, subsidised by Social and Cultural deductions)	
SACEM	France	N	Y (for symphonic music on TV)
SGAE	Spain	N (but higher licensing tariff for classical music)	Y (for symphonic music on TV, and on radio for 'serious music, opera, *zarzuela* [Spanish operetta] symphonic works etc.')
SABAM	Belgium	N	Y (for symphonic, chamber, 'serious music' on radio and TV)
KODA	Denmark	Y (for 'complex/score music'; also bonus for world premieres in Denmark)	N
STIM	Sweden	Y (in 2004 for 'complex/large-scale' works; weightings subsequently removed)[2]	
ZAIKS	Poland	Y (dependent on instrumentation)	Y (for broadcasts over 30 minutes)
TEOSTO	Finland	N	N
ARTISJUS	Hungary	Y (dependent on instrumentation, subsidised from background 'mechanical' [i.e. recorded] public performance collections)	Y (dependent on instrumentation)
OSA	Czech Republic	Y (dependent on instrumentation and duration)	

[1] Sources: PRS international market focus pamphlets and issues of members' magazine (*M*) volumes 7–12 (1999—2004); information checked, updated, and supplemented up to July 2017; particular thanks to the PRS (International Department) and for Harriet Wybor's generous assistance.
[2] Examination of the circumstances surrounding this decision would make an informative comparison to this chapter's chronicle and analysis.

Figure 1.2 (Continued)

Reference follows to a decision to create a specific revenue pool for serious music concerts with 'a reasonably substantial amount of revenue from other sources to be added by way of subsidy.'[25] In other words, licence revenues from all serious/classical music concerts in a given year were paid into the same pot, topped up with general revenue so that the distributable amount was more than 100% of gross collections, then divided up into "points" with fixed values for distribution purposes, weighted exponentially towards longer works and larger forces. Classical publishers and composers therefore benefitted not only through the subsidy, but also because of the pooling (which made royalties predictable) and weighting towards the more labour-intensive compositions. Instrumentation was not taken into account in allocating royalty points for radio and television broadcasts, but longer pieces were rewarded with a higher rate per minute ("bonus for length"), in accordance with the CISAC principle, as outlined by Ehrlich.[26]

How this dispensation disintegrated is a function of general cultural change and specific events in the 1990s. The previous decade saw publishing and recording companies incorporated into global conglomerates, invariably dominated by pop and other commercial musics and empowering these "majors" within the PRS. As Andrew Potter, then Chairman of the Society, remarked: 'PRS stopped being a gentleman's club and became a business.'[27] Signs of change are found in the 1988/89 *PRS Yearbook*, which described the abolition of royalty weighting according to instrumentation, and declared that a wider range of performances would benefit from subsidy via a new 'semi-classical' category.[28] A review of the broadcasting bonus for length multiplier was also announced, while additional notes made the pointed observation that 1987 had 'produced payments that were disproportionate in relation to those [payments] applicable to larger [presumably popular] ones'.[29] Significantly, the more neutral term *serious* music had become the stylistically marked (othered?) *classical* music. Attempts in the late 1980s to raise tariffs for live concerts of all genres were only partially successful, leading to a new live music policy in 1992 where both classical and popular concerts held at a list of several hundred 'significant venues' were guaranteed royalty distributions, subsidised from general (live) revenue.[30] This marked a shift towards parity of treatment, distributionally speaking, for pop and classical concerts; previously, only popular music events earning over a certain licence fee had been distributed, while *all* classical concerts had been eligible for distribution.[31]

The primary catalyst for a further raft of distribution policy changes was a referral—by the Office of Fair Trading (OFT) to the Monopolies and Mergers Commission (MMC)—to investigate the PRS. An OFT press notice referred to

> complaints made by composers of less popular forms of music that they were receiving inadequate royalty payments [and] lacked sufficient representation; [and that] the revenue distribution policies recently adopted by the Society [i.e. the 1992 live music policy] unduly favoured composers and publishers of more popular forms of music.[32]

Perhaps surprisingly, then, this was no flexing of the muscles of the majors seeking more power, but a revolt from "below". (The complainants are understood to have included classical composers, as the press notice, indeed, implies.) The PRS's voting structure has arguably tended to perpetuate financial inequality among its members by linking voting rights, and therefore influence on policy, to earnings.[33] Conducted in 1995, the MMC investigation reported in February 1996. Its authors called for a review of the live music distribution policy and alluded to the possibility of statistically "sampling" all areas of public performance (see Figure 1.1). They further commented:

> The classical music subsidy . . . has been in place for many years and appears from the evidence provided to us to have the broad approval of both writer and publisher members.[34]

The PRS's subsequent Distribution and Data Review became increasingly imbued with the ethos of cost-benefit analysis, concluding that 'we need to ensure that the resources we devote to collecting and processing performance data are in proportion to the revenue at stake.'[35]

On the subsidy itself, a PRS questionnaire divided opinion: 48% of members were found to be in favour of it, 48% against, and 4% had no view, to which the Board responded that it planned 'no action at present, and has noted this response.'[36] The reassuring tone soon became more measured ('the classical music-subsidy is now being re-evaluated'),[37] and in early 1999 a Subsidies Taskforce was set up to 'ensure . . . any support of subsidy payments will adhere to the MMC instructions . . . [in order to] distinguish clearly between distribution rules and cultural support and donation.'[38] By then, however, the die had been cast. In fact, a December 1998 press release had announced the phasing-out of the CMS and the implementation of the new live music policy.[39] In practice, this meant that the last major classical distribution under the old (1992) policy, with its 'significant' venues and fixed royalty values incorporating a full subsidy,[40] took place in July 1999; that classical concerts from the start of 1999 were "sampled", with only concerts generating a licence fee of £75 or more being guaranteed distribution, and sample rates decreasing according to box office value;[41] and that the subsidy was to disappear completely by 2001.

In amelioration, the PRS initiated a gradual escalation of the tariff ("LC") charged to classical concert promoters, rising from 3.3% initially to 7.3% by 2007, in order to maintain revenue in the live classical sector by increasing collections rather than supplementing them from other revenue areas.[42] (This is comparable with the current practice of the Spanish society Sociedad General de Autores y Editores (SGAE); see Figure 1.2). Additionally, a new £1 million fund to support contemporary music was announced, which effectively enhanced an existing committee that dealt with Donations & Awards, but which was soon branded the PRS Foundation.[43] While this money was available on application to composers and songwriters of any genre with a demonstrable need for support, the timing of PRS communications suggest this was intended to be understood as one way of replacing the CMS.[44]

Reaction, Counter-Reaction, and Debate

The first salvo in response to the withdrawal of the CMS came from a group subsequently known as the Classical Music Alliance (CMA).[45] A letter of protest was signed by Donald Mitchell (chairman of the Britten Estate and former PRS Director) and leading composers Harrison Birtwistle, Peter Maxwell Davies, and Mark-Anthony Turnage.[46] John Tavener and Paul McCartney, among others, were subsequently identified as supporters.[47] The letter rehearsed several arguments that would characterise subsequent debate: that compared with mainland European societies, classical concert tariffs were low; that the subsidy therefore brought royalties up to an appropriate (that is, comparable) level; that PRS members were insufficiently consulted; that the timing was poor (perhaps a reference to the press release issued just before Christmas); and that the effect of removing the subsidy on the UK classical music industry, especially 'young British composers of the future', was great relative to its cost and the lack of tangible effect on other members' earnings.

Two further arguments were added in a letter sent a week later by representatives of leading contemporary classical publishers.[48] The first was a utilitarian argument about the labour and cost of preparing performance materials (that is, scores and parts) for contemporary classical performances, and the consequent need for long-term investment that might never be recouped.[49] The second was that removing the CMS was 'the last straw' following a series of changes adversely affecting classical music, in particular the removal of the instrumentation multiplier at the turn of the 1990s, and the removal of the radio bonus for length in 1998.[50] Unrepentant, Hutchinson responded by defending the new system's greater fairness and transparency as a consequence of the straight line between collection and distribution of concert revenue;[51] the avoidance of problematic value judgements and differentiation between genres; the fact, based on the aforementioned questionnaire, that supporters of the scheme did not form a majority of the membership; and that the largest beneficiaries of the subsidy were not young British composers, but the estates of deceased composers and members of overseas PROs affiliated to the PRS.[52]

The Guardian newspaper also hosted the debate, with composer Colin Matthews echoing the 'last straw' argument,[53] and drawing a repost from Andrew King of pop publisher Mute Song:

> Once again the grandees of the world of classical music emerge from their rural retreats . . . The beneficiaries of this scheme [the CMS] have kept very quiet about it until, as a result of a widely supported effort

to bring the PRS out of its fustian gloom by updating its business practices . . . this subsidy . . . is to be removed . . . These people have always
insisted that only their value judgements, which are consistently self-
serving, have any merit.[54]

King's combative tone typifies a certain view of the classical music industry, problematises the sector's presumed claim to the "transcendence" of its
music, and points to broader questions concerning the genre's relevance and
purpose at the turn of the century (and, indeed, since).[55] There was an irony
in King attacking a genre that effectively gave rise to the musical work/copy-
right concept on which all pop publishers' business models rely. Nevertheless, the heightening of rhetoric continued when Hutchinson's provocatively
quoted a comment (attributed to Mitchell) from the MMC report—that 'the
moral basis for PRS "depended on its being perceived as fairly representing
the interests of every sector of the membership and serving impartially the
creators and their publishers across the musical spectrum".'[56] Aggravated,
Mitchell duly rose to the challenge:

> Turning his fire on me will not save Mr Hutchinson when he has to face
> the cultural and political fall-out from the assault he is leading PRS to
> mount against the very sector which founded PRS in 1914. The Soci-
> ety's creators must be turning in their graves.[57]

The very public debate soon migrated to the pages of industry journal *Classical Music*, whose editorial observed how 'the PRS has a long history of
upsetting its classical members', adding the context of the Significant Venues
scheme and the lack of financial rewards accruing to classical composition.[58]

The CMA sought government mediation, and a Select Committee hearing chaired by Labour MP Gerald Kaufman was held in mid 1999. Several
new ideas and observations were developed by the witnesses and their in-
terlocutors: that classical composers and publishers might form their own
collecting society to break PRS's monopoly, a prospect the Chief Executive
of Boosey & Hawkes considered unviable, however;[59] that new classical
music is disseminated overwhelmingly through infrequent live performance,
whereas more popular genres place greater emphasis on recordings and
broadcasts;[60] that the CMS contained anomalies, for example, that popular
works performed in classical concerts would receive it, but not vice versa
because the subsidy was awarded to licensable events, rather than to individual works. As Kaufman elaborated:

> In any kind of logic whatsoever, the internal PRS Subsidy is anomalous
> and unjustified . . . On the other hand, any kind of subsidy from the
> Arts Council or anywhere else is not going to provide an impulsion for
> performance in a way that the PRS subsidy has done.[61]

The rhetoric of taking money from genres other than classical music was stressed by those opposing the subsidy,[62] upheld by the Committee,[63] and even acknowledged by some of its defenders (such as BASCA), although the reality of this characterisation was, had been, and continued to be disputed in other quarters.[64] Nevertheless, the PRS's decision, and its right to make it, was condoned by politicians perhaps imbued with the government's contemporaneous "Cool Britannia" agenda,[65] wherein cultural advocacy and ambassadorship was associated with popular music, typified by Britpop, rather than with "art" music.

As the impact of the new policy began to be felt, attention was redirected to another of its controversies: the statistical sampling of live classical performances. Sally Cavender (Faber Music) tactically echoed the market-oriented rhetoric of the policy's proponents:

> [Statistical] sampling is fine for pop, but not for classical music. The system just doesn't meet the needs of our market segment. We don't want handouts—we want payment because our pieces are being played.[66]

A *Guardian* editorial in January 2001 even called on Culture Secretary Chris Smith to intervene—rather late in the day, given the Select Committee had concluded in 1999, observing that 'PRS's approach, which links box-office success to the likelihood of a composer being rewarded, will encourage a play-safe approach and discourage risk-taking.'[67] Faber's Richard Paine had already criticised the policy's unabashed commercialism, claiming it would 'inevitably favour the established and successful composers at the expense of the up-and-coming.'[68] Ironically, PRS had often made similar arguments to criticise the failure of the CMS to support living or young composers. It repeatedly quoted statistics on the percentage of subsidy paid to estates of deceased composers and affiliate societies, although some of those estates were quick to retort that such money was redistributed through schemes to support young musicians or new music.[69]

Analysis, International Comparisons, and Consequences

What are we to make of the above episode? What does it tell us about classical music, copyright, and British cultural politics? Composer and long-term PRS board member Edward Gregson now believes that the CMS 'emerged as a "problem" [because of] the increasing presence and variation of pop board members', who were concerned exclusively with financial "bottom lines".[70] Sarah Rodgers feels that while the MMC report did not threaten the classical subsidy directly, it 'opened a chink' in the longstanding settlement described by Ehrlich.[71] She believes that this allowed pop publishers, who had moved away from "gentlemanly" congeniality and towards a market-driven foregrounding of individual corporate interests, to argue away the subsidy by promulgating the "level playing field" argument.[72] The Arts Council's belief at the time that the 'view of PRS' General Council . . . [is] that the cultural consensus underlying the [CMS] has broken down' offers a broader context,[73] as do parallels the same organisation drew with the fact that its own funding for music had, until the mid-1980s, been directed exclusively towards classical music. To recall the start of this chapter: if popular songs were to be conceived as 'works', they could now be considered art; but British classical music, by the same token, was now effectively stripped of its transcendent artistic status and exposed, unprecedentedly, to the harsh realities of the commercial music industry.[74] In fact, the Arts Council advocated reorienting subsidy across many minority genres, couching the argument in instrumentalist terms to argue that 'investment in uncommercial repertoire—R&D expenditure—is essential for the long-term health of the music industry.'[75] The PRS did not adopt its suggestion.

A lynchpin of arguments in favour of the subsidy was greater parity with overseas affiliates, particularly in mainland Europe where most societies did (and still do) apply royalty weightings that benefit classical music (Figure 1.2), even if they are not always framed as such. Moreover, mainland European societies generally achieve higher concert licensing tariffs.[76]

Why did something that is politically possible in other countries become untenable in the UK? The enormous success and strength of the Anglo-American popular music industry looms large, both culturally and organisationally; Rodgers, for example, observes the greater regard other European countries pay to classical music traditions, be they long and unbroken or identified with national independence movements.[77] Similarly, PRS's voting structure is not replicated in other European collecting societies, where major publishers tend to have less influence. Since the 1980s, British political culture has tended to view classical music with suspicion: for some on the Left, its perceived elitism and lack of popular support can be problematic; on the Right, its hunger for public funding and subsidy compare unfavourably with the commercial success of popular music, coupled with the fact that, since the 1990s, some "classical" music has also crossed over (and been explicitly marketed) to become "commercial".

As for the episode's consequences: this chapter has so far documented a deep rift between the UK's classical composing and publishing community and its leading music copyright organisation. Some classical publishers and composers, however, defended the logic and, perhaps, the inevitability of removing the subsidy, not least PRS Chairman Andrew Potter (who also worked for Oxford University Press) and David Bedford (Potter's successor at the PRS). Others accepted the Board's decision but continue to believe, as Gregson argues, that 'support of classical music through distribution enhancement is justifiable.'[78] He continues:

> I tried to argue that . . . supporting classical writers and publishers in some kind of enhanced manner . . . would benefit the music industry as

a whole, as so many classically trained composers were, and still are, a vital part of the pop and media world. Sadly, that argument fell on deaf ears![79]

Discontent arising from the loss of the CMS was manifested both trivially—one anecdote tells of a classical publisher popping PRS-branded balloons at a sponsored classical event—and as a lasting blow to trust and confidence. A more positive outcome, recommended in civil servant Richard Hooper's review of PRS for Music in 2013, has been the appointment of a Classical Account Representative (Naomi Belshaw, 2014–16; Harriet Wybor since 2016). The role 'acknowledged the need to build bridges' with the community, as composer Gary Carpenter observes.[80]

For Rodgers, it is as much a matter of the "soft" skills of understanding the language and milieu of classical music as it is "hard" policy,[81] although she also talks of a transformation from royalties forming a reliable 'central plank' of composers' incomes to composers having to earn from parallel musical activities.[82] However, the flow of new entrants to the British composing community has certainly not dried up in line with some of the direr predictions of the CMA. If anything, the community is larger, and more diverse, than it was at the turn of the century. Rodgers, Wybor, and Gregson all acknowledge that conditions in the UK today make it very difficult, but not impossible, to pursue a career exclusively as a classical composer.[83] At the same time, classical music is now less narrowly defined than it once was, with a broader range of opportunities, particularly for collaboration. Wybor points to new priorities for PRS for Music in improving reporting and responding quickly and effectively to 'new forms of the market [with] simple and effective licensing solutions.'[84] One example is a new tariff for cinema simulcasts, introduced in 2013 to meet the growing popularity and value of live cinema relays of opera house productions.[85]

Copyright Challenges and Classical Music

Professional and academic discourses on copyright law and practice have diverged in recent decades in response to such technological and cultural changes as (unlicensed) digital sampling and the (illegitimate) online dissemination of music.[86] To borrow John Oswald's observation, cited by Simon Frith, 'the legal challenge of digital technology is . . . that it blurs the boundary between production and consumption.'[87] This also weakens the strong work-concept on which copyright relies. Frith notwithstanding, academic literature tends to be situated in an American rather than European context, which highlights a further divide: between economically-based property theories of copyright prevalent in the US (and to an extent other English-speaking countries) and the inalienable *droit d'auteur*, a concept closer to that of human rights that emphasises moral rights and is fundamental to European civil law jurisdictions. Ideological backdrops similarly range from

Ronald Bettig's explicitly Marxist perspective,[88] to out-and-out neoliberal capitalism, sometimes masquerading as quasi-socialist "sharing", to which we will return. Classical music is rarely explicitly considered in either industry or academic discourses.[89]

In terms of changing copyright practice, Lawrence Lessig's theories have been highly influential, being realised through licensing options that allow for different degrees of creators' control, as outlined by the California-based organisation Creative Commons.[90] Lessig's central premise is that digital technology and, relatedly, postmodern aesthetics have enabled society to recapture a kind of prelapsarian state of engaging with cultural products, rather than passively consuming them, as in the industrial age: RW (read-write) rather than RO (read-only) culture. Although Lessig's differentiation of commercial and "sharing" economies and his ambitions to deregulate amateur creativity and simplify copyright are laudable,[91] he appears to conceptualise musical creativity exclusively in terms of digitally manipulating existing commercial recordings. Lessig, and indeed others, have generally overemphasised the importance of (artistic) sampling, which, although prominent in certain genres, is not ubiquitous in mainstream rock and pop, let alone classical music. (Neither is it anything new conceptually, as the history of musical borrowings in classical repertoire attests.)[92] His perception does, however, further illustrate how far the public image of musical creativity has moved from the classical model of the individual composer notating scores in isolation.

Lessig has also recommended shorter copyright terms,[93] and a reversion to the pre-1976 US (non-Berne Convention) principle of calculating copyright duration from the date of registration rather than from the death of the author (the *post mortem auctoris* or "pma" principle).[94] This is a typical revelation of the conceptual split between property theory (copyright as a commodifiable, intellectual "product") and *droit d'auteur* (copyright as an individual quasi-human right, inheritable by descendants). Crucially, it discounts the possibility that in some genres, such as classical music, successful reception and dissemination might be achieved over decades rather than years. Moreover, given Lessig's hope to simplify copyright, it is hard to see this being achieved by replacing the simple "pma" principle with one that requires knowledge of dates of publication and potential renewals at work level. Indeed, the US copyright situation before 1976 was considered highly problematic in the industry.[95]

Lessig's manifesto, particularly concerning decriminalisation, implies great change, although his influential Creative Commons schemes have demonstrated their ability to coexist with, rather than overturn, extant copyright protection. Change more radical still was proposed in 2017 by the UK Pirate Party:

> Copyright should give artists and innovators the chance to make money from their work; however, that needs to be balanced with the rights of

society as a whole. We will work for copyright reform and reduce copyright terms to 10 years [from creation/publication] to balance everyone's needs.[96]

The party previously advocated a copyright term of 5 years from creation, renewable once. While European Pirate Parties generally present themselves as part of the radical left, the Deputy Leader of the Swedish Pirate Party (the original Pirate Party) revealed a nakedly neoliberal face when taken to task by *Classical Music* in 2009:

> *Classical Music*—Do you think that classical composers would be able to earn a living under this system [a 5-years-from-creation copyright term]?
> *Christian Engström*—They will have to adapt their business model, that is what it is like being an entrepreneur, running a company which is in effect what most cultural work is. If you can't make a profit from it, unfortunately you have to do something else. It is called a market economy and that is the way it is.[97]

Representatives of BASCA quickly pointed out that this would 'destroy the economic model of any collecting society' and therefore also the chance to benefit even from this limited term.[98] In the later UK manifesto, however, reference appears to be made to subsidising culture.[99] It is striking that countries that enjoy high levels of cultural and welfare spending, such as those in the Nordic region,[100] also have the highest popular support for Pirate Parties—perhaps implying that the Pirates' supporters believe a *social-democratic* model could provide an alternative to comprehensive copyright protection. Yet, states like Norway and Denmark offer basic incomes *as well as* publicly-funded commissions for their composers, with copyright income *on top* (which itself may be weighed towards serious music; see the policies of TONO and KODA outlined in Figure 1.2). For regimes where art music thrived without copyright protection, we must look not to modern social-democratic states but to older, feudal structures such as those of pre-modern Europe, where composition was predicated upon extensive ecclesiastical or aristocratic patronage.

Conclusions

Despite their obvious flaws and apparent lack of consideration for classical music, the critiques and proposals we have examined do highlight that a reductive approach to distributing copyright royalties risks exacerbating the flow of a large percentage of available revenue to a small number of recipients. Notwithstanding the specific nature and needs of a genre such as classical music, collecting societies must consider how this balance is managed if they are to retain the confidence and support of their stakeholders.

Anderson, indeed, recalls the 'founding concept of the PRS as a collective . . . [where] almost everyone got something.'[101] Distributions of "black box" income, framed by PRS in terms of "unlogged performance" or "special" allocations but abolished in 1999, once offered emerging writers modest but tangible financial support.[102] The social and cultural funding offered, and promotional work undertaken, by mainland European collecting societies have consequences beyond their immediate benefits to the recipient—not least, as highlighted by Michael Freegard, the achievement of higher licensing tariffs than those gained by PRS for Music, in part because of the greater public and political awareness such work enables.[103] Collective licensing will always be necessary for public reception and the majority of live performances, and will maintain bargaining power when negotiating blanket broadcast licenses. However, technologies that promise shorter, immutable value chains from music users to copyright owners, such as Blockchain, threaten to undermine the collecting societies' role, particularly in online arenas.[104]

These tensions throw the focus back on to value of collective copyright licensing as a collective. As writers collaborate across genres, and publishers understand that they face the *same* types of challenges that writers face, the benefits of the collective become more obvious, particularly for new entrants to the profession. Indeed, arguably the greater benefit is the equality principle, whereby all writers and publishers, irrespective of their experience or status, receive the same per-work royalty rate for the same usage category and type. This principle does *not* play out when publishers license music directly, for example, mechanical rights for most feature film and advertising usages, known as synchronisation or "sync" rights. The idea of new music, including (and perhaps especially) classical music, as a kind of R&D laboratory for innovative ideas that go on to benefit the mainstream has been espoused in many quarters, from the Arts Council to the Pirate Party.[105]

While this argument leans rather heavily on economic instrumentalism, it does at least support the concept of incentivising, and rewarding, work beyond the immediately popular or profitable, whether through direct public funding or internal collecting society distribution policies. The latter need not take the form of explicit subsidy from one section to another, as revenue pooling itself has a democratising effect. (This is still carried out to a considerable extent within PRS for Music, as with other PROs.) Some kind of emerging writer allocation, in the form of a minimum royalty payment guaranteed for the first years of membership, would help ameliorate distribution inequality and provide rudimentary support for new writers. The PRS actually operated such a guarantee, for the first 2 years of membership, as part of its unlogged performance allocation between 1992 and 1999.[106]

Copyright legislation has developed in tandem with, and in response to, specific times and places. For musical copyrights, the work-concept as developed in the early nineteenth century in the context of European classical music remains paradigmatic; it has proved remarkably adaptable to different forms and contexts. Although the work of Goehr and others means that the work-concept is understood in musicology, the idea's debt to classical music is insufficiently recognised in the music industry. After all, it informed part of the Berne Convention, a genuinely democratic and internationalist late nineteenth-century initiative whose precepts resonate today, even as they are challenged.[107] If copyright generally and Berne's principles in particular are to continue to thrive, a wider understanding of how they benefit individual creators (especially morally), and hence also those who appreciate their work, is important. As for collecting societies and other cultural institutions, the message of this chapter points to the need for acknowledgement and understanding of generic difference, in terms of language and support. This may go beyond the well-trodden pop/classical binary.

Consider, lastly, non-Western "classical" music, long positioned by Western writers and scholars within the realm of ethnomusicology or, even more problematically, "world" music. How should copyright societies across the world treat such music? In what ways should (and do) they distinguish between "their" and "other" classical musics?[108] What role, if any, should they have in encouraging, or incentivising, the development of such traditions?[109] These questions are pointers both to further research and towards a potential enriching of global cultural practice.

Notes

1. I would like to thank Gary Carpenter, Sarah Rodgers, Edward Gregson, Harriet Wybor, and Julia Haferkorn for their thoughtful comments that informed this chapter.
2. 'Classical music' is used throughout the chapter to denote art music (that is, music made primarily for purposes other than entertainment or profit) typified by a division of labour between composer and performer and achieved through the use of notation. The classical music referred to is implicitly Western; the first part of this definition could also apply to non-Western classical music, but not necessarily all of the second part. While the term is admittedly contested and polysemous, it (and its cognates in other languages) is commonly used in public with such meanings. For further discussion, see my article 'Vive la différence', *M* [PRS Members' Music Magazine], 12 (2004), 16–18.
3. See Lydia Goehr, *The Imaginary Museum of Musical Works: An Essay in the Philosophy of Music* (2nd edn; Oxford: Oxford University Press, 2007), 2–3.
4. Goehr, *The Imaginary Museum of Musical Works*, 206.
5. Anne Barron, 'Harmony or Dissonance? Copyright Concepts and Musical Practice', *Social and Legal Studies*, 15/1 (March 2006), 25.
6. Friedemann Sallis, *Music Sketches* (Cambridge: Cambridge University Press, 2015), 2–3.
7. Goehr, *The Imaginary Museum of Musical Works*, 218.
8. Goehr, *The Imaginary Museum of Musical Works*, 227.
9. Drawing on Carl Dahlhaus, Sallis discusses how 'Beethoven . . . claimed for music the strong concept of art . . . [for] an instrumental composition could now exist as an "art work of ideas" transcending its various interpretations.' Sallis, *Music Sketches*, 20. Nicholas Cook also links Beethoven's (Dahlhaus-identified) conception of music—an ideal, imaginary realm—to the composer's profound

deafness. See Nicholas Cook, *Music: A Very Short Introduction* (Oxford: Oxford University Press, 1998), 26.

10. See Friedemann Kawohl, 'Commentary on the Prussian Copyright Act (1837)' and Ronan Deazley, 'Commentary on *Copyright Amendment Act* 1842', in *Primary Sources on Copyright (1450–1900)*, ed. Lionel Bently and Martin Kretschmer (Arts & Humanities Research Council, 2008), www.copyrighthis tory.org (accessed 5 June 2017). France had already protected performances through the Revolutionary laws of 1791/93, as noted by Goehr.
11. Goehr, *The Imaginary Museum of Musical Works*, 219.
12. See also Jason Toynbee, 'Musicians', in *Music and Copyright*, ed. Simon Frith and Lee Marshall (2nd edn; Edinburgh: Edinburgh University Press, 2004), 126–8.
13. See Ron Moy, *Authorship Roles in Popular Music: Issues and Debates* (New York: Routledge, 2015).
14. Incidentally, classical (and all) performers have enjoyed explicit protection of their recorded performances as intellectual property since the World Intellectual Property Organization (WIPO) instituted the 1996 Performances and Phonograms Treaty.
15. Classical publishers usually require copyright to be assigned for its full term, although it can also be reassigned or fixed-term licensing agreements can be negotiated.
16. PRS, like other PROs, acquires control of the performing right through legal assignment, and shares royalties between music/text authors and publishers. This legal and distributive principle is also applied to the mechanical right by societies in mainland Europe.
17. Cyril Ehrlich, *Harmonious Alliance: A History of the Performing Right Society* (Oxford: Oxford University Press, 1989), 157.
18. Arts Council, 'Specific Comments on the PRS' Decision to Phase Out Its Old-Established Classical Music Subsidy', in House of Commons, 'Culture, Media and Sport Committee—The Performing Right Society and the Abolition of the Classical Music Subsidy' (1999), www.publications.parliament.uk/pa/cm 199899/cmselect/cmcumeds/468/46803.htm (accessed 17 November 2016).
19. House of Commons, Question 67 of 'Examination of Witnesses'.
20. Terri Anderson, *Giving Music Its Due* (London: MCPS-PRS Alliance, 2004), 132, 138.
21. George Benjamin, quoted in Stephen Moss, 'Used Notes Only', *The Guardian* (11 January 2001), www.theguardian.com/culture/2001/jan/11/artsfeatures (accessed 9 June 2017).
22. Ehrlich, *Harmonious Alliance*, 155–6.
23. See 'General Fees Distributions', *Performing Right*, 6 (November, 1971), 40–1.
24. PRS, 'How PRS Helps Serious Music', *PRS Yearbook* (1978), 66–7; emphasis added.
25. *PRS Yearbook* (1978), 66.
26. Concert performances attracted a similar bonus until 1988.
27. Andrew Potter, quoted in Anderson, *Giving Music Its Due*, 100.
28. *PRS Yearbook* (1988/89), 65. The new category explicitly included 'avant-garde jazz' performed to audiences 'there primarily to hear the music' in the context of 'undisturbed listening', echoing the society's 1971 terminology describing 'serious' music. Two years later, 'semi-classical' became 'light classical'. See *PRS Yearbook* (1990/91), 74.
29. The bonus for length for TV broadcasts was abolished in 1988; for radio it was retained until 1998. See *PRS News*, 27 (October 1988), 12–13; and *PRS News*, 49 (May 1997), 10.

30. This policy also abolished the 'light classical' category and is detailed in a supplement to *PRS News*, 33 (Autumn 1991), 2–5.
31. The 1992 policy was, however, amended the following year to allow classical members to be paid for performances at 'non-significant' venues on a claims-only basis. In parallel, the subsidy for popular concerts was removed, perhaps shoring up resentment from that sector towards the continuing subsidy for classical music. See *PRS News*, 38 (Autumn 1993), 2.
32. OFT, *Press Notice*, 54/94 (30 November 1994).
33. PRS for Music, "PRS Membership Categories", www.prsformusic.com/about-us/governance/prs-membership-categories (accessed 6 June 2017).
34. MMC (now the Competition and Markets Authority), *Performing Rights: A Report on the Supply in the UK of the Services of Administering Performing Rights and Film Synchronisation Rights* (February 1996), http://webarchive.nationalarchives.gov.uk/20111202195250/http:/competition-commission.org.uk/rep_pub/reports/1996/378performing.htm, Section 2.82 (accessed 17 November 2016).
35. *PRS News*, 52 (Summer, 1998).
36. See *PRS News*, 47 (Autumn 1996), 7.
37. *PRS News*, 52 (Summer, 1998), 18.
38. *PRS News*, 53 (January 1999), 3.
39. This dates the decision to remove the subsidy to that December's board. Only two of its members voted against the decision.
40. Which at this time boosted live classical revenue to the tune of 170% of receipts.
41. The threshold for guaranteed payment was reduced to £50 in 2000. Since 2004, all such concerts have, in principle, been distributable.
42. However, following a referral by the Association of British Concert Promoters to the Copyright Tribunal, the tariff was settled at 4.8% in December 2003.
43. The Foundation's funding model was also different, and less politically contentious. While Donations & Awards had been funded with a percentage of distributable revenue, the Foundation was, and remains, funded by non-licence revenue (essentially bank interest on funds awaiting distribution). See also www.prsformusicfoundation.com.
44. For example: the Foundation's announcement in July coincided with the final fully-subsidised distribution of classical concert revenue. See *PRS News*, 55 (August 1999), 1–2. Sarah Rodgers (former Chairman of BASCA's Concert Executive) confirms that 'creation of the PRS Foundation, at the suggestion of John Hutchinson, was definitely a gesture of compensation towards the disenfranchised classical members.' Rodgers, correspondence with the author, 5 July 2017.
45. See Andrew Stewart, 'PRS Under Fire From Classical Music Pressure Group', *Classical Music* (6 March 1999), 5.
46. See Donald Mitchell, 'Classical Concerts Income "Halved"', *The Times* (23 February 1999), 19. Other signatories included conductor Simon Rattle and composer/broadcaster Michael Berkeley.
47. See Stewart, 'PRS Under Fire From Classical Music Pressure Group'.
48. Trevor Glover [Boosey & Hawkes], 'From Mr Trevor Glover and Others', *The Times* (1 March 1999), 21. Other signatories were Chris Butler (Novello), Sally Groves (Schott), Martin Kingsbury (Faber Music), Ben Newing (Universal Edition), and James Rushton (Chester Music).
49. This was an (intentionally?) ironic echo of the PRS's own former view, as expressed in its 'How PRS Helps Serious Music' features, published annually between 1978 and 1988.
50. See notes 28–9.

51. That is, the total concert royalty equalling the licence fee minus an administration charge (20% as of December 2016). This is further divided, proportionately according to duration, between the copyright works in the programme. For more on "straight-lining", see Figure 1.2 and Moss, 'Used Notes Only'.

52. John Hutchinson, 'End of "Subsidy" for Classical Music', *The Times* (1 March 1999), 21.

53. Colin Matthews, 'Cough up, PRS', *The Guardian* (13 March 1999), www.theguardian.com/theguardian/1999/mar/13/guardianletters (accessed 8 June 2017).

54. Andrew King, 'Pay Scales', *The Guardian* (15 March 1999), www.theguardian.com/theguardian/1999/mar/15/guardianletters (accessed 8 June 2017).

55. See, for example, Norman Lebrecht, *When The Music Stops: Managers, Maestros and the Corporate Murder of Classical Music* (London: Simon & Schuster, 1996). Conversely, this air of fatalism inspired defensive apologias such as Julian Johnson's *Who Needs Classical Music? Cultural Choice and Musical Value* (Oxford: Oxford University Press, 2002).

56. John Hutchinson, 'Discord in Musical Fraternity', *The Guardian* (23 March 1999), www.theguardian.com/theguardian/1999/mar/23/guardianletters (accessed 8 June 2017).

57. Donald Mitchell, 'Oscars Won't Make Up for a Cut in Composers' Royalties', *The Guardian* (27 March 1999), www.theguardian.com/theguardian/1999/mar/27/guardianletters (accessed 8 June 2017).

58. Keith Clarke, '[Editorial]', *Classical Music* (3 April 1999), 3.

59. House of Commons, 'The Performing Right Society and the Abolition of the Classical Music Subsidy', Question 4 of 'Examination of Witnesses'.

60. House of Commons, Question 81 of 'Examination of Witnesses'. In the same report, see also: 'Memorandum submitted by the Publishers of *Classical Music*', Section 2; and 'Memorandum submitted by The Classical Music Alliance', Section 3.1.1.

61. House of Commons, Question 58.

62. This had been pre-empted in another part of King's letter: 'The classical music subsidy operated by the Performing Right Society has taken money earned from performances of works by other composers of all genres and types and given it to the rights owners of so-called "classical" works.' King, 'Pay Scales'.

63. House of Commons, 'Conclusions', Sections 42–3.

64. For example, the PRS's former CEO Michael Freegard, as reported by Anderson:

    UK writers and publishers saw deductions of all kinds (such as affiliate societies' social and cultural deductions) as 'members' money being taken': Freegard's standpoint was and is that the revenue collected by PRS 'was not anyone's money until it was distributed.'

    Anderson, *Giving Music Its Due*, 106. See also Matthews's letter to *The Guardian* (13 March 1999), which refers to 'unallocatable [general] income which would not, and will not, find its way to [other niche genres].'

65. Indeed, the transcript alludes to this term, along with its iconic representatives, Oasis.

66. Sally Cavender, quoted in Moss, 'Used Notes Only'.

67. 'Air on a Shoestring', *The Guardian* (11 January 2001). www.theguardian.com/theguardian/2001/jan/11/guardianleaders (last accessed 1 July 2017). This editorial is likely to have been penned by then editor Alan Rusbridger himself, whose interest in classical music is well documented.

68. Richard Paine, 'Young Composers', *The Times* (20 September 1999), 19.

69. See, for example, the enduring grant-giving programme of the Britten-Pears Foundation (www.brittenpears.org/grants, accessed 7 June 2017). Illustrating the swiftness and sharpness of change in the 1990s, PRS itself had formerly acknowledged that while the subsidised classical concert royalty section most

benefitted the estates of frequently performed early and mid twentieth-century composers, their publishers were 'thereby helped to invest in the new generation of composers who have yet to establish themselves'. *PRS Yearbook* (1986/87), 102. The point is made in every *Yearbook* from 1978 to 1989.

70. Edward Gregson, interview with the author, 8 September 2016. Gregson points out that in 1995, a third of the board were "classical" members, divided equally between composers and publishers. As of September 2016, only three publishers and one composer—Gregson himself—were identifiably classical.

71. Sarah Rodgers, interview with the author, 3 August 2016.

72. Indeed, Hutchinson told the Select Committee that it became clear . . . that hidden subsidies were totally inconsistent with the principles set out by the MMC . . . For a subsidy to be transparent, members needed not only to know how much they were contributing but to whom and why; within a confidential distribution system, that is just not possible. House of Commons, Question 87. However, less objective motivations have also been suggested. An industry anecdote tells of a prominent pop/media composer agitating pop music publishers to demand the Board abandon the CMS after a performance of a large-scale work of his had been classified "non-classical." In pondering this suggestion, the importance of personal relationships in the music industry, and the presence of strongly distinctive personalities, should certainly be borne in mind.

73. House of Commons, 'Specific Comments on the PRS' Decision to Phase Out Its Old-Established Classical Music Subsidy'.

74. That said, even under the previous consensual settlement, "serious" composers had been vulnerable to the market. As Peacock and Weir observed in the 1970s, 'there must be few professions who have to face up to the fact that their professional evaluations of their creations are so much at variance with the judgement of the consumer expressed in what the latter is willing to pay.' Alan Peacock and Ronald Weir, *The Composer in the Market Place* (London: Faber, 1975), 31.

75. House of Commons, 'Specific Comments'.

76. For a selection of rates, which reach as high as 12.5% of gross receipts (Belgium's SABAM), see PRS, 'Overseas Live Classical Concerts Tariff', M, 11 (Spring, 2004), 27.

77. Rodgers references the German term *Ernste Musik* (serious music), which is opposed to *Unterhaltungsmusik* (entertainment music). This opposition, as understood, has been associated with German-language collecting societies, notably the Gesellschaft für musikalische Aufführungs- und mechanische Vervielfältigungsrechte (GEMA), but is also a wider cultural-societal concept in German-speaking (and Nordic) countries. Rodgers, interview with the author.

78. Gregson, interview with the author.

79. Gregson, correspondence with the author, 28 June 2017.

80. Gary Carpenter, interview with the author, 8 June 2016.

81. As an example, a PRS scheme launched in 2004 to allow writer-performers to report for distribution performances in non-concert venues was entitled "Gigs and Clubs", despite all music genres, including classical, being eligible.

82. Rodgers, interview with the author.

83. The main challenges are a lack of money in the sector, the number of aspiring professional composers competing for limited resources (financially and in terms of identifying suitable performers). The latter suggests that potential professionals have not been put off by the former, although Rodgers notes that this is true only because of a context of lower (financial) expectations. Again, this is not entirely new: Alan Peacock and Ronald Weir refer to the supply of new classical music 'being "wildly" in excess of demand', given the 'limited nature of the market.' Peacock and Weir, *The Composer in the Market Place*, 162.

84. Harriet Wybor, interview with the author, 20 July 2016.
85. While PRS, like most PROs, does not control opera and other such dramatico-musical "grand right" performances directly, it does license secondary usages.
86. Professional and academic discourses tend to focus on recordings rather than scores, not because sheet music copyright is not infringed on the Internet (which simply provides a new and more convenient locus for the long history of sheet music piracy), but because, by its nature, such infringement is on a relatively smaller scale and attracts less publicity.
87. Simon Frith, 'Music and Morality', *Music and Copyright* (1993), 19.
88. See Ronald Bettig's *Copyrighting Culture: The Political Economy of Intellectual Property* (Westview: Avalon, 1996), especially Chapter 8: 'Intellectual Property and the Politics of Resistance', 235–45. See also: Siva Vaidyanathan, *Copyrights and Copywrongs: The Rise of Intellectual Property and How It Threatens Creativity* (New York: New York University Press, 2001); Lee Marshall, *Bootlegging: Romanticism and Copyright in the Music Industry* (Thousand Oaks: Sage, 2005); and Joanna Demers, *Steal this Music: How Intellectual Property Law Affects Musical Creativity* (Atlanta: University of Georgia Press, 2006).
89. A notable exception is Amanda Scales's '*Sola, Perduta, Abbandonata*: Are the Copyright Act and Performing Rights Organizations Killing Classical Music?', *Vanderbilt Journal of Entertainment Law and Practice*, 7/2 (Spring, 2005), 281–99. While Scales acknowledges some of the obvious differences between classical and popular musics, her US-focussed article contains a number of problematic generalisations and inaccuracies, of which the most serious is the claim that 'for their trouble, the PROs keep fifty percent of the money they collect' (p. 285). Average administration rates are nowhere near that high: see note 51 of the present chapter for PRS for Music's *highest* rate.
90. See Lawrence Lessig, *Remix: Making Art and Commerce Thrive in the Hybrid Economy* (London: Bloomsbury, 2008). For licensing schemes, see www.creativecommons.org (accessed 4 July 2016).
91. See Lessig, *Remix*, 254–72.
92. Surprisingly, Scales (see note 89) foregrounds this weak work-concept tradition in classical music, which has largely been overshadowed by the Beethovenian strong work-concept. See Scales, '*Sola, Perduta, Abbandonata*', 294. Quotations and other musical borrowings, including a kind of acoustic 'sampling', are indeed features of certain late twentieth- and early twenty-first-century approaches of a postmodern hue, from Luciano Berio to Michael Finnissy.
93. See Lessig, *Free Culture: How Big Media Uses Technology and the Law to Lock Down Culture and Control Creativity* (New York: Penguin, 2004), 292–3; also available at www.free-culture.cc/freeculture.pdf.
94. An enduringly democratic, inclusive benefit of the Berne Union is that any creative individual can generate a copyright simply by fixing their creativity, thereby acquiring legal economic potential and protection of moral rights for life and beyond (50–70 years or more in Berne jurisdictions).
95. See Peacock and Weir, *The Composer in the Market Place*, 163.
96. Pirate Party, 'Our 2017 General Election Manifesto', www.pirateparty.org.uk/sites/default/files/library/OpenManifesto.pdf (accessed 9 June 2017), [9].
97. Christian Engström. 'Q&A', *Classical Music* (6 June 2009), 17.
98. Sarah Rodgers, David Bedford, and Patrick Rackow, 'Tackling the Pirates', *Classical Music* (4 July 2009), 69.
99. 'Artists should be the focus of culture sector funding.' Pirate Party, 'Our 2017 General Election Manifesto', [9].
100. Nordic countries are often viewed as creative paradises by stressed, cash-strapped British composers. Iceland, Norway, and Denmark, for example,

provide lifetime income guarantees for composers and other artistic creators. Sweden replaced such guarantees in 2010 with long-term (ten-year) grants, awarded to a wider range of recipients. Daniel Carlberg (Föreningen svenska tonsättare [Society of Swedish Composers]), correspondence with the author, 14 September 2016.

101. Anderson, *Giving Music Its Due*, 137.
102. My own experiences as a composer member (since 1998) and former employee of MCPS-PRS (2001–07) support this observation. As an aside, when I first joined the society, it seemed to me an almost magical thing to be rewarded financially for the ongoing performance life of music I had *already written*.
103. See Anderson, *Giving Music Its Due*, 105–6. The rebranding of PRS ('PRS for Music' since 2009) was surely an attempt to increase its own public and political recognition.
104. For an explanation of Blockchain technology and the extent (and limits) of its potential to facilitate royalty distributions, see Jeremy Silver, 'Blockchain or the Chaingang? Challenges, Opportunities and Hype: The Music Industry and Blockchain Technologies' (Centre for Copyright and New Business Models in the Creative Economy (CREATe): 2016), https://zenodo.org/record/51326/files/CREATe-Working-Paper-2016-05.pdf (accessed 14 June 2017). At the time of writing, societies seem to view the technology as a useful tool rather than an existential threat.
105. Many examples from classical music could be cited. Perhaps the most obvious is how Karlheinz Stockhausen's experiments with electronic music informed more mainstream, popular music, including The Beatles, for example, the band's 'Revolution #9' collage. An anecdotal illustration of Stockhausen's (sometimes unwitting) influence on electronic dance music is found in Dick Witts, 'Stockhausen Meets the Technocrats', *The Wire*, 141 (November, 1995), 33–5.
106. The suggestion also has contemporary resonance with proposals mooted across the political spectrum to consider universal basic income.
107. Moreover, its initial 1886 signatories were not limited to European nations, but included Tunisia, Liberia, and Haiti.
108. An indicative example is the treatment of Indian classical musics by the PRS. Previously deemed non-classical for programme classification purposes, such programmes are now classified as classical, thereby accruing the higher concert tariff "LC".
109. Michael Church, indeed, identifies most of the world's classical music traditions *other* than Western as endangered. See Michael Church (ed.), *The Other Classical Musics: Fifteen Great Traditions* (Woodbridge: Boydell Press, 2015), 17.

2 "Growing a Forest"

The Changing Business of Classical Music Publishing

Sarah Osborn

Musicians intersect with music publishers daily. Superficially, this is obvious: students, teachers, and professional musicians spend much of their time learning and performing repertoire from the classical canon. Yet, the role of a music publisher is little understood because the transactional relationship that allows the supply of sheet music is just one part of the rich, multifaceted role publishers play in cultural life. To recognise their broader role, we must first look to the fundamental link between publishing and copyright. The latter is the bedrock of the business, and to recognise its principles, however nebulous they can sometimes appear, is to understand its inherent stresses, strains, and rewards. This strand of intellectual property law gives composers the ability to control how their work is used, and to be paid for this use. As with any kind of property, intellectual property can be sold (assigned) or rented (licensed). Ordinarily, composers assign their works to a publisher in return for a share of the royalty income.[1] It then falls to the publisher to find ways to generate revenue through, for example: the hire or sale of sheet music; licensing live performance; radio broadcast; "fixing" music to images in films, television, advertisements, games, and so forth (commonly referred to as synchronisation or "sync" rights); or encouraging music to be commercially recorded and/or streamed online.

Classical music publishing is therefore an inherently speculative business in which high risk can yield high reward. Ross Hendy (Managing Director, New Zealand's Promethean Editions) explains his approach as 'a perilous balance of personal taste . . . punting on music that I believe will engage the audience.'[2] The approach is straightforwardly capitalist:

> "Good" art will compete against "bad" art . . . ris[ing] above to create a natural supply and demand. This can, and must be, measured by popularity. The content or creator must outperform their competition. As a consequence, we have to be [arbiters] of taste, quality, and commercial realities.

Yet to "build" a catalogue, publishers must also consider and balance a composer's short- and long-term prospects: musical tastes come into and out of fashion; and a significant amount of time and money needs to be invested, especially in early-career composers, before their reputation is established. A publisher must therefore forecast the likelihood of achieving a reasonable return on their investment over a number of years. To minimise the risk, a successful publishing house will usually have composers at different stages in their career (not to be confused with age) and/or to fulfil a specific role or purpose, such as writing music for children or because they are active in the "sync" market. Such specialisms also help define a publisher's aesthetic although in reality catalogues frequently encompass a broad range of musical styles: Oxford University Press (OUP), for example, is renowned for its choral music but also has a rich orchestral and chamber music catalogue; at Boosey & Hawkes, Karl Jenkins, famed for wildly popular classics such as *The Armed Man: Mass for Peace* (1999), sits comfortably alongside Harrison Birtwistle, renowned for modernist works such as *The Triumph of Time* (1971–72); and at Music Sales, Judith Weir, the UK's current Master of the Queen's Music, is as much part of the publishing "house style" as Nico Muhly, Joby Talbot, and Ludovico Einaudi.

This is not to imply that the older generations subsidise the younger, although the historical ability of a household name such as Sergei Prokofiev or Benjamin Britten to provide stable revenue is naturally related to a publisher's attitude to risk when signing new composers. At the same time, publishers must plan well in advance for the expiration of a composer's copyright (that is, when their works fall into the public domain and private ownership ceases).[3] Finding and nurturing composers, securing commissions, generating performances, seeking exposure through recordings and broadcasts, and fostering an online presence are therefore essential parts of a publisher's remit. This quasi-curatorial role, coupled with building a catalogue of musical works, is the lifeblood of publishing. With copyright lasting for the life of the composer plus 50–80 years beyond their death depending on the territory,[4] publishers must have a continual pipeline of "in-copyright" works in their catalogue. An analogy cited by a seasoned music publisher once likened her role to being custodian of a forest. She would select young saplings for the forest and, with encouragement and nurture, they would grow into mighty oaks. The mature trees formed the backbone of the forest but would eventually die. Without a continuous planting cycle the forest would eventually disappear and the land become barren.

Once a work falls into public domain, a publisher can still hire and sell the work but is no longer able to collect any copyright-related income. For the publisher, then, it is imperative to maximise income from "evergreen" pieces,[5] in part to allow continued investment in the next generation of composers. To develop and guide composers, and to introduce their music to conductors, soloists, performers, and artistic administrators, is typically very time-consuming and labour-intensive. Additional costs, such as editing and typesetting scores and parts, have to be recouped from earnings before profit on a work is seen. Not every work written will be a masterpiece or even become part of the established repertoire. Although publishers accept this risk as part of their business model, each house typically has a very large number of works with unrecouped costs. In principle and, hopefully, practice, a much smaller number of income-generating works more than compensate for this deficit. In such an uncertain environment—where there are no guarantees of success, and numerous works are written each year—risk and reward must be assessed continually. Faith and trust between publishers and composers is therefore critically important. Indeed, a further nuance to the risk is the influence publisher has (or, typically, lacks) over the creative process itself. Composers tend to self-evaluate the success of their work; there is no true equivalent to the literary world, where an editor guides the publication process with their suggestions.

"Storm Clouds Gathering . . ."

Publishers have long assumed the role of *de facto* gatekeepers. Until the emergence of the Internet in the 1990s, publishers were the primary source of information about contemporary music and composers. In the way that travel agents held the monopoly for booking holidays throughout the 1970s and 1980s, publishers dominated access to new music, effectively controlling the number of composers in the marketplace. For a composer, then, the landscape was very simple as the correlation between being published and being successful was clear to see.[6] These facts explain why, historically, composers have viewed being signed to a publisher in great esteem, and why, conversely, resentment towards publishers grew. Today, the situation is very different. The perceived stranglehold publishers had over the supply chain has weakened and the Internet has given composers a shop window to the world, empowering them to bypass traditional publishing models (if they wish). This "democratised" space not only encourages self-publishing composers, whose websites promote, market, and sell their music, but also brings composers, artistic decision-makers (i.e. orchestra managers, conductors, and festival directors), musicians, and audiences closer together. The tools to produce, print, and distribute music also became easier and cheaper to access, as music-notation software such as Sibelius and Finale were adopted widely.

The late 1990s also witnessed the dawn of the "experience" economy, which manifested itself in music through a surging number of site-specific, immersive concerts. Often performed in non-traditional, small-capacity venues, such performances were antithetical to usual publishing models, whose economic feasibility relies on multiple performances in medium- to large-sized venues (to recoup expenditure for costly first performances). Savvy artistic programmers also spotted an opportunity in the disruption of the traditional publisher-composer relationship. To work with unpublished composers could complement the "experience" economy more readily than to pair with a published composer; to discover a composer whose world revolves around Kreuzberg or Dalston (fashionable parts of Berlin and London respectively) to create a project in an unconventional venue was, and remains, an attractive option—more attractive to many programmers than, say, offering another piece of music for standard forces by an established composer in a traditional concert hall.[7] The flexibility to offer "all-in" fee packages for such projects also simplified the deal-making process—or, viewed more sceptically, took advantage of composers inexperienced in negotiation and/or naïve about rights.[8] If the establishment was no longer seen as "cool", or even something to aspire to, then the stigma attached to being an unpublished composer diminished. Indeed, this process also coincided with a number of unpublished composers being appointed to positions in conservatoires and universities. While some have gone on to be published, at the time of their appointment Philip Cashian (Royal Academy of Music), Joe Cutler (Royal Birmingham Conservatoire), and Christopher Fox (Brunel University) were all self-published.[9]

The next event, indeed, was less specific to publishing but more profound: the "credit crunch" of 2007/08 and the subsequent global financial crisis further disrupted high-street and household budgets. With its large independent sector, music retail was particularly vulnerable, not least because space-restricted high-street shops could only ever offer a fraction of the publications that were actually available. Faced with rising rents, wages, and other overheads, and struggling to compete with prices and availability online, many retailers closed or diversified. In London, two high-profile casualties were Chappell of Bond Street, which after its takeover by Yamaha turned its focus to instrument sales, and the Boosey & Hawkes music shop, a presence on Regent Street since 1930. The trend was not confined to London or, indeed, the UK: towns across the country and abroad lost, and continue to lose, their sheet music retailers.

Publishers faced a dilemma: continue to support the remaining retailers, the historical lifeblood of the supply chain, or move into competition with them by growing Business to Consumer (B2C) selling channels to mitigate the aggressively lower prices of retailers such as Amazon. Inevitably, perhaps, the opportunity to cultivate a direct relationship with the customer prevailed. Publishers could finally harvest data to enable them to understand their customers and their preferences, aiding product development and marketing. However, the shift from a basic B2B (Business to Business) to a mixed B2B/B2C model put considerable strain on the relationship between publishers and retailers. Accusations were rife that publishers were abandoning the sector, and retailers pushed for more generous trading terms to compensate.[10] Despite attempts by the Music Publishers Association (MPA) to work with the Music Industries Association and its members, suspicions that publishers could, and should, have done more to halt the sector's decline were prevalent throughout the 2000s.

Illegitimate online alternatives to traditional retail represent a further threat to publishers. Exemplified in public consciousness by websites such as Pirate Bay—a website popular for recordings and films but which also facilitates the illegal sharing of sheet music—a greater threat to sheet music publishers is the International Music Score Library Project (IMSLP), which bills itself as a 'community-built library of public domain sheet music [that] *strives to* comply with Canadian copyright laws.'[11] Meeting this objective requires *users* to understand public domain and non-public domain thresholds and, more crucially, to distinguish between graphic rights and the right in the musical work itself, often referred to as the underlying right. In the UK, the graphic right subsists until 25 years after the date of publication, hence it is common for printed editions to be in copyright even if the constituent musical work is not. A parallel here can be drawn with YouTube, which belatedly agreed to its responsibility to be licensed on behalf of its users, accepting that it impractical for either the user or the copyright owner to have a direct licensing relationship for user-generated content (UGC). Such sites still rely on a "take-down" system, effectively shifting responsibility for policing UGC to the copyright holder. Legally, there is no difference between a music teacher inadvertently uploading an in-copyright score to IMSLP and profit-making websites operating under "safe harbour" laws that exist to protect such accidental copyright infringers.[12] The music industry continues to lobby the EU to close what it considers a loophole.[13]

"Branching Out . . ."

The confluence of these challenges impelled publishers to respond. Recognising they were losing the battle to educate the public about copyright law, the music industry resolved to do more to promote legal (i.e. licensed) alternatives. This has been most successful in the recorded sector, for example, Spotify, but sheet music is yet to find a comprehensive solution. The MPA took a significant step forward in 2013 by establishing a Schools Printed Music Licence, which permits (under certain conditions) the copying of sheet music for use in a school. By legitimising a longstanding and prevalent area of infringement, a new income stream was opened up that enabled publishers to be compensated for income lost from primary sales. These efforts have been made against the backdrop of a UK government and EU reviews of copyright in 2011 and 2013 respectively.[14] The UK music industry argued that copyright itself was not broken, and that no single step in evolution of formats (e.g. sheet music, gramophone, LPs, cassettes, CDs, downloads, streaming) had compelled law to be rewritten, but that a more robust and simpler framework for enforcement and licensing were required.[15] Yet, with copyright reform mooted, uncertainty reigned. Publishers feared that any changes would harm them (and, by extension, the composers they represent), with government dazzled by the tech "giants", who, it was perceived, believed copyright law limited growth. Publishers became more cautious with new signings, which only further encouraged composers to self-publish.

Similarly, the rise of the freelancer—managers, editors, website designers, social media marketers—and the accompanying "gig" economy has allowed composers to handpick their support team, bypassing (through choice or otherwise) the services a publisher can provide or facilitate. Although this requires composers to bear and manage such costs, publishers have responded with a range of "hybrid" models to try to tap into this scene. The New York branch of Boosey & Hawkes took the lead, setting up an "Emerging Composers" scheme in 2008.[16] Its try-before-you-buy approach offered composers the opportunity to work with a publisher without locking either side into a long-term deal. Although no longer active, the scheme's alumni include Anna Clyne, who has achieved international performances, recordings, and a full-service publishing agreement.[17] Across town, Norman Ryan (Vice President, Composers & Repertoire, European American Music) was working on something even more ambitious: Project Schott New York (PSNY) was the first digital music publishing edition to be developed by a major music publishing house. The initiative put composers in the driving seat, allowing them to curate media-rich resources for programmers to explore, and to manage their own publication schedule. Its roster currently includes over fifty composers.[18] In Europe, Ricordi Berlin launched RicordiLab—essentially a composition competition, with open-call invitations issued to emerging composers to submit scores for consideration by a panel of experts, the reward being an initial three-year association with the publishing house.[19] Such transparency around signing composers was, and remains, rare.

The days of composers completing their academic studies before participating in such "emerging composer" schemes as the London Symphony Orchestra's Panufnik scheme or the London Sinfonietta's Blue Touch Paper project to help secure a publishing deal seemed distant.[20] Indeed, the tide had begun to turn in the 1990s, when many prominent composers were quietly dropped by their publishers and had to seek new publishing arrangements (University of York Music Press was founded in 1995 to provide a home for such composers).[21] With cuts to public subsidies via the Arts Council rife, less money also had to stretch further. For composers at the start of their career, the prospect of sharing with a publisher the little money that was available for projects made a publishing agreement less attractive; others preferred not to "sign away" control of their copyrights, viewing that path as contrary to the new "freedom" of digital. Composers began to actively question the very benefits of being published. Graham Fitkin is an interesting example of someone who found a middle way, working with a publisher for his orchestral works and publishing smaller pieces himself, as he declared:

> Nowadays it is very feasible to distribute music over the web, and of course do all the other things associated with it, score setting, recording, liaising with geographically separate musicians etc. that I tend to be

involved in it all. In the past you'd need to get a photographer, printer, designer, someone to set the music, etc. and now (unfortunately!) you can do it all yourself.[22]

A related factor was the rise of co-commissions. By the mid 2000s, the costs for commissioning a new work had become increasingly untenable for a single organisation to cover. In any commission scenario the composer's commission fee is one of several costs, which also include the licence required to cover performing right fees and the purchase or hire of the music from the publisher (which itself includes a surcharge for giving the premiere performance, and often involves a further contribution towards the editorial and production costs of manufacturing the score and parts). Extra rehearsals are often needed due to the unfamiliarity of the music and, depending on the instrumentation, further costs can be incurred to hire specific instruments or musicians. The issue is particularly acute for large-scale works such as orchestral pieces or operas, so to offset such costs organisations began to collaborate by forming consortia to share the cost. As well as minimising expenditure, the work is also given the best possible start by receiving multiple performances, often across different continents. This approach to commissioning new work is now embedded in the new music scene and is frequently a stipulation or prerequisite of funding. This shift, however, has not been trouble-free. Co-commissions have both shrunk the market, resulting in fewer commissions and projects overall, and contributed to the prevalence of composers being dropped and the industry's underlying sense of precariousness.

The collapse of United Music Publishers (UMP) in early 2014 was a stark reminder of the sector's fragility.[23] The acquisition by Music Sales (owned by Robert Wise and family) of one of the most prominent catalogues it distributed, Alphonse Leduc, ultimately rendered UMP financially unviable. Leduc followed other historic names in classical music—Schirmer (1986), Chester Music (1988), Novello (1993), Rhinegold Education (2010), and Chant du Monde (2016)—in being subsumed into this giant publishing house. But Music Sales was not alone in eyeing expansion: Universal Music Publishing was also making moves to bolster its presence in the classical music market. Editio Musica Budapest was sold to Universal in 2006; the Italian Ricordi group of companies and French Editions Durand-Salabert-Eschig (itself a composite of three previously independent catalogues) followed a year later. Independent stalwart Boosey & Hawkes was sold in 2008, becoming part of a new publishing group that later expanded to include Rodgers & Hammerstein. In 2017 it was sold again to Concord Bicycle Music, a large US independent recorded music and publishing company. In a few short years, some of the most longstanding and respected publishers had been sold or acquired, changing the ownership landscape forever.

As Helen Wallace describes in her history of Boosey & Hawkes, the period after the turn of the twenty-first century saw a 'world [that] was shrinking:

music publishers were under pressure and needed each other to keep afloat. The buzz words were "outsourcing" and "exploiting synergies".'[24] Besides increasing market share through acquisition, strategic partnerships grew in prevalence in a bid to reduce duplication, share expertise, and lower overheads (a trend, as we have seen, that continues today). Boosey & Hawkes entered into a strategic partnership with Schott Music in 2004, outsourcing sales, marketing, and distribution (of the former's print catalogue) in exchange for royalty processing and copyright control services. Schott has likewise enjoyed longstanding cooperation with Universal Edition, jointly publishing the Wiener Urtext Edition since the 1970s, as well as sharing offices for their respective outposts in London and providing reciprocal hire library and copyright services in mainland Europe. A joint publishing programme also operates between Faber Music and Edition Peters, who, since 2014, have drawn on each other's strengths in the UK and Germany respectively, and provided distribution and digital partnerships through the offshoot venture Tido. Reciprocal distribution agreements have been commonplace for many years, but increasingly these are being replaced by joint ventures, where risk and reward are shared.

"Out of the Woods?"

While traditional publishers were busy restructuring and streamlining, a new form of publishing quietly began to gain traction. Recognising that there was a raft of experienced composers who had previously been published but now found themselves "homeless", and a swathe of younger composers for whom the traditional publishing model was either unappealing or unavailable, Dan Goren set out to define a new path that bridged the gap between self- and fully-published status. The result, Composers Edition (f. 2011), enabled composers to retain their rights (thereby not surrendering copyright) and to benefit from belonging to a collective (being in need of logistical support). This "third way" asks composers to pay a subscription fee to access marketing and distribution support but is deliberately limited, with no editorial intervention, licensing, or copyright services. Similarly, the business of securing performances and promotion is left principally to the composer, but being a member of a roster alongside fellow professionals helps to raise profile and to foster a sense of cohesion.

That some composers now pay to be published, having once received an advance and/or a "golden hello", illuminates the extent of recent change in the publishing world. In the late twentieth century it was common for a composer to negotiate an annual retainer with their publisher and, in addition, to receive a share of income generated.[25] A similarly radical shift has affected deal terms. Custom dictates that composers assign works to their publisher for the life of the music's copyright, thereby separating the composer from their creations such that should the composer part ways with the publisher, the works would remain with the original publisher. The practical advantages to this arrangement are essentially twofold: it maximises the publisher's opportunity to recoup monies invested; and it offers the assurance that a rival publisher cannot benefit from these initial efforts to establish the work. Whereas a composer's place on a publisher's roster was once virtually guaranteed for life, we have seen that by the turn of the century this was no longer so, and that commercial realities were forcing publishers to reassess their stance. Split catalogues, however, are not ideal, as they can frustrate the composer and confuse the customer. Many a time has a publisher approached a conductor, drummed up interest in a composer, and suggested works for consideration, only to discover that an alternative work by the composer—one published by a rival house—is to be programmed. The pragmatic publisher takes the view that all interest in a composer is welcome, but questions of feasibility naturally arise if this scenario plays out repeatedly, particularly for the original publisher with nothing "new" to promote.

The spectre of publishers embracing the digital world has long intrigued industry-watchers. It would be an easy mistake to conflate digital and e-commerce. (The latter, as we have seen, was central to publishers' development strategies in the early 2000s.) Publishers flirted with digital publishing by offering digital downloads of the best-selling publications for consumers to print and own. Faber Music, for example, launched www.choralstore. com to move into an area where, historically, musicians had turned to illicit photocopying either for speed or through casual ignorance of the law. Schott, meanwhile, launched www.notafina.de. Still a stubbornly small revenue stream for most publishers, digital editions have not yet emulated the successes of e-books and recorded music downloads. The sight of musicians performing from tablets is admittedly becoming more common, despite the limitations of size, glare, and undesirable brightness in concert. (An oversized, backlit tablet may emerge as the preferred solution, but no clear market leader currently exists.)

Such barriers to a full transition to digital publishing remain. Indeed, cost is another major factor, both for cash-strapped, publicly funded performing organisations and for publishers, who would have to invest vast sums to prepare files for digital delivery—assuming, of course, that agreement could be reached on a common file standard to facilitate open software. The cost-benefit ratio and demand are currently insufficient to persuade publishers to invest heavily in this area. At the same time, a growing "digital warehouse" has enabled some welcome, if incremental, advances. Publishers, for example, now have the ability to email replacement parts for lost or damaged music. Online score libraries for conductors and artistic decision-makers to peruse have likewise simplified operations; no longer must costly physical scores be made-to-order and posted.

In a mixed economy of published, self-published, and hybrid publishing, does the traditional publishing model stand up? Composers who still operate on an international platform, writing works for established forces of opera, orchestra, string quartet, and so on, may well have little reason to doubt so. The ability to have music promoted worldwide and to be part of a select, curated group of composers still carries weight, attracts prestige, enhances careers, and helps distinguish composers in a crowded marketplace. Indeed, publishing will lose its way the day it disengages from musicians or the public they serve. Gained over many years and decades, publishers' knowledge of repertoire is a rich resource for programmers and musicians alike. Publishers must continue to discover and develop composers, however great or changeable the circumstances of the day. Above all, publishers must remember to facilitate, to think creatively about licensing conundrums such as the portability of digital services across borders, and to strive to ensure that each side of the mutually dependent composer-publisher-performer triangle benefits. No longer does a publisher have to think purely about "growing a forest"; it also needs to be aware of all the hidden or unexpected dangers it could encounter: the threats of urban development, deforestation, and disease each have the potential to destabilise; our "trees" are the composers and the role they and their music play in the world. The reward for the publisher, then, is to watch a composer flourish, to fulfil a creative vision, and to enable audiences to respond favourably to new music.

Notes

1. This percentage varies according to the contract agreed and its range can be large (from 5% to 75%), depending on the nature of the use.
2. Ross Hendy, 'Promethean Unbound', public lecture, University of Auckland, New Zealand, 12 September 2012.
3. Copyright is the umbrella term that encompasses the various different rights, the most common of which are performing, mechanical, sync, and graphic/print rights.
4. Most of Europe is life plus 70 years, the exception being Spain, which is life plus 80 years. Japan, China, and Canada are life plus 50 as is most of the Middle East.
5. 'Evergreen' continues our analogy but also happens to be a term used by music publishers, irrespective of genre, to describe works that are perennially popular and which can be relied upon to generate a minimum level of annual income without extensive marketing or promotion. Typical examples include Carl Orff's *Carmina Burana* (1937) and Ralph Vaughan Williams's *The Lark Ascending* (1914, rev. 1920).
6. Exceptions that prove the rule include Gavin Bryars, who did not sign to a publishing house (Schott Music) until 1994 when he was in his fifties.
7. For example, Catherine Kontz, Laurence Crane, and Matthew Shlomowitz frequently work in or around Dalston in East London. The success of venues such as London's Café Oto epitomised this broadening of the range of classical and cross-classical venues.
8. To define "all-in": instead of itemising the cost of individual elements of a project, for example, the commission fee, hire fees, and production costs, the composer is offered a lump sum to cover all costs associated with the project.
9. Word-of-mouth and recommendations more generally play a significant role in promoting such "underground" classical music cultures. Purchasing objects is

a tactile experience; music has to be experienced. This brings greater risk from the consumer's perspective because of the implied expense, be it financial or simply the time required to invest in the experience. Recommendations therefore accrue greater importance for musical experiences, and nowadays these are just as likely to derive from social networks, blogs, friends, and, indirectly, celebrities, as from existing "authoritative" voices such as journalists, critics, and DJs. In the relatively small market of contemporary classical music, recommending voices are amplified.

10. These terms included larger trade discounts and moving to consignment stock (or "sale or return") models. Ceasing to offer financial support for retailers to visit the Frankfurt Music Fair further worsened relations. This annual trade fair offered publishers the opportunity to showcase new products and to broker major sales orders with retailers.

11. imslp.org (accessed 25 October 2017); emphasis added.

12. In the EU, E-Commerce Directive (2000/31/EC) introduced "safe harbours" to protect websites that did not realise they were hosting, or enabling the use of, copyright material. In return, such sites were compelled to remove content once notified of infringement. For further information, see http://eur-lex.europa. eu/legal-content/EN/TXT/?uri=celex%3A32000L0031 and www.m-magazine. co.uk/what-is-safe-harbour (both accessed 1 October 2017).

13. PRS for Music has led lobbying in this area since 2014. See, for example, www. prsformusic.com/what-we-do/influencing-policy/transfer-of-value (accessed 5 November 2017).

14. See Ian Hargreaves, *Digital Opportunity: A Review of Intellectual Property and Growth* (Department for Business, Innovation and Skills, 2011), www.gov.uk/ government/publications/digital-opportunity-review-of-intellectual-property-and-growth; European Commission, *Public Consultation on the Review of the EU Copyright Rules* (2013–14), http://ec.europa.eu/internal_market/consulta tions/2013/copyright-rules/index_en.htm (both accessed 31 October 2017).

15. For UK Music's responses, see www.ukmusic.org/assets/general/UK_Music_ EU_Consultation_Final.pdf and www.ukmusic.org/assets/general/UK_Music_ Response_to_Independent_Review_of_IP_and_Growth_4th_March_2011.pdf (both accessed 31 October 2017). British law is governed by the Copyright, Design and Patents Act (CDPA, 1988), which succeeded the Copyright Act (1956). The CDPA was introduced, in part, to recognise broadcasts.

16. See www.boosey.com/cr/news/Boosey-Hawkes-Launches-Emerging-Composers/ 11621 (accessed 5 May 2017).

17. A full service agreement refers to a deal whereby the publisher is assigned the copyright in the works covered by the agreement and undertakes to promote them to the best of its ability—as opposed to a distribution-only model.

18. See European American Music Distributors Company, 'Composers', www. eamdc.com/psny/composers/ (accessed 17 August 2017).

19. See The Composer's Site, 'Ricordi Berlin Calling for Works', www.composers site.com/content/ricordi-berlin-calling-works (accessed 17 August 2017).

20. The LSO scheme (https://lso.co.uk/lso-discovery/the-next-generation/panufnik-composers-scheme.html) has operated since 2005 and offers six composers the opportunity to write for and rehearse a piece with the orchestra. Blue Touch Paper (www.londonsinfonietta.org.uk/opportunities/blue-touch-paper) was launched in the early 2000s and evolved from a simple commission opportunity to encouraging cross-disciplinary collaboration.

21. Anthony Gilbert was quick to join UYMP; his compatriots Simon Bainbridge and Robert Saxton followed.

22. Graham Fitkin, interview with Bob Briggs, March 2011, www.musicweb-international.com/SandH/2011/Jan-Jun11/fitkin_interview.htm (accessed 31 October 2017).
23. UMP's story warrants its own volume. The business fell into two parts: a modest catalogue of house composers such as Edward Cowie, Stephen Montague, and Diana Burrell, and a much larger distribution arm specialising in French catalogues. Cost-saving measures, such as relocating from its prime central London premises to the city's outskirts, could not save it from unsustainable trading conditions and overheads. UMP eventually ceased trading with a management buyout of its copyrights and the catalogues it distributed dispersed among other publishers.
24. Helen Wallace, *Boosey & Hawkes: The Publishing Story* (London: Boosey & Hawkes, 2007), 223.
25. This income would either be split and shared immediately with the composer or would be set against production costs and distributed (in accordance with the agreed contract) only once those costs had been recouped. Traditionally, hire fees were the most reliable source of income and a composer could expect to receive 25%–50% on average, depending on the type of deal they had agreed.

3 Evolving Business Models in the Classical Record Industry

Marius Carboni

Major and independent labels serve classical music, as they do other musical genres. The three "majors" are Warner Music Group (WMG), Sony, and Universal Music Group (UMG).[1] The number of "independents" is too great to list, but the most influential include Naxos, Hyperion, Chandos, and Harmonia Mundi. Smaller independent labels include Signum, Delphian, Avie, ECM, Channel Classics, and Champs Hill. For the broadest picture, further classifications are necessary, for example, to recognise: niche labels dedicated to particular types of classical music, such as NMC (contemporary-classical) and Toccata Classics (repertoire rarely or not yet recorded); labels that are artist-led, such as Coro (The Sixteen), Gimell (The Tallis Scholars), and Soli Deo Gloria (Sir John Eliot Gardiner and his three Monteverdi ensembles); those founded because of their association with, or ownership by, a particular venue, opera, or orchestra (LSO Live, Hallé, Wigmore Hall Live, and Opera Rara); and other labels with non-traditional objectives, such as Project Odradek and TwoPianists.[2]

Drawing on interviews, recent literature, and industry data, this chapter scrutinises current classical music record industry practices and business models and asks what the future holds for the relationship between artists, consumers, and those working in the sector. To address these issues is to recognise that the responsibility of the classical artist to music marketing and promotion has grown significantly in recent years. The ways in which classical music reaches and is used by the consumer is therefore at the heart of this chapter. Indeed, a key area of artistic and financial interest (to both label and artist) is the increasing deployment of the artist as a "conduit" to the consumer, with the artist maintaining a close relationship with their fan base and reaching out to new consumers. Many musicians manage this process themselves, with or without help from an intermediary. The presence and activity of artists on social media, for example, is nowadays commonplace and fascinating to chronicle, with the number of likes, shares, retweets, and other forms of engagement easy to see.

Equally, the historical context of such phenomena is central to understanding how marketing and record industry structures are, in fact, intrinsically linked. Marketing techniques more typical of popular music—television advertising, releasing singles to maximise airplay, advertising in non-classical media—characterised the pioneering commercial successes of the late 1980s and early 1990s, epitomised by Nigel Kennedy's EMI recording of Antonio Vivaldi's *Four Seasons* and The Three Tenors' FIFA World Cup-affiliated PolyGram album *Carreras Domingo Pavarotti in Concert*. It is no exaggeration to say that these two campaigns prompted major record labels' classical music divisions to be radically restructured—and changed the genre itself. Twofold, or tiered, operations emerged: "core" classical, targeting the more knowledgeable classical consumer; and "strategic" classical, creating projects to reach a consumer base not necessarily as interested in, say, the intricacies of musical interpretation.

Labels therefore became keener to understand their audiences, to tailor their products accordingly, and to address the type of structural deficiency David Kusek and Gerd Leonhard would later identify:

> Most recorded music has been mass marketed from record labels to the fans. For the most part, the labels had no real idea who was purchasing their CDs and had no way of establishing a direct relationship between the fans and the artist or label. Direct marketing, when properly done, is a way of establishing and building a direct relationship between the company producing the product or service, and its customers.[3]

The crux, then, is connectivity. One notable example is how the close contact Coro maintains with its core market. The Sixteen's impressive social media presence is strategic,[4] as Cath Edwards (Label Manager, Coro) comments:

> We have to be very coordinated because the group as a whole deals with recordings, concerts, commissions, and education projects, which need to be communicated to the correct audience at the right time.[5]

While Edwards's final point is a truism, it also hints at the danger that the division between core and strategic markets bifurcates the sector. As Louis Barfe has argued, '[t]he packaging of classical repertoire in a similar manner to pop music has created a crossover market while, to some degree, ghettoizing the legitimate concert scene.'[6]

'Legitimate' may be the loaded adjective here, but it is true that innovative and varied forms of promotion used for recordings have not always transferred well to classical music's concert scene. Certain audiences expect and prefer a traditional concert layout, whereas others enjoy alternative presentations. Concerts presented by the British impresario Raymond Gubbay highlight this: "Handel by Candlelight" and "Space Spectaculars" transform the concert into a multimedia "event", employing large venues and vivid lighting.[7] Similarly, although the crossover market Barfe cites has undoubtedly attracted new audiences to classical music, not all labels, and particularly not independents, are interested in releasing products along these lines.

Turning to the majors, Patrick Lemanski (Head of Classics, Warner Music UK) explains how WMG relies on a mix of physical and digital marketing:

> Magazines are not cheap [to advertise in] but of course they are still worth doing in both print and digital versions. Our [consumer base] spend tends to be 70% traditional supports and 30% online, such as Google Ads. 70% [of revenue] is still physical sales in classical. That's the reality of the market.[8]

The obvious and inevitable dilemma for Lemanski and others is that in the UK, the committed classical record buyer is more likely to read *Gramophone*, *BBC Music Magazine*, or a specialist instrumental or vocal magazine such as *The Strad*, *Opera,* or *Pianist*, yet younger consumers prefer online access. Moreover, Chaz Jenkins (Founder, Fumubi and Partner, Chartmetric) questions whether it is even possible to identify a typical classical consumer accurately:

> No one knows whether it is the mythical "male-over-55". There is probably a diehard set of classical consumers who fit this demographic but their contribution to overall revenues is almost certainly far, far smaller than we would normally believe.[9]

Furthermore, Jenkins suggests that the concept of genre itself is less relevant than ever:

> Genres were a useful way for labels, retailers, and the press to categorise music for their own purposes, but very few people were fans of only one genre. And the chances are that if they were, they knew so much about the genre and the artists that they were immune from marketing activity. Today, there are only two genres: 'music a person likes' and 'music a person doesn't like'.[10]

The prevalence today of streaming only encourages this view, yet specialist labels such as Soli Deo Gloria (SDG), the label of the Monteverdi Choir and Orchestras, must continue to innovate to survive. Isabella de Sabata (Director, SDG) describes how the label

> started a subscription series for our Bach Pilgrimage project [the year-long tour during which a remarkable 28-album (56-CD) *Bach Cantatas* series was recorded] and it caught the public's imagination . . . offer[ing] a discount on the recordings in exchange for signing up to our subscriber mailing list . . . This provided a solid base of potential buyers on which to build.[11]

Likewise, Steve Smith (Co-founder, Gimell Records) defends the need for marketers to take a broad approach as he outlines a seven-point marketing plan for one of his choral artists:

1. *Gramophone* and *BBC Music Magazine* half- or full-page advert;
2. *Early Music Today* (or another of the Rhinegold stable of magazines) and *Classical Music*;
3. Non-music publication such as *The Big Issue*;
4. Plan press campaign up to six months before release date with finished review copies ready (and up to twelve months for especially important releases);
5. Long-lead (e.g. magazines) contacted first, then short-leads (e.g. newspapers and radio);
6. BBC Radio 3's *Record Review* to receive a copy as early as possible, maximising the chance of review [the Saturday programme follows the typical Friday release date];
7. YouTube video of new release, with excerpts and explanation of works.[12]

To this excellent overview of a classical campaign we can add analysis of sales trends, of which labels must obviously keep abreast. Kim Bayley, Chief Executive of ERA (Entertainment Retailers Association), confirms that the CD format remains the most popular format for classical albums, representing 71.9% of UK sales in 2016 according to the Official Charts Company.[13] This low and static market share for streams—0.9% in 2015 and 2016—confirms the suspicion that classical music lags behind other genres' embrace of digital.[14] (To aid comparison, UK market share for total classical music sales, including physical copies, was 3.1% in 2016.)[15]

Metadata—the mechanism that facilitates browsing of music online—and concerns about sound quality go some way to explain the problem. Metadata should include the details the listener needs to access a specific piece of music, for example, its title of work, composer, performer, the recording to which it belongs, the year it was recorded, its label, and so on. Unlike popular music, classical music finds this difficult because its vast repertoire sees works typically being recorded multiple times (by various interpreters). The genre therefore requires a more involved, and discographically precise, system to function properly and accessibly. The consumer can be easily frustrated by locating, say, the correct movement but an unwanted version, or a piece may be filed under the soloist's name, as in popular music, rather than the composer's.

Jenkins embellishes, and in some ways contradicts, this argument:

If anybody is responsible for the poor metadata, it's the labels themselves, who supply poor metadata to the services. Labels have had almost two decades to address this issue. Some did right from the start of the digital revolution, whilst others still complain but do nothing to address the issue, and when they do address it, they specify metadata that suits their preconceived idea of what a classical consumer wants (in other words, what *they* want) rather than what consumers actually want. There are literally millions of consumers who are more adept at finding classical music, and any other type of music, on streaming services.[16]

More work is needed to understand the preferences of online consumers who listen to classical music (whether or not they would principally define themselves as classical enthusiasts), for we can deduce from Jenkins's argument three further hypotheses: that the official data we have seen may not capture the full reality of online classical music listening; that a majority of consumers crave quality but regard such details as opus numbers or even movement titles as less important; and that the classical music recording industry and many of its consumers are therefore at odds.

Recent efforts to promote downloads with high sound quality have sought to address fears in the second area. Signum reports that the number of high-definition downloads are growing;[17] Linn Records also has a particular focus on high-quality releases,[18] and the trend has prompted www.findhdmusic.com to compile a directory of labels offering high-definition recordings. How the industry continues to adapt to, and commercially exploit, such technologies is surely key to its future prospects. We might heed the advice of Glenn Gould, the stellar twentieth-century pianist who abruptly abandoned live performance in his early thirties for the seclusion of the recording studio:

> At the center of the technological debate, then, is a new kind of listener . . . For this listener is no longer passively analytical; he [*sic*] is an associate whose tastes, preferences, and inclinations even now alter peripherally the experiences to which he gives his attention, and upon whose fuller participation the future of the art of music waits.[19]

Over a half-century old, Gould's remark remains relevant, particularly in a world in which the Internet is revolutionising approaches to music listening and artist-consumer interaction. More recently, Joshua Fineberg has observed:

> [T]he virtual community phenomenon is not confined to recordings. The rise of online communities means that a few thousand people scattered throughout the world can actually be reached in a coherent way: Look at how international festival audiences have become.[20]

Increasingly, then, artists are keeping in closer contact with their potential consumers. For SDG's acclaimed Bach Cantata series, for example, Sir John

Eliot Gardiner unusually wrote a diary to record his 'thoughts and analysis of the music and personal remarks about the events of the tour.'[21] To extend our discussion of Coro, Edwards explains the new norm in social media strategy, whereby various online media channels are 'pulled together . . . in one place.'[22] The majors, too, understand the new significance of social media to classical music. Lemanski describes how 'we encourage artists to blog and tweet but we'll work with them or their management if they don't.'[23] Indeed, violinists Leonidas Kavakos and Anne-Sophie Mutter are two further classical musicians whose social media activity has been pioneering: the former hosts live Facebook question-and-answer sessions for his fans;[24] the latter posts video clips of her on-tour activities, introducing her fellow musicians and sharing photos of rehearsals.[25]. In truth, there are now numerous examples of such online behaviour, albeit not usually as personal in approach; agents or press officers manage many social media accounts. Signum encourages their artists to be social media-savvy, even providing a "social media best practices" guide for them to use.[26] The label also carefully monitors its plays, likes, comments, and shares on Spotify, YouTube, Apple Music, and Facebook, and ensures its branding is consistent across online platforms.

Although, as we have seen, CD sales remain vital to the sector, industry managers realise that this may change and must plan accordingly. As Smith comments:

> Three or four years ago Gimell were selling more downloads than CDs. In 2008 we launched the second-ever website to sell high-resolution downloads, and that significantly boosted our digital income for many years (the site was closed in 2017). We also had a long-term hit on iTunes when our recording of Tallis's *Spem in alium* was featured in the book *Fifty Shades of Grey*. Now [in 2017], sales of downloads have plummeted as customers switch to streaming services but the income from streaming is a small fraction of our former earnings from downloads.[27]

Similarly, on the split between downloads and streaming, Long states:

> Downloading and streaming income is about even now [at Signum]: year-on-year [May 2015–16], there's been a 50% increase . . . It's about people downloading differently—so in blocks (e.g. Mahler 1, 2, 3 as a [bulk] download, or 4, 5, 6, or 7, 8, 9) [rather than individual tracks].[28]

Alison Wenham (CEO, Worldwide Independent Network) has sympathy for the challenge such smaller classical labels face in this area:

> The structural issues in classical market make it very difficult for streaming services to present classical music to their subscribers. Streaming

services are predicated on pop music, and sign-posting is lamentable [for classical], which is a huge disservice to labels and consumers. So, until this issue is addressed, classical music will continue to suffer in the streaming market.[29]

To metadata and sound quality, then, we can add the very presentation of classical music itself, which is marketed and sold in many different ways: the presentation of products can be focussed on their composer(s), performer(s), conductor, historical period, subgenre, instrument, or ensemble (that is, the instrumental medium), occasions ("Classics for Weddings"), soundtracks, or even mood ("Relaxing Classics") or a combination of these features and qualities. While this versatility is in many ways appealing for marketers, the unavoidable truth is that classical music as a marketable *genre* is incredibly wide ranging.

This does not, however, deter the majors in their efforts to support streaming. As Lemanski adds:

> Downloading is declining rapidly . . . There's a big difference in income between streaming and downloads. A year ago, digital revenue was 70% for downloading and [for] streaming, 30%. Twelve months on it's the opposite; now it's all about Spotify, Apple, Deezer, Amazon, and the classical music-dedicated sites, such as Primephonic.[30]

Some labels, indeed, have their own streaming service, for example, Deutsche Grammophon's DG Discovery, while others have collaborated with other operators, albeit with little success to date: Composed, a joint venture between Global (owner of Classic FM) and Universal (owner of Decca and Deutsche Grammophon), closed in 2016.[31] Jenkins detects a sea change in labels' attitude to streaming:

> The overall music industry is growing again, with growth entirely driven by streaming. But until this year [2017], even the pop labels have been fighting against streaming—not trying to maintain physical formats or downloads specifically, but to maintain the economics of "albums". All labels, pop *and* classical, like to believe that consumers like the album concept. But they're fooling themselves. Most consumers simply like music and they like artists. It's only labels who like albums as the economics of the format suit their traditional business models.[32]

This point is strengthened by Chandos's decision to make its new releases and back catalogue available on streaming platforms in 2018. By alluding to labels' conservatism, Jenkins also suggests that other (non-classical) genres have more in common with classical music that we might commonly imagine:

Rap, dance, and electronic music perform well in the streaming environment . . . Artists such as Drake [the Canadian rapper] have a set of collaborators similar to the breadth of guest soloists and conductors in classical. This collaboration is positive as it broadens the potential to increase audience engagement.[33]

Classical music also naturally shares with these genres a connection to the recent renaissance of vinyl. While its overall demand (low) and production costs (high) are prohibitive, marketers increasingly look to it to mark a special release—for example, Paul McCreesh and the Gabrieli Consort and Players' *A New Venetian Coronation* on Signum (SIGLP287; 2013)—or to reissue back catalogue. Nevertheless, sales are increasing fast: UK classical vinyl sales rose from 1,518 in 2014 to 19,764 (so far) in 2017.[34]

Nevertheless, the record industry continues to prioritise CDs. Witness a recent (late 2016) Decca/DG edition of Mozart's complete oeuvre to mark the 225th anniversary of the composer's death: an understandably very expensive 200-CD set that, remarkably, lacks a digital option to "buy now".[35] Moreover, not all companies engage with streaming: Hyperion's catalogue is unavailable in the format, as Simon Perry (Director, Hyperion) comments:

> We provide some tracks of some of our artists for Apple playlists [such as Stephen Hough and Angela Hewitt]; the resulting payback is 50% of the streaming revenue comes from just 4% of users.[36]

Moreover, Smith regards streaming as plainly untenable in business terms:

> It [is] a terminal threat to what we [Gimell] do; the most important fact is how it pays—and it is not a sustainable model. We have to recoup upfront costs of each recording and the streaming model makes it hard to cover these, even if our recordings are played many times. Our customers would have to stream an album many more times than they usually listen to a CD or download for us to recoup the same income.[37]

At the same time, labels that possess significant back catalogues, and prefer to capitalise on those catalogues rather than focus on new releases, can (and do) reach a different conclusion to Smith. As Lemanski recalls:

> One of the differences between Harmonia Mundi [where Lemanski was UK Managing Director] and Warner Classics is the emphasis on back catalogue. For an independent label, income from back catalogue could represent 50% of income; for a major label like Warners it is 80%-plus.[38]

Similarly, the classical music industry has not yet realised the potential of YouTube, which already has a tremendous influence in popular music and, indeed, a roster of self-made "YouTubers". The development of instrument-specific YouTube channels such as Clarinet Mentors (f. 2012 by Michelle Anderson) and the Violin Channel (f. 2009 by Geoffrey John Davies), and initiatives such as the YouTube Symphony Orchestra (f. 2009, the first-ever "online collaborative" orchestra), will be intriguing to watch.[39] Excitingly, such online trends would not appear to represent a typical, or incremental, evolution for the record industry, which explains why their potential is great yet disruptive and divisive, too. As Jenkins remarks:

> Streaming is *not* a continuation of the development of "formats" from vinyl to cassette to CD to downloads . . . With streaming, consumers do not pay for a format or even the music, they pay (or an advertiser or sponsor pays) to be able to access music. Labels only receive revenue if people listen to the music.[40]

Classical music's record industry is more diverse than ever, with a huge range of products, a seemingly divided consumer base, and an equivalently wide variety of musical tastes, access preferences, marketing strategies, and industry opinion. If classical music lags behind other musical genres, then in part this is because of its consumers' different expectations. But a further factor, as we have seen, is the sector's own diversity, which means it does not (and probably cannot) take a common view on its future when it considers how to approach the dominant and nascent formats or, indeed, their marketing. Yet, this fragmented picture is surely inevitable given the pace of technological change and the specialised nature of most classical music. These facts should not tempt us to talk down the sector or to label it as "in crisis", as so often seems to happen. On the contrary, its musical and strategic multiplicity is to be celebrated.

Notes

1. To understand how mergers and acquisitions left just three major record companies in their wake, see Patrik Wikström, *The Music Industry: Music in the Cloud* (2nd edn; Cambridge: Polity, 2013), 73–81.
2. The US-based Project Odradek (f. 2012 by John Anderson) promotes a meritocratic process of selection by inviting aspiring and established artists to submit their demos to a blind judging panel. Nina Schumann and Luis Magalhães founded TwoPianists as a duo (f. 1999) that subsequently expanded into an independent record label (2008).
3. David Kusek and Gerd Leonhard, *The Future of Music: Manifesto for the Digital Music Revolution* (Boston: Berklee Press, 2005), 66.
4. See, for example, www.facebook.com/pg/The-Sixteen-32607011699/community/?ref=page_internal%29, https://twitter.com/TheSixteen, and www.youtube.com/user/16choir (all accessed 17 July 2017).
5. Cath Edwards, interview with the author, 4 August 2016.

6. Louis Barfe, *Where Have All the Good Times Gone?* (London: Atlantic, 2004), 340.
7. See www.raymondgubbay.co.uk (accessed 12 August 2016).
8. Patrick Lemanski, interview with the author, 16 August 2016.
9. Chaz Jenkins, interview with the author, 30 June 2017.
10. Jenkins, interview with the author.
11. Isabella de Sabata, interview with the author, 3 August 2016.
12. Steve Smith, interview with the author, 18 August 2016.
13. Kim Bayley, correspondence with the author, 21 June 2017.
14. See British Phonographic Industry, *All About the Music 2017—Recorded Music in the UK: Fact, Figures and Analysis* (London: BPI, 2017), 38.
15. Greater success in terms of volume is attached to contemporary composers whose music straddles what we might call classical minimalism and ambient pop—in truth the classification is musicologically awkward—for example, Ludovico Einaudi, Nils Frahm, and Joep Beving. In 2015, indeed, five of Einaudi's tracks were streamed more than a million times. See BPI, *All About the Music*, 38.
16. Jenkins, interview with the author, 30 June 2017.
17. Steve Long, interview with author, 1 August 2016. We can define 'high-definition' as 20- and 24-bit as can be conveyed by, say, DSD, FLAC, AIFF, and WAV formats; CDs are designed to resolve to 16-bit only.
18. See www.linnrecords.com/linn-formats.aspx (accessed 21 August 2017).
19. See Glenn Gould, 'The Prospects of Recording', *High Fidelity*, 16/4 (April, 1966), 46–63, www.collectionscanada.gc.ca/glenngould/028010-4020.01-e.html (accessed 1 December 2017).
20. See Joshua Fineberg, *Classical Music, Why Bother? Hearing the World of Contemporary Culture Through a Composer's Ears* (New York: Routledge, 2006), 70.
21. Anonymous [Monteverdi Choir and Orchestras], 'Soli Deo Gloria: About the Cantata Series', www.monteverdi.co.uk/sdg/cantatas (accessed 5 August 2016).
22. Cath Edwards, interview with the author, 5 July 2017
23. Patrick Lemanski, interview with the author, 16 August 2016.
24. See Leonidas Kavakos, "Leonidas Kavakos", www.facebook.com/leonidas.kavakos.violin (accessed 10 July 2016).
25. See Anne-Sophie Mutter, "Anne-Sophie Mutter", www.facebook.com/annesophiemutter (accessed 10 July 2016).
26. Long, interview with the author.
27. Smith, interview with the author.
28. Long, interview with the author. Downloading was, and to a large extent remains, track-based, being geared to popular music. For the classical sector, the market has matured with consumers downloading whole (and multiple) symphonies and operas.
29. Alison Wenham, interview with the author, 19 September 2016.
30. Patrick Lemanski, interview with the author, 16 August 2016.
31. See Rhian Jones, 'Classic FM and Decca Launch Streaming Service', *Music Week* (11 November 2014), www.musicweek.com/news/read/classic-fm-and-decca-launch-classical-music-streaming-service/060090 (accessed 5 August 2016).
32. Jenkins, interview with the author.
33. Jenkins, interview with the author.
34. The latter figure captures 2017 sales up to 12 November. Figures courtesy of the Official Charts Company (www.officialchartscompany.co.uk).
35. See Universal Music, "W.A. Mozart. The New Complete Edition", www.mozart225.com.

36. Simon Perry, interview with the author, 11 November 2017.
37. Smith, interview with the author.
38. Lemanski, interview with the author.
39. See, respectively: www.youtube.com/user/ClarinetMentors; www.youtube.com/user/theviolinchannel; and www.youtube.com/user/symphony (all accessed 16 October 2017).
40. Jenkins, interview with the author.

4 Managing Artists in the Classical Sector

Definitions and Challenges

Atholl Swainston-Harrison

To define and scrutinise artist management in the context of classical music today is to encounter immediate difficulties surrounding the ways in which the practice is typically discussed and perceived.[1] Indeed, some within the classical music sector find it uncomfortable to talk about business in the same breath as art. The role of an artist manager is also often misunderstood, for it far exceeds the caricature of someone who simply finds work for the artist and pockets their agreed commission: artist management also requires nuanced knowledge of the media, audiences, broadcasting, promotion, taxation, legal affairs, travel, and even politics. This chapter aims to deepen understanding of artist management, including the particular challenges managers face today. Given its significance to musicians and the wider industry, it is surprising how little has been written about the practice of managing classical artists; Christopher Fifield's book on pioneering British agency Ibbs and Tillett (1906–90) is an admirable exception.[2] Figures such as Emmie Tillett, Harold Holt, Joan Ingpen, Hans Ulrich Schmid, and Lies Askonas laid the foundations for today's major agencies, including HarrisonParrott (*sic*) (f. 1969),[3] Askonas Holt (f. 1998, but traceable to 1876),[4] and Ingpen & Williams (1946–2016, now operating as Grove Artists).[5] The world's oldest family artist management agency by name—that is, continuously operated under the same name—is Helsinki-based Fazer Artists (f. 1903), an agency that was instrumental as a gateway between Russia and the West in the twentieth century.[6] Astrid Becker and Cornelia Schmid have documented the influence of Hans Ulrich Schmid,[7] the 1959 founder of Konzertdirektion Schmid. Schmid's daughter, Cornelia, took over the management of this successful (now multinational) agency in 1994.

Bankruptcies, mergers, acquisitions, and "spin-offs" have transformed the landscape of artist management over the years. One of today's biggest names, Columbia Artist Management, Inc. (CAMI), was formed when several smaller companies amalgamated in 1930.[8] More recently, Van Walsum Management was sold to International Classical Artists (now Wright Music Management) in 2010. Examples of spin-offs, which typically account for today's proliferation of *boutique* agencies, include Keynote Artist Management (f. 2013), founded by Libby Abrahams (previously Vice-President of International Management Group, better known as IMG Artists), and

Enticott Music Management (f. 2014), founded by Kathryn Enticott (also once of IMG Artists). A spin-off agency implies a small roster of artists, with significant artists sometimes having followed the manager to the new agency. The question "is bigger or boutique better for artist representation?" has long encircled the sector. This is a flawed perspective, however, as it is the artist's relationship with the individual manager, not corporate loyalty, that counts among artists. Determining factors are the "chemistry" between artist and manager and, irrespective of the size of the company, the workload of the manager and, in turn, the time available for the artist. Similarly, there is no ideal number of "artists per manager"; artists' needs can vary tremendously. Arguably, larger agencies can act more quickly than smaller agencies, for example, sourcing artists from within their rosters in the event of cancellations. At the same time, smaller companies typically enjoy closer networks, particularly in opera, where such "referrals" are made on the understanding that the favour will be repaid.

For the aspiring artist, the question of how to find and agree representation can be a vexed one. The process can seem clandestine and complicated because, in truth, the question has no single answer: some managers look to international competitions; others rely on word-of-mouth recommendations, perhaps drawing on their conservatoire connections; and others simply attend concerts to scout the most promising talent. The decision to sign an artist is preceded by a period of research, with the manager attending performances, checking social media profiles, and seeking advice from colleagues. The dynamic between manager and artist is paramount, and this entails not just interpersonal factors, but also a shared understanding of the musician's artistic identity and its importance in a competitive market. Appreciating that successful careers, particularly of conductors and soloists, can take many years to establish, managers must also form a judgement on the artist's long-term prospects, for example, their staying power or even their potential to reinvent themselves. These considerations can be influenced by other factors, such as the artist's interests in perhaps visual art, other performing arts, or other interpreters of the repertoire, any of which might give a clue to the musician's artistic capacity. Another important question is, "does the artist have something to say about the repertoire they perform?" Because if an artist is unable to demonstrate a perspective, or to communicate their identity, then it is unlikely an artist manager will be interested in signing them. Auditions, particularly for singers, are another way for managers to form judgements, but it is not unheard of for an artist's Internet footprint (YouTube videos, typically) to influence decision-making. Artists must therefore consider carefully what recordings of them are publicly viewable online.

Definitions

At this point, let us to define *agent* and *artist manager*. In the popular music sector, these responsibilities are distinct: the agent takes a booking and services the engagement; the manager outlines a strategy for the artist to help realise their goals. Both take a commission for their work. Due to the generally much lower fees artists earn in the classical sector, the two roles are carried out by one person: the artist manager.[9] In many territories the authority of a manager to act on their artist's behalf is defined according to the law of Principal and Agent: the manager is regarded as an agent acting on behalf of their principal (here, the artist), with no other legal authority.[10] In practice, the manager's experience is invoked by their guidance of the artist's decision-making and their strategic implementation of those instructions. This practice, indeed, has sustained the artist/manager relationship for many decades. However, as we shall see, stagnant artist fees, intense workloads, and increasing demands are beginning to call its sustainability into question.

Let us first examine artist representation in different territories: *Local* managers administer representation in one country or, sometimes, a small number of countries. *Regional* managers' area of representation covers larger territories, generally following continental borders, such as North America or Europe. *Worldwide* or *General* management may therefore seem self-explanatory, but the important difference for the artist is that the General Manager holds their diary, works closest with them, and assumes overall authority to represent them to all sections of the music community. Both General and Local Managers should learn of all the aspirations, strengths, and weaknesses an artist possesses, while being tasked with presenting the artist's unique qualities to the outside world. It is this human aspect that far surpasses anything written down in an agreement, but which also marks the tension between the personal and professional nature of the role.

Some artists have no need for a Local Manager as their General Manager is able to cover all territories appropriate to their activities. The role of a Local Manager, if required, is primarily concerned with market effectiveness, such as overcoming particular language or contractual intricacies (in Japan, for example, knowledge of public broadcasting media terms can be vital) and maximising opportunities for the artist (an early music specialist, to take another example, might be guided towards The Netherlands, where audience support for that genre is strong). Although competitive in nature, the relationship between General and Local Management companies is vital to an artist's success and must therefore be based on mutual trust and an interest in the artist being represented well. In such a relationship, the General Manager would still take a commission from any engagement the Local Manager might source, but at a lower rate: perhaps 5%–10% or as negotiated according to the amount of work involved. Because of the involvement of two companies, the artist might pay more commission than usual, but this would be a strategic decision agreed on by all parties.

Complications can arise when an artist is offered an engagement directly by a promoter, despite a Local Manager being in place. If the artist relays the offer directly to the General Manager, the question arises as to whether the Local Manager is entitled to a commission. If the General Manager appointed the Local Manager, there is usually an established relationship in place that would respect the commission claim of the Local Manager. Similarly, if the artist appointed the Local Manager, perhaps before the General Management relationship started, the commission claim is also likely to be respected, as there is often a personal bond between the artist and their Local Manager (particularly if the manager gave the artist their first "leg-up") and the General Manager would be reluctant to end such an arrangement. Occasionally, artists take the position that an engagement should be commission-free, for example, if an offer of work was made through personal connections. However, this is clearly not a professional perspective if a contractual relationship is in place: all engagements contribute to the aims and strategy an artist and manager discuss and agree.

Even so, there are few fixed terms or standards of practice between artists and artist management companies: contractual terms, including retainers and commission rates, vary wildly and are based solely on the business model of each individual management. Generally, *commission* is defined as a fee for services rendered and is expressed as a percentage of the artist's fee. Depending on the management company's own business practices, the commission is usually taken from the artist's gross fee, before any deduction for tax.[11] Travel and accommodation expenses are sometimes paid separately to the fee, in which case it is customary for them to be ignored for commission purposes. A *retainer* is a fixed amount of money paid by an artist to a management company either regularly or as a one-off; it is typically a non-refundable payment for the manager's time, services, and "investment" in establishing and promoting the artist's career. This is not the model that is practiced in the classical music world as a whole. In the United Kingdom, if a fixed, regular fee is due from the artist, the law requires that it must relate to a specific service that the artist and manager have agreed in advance. Retainers in this sense are illegal,[12] since fees cannot be undefined for "general" services and must therefore be declared transparently and revisited periodically. Such principles, indeed, are useful regardless of legal requirements: ill-defined terms only breed resentment or worse should disagreements ever arise.

To that end, Figure 4.1 reproduces guidance the International Artist Managers' Association (IAMA) gives its members as they prepare to take on artists.[13] The principal areas in which agreement must be reached are the territories the agreement covers, the capacity of representation, commission rates, and termination. The spirit and letter of the agreement must pre-empt and thus minimise the prospect of disagreement, comprehensively defining the processes (and, implicitly, the challenges) that characterise the artist-manager relationship in today's classical music industry.

- There should be a clear statement of intent by the artist management company (AMC) setting out the goals of artist representation and stating clearly that all inquiries, engagements, and royalties fall within the bounds of the contract. If, for any reason, the artist believes that some engagement(s) should not be covered under the terms of the contract, it should be settled with the AMC before the terms of the agreement are signed.
- Any statement of intent should include wording to the effect that the AMC and Artist have a co-responsibility in developing a career strategy and artistic development and that the AMC shall use its best endeavours to procure engagements and offer appropriate, professional career advice.
- The date on which the agreement commences must be stated, as well as the termination notice term by either party (AMC/Artist). IAMA recommends that this notice period be three months. Notice must be given in writing by the terminating party.
- In the event of termination, the agreement should clarify the procedure for dealing with commission concerning future engagements and how to deal with those engagements that are not yet contracted.

Territories and Management Relationships

- The agreement should state the territory(ies) or country(ies) for which it is valid and if the AMC representing the artist is doing so as a General or Local Manager.
- The agreement should state if the Artist Manager is the sole and exclusive representative and can enter into agreements on behalf of the Artist. If the agreement is for General Management, the procedure for appointing Local Managers should be clearly understood and agreed to by both parties.

Commission Rates, Tax, and Services

- The agreement should establish: commission rates which need to be understood as being over and above any state taxes applied; and a payment structure for commission and fees, e.g. how commission will be levied and when. This should be reflected in writing.
- A plan for dealing with expenses should be established before commencement of the agreement. It should be stated in writing what expenses should be regarded as extra and therefore settled by the Artist. Should the Artist agree to a certain expenditure limit without prior consultation, then this should be stated and when incurred, communicated to the Artist as soon as practicable.

Figure 4.1 International Artist Managers' Association (IAMA) Guidelines for Prospective Artist Managers

Contemporary Challenges

Artist management faces many specific challenges—the number of chamber music ensembles on management rosters has, for example, fallen markedly in recent times[14]—but for the purposes of this chapter, we can group and assess three areas that are most significant and topical: commission rates and the commission model; exclusivity, termination, and handover; and the Internet, social media, and online communication.

Commission Rates and the Commission Model

A 2016 survey of IAMA members revealed that commission rates are rising—not significantly for companies already charging around 20% commission, but more substantially for companies that had operated in the 10%–15% bracket. The increase in percentage rates can be explained by the central challenges artist management companies have faced over the past ten years, including unpredictable currency depreciation/appreciation (for example, the Swiss Franc against the Euro, or the British Pound after 2016's Brexit referendum);[15] continually rising costs of having an office and staff, particularly in a major capital such as London; and a worldwide economic downturn that has generally seen performance fees stagnate and levels of private sponsorship and public subsidy decrease. Figure 4.2 illustrates the range of commission rates IAMA members charge for different types of engagements, such as conducting, operatic, and soloist. Many factors determine the variation in rates: the figures alone cannot define the level of service an artist management company provides, that is, the precise tasks a manager carries out on their artist's behalf; different types of engagements also place different administrative burdens on the artist manager (compare, for example, a chamber ensemble flying to another country for a one-off engagement to a singer being booked for an opera's month-long run). Important caveats to these findings include geographical factors, such as in France, where laws prescribe that promoters can pay no more than the equivalent of 10% of the engagement fee directly to the management company, which can fail to meet contractual obligations (if, say, the commission percentage agreed is greater than 10%) and result in the management company having to invoice the artist for the difference.

Straight commission, the simplest and most traditional model of artist-manager engagement, is likely to dominate for the foreseeable future, despite the financial risks it poses to the manager. When taking on a young artist, it can take three years or longer before a manager is adequately compensated for their time, effort, and expertise. The hope, of course, is for the artist to succeed reputationally and commercially, and for engagement fees to rise. However, because this trajectory is obviously neither guaranteed nor determined entirely by the manager or the artist, the manager is vulnerable to the risk of earning very little or nothing. Moreover, some record companies have recently sought commission on the live work of young artists

Managing	10%–12.5%	15%	20%	>20%
Singers (Concert)	29%	48%	23%	0%
Singers (Opera)	69%	26%	5%	0%
Conductors (Concerts)	19%	42%	38%	1%
Conductors (Opera)	14%	45%	40%	1%
Instrumental Soloists	19%	35%	45%	1%
Chamber Ensembles	14%	40%	45%	1%

Figure 4.2 Declared Commission Rates, as of April 2016[16] (percentage of IAMA members charging in each category)

signed to them, prompting difficult conversations between all parties given how little emerging artists typically make.[17] Sensitive to their profession's stereotype ("the greedy agent"), managers themselves can be suspicious or even disparaging about anyone who breaches traditional models by charging artists substantially above industry norms. In reality, profit margins in this labour-intensive profession are very slight.[18] While charging a higher commission can be a way forward for some companies, there will always be a limit to how much rates can be increased. With the commission model potentially under strain, there have been calls within the profession to negotiate specific service packaging deal with artists.[19] Such deals could mean that artists do more of their own logistical work, allowing managers to devote more time to representation.

Additionally, legal and financial compliance has become increasingly burdensome for artist managers. The UK, for example, has very strict laws on the treatment of client money, requiring companies to hold client money in separate bank accounts.[20] Coupled with demands from the banking sector,[21] this has prompted some companies to abandon the traditional model of invoicing and collecting engagement fees on behalf of the artist (before deducting their commission and transferring the remainder to the artist). Instead, engagement fees are paid directly to the artist, with the management company invoicing the artist for their commission. This, however, places artists into the position of fee collector, which is onerous and potentially calamitous when public funds are delayed or, worse, commercial promoters go bankrupt. Moreover, although the European Union sets clear terms for commercial settlement,[22] there is no international consensus on what is considered acceptable. In Italy, for example, no operatic artist contract is even technically valid unless the opera house issuing the contract has approved the production budget—a lengthy process subject to the capricious nature of public funding, such that artists must often undertake engagements in good faith. Here and elsewhere, then, artists can be forced to wait for long periods of time before they are paid, potentially straining their relationships with promoters and, indeed, managers. Yet, the alternative—to reject work out of principle—is unlikely given the competitive nature of the field.

Exclusivity, Termination, and Handover

A fundamental principle of artist representation is *exclusivity*, whereby managers are contractually authorised to represent artists worldwide or in certain countries or territories, typically abiding by the Local/General principles outlined earlier in the chapter. Non-exclusive arrangements exist, mostly in mainland Europe, but are not common. Exclusivity defines relationships within the profession clearly and implies that the artist consents to grant the management(s) the permission to negotiate contractual terms and to enter into an engagement on their behalf. The umbrella organisations IAMA and the Association Européenne des Agents Artistiques (AEAA) jointly maintain a database (www.classicalmusicartists.com) to list relationships of exclusivity, enabling promoters to source artists easily.

Countries such as Switzerland and Germany do not recognise the legal status of exclusivity. International artist management operates in spite of this because exclusivity is recognised across the profession as being the clearest way of defining who represents whom. This situation is a strong argument for the standardisation of law; when national laws disadvantage companies, particularly in the context of accepted common practice within the EU, they should be harmonised. Indeed, in Italy, artist managers were disadvantaged by legal changes in the 1970s that relegated their role to that of a secretariat, implying a support service rather than an entitlement to represent the artist. Similarly, France's prerequisite for a foreign EU company to be licenced to operate as a business is still technically enforceable. Such cases highlight the nuanced realities of supporting an artist's career across international boundaries. Consider also that tax, social security, and immigration laws vary tremendously between territories, and it becomes clear that the artist manager must develop expertise in these areas and know to draw on specialist advice whenever necessary.

The most sensitive area of the artist-manager relationship is when an artist changes management companies, not least because the artist is usually still contractually bound to their present manager. Historically, such "poaching" was almost taboo. Policing the practice is one reason why the British Association of Concert Agents (BACA, the forerunner of IAMA) was founded in 1954. Today, on the contrary, artist choice is accepted and understood. A manager might well know that the time is right for the artist to seek new pastures because a limit has been reached, and consent for such a change is typically mutual. Nevertheless, such "handovers" can test the outgoing and incoming managers' ability to maintain sufficient business perspective and to act in the artist's best interests.

Once the artist gives notice to their manager, or vice versa, the terms of the original agreement are invoked. Future engagements often stretch beyond the typical termination period of three-to-six months and performance schedules planned two-to-three years in advance can be a challenge during any handover. A general rule is that any commission for engagements agreed before the handover would still be due to the outgoing manager, although it sometimes serves everyone's interests to agree a buyout of such commitments, severing the existing relationship quickly and cleanly. Such an arrangement also solves the more ambiguous area of "pencilled-in" or expected dates, which the outgoing manager may well be holding in the artist's diary. Such dates can be negotiated to agree who will service them and follow up with the promoter: some companies choose to offer a 50% buyout on all unconfirmed arrangements; others prefer a more detailed agreement with a sliding scale of fees (since the further ahead an engagement, the greater the risk that it may not happen). Artists must bear in mind that the incoming manager is not obliged to deal with the outgoing manager and that because the classical music world is relatively small, respect for professional standards, courtesy, and, of course, the legal agreements themselves are paramount.

The Internet, Social Media, and Online Communication

The Internet is much vaunted for its ostensible ability to bypass intermediaries, but as we have seen, to describe artist managers as such would be to oversimplify their role. Used well, online technology is nevertheless invaluable to a classical artist, whose challenge is to source and make available high-quality content, while minding that online footprints endure. In practice, the artist and manager often share this responsibility. Public broadcasters were once reluctant to part with audio-visual material. But as their demand for and use of rights rises—while the fees they offer stagnate or even fall—a compromise has ensued where access to a limited use and length of material can be offered subject to rights clearance. If the artist has a relationship with a record company, then it is very important to negotiate what material an artist can share on their website. A dialogue between all parties—artist, manager, and record company—will ensure that a mutually acceptable balance between promotion and commercial return on a recording is struck. Recently, however, IAMA members have reported that labels' greater demands for exclusivity have clouded these discussions. The underlying apprehension, of course, is streaming, as labels are forced to confront new realities of consumer expectation and choice. Social media presents artists and managers with a similar dilemma. Artists who have mastered audience-friendly activity online are often applauded; indeed, promoters will appreciate an artist's social media following as they ponder potential ticket sales. However, as social media and technology continue to develop, it is becoming critical for artists to receive independent advice, and some managers now engage PR consultants and social media experts for guidance—a service paid for by the artist. Many high-profile artists use specialists to update social media for them, but arguably this is inauthentic and undermines the spirit of the medium. Essentially, the challenge for the artist manager in this landscape is to advise the artist if their performing persona is at odds with their online identity.

As the challenge of servicing an artist's career grows more complicated, there is ever greater reliance on online communication as modern management practice. The ability of managers to act quickly and flexibly, usually by email, is particularly tested in the international arena or when opportunities arrive at short notice. Insecurity of funding, for example, can lead promoters to announce decisions much later than managers would prefer. Indeed, artist management is increasingly email-led. The volume can be overwhelming and also introduces a uniquely twenty-first-century problem whereby the "paper trail" becomes more prolonged, fragmented, and open to (mis)interpretation than it once was. Globalisation fosters new connections between people and markets; email entails a reliance on the written word between people who have probably never met or even spoken to each other. Correspondence can be misconstrued, due to style of expression or when English, the most common business language, is not the user's first language. Now recognised as a legal form of concluding contracts in the EU, email is unlikely to disappear. If anything, communication is becoming more rather than less fractured, as various types of social media are also used for communicating legal terms.

§

Despite the demographic, technological, and commercial challenges classical music faces, opportunities for artists (and, by extension, managers) are being found thanks to global development and the very qualities that define a positive artist-manager relationship: reputational growth, a nuanced understanding of markets, sound artistic and commercial judgement, and trust between the artist, manager, and, in turn, promoters. Managers do report that their workloads have increased in recent years, and this concern warrants further scrutiny. Indeed, the absence of scholarly or industry-led research on the role of the artist manager is telling; the sector goes beneath the radar, largely invisible to audiences and academics alike. Conversely, cause for great optimism resides in the increasing trade with Chinese promoters. China and South Korea, in particular, have developed their infrastructure for classical music concert performances rapidly this century, and the number of young prize-winning musicians from these countries has likewise grown. While the question "does the number of artists outstrip demand?" will continue to be posed, particularly in conservatoires, many excellent musicians will lack representation because the capacity of artist management companies is finite. From the perspective of artist management itself, however, this deficit shows how managers' ability to nurture talent is understood, and that, in the classical music industry at large, the sector has retained its prestige, value, and remarkable resilience.

Notes

1. I am grateful to Brian Goldstein (GG Arts Law, New York) and James Brown (Managing Director, Hazard Chase) for their advice during my research for this chapter.
2. See Christopher Fifield, *Ibbs and Tillett: The Rise and Fall of a Musical Empire* (Aldershot: Ashgate, 2005). Robert Leigh Ibbs and John Tillett founded the agency, which was managed after Tillett's death by his widow Emmie. Paul Allen's *Artist Management for the Music Business* (3rd edn; Oxford, United Kingdom: Focal Press, 2014) is a fixture on music business reading lists but does not discuss classical artist management specifically.
3. See Harrison Parrott, "About HarrisonParrott [sic]", www.harrisonparrott. com/about-us (accessed 20 December 2017).
4. See Askonas Holt, "History", www.askonasholt.co.uk/about/history/ (accessed 20 December 2017).
5. See Groves Artists, "About Us", www.grovesartists.com/about-us/ (accessed 20 December 2017).
6. See Fazer Artists' Management, "History: Years 1890–1925, The Times of Edvard Fazer", www.fazerartists.fi/company/history/1890-1925/ (accessed 10 August 2017).
7. See Hans Ulrich Schmid, *Aber spielen müssen Sie selber: Aus den Erinnerungen eines Impresarios*, ed. Astrid Becker and Cornelia Schmid (Hildesheim: Georg Olms Verlag, 2013).
8. See Columbia Artists, "History", http://columbia-artists.com/?topic=history (accessed 20 December 2017).
9. This explains the anomaly that while artist representatives are referred to as "artist managers", the companies they run are usually called "agencies".
10. This principle is longstanding. See, for example, Joseph E. Stiglitz, 'Principal and Agent', in *Allocation, Information and Markets*, ed. John Eatwell, Murray Milgate, and Peter Newman (London: Palgrave Macmillan, 1989), 241–53.
11. In the classical sector, all income, including royalties, longer-term contracts, sponsorship, endorsements, broadcasting fees, and repeat fees, is generally commissionable.
12. See The Conduct of Employment Agencies and Employment Business Regulations (2003), www.legislation.gov.uk/uksi/2003/3319/contents/made (accessed 19 December 2017).
13. The International Artist Managers' Association (IAMA) is the only worldwide association for classical music artist managers and concert agents. See www. iamaworld.com/history.aspx (accessed 19 December 2017).
14. The decline is due to the substantial time needed to service chamber music engagements and the comparatively small financial return. If this trend continues, chamber music's exposure may be compromised.
15. Such volatility is problematic in most businesses, but acutely so in artist management given that the marketplace is international and contracts are typically signed months, sometimes years, in advance of engagements.
16. Survey data was collated in April 2016. 62% of IAMA's Full Members participated in the survey.
17. Technically, we might call this a '180-degree' contract, since it covers two areas—recording and live performance—of the four covered by 360-degree contracts. See also: Lee Marshall, 'The 360 Deal and the "New" Music Industry',

European Journal of Cultural Studies, 16 (2013), 77–99; Matt Stahl and Leslie Maier, 'The Firm Foundation of Organizational Flexibility: The 360 Contract in the Digitalizing Music Industry', *Canadian Journal of Communication*, 37 (2012), 441–58.

18. In the UK, accounts of incorporated companies, including artist management companies, are publicly available from Companies House; see www.gov.uk/get-information-about-a-company (accessed 20 December 2017)

19. A management company might, for example, offer a PR consultancy package or charge separately for services relating to visa/immigration matters.

20. See The Conduct of Employment Agencies and Employment Business Regulations (2003), www.legislation.gov.uk/uksi/2003/3319/contents/made (accessed 19 December 2017). The 2016 IAMA survey also indicated that 50% of its members operate client accounts and that the majority of such members are UK-based.

21. Since 2008, banking regulations have become more stringent in the UK and elsewhere.

22. For more on the EU's efforts to deter late payment for commercial transactions, see Directive 2000/35/EC, http://eur-lex.europa.eu/legal-content/en/TXT/?uri=CELEX%3A32000L0035 (accessed 17 December 2017).

5 On Classical Music Competitions

Glen Kwok and Chris Dromey

Competitions have long been a mainstay for classical musicians of all ages and proficiencies: emerging and established, amateur and professional, solo and ensemble. By enabling musicians to judge their level of performance against fellow performers on local, regional, national, or international stages, competitions represent more than the act of competing: they are also a vital means for classical musicians to promote themselves, to gain recognition, and, potentially, to launch their careers. Yet, as competitions have multiplied and diversified, particularly over the last half-century, questions surrounding their viability and legitimacy have gradually grown louder. The global financial crisis has jeopardised economic support for the arts and caused several competitions to close, sometimes after decades of operation, for example, Paris's quadrennial Rostropovich Cello Competition (1977–2009). Nevertheless, it is encouraging that most established competitions continue and, as we shall see, that new competitions are continuing to appear.

This chapter charts the mechanisms and dynamics of how classical music competitions operate. In so doing, it also addresses certain fundamental and topical questions that aspiring musicians, professionals working in the competition world, and critics of competitions will surely recognise given their relevance to musical life today: How do competitions vary? What purpose are they intended to serve? What are their benefits and, indeed, their drawbacks? The chapter falls into four related sections: a brief historical overview of competitive music-making, providing context for how and why classical music competitions proliferated in the post-war era; a more substantial chronicle of today's scene, with a practical focus on different types of competitions in which musicians of international standing compete today; and a two-part appraisal of competitions' efforts to innovate, examined in light of the complex, sometimes controversial issues, such as bias and musical judgement, these events provoke.

The history of competitive music-making is fascinating but from a contemporary standpoint it is easy to overlook.[1] In a modern sense, our understanding of the subject can be traced to late eighteenth-century Britain, with its panoply of brass band contests, competitions for choirs, singers, and solo instrumentalists, as well as its revival of the *eisteddfodau*. This latter example, however, points us in the direction of the eighth-century Welsh festivals in which bards competed; in fact, the earliest known musical contests took place alongside the Pythian Games (sixth century BC), from which a new, prize-winning class of musician emerged. Another important link between the distant and recent past is the establishment of influential European guilds that patronised music and poetry, flourishing across northwest Europe by attracting troubadours and trouvères to perform. As *Puys* evolved into competition-based festivals and gained popularity in the fifteenth century, new treatises on performance and composition scrutinised the emerging links between competition and adjudication.

By the nineteenth century, a competition *movement* could be recognised. Contests were formalised, patronised, and popular, with audiences attracted as much by musical rivalry as by the higher-quality performances now on offer. One example, notable for its age, is the British Open Brass Band Championship (f. 1853 in Manchester, now held in Birmingham). Widely emulated, the Stratford Festival (f. 1882; now known as the Stratford & East London Music Festival) was a wholly musical occasion, managed by teachers and choirmasters and imaginatively split into twenty classes and five sections of competition. Founded by John Spencer Curwen (son of John Curwen, proponent of "Tonic sol-fa" pedagogy), this pioneering event gave competitions an educational subtext and bestrode amateur and professional music-making.[2] In parallel to such events, one-off competitions pitted solo instrumentalists against each other, either for entertainment, patronage, appointment, or simply to debate the merits of the musicians involved. A famous example is an 1837 benefit concert (hosted in Paris by Princess Cristina Belgiojoso), during which the rivalry of celebrated pianist-composers Franz Liszt and Sigismond Thalberg was brought to a head.[3] Such "duels" have a modern equivalent in the showy, sudden-death stages of "reality" television contests, which are typically pop-based but have (controversially) reached classical music, for example, the BBC's *Classical Star* (2007) and *Maestro* (2008).[4]

The foundations were laid for competitions to flourish in the twentieth century—an era that informs our present understanding of how a classical music composition is modelled, with entrants usually restricted by an upper age limit, performances heard before a jury, works set from the repertoire (sometimes with a specially commissioned test piece), and the latter stages of competition often held publicly. Significantly, the period also gave rise to events such as the annual Queen Elisabeth Competition (Brussels, f. 1937 as the Concours Eugène Ysaÿe), which is held to be the most challenging of all competitions.[5] The cachet associated with such events swiftly enhanced winners' standing. In the interwar era, Soviet musicians were the significant beneficiaries: violinist David Oistrakh won the first Concours Eugène Ysaÿe, pianist Emil Gilels won the second, catapulting both musicians to further international success.

The World Federation of International Music Competitions (WFIMC, the governing body of many of the world's leading competitions) is a useful yardstick by which to measure the growth of competitions over the last half-century: the organisation grew from 24 members in 1965 to 123 in 2017.[6] Of its current members, those for piano—that is, single-discipline competitions devoted to the piano—are the most common (40 of 123); a further 24 multi-discipline competitions feature the piano on a rotational basis. This abundance is reflected globally: according to Gustav Alink, founder of the Alink-Argerich Foundation that publishes an annual catalogue of international piano competitions, the total exceeds 300, a six-fold increase since 1965.[7]

More broadly, classical music competitions today serve every discipline and family, including conducting, composition, and ensembles. One of the newest competitions, for example, offers traditional and "open" categories: the "M-Prize" Chamber Arts Competition (f. 2016, based at the University of Michigan) adds to the standard strings and winds ensembles a third category for

> any instrumentation including, but not limited to: percussion; voice; technology including . . . turntables, laptops, and/or visual media; ensembles whose work contains a significant amount of improvisation including . . . jazz, bluegrass, world music, and/or free improvisation.[8]

The phenomenal breadth of competitions reflects the ways in which classical music has evolved since the turn of the twentieth century. Chamber competitions such as the M-Prize respond to trends we now consider historical, for example, the proliferation of the Pierrot ensemble and the saxophone quartet, and take a broad perspective on interdisciplinary and cross-genre creativity.

At the same time, many competitions remain dedicated to single disciplines. Just as the Chopin (Warsaw, quinquennial since 1927), Busoni (Bolzano, biennial since 1949),[9] Leeds (triennial since 1961),[10] Van Cliburn (Fort Worth, quadrennial since 1962), and Hamamatsu (triennial since 1991) competitions attract the world's best young pianists, violinists vie for the Paganini (Genoa, since 1954, now biennial), Indianapolis (quadrennial since 1982), Joseph Joachim (Hannover, triennial since 1991) and Michael Hill (Auckland, biennial since 2001) titles. Prominent string quartet competitions are held in Banff (triennial since 1983) and Bordeaux (originally Evian, triennial since 1981); further single-discipline competitions include the Mirjam Helin International Singing Competition (Helsinki, quinquennial since 1984), BBC Cardiff Singer of the World (biennial since 1983), the USA International Harp Competition (Bloomington, triennial since 1989), and the Kobe International Flute Competition (quadrennial since 1985).

Many classical music competitions are dedicated to specific composers, for example, (to add to those listed above) the International Jean Sibelius

Violin Competition (Helsinki, quinquennial since 1965, Sibelius's centenary) and the International Franz Liszt Piano Competition (Utrecht, triennial since 1986, the centenary of Liszt's death). Such competitions naturally place a focus of their eponymous composers, although music by other composers also features. A further category of competitions invites applicants from multiple disciplines and has two subsets: those that present a single discipline each time they are held but "rotate" them annually or biennially; and those that present multiple disciplines simultaneously but which change the discipline each year. The Queen Elisabeth, for example, rotates between violin, piano, cello (since 2017), and voice (since 1988) on a four-year cycle. The Geneva International Music Competition (f. 1939) is more changeable: in 2018 it offers piano and clarinet categories, having hosted composers, pianists, and string quartets in recent years, and a still greater range of instrumentalists historically. A comparable example is Munich's ARD International Music Competition (Germany's largest competition, f. 1952), whose range is such that it may offer guitar, piano, oboe, and violin one year, then voice, viola, trumpet, and piano trio the next.[11] Conversely, the International Tchaikovsky Competition (Moscow, quadrennial since 1958), is a hybrid, offering four categories—violin, piano, cello, and voice—simultaneously, but only once every four years.

The relationship between competitions, the music they select for performance, and the classical canon is an absorbing subject. While research has tended to focus on competitions' histories and psychological factors, the range of music typically required to enter a competition not only incentivises participants to master the repertoire (developing their repertoire base and versatility), but also expands the repertoire itself. While smaller competitions may call only for a single work or concerto movement to be performed, the larger international events can demand over three hours of music, spanning historical periods and sometimes including a newly commissioned work.[12] The Busoni, for example, asks for 45-minute and hour-long programmes, a 40-minute chamber ensemble programme, and an approximately 40-minute concerto for its final round. The impact of commissioning new music, meanwhile, is twofold: for participants, learning a piece with no performance history in a defined time period is often a new experience in itself; and the benefits for living composers, new music (an often embattled genre), and, indeed, the competitions themselves, are mutual. A prominent example is BBC Young Musician of the Year (London, biennial since 1978) and modern percussion repertoire, both of which have been galvanised by the category's introduction in 1994.

Similarly, collaboration is now an important feature of many competitions, from working with a specialist accompanist as a solo musician to performing with an established artist or chamber ensemble. Many piano competitions feature a chamber music round in which, for example, the pianist is asked to perform a piano quintet with a renowned string quartet. At the Van Cliburn International Piano Competition, for example, pianists performed alongside the Takács Quartet (more recently, the Brentano Quartet). At Calgary's triennial Honens International Piano Competition (f. 1992 as the quadrennial Esther Honens International Piano Competition), contestants play part of their semi-final round with guest artists: such musicians have recently included violist Hsin-Yun Huang, clarinettist James Campbell, and singer Isabel Bayrakdarian. Contestants fortunate enough to reach the finals of some of the larger events are also granted the opportunity to perform with a professional orchestra.

Despite their proliferation, the essential structure and format of competitions have not changed dramatically in recent years. Perhaps the chief differences lie in the exposure they provide to their participants and, relatedly, in post-competition expectations. Before the digital age, the focus fell largely on the winners, but today's social and musical landscape is such that competitions, historically vast in number, produce record numbers of winners, yet concert opportunities have actually declined.[13] These facts have skewed the ratio of competition winners-to-opportunities, ultimately creating an oversupply of concert artists. As Lisa McCormick has argued, there 'are now so many competitions that the prize-winning musician is no longer exceptional'.[14] Except, the very act of entering a classical music competition requires intensive practice, coaching, and trial performances, and nurtures educational and personal discipline, confidence, and comfort (with the practice and etiquette of performing under pressure). To be judged as a formative classical musician against peers and by a jury is exceptional in itself, especially in a high-level, international context when juries can nowadays include not only "star" names, but also other experts such as conductors, artist managers, and critics.[15] Moreover, we can add another tangible benefit—exposure—to those we have chronicled, for social media has quickened the pace of wider coverage of classical music competitions, as has the decision of many competitions to live-stream or archive performances online.[16]

Nevertheless, broader questions have been asked about the philosophy and practice of competitive music-making and continue to warrant scrutiny, for example, on the fairness of adjudication, and whether competitions can withstand either the polystylism of twenty-first-century musical life or attendant fears about musical judgement in general. It is against this precarious backdrop that a jury member must form a judgement on the relationship between the music and its expressive interpretation in performance. Further subjective considerations influence and moderate their verdict, from the music's difficulty and stylistic conventions, to technical matters particular to the instrument(s) or voice. Given these parameters, jury members are not merely adjudicators; they are aestheticians, historical musicologists, analysts, and audience members—not to mention typically performers themselves. Martin Cooper laid bare the paradox: 'Does A play Bach better than B plays Beethoven is a question that cannot logically be put, let alone answered.'[17]

Unsurprisingly, then, opinions on the desirability of certain expressive qualities vary, affecting not only a competition's outcome, but also the pedagogy that trains musicians and encourages them to compete. Moreover, research has shown that the consistency and reliability of rankings by adjudicators can be very low. Harold Fiske, for example, asked experienced adjudicators to rate a set of performances on their overall musical quality, but only he knew that each performance was presented twice, producing inconsistent scores for each performance.[18] Similarly, Renato Flores and Victor Ginsburgh analysed the Queen Elisabeth Competition over a ten-year period and found that competitors appearing on the final day stood a much greater chance of being ranked higher.[19] Whether due to adjudicators' fatigue, adjusted expectations, or greater appreciation of the music over time, the process of hearing the same pieces repeatedly seemingly caused criteria to be relaxed as the competition progressed. Many competitions, including the Queen Elisabeth, have since introduced pre-competition screening, serving to reduce the number of competitors appearing before juries in the public rounds of competition and thereby lessening the dangers of fatigue.[20]

The related psychology behind expectation, of who *should* perform well, is another longstanding, confirmed bias. George Duerksen, for example, presented listeners with two recordings of an identical performance but labelled one as professional, the other amateur—the latter received much lower marks.[21] Because such bias points both to greater risks (for example, partiality concerning gender, race, or sexuality) and to other influences (bodily gestures, facial expressions), some orchestras audition "blind", with candidates performing behind a screen. In popular music, *The Voice* made this same tactic its raison d'etre when in launched in the Netherlands in 2010. The trade-off is clear: bias is countered, however musicians cannot exploit the sort of visual, extramusical information that, for better or worse, has been an historical sway on their audiences. As Robert Schumann remarked on Liszt, 'if [he] played behind a screen, a great deal of poetry would be lost.'[22]

Competitions, meanwhile, have taken different steps to address concerns. To be accepted into the WFIMC, for example, competitions must agree that no more than half of its jury members hail from the competition's host country. The rule's implicit aim is obvious: to thwart potential geographical bias. Such "political" factors inevitably underlie, and risk undermining, the competition movement given its global reach.[23] Indeed, some commentators have called for competition organisers to go further, for example, by publishing adjudicators' scores post-competition or even after each round. The "Chopin" did so in 2015, revealing its final's scores, including how each jury member scored each participant.[24] Further policies include "no-discussion" rules forbidding jury members from conferring, enforced abstentions where jury members have a student in competition (as Warsaw's scores exemplify), and computerised scoring systems to adjust scores in order to calculate a jury's overall statistical voting distribution. Competitions' safeguards seek to uphold their integrity and answer the accusations they sometimes face, which tend to centre on nepotism, opaqueness, and, relatedly, score manipulation.[25]

The value of classical music competitions has changed as they have evolved and proliferated. Winning one may no longer guarantee that a career will flourish, but competitions remain popular, harnessing a natural instinct to compete and working tirelessly to discover and nurture talent. The different tastes, pedagogical styles, and performance traditions that problematise competitive music-making are also its lifeblood. To what end would classical music competitions otherwise exist, if not to foster discussion about how the genre is interpreted and to showcase excellence? The counter-argument is to fear that the strictures and pressure of competitions can have a homogenising influence on classical music practice. While competitions' modern variety partly assuages such concerns, we might ponder how an iconoclast such as Glenn Gould would have fared in a competition environment that inescapably rewards the majority view, even as it strongly prizes musical versatility.[26]

Should classical music competitions be *more* transparent about their criteria and scoring? The dilemma is that to go beyond the exemplar of the "Chopin" would introduce new risks. To publish a breakdown of scores for all rounds would be to reveal the losers and the margin of the "defeat", potentially harming participants psychologically. It could even nudge competitions in the direction of "reality" contests, whose wild success is based on their docudrama, charting contestants' musical and emotional highs and lows. Such invasiveness—exploitation, some argue—is anathema to classical music competitions, whose musicians are typically young adults and still developing. Competitions such as Indianapolis's seek to nurture and, increasingly, to mentor their participants. Financial advice is particularly important because cash prizes have risen rapidly in recent years as competitions have grown in number and themselves vie for attention and prestige: the aforesaid M-Prize awards its winner $100,000.[27]

Competitions are also beginning to broaden their scope. In May 2018, the first Leeds Piano Festival will extend that city's prestigious competition by featuring alumni (Lars Vogt, Alessio Bax, and Sunwook Kim) alongside younger pianists. Such initiatives are another form of mentorship, adding to the more typical guidance on public speaking, media skills (including social media and website design), publicity materials, and travel. For winners, in particular, further career-related rewards include the provision of engagements and recording opportunities and the arrangement of meetings and auditions with conductors or artist managers. Such guidance is intended to relieve the pressure on a winner, thrust into the limelight with career-changing decisions to make. Indeed, young winners have often accepted too many post-competition concerts, without adequately considering the probability of exhaustion, stress, or below-par performance. Efforts to educate and mentor participants, subvert the traditional argument that competitions risk artificially accelerating classical musicians' careers.[28] Although the complaint is perhaps more relevant to competitions for particularly young musicians, the "Menuhin" competition (biennial since 1983; officially the Yehudi Menuhin International Competition for Young Violinists, for musicians under 22) was an early pioneer in mentoring participants and encouraging interaction between its competitors.

The results of recent competitions are no exception. When cellist Sheku Kanneh-Mason won the 2016 BBC Young Musician, the discussion around his win was tellingly alive to the dangers of hype and expectation. Former winner Nicola Benedetti was employed to mentor all three finalists in 2016,[29] Julian Lloyd-Webber remarked (seconds after Kanneh-Mason was crowned) that 'I hope he is not now rushed into doing too much too soon—he has all the time in the world',[30] and the sentiment is clearly shared by Kathryn Enticott (Kanneh-Mason's General Manager), who recalls seeing 'the final and . . . [thinking] "I *have* to work with this guy" ' but is quick to stress the importance of

> taking a long-term view . . . staying grounded . . . ensuring it doesn't go to his head . . . and [preventing] things from happening too quickly in the wrong way: you can be exceptionally talented and your career can plummet in a year or two if it's not handled in the right way.[31]

Chairing that year's jury, composer Dobrinka Tabakova tearfully prefaced her announcement of the results by acclaiming the competition's capacity to 'shut the door to the crazy mediocrity . . . sweeping our country.'[32] Her logic is closer to Lloyd-Webber and Enticott than it might appear, for while the opportunities and dangers surrounding classical music competitions have new, modern contexts, their overriding motivation endures: to showcase, and safeguard, musical talent.

Notes

1. This section interpolates and develops previously published research. See Christopher Dromey, 'Competitions: Classical and Popular', in *Music in the Social and Behavioral Sciences*, ed. William Forde Thompson (London: Sage, 2014), 207–9.
2. See Annie J. Curwen, 'The First Competition Festival', *Musical Times*, 72/1056 (February 1931), 160.
3. See E. Douglas Bomberger, 'The Thalberg Effect: Playing the Violin on the Piano', *Musical Quarterly*, 75/2 (Summer, 1991), 198–208.
4. See also note 32.
5. See Thierry Bouckaert, *Elisabeth's Dream—A Musical Offering: Fifty Years of the Queen Elisabeth Competition*, trans. Peter King and Sara Montgomery (Brussels: Complexe, 2001).
6. Benjamin Woodroffe (Secretary General, World Federation of International Music Competitions), interview with the author, 5 August 2017.
7. See Alink-Argerich Foundation, Piano Competitions Worldwide: 2017–2018–2019, www.alink-argerich.org/books/detail/id/23 (accessed 5 August 2017).

8. See 'M-Prize Competition Guidelines', http://mprize.umich.edu/resources/MPrize2016_Guidelines.pdf (accessed 31 October 2017).
9. Unusually, the Busoni—the Ferruccio Busoni International Piano Competition, to give its proper title—was held annually until 2003, when it became a biennial competition.
10. See Fanny Waterman and Wendy Thompson, *Piano Competition: The Story of the Leeds* (London: Faber, 1990).
11. ARD, or Arbeitsgemeinschaft der öffentlich-rechtlichen Rundfunkanstalten der Bundesrepublik Deutschland, is a German consortium of nine local public broadcasters.
12. The WFIMC itemises its members' commissioned works: see www.wfimc.org/Webnodes/en/Web/Public/Competitions/Commissioned+works (accessed 6 November 2017). Incidentally, official competitions for composers are less common than for performers. Ordinarily, composers look instead to answer "calls for scores" issued by ensembles, organisations, and special events such as the Huddersfield Contemporary Music Festival (HCMF). The International Society for Contemporary Music (ISCM) monitors such opportunities: see www.iscm.org/article-tags/composers-competition). Nevertheless, certain competitions, as we have seen, include a category for composers in tandem with other disciplines. Also noteworthy is the historically important Prix de Rome (1663–1968), which began as a scholarship for French painters and sculptors, with music added in 1803, and was replicated abroad.
13. This is because the number of orchestras worldwide has fallen, and because many existing orchestras' seasons have been shortened. In the United States, for example, strikes/lockouts and bankruptcies have afflicted several orchestras, and the symphony orchestras of Honolulu (1900–2009, since revived as the Hawaii Symphony Orchestra), Syracuse (1961–2011), and New Mexico (1932–2011) have closed. See Philip Kennicott, 'America's Orchestras are in Crisis', *New Republic* (26 August 2013), https://newrepublic.com/article/114221/orchestras-crisis-outreach-ruining-them (accessed 12 December 2017).
14. Lisa McCormick, *Performing Civility: International Competitions in Classical Music* (Cambridge: Cambridge University Press, 2015), 2.
15. While involving people who lack discipline-specific expertise (e.g. technique) might once have seemed anomalous, competitions grant contestants valuable access to such industry figures, who understand, by virtue of their profession, what it takes to succeed. Assembling a strong and rounded jury is an art in itself.
16. Indeed, another very simple but important benefit is that competitions attract music critics. Musicians prize the opportunity to be reviewed because it can be difficult to obtain, can contribute to publicity material, and can reach a discipline-specific audience, for example, upcoming violinists appearing in the pages of *The Strad*.
17. Martin Cooper, 'Competitions' [*Daily Telegraph*, 20 January 1980], in *Judgements of Value: Selected Writings*, ed. Dominic Cooper (Oxford: Oxford University Press, 1988), 152.
18. See Harold E. Fiske, *The Effect of a Training Procedure in Music Performance Evaluation on Judge Reliability* (Ontario Educational Research Council Report, 1978).
19. See Renato Flôres and Victor Ginsburgh, 'The Queen Elisabeth Musical Competition: How Fair is the Final Ranking?', *The Statistician*, 45/1 (1996), 102.
20. Screening practices vary. Some competitions employ entirely different juries for screening rounds, while for others, such as Indianapolis's, the president of the "proper" competition jury also chairs a screening jury months before the main competition, but membership of the two juries does not otherwise overlap.

21. See George L. Duerksen, 'Some Effects of Expectation on Evaluation of Recorded Musical Performance', *Journal of Research in Music Education*, 20/2 (Summer, 1972) 268–72.
22. Robert Schumann [March, 1840], quoted in Konrad Wolff (ed.), *Robert Schumann on Music and Musicians*, trans. Paul Rosenfeld (New York: Pantheon, 1946), 156.
23. The Federation also recommends that juries comprise seven or more adjudicators. A less subtle example of politicking affecting musical judgement (in popular music) is the annual Eurovision Song Contest (f. 1956). Originally judged by national juries, then voted for by the public, and nowadays by a mix of the two, the contest gives each country equal weighting, no matter its size. As several European nations devolved in the late twentieth century, so Eurovision voting blocs became more pronounced. Countries tied by their geography or politics continue to reward each other's entries, amusing and frustrating commentators in equal measure. See Ivan Raykoff and Robert Deam Tobin (eds.), *A Song for Europe: Popular Music and Politics in the Eurovision Song Contest* (Aldershot: Ashgate, 2007).
24. See http://test12.nifc.pl/u299/final_oceny.pdf (accessed 1 December 2017).
25. Several recent flashpoints are detailed in Stuart Isacoff, 'Competition Judging: Keeping Evil Out of the Jury Room', *Musical America* (3 February 2015), www.musicalamerica.com/news/newsstory.cfm?storyID=33290&categoryID=7 (accessed 28 November 2017).
26. The speculation is slightly casuistic, and not only because Gould was such a one-off: we know he avoided competitions, save for a prize-winning appearance in 1944 at Toronto's first Kiwanis Music Festival in 1944, aged just 11.
27. More generally, "placed" musicians and, in certain cases, finalists and semi-finalists, may also receive financial reward. Some competitions also offer "in kind" rewards, for example, the loan of priceless instruments and other equipment, such as bows. The USA International Harp Competition goes further, awarding its winner a Lyon and Healy Concert Grand Harp.
28. As Cooper also argued: 'In a field where real progress is of its very nature slow, since it involves the whole personality, competitions demand an artificial acceleration, a process comparable to inducing the birth of a child.' Cooper, 'Competitions', 153.
29. Saxophonist Jess Gillam and horn player Ben Goldscheider were the other finalists.
30. Julian Lloyd-Webber, interviewed by Alison Balsom and Clemency Burton-Hill after the BBC Young Musician Final, Barbican Hall, London, 15 May 2016.
31. See Kathryn Enticott, interviewed *in Young, Gifted and Classical: The Making of a Maestro* (BBC Four, 2006).
32. Dobrinka Tabakova, announcing the result of the BBC Young Musician Final, 15 May 2016. Tabakova's tacit target was presumably shows such as *The Voice*, *The X Factor*, and their international imitators, whose success has transformed the meaning of competition in music more broadly. In truth, such programmes are throwback to the first televised talent contests, for example, *Opportunity Knocks* (1949–90), and while some finalists enjoy prolific sales in the short term, only a handful of winners have attained lasting fame and commercial success. Tabakova's 'mediocrity', then, is an imperfect antonym for the ideals of artistic dedication and longevity that classical music competitions such as the BBC Young Musician are designed to encapsulate, value, and reward.

Part II
Identity and Diversity

6 Uncertain Capital

Class, Gender, and the "Imagined Futures" of Young Classical Musicians

Anna Bull

In January 2016, Ed Vaizey, the UK's then Culture Secretary, told the classical music sector that it must make a 'step change' towards becoming more diverse and urged the need for clear targets to achieve this.[1] Such pressure coincides with an emerging body of research on inequalities in the creative and cultural industries in the UK.[2] For example, Dave O'Brien, Daniel Laurison, Sam Friedman, and Andrew Miles have demonstrated that there is a 'class ceiling' for those working in these industries, which under-represent those with working-class backgrounds, and that the music industry is one of the most unequal professions.[3] Their data does not reveal whether the structure of these inequalities is the same for classical music as it is for music more broadly. As Christina Scharff has noted, there is a lack of data on the class origins of classical musicians in the UK,[4] but as we shall see, the available evidence confirms assumptions that the profession is predominantly middle class.

This chapter examines the formation of class inequality in the classical music industry by drawing on qualitative data on the aspirations and pathways of young classical musicians from southeast England. It explores how patterns of class inequality among young people playing in classical music ensembles shape their aspirations, shows how these intersect with gender, and contextualises this within patterns of class inequality in classical music more widely. The theoretical focus of this chapter foregrounds class and explains gendered patterns through this lens.[5] The chapter first scrutinises the concept of class, then summarises research on class and classical music production before introducing the study from which data is drawn. It then describes how classical music works as a form of uncertain capital among the study's young musicians, whose class and gender positions strongly influenced their choices about whether to enter the profession.

Theorising Class and Culture

Contemporary associations between class and classical music are under-studied. It is possible to draw a strong correlation between being middle class and listening to classical music, as this chapter will outline. However, the mechanisms by which this occurs have been insufficiently examined, and economic factors, such as the prohibitive costs of lessons and instruments, have been seen as the primary driver of this correlation.[6] This chapter contends that social and cultural factors, intersecting with such economic factors, are equally important. The study of class has a long intellectual and political history,[7] but one way to approach it is to understand it as a set of theories that attempt to explain how economic inequality shapes identity and is reproduced. Stark differences in life expectancy, educational outcomes, occupational stratification, and health and well-being that map onto economic inequality can then be understood and addressed.[8] As such, there are various ways of measuring class. The UK government's measure draws on a key strand of sociological theory on class, using occupation as the key indicator. This chapter draws on a second, broader tradition of thinking about class: focusing on the interplay of material and cultural aspects of social life to examine how identities formed around economic inequalities become "sedimented", being passed between generations through shared norms and cultural practices.

The most successful examples of such work draw together aspects of lived experience, such as cultural taste, leisure practices, morality, aspirations, and ideas of self-worth, alongside wider patterns of economic inequality to theorise how certain social groups retain power and status in society.[9] Pierre Bourdieu's work on different forms of 'capitals' as resources that are convertible to one another is helpful here.[10] Bourdieu describes three main forms of capital: cultural, social, and economic, which can each in turn manifest as symbolic capital or prestige. These influential ideas recognise that social and cultural resources can confer status and can be converted into different types of resources.

Bourdieu theorises cultural capital very broadly, encompassing educational qualifications, bodily manner, mode of speech, and the possession and knowledge of cultural artefacts.[11] The most helpful sociological work following Bourdieu in this area explores how people's assumptions around what forms of culture are valuable shape their investment in them. For example, in a study of black middle-class parents in London, Carol Vincent, Nicola Rollock, Stephen Ball, and David Gillborn found that extracurricular instrumental music tuition was the second most popular activity for parents to choose for their children (after sports).[12] This was in some cases a conscious choice by parents of 'traditional, high status cultural knowledge',[13] such as encouraging their children to learn orchestral instruments in order to work against stereotypes of young black people who risked 'being positioned as marginal, less capable or deserving than their White peers'.[14] The assumption that classical music can be converted into other kinds of social resource is borne out another study of culture and class in the UK, which found that 'familiarity with classical music still acts as a form of institutional cultural capital' due to its use—especially opera—by elite groups for the purposes of networking and displaying cultural knowledge.[15]

A limitation of Bourdieu's work is that he fails to pay sufficient attention to people's affective engagement with culture, that is, the pleasure and fulfilment they may obtain from accruing cultural knowledge and skills. This is important not only in order to make a sociological account of the world recognisable to the people it is describing, but also because the pleasure people may take in listening to or playing classical music has social effects.[16] Pleasure threatens to interfere with the (conscious or unconscious) rational decision-making of the strategic actor that Bourdieu describes, and to derail their capital-accumulating "game". Classical music is an interesting way to explore this problem with Bourdieu's work because it appears that, in general, following classical music as a career does not lead to economic rewards: Mari Yoshihara's study of Asian-American classical musicians shows that pursuing a career in classical music tends to lower rather than raise a musician's class position;[17] similarly, the UK's Musicians' Union found that 56% of classical musicians in 2012 earned less than £20,000 per annum.[18] To scrutinise the classed and gendered dynamics of the choices of young people considering entering this profession is to explore whether the anticipated pleasure and fulfilment of a musical career can override such economic considerations—and to interrogate the extent to which such affective or emotional engagement challenges Bourdieu's model that people strategise for longer-term "capital accumulation".

Classed Patterns of Classical Music Consumption and Production

The aforesaid lack of existing data on the class background of British classical musicians is unsurprising given the broader lack of sociological attention to classical music as contemporary social practice. There are relatively few empirical sociological studies of classical music cultures, institutions, and practices.[19] Yoshihara and Hall have analysed class and classical music in the US and Australia respectively, but the only existing theoretically informed work on class and classical music in the UK is Scharff's work on young female classical musicians and class inequality.[20] These musicians perceived their industry as having become *more* middle class over time, and those who were not from middle-class backgrounds described feeling 'intimidated' or like an 'outsider'.[21] Similarly, Savage, drawing on data from Bennett et al.'s study of class and consumption in the UK, found in a representative sample of the UK population that people with degrees were six times more likely to listen to classical music than those without.[22] Particularly for white respondents, Bennett et al. found that 'classical music remains attuned to class' and among this group, for the working class, it evokes 'a response which is much more complex than a straight rejection or distaste for it', for example, distancing themselves from it.[23] From the limited data already available, then, it already appears that the middle classes predominate in both the consumption and production of classical music.

Similarly, in education, a recent Associated Board of the Royal Schools of Music (ABRSM) report found that 90% of children from AB backgrounds (the most privileged) had ever played an instrument,[24] against 74% from grades C1 and DE (lower socio-economic groups).[25] This reflects a long-term pattern for music exams to be predominantly undertaken by the middle classes, as David Wright has described.[26] The ABRSM study also found that the main reason both children and adults gave for choosing not to play a musical instrument is a lack of interest, or if they had learnt and given up, the main reason given was having lost interest.[27] By contrast, the cost of lessons was only the seventh most important factor for those who had given up playing and the second most important factor for those who had never played. This suggests that economic barriers are not the principal explanation for why people do not play an instrument.

Examining pathways for music education at tertiary level reveals similar "classed" patterns of self-elimination and exclusion. A recent (2007–11) study of admissions data centring on music and music technology degrees in the UK (excluding conservatoires) demonstrates a clear class divide between those studying the two subjects: the former predominantly middle class; the latter tending to be working-class boys.[28] This trend would appear to extend to music conservatoires. In 2006/07, *no* pupil who had received free school meals at age 15 (a standard measure of deprivation in the UK) had progressed to any of the UK music conservatoires four years later.[29] Supporting this finding, data from the five top conservatoires in the UK in 2012/13 shows that only 3.9% of students came from 'low participation neighbourhoods' (the lowest quintile of the UK, by area, for participation in tertiary education), against 9.8% across all tertiary music degree courses.[30] There is also a genre divide between different types of musical knowledge. As Georgina Born and Kyle Devine observe, music degrees tend to include a large component of classical music and to require the ability to read standard staff notation, whereas music technology degrees do not tend to require such knowledge, relying instead on different forms of notation and knowledge, such as music technology software.[31] Born and Devine argue that a 'confluence of an array of historical trajectories' is responsible for this divide, including musical, technological, industrial, social, educational, political, and policy-related changes since the 1990s.[32]

The Study

This chapter seeks to understand class inequalities in classical music in relation to young people's educational pathways by breaking the process of formation of these inequalities into two stages. The first stage examines the first few years of engagement with classical music learning and performing, as well as how children and their parents negotiate transitions in education such as between primary and secondary school.[33] A second stage, a particular focus of the chapter, examines further transitions from school, through higher education, to the music profession. Accordingly, it analyses the decisions young people make (on whether to continue studying classical music) against the backdrop of wider social inequalities surrounding class and gender. The data of this ethnographic study derives from a broader project conducted in 2012/13 on the "classed pathways" of young members of four classical youth ensembles (a choir, two orchestras, and an opera group) in a south-eastern English county, whose largest city is here anonymised as 'Whitchester'. I participated as a cellist in the two orchestras and as *répétiteur* for the opera group, and observed the choir's rehearsals and concerts. I also organised 37 semi-structured interviews and three focus groups with young people and interviewed nine adults involved in the running of these groups.[34] Rather than a mere snapshot, the study, conducted over 18 months, allowed the aspirations and pathways of young musicians to be followed and scrutinised.

The middle classes can be seen to have common norms and practices, such as protecting their position through education.[35] But to understand them as a political group they must be analysed by subcategory, for example, public and private sector employees,[36] or 'managerial' and 'professional' classes, with their different lifestyles and experiences.[37] It is also possible to describe such different middle-class "fractions" in terms of their length of tenure in the middle class, for example, 'new' or 'established'—a relatively objective measure of class on which the present study and its analysis draw.[38] This, then, is effectively a study of different middle-class fractions with quite different experiences of classical music education and of being middle class. Easily a majority among participants (n=28), the first group comprises children of the professional middle classes, who tended to live in or near Whitchester, and whose parents (and sometimes grandparents) had attended university. Another group of upper-middle class participants (n=4) had been educated privately since primary school.

A third group (n=4) comprised the children of the 'new' middle classes, or those who were striving to enter the middle class, whose parents had not attended university. These musicians were more likely to live in rural areas or small towns beyond Whitchester. Finally, the sample included one participant who could clearly be categorised as working-class according to the aforementioned scheme of Diane Reay, Gill Crozier, and David James.[39] These groupings are, to some extent, ideal types, as boundaries were not always clear-cut. These groups also revealed divisions according to the type of instrument participants played: the new middle-class group were most likely to be brass players, while string players were almost exclusively from the professional middle or upper-middle class group. For the 'new' middle-class group classical music also took on a particular meaning, symbolising entry into the 'proper middle class', as brass player Owen described. By contrast, for the professional middle-class and upper-middle-class young people, playing classical music was unremarkable and did not take them out of their usual social circles.

Uncertain Capital

The following analysis focuses on how inequalities affect young people's pathways once they are already heavily engaged in classical music. Participants had typically been learning their instrument for 5–15 years; sometimes longer. As we shall see, their gender and class positions mapped closely onto the ways in which they imagined their futures would unfold as well as their actual pathways during the course of this study. Using data about young people's class, gender, career choices, and aspirations, a clear pattern emerged.[40] Specifically, three groups can be classified according to their self-perceived understandings: the "bright futures", the "masters of the musical universe", and the "humble and hardworking" (see Figure 6.1).

The first group encompasses those who, despite excellent musical ability (for example, having achieved Grade 8 standard and participating in prestigious, selective schemes such as a junior conservatoire programme), had decided not to pursue music as a career. As 18-year-old violinist Bethan remarked just before embarking on undergraduate study at Oxford (having been asked what she had in common with the other members of her orchestra):

> Well I guess everyone here is very disciplined, you know, they're all clearly working very hard and going to have *bright futures* [laughs—emphasis added]. And I think—I've been practising the violin every day since I was six—not that I practise every day [laughs] but it's a good way to get into that kind of mindset where you just keep going and what you do pays off.

The "bright futures" group	• From the professional or upper-middle classes • Did not pursue music as a career
The "masters of the musical universe" group	• From the professional or upper-middle classes • Exclusively male • Pursued music as a career and anticipated holding a position of power or prestige
The "humble and hardworking" group	• From the professional or new middle classes • Pursued music as a career but did not expect high status or rewards

Figure 6.1 Classifying the Study's Groups of Young Musicians

Such striking, earnest confidence in the 'bright futures' in store for her and her fellow musicians were not specific to music—at least not for herself, as she had no inclination to become a professional musician—but rather were a general faith in future rewards for present effort.

Bethan also described how such a mindset ('what you do pays off') helps with schoolwork, that is, discipline and hard work beget success. Indeed, working in a disciplined manner with a view to future proficiency, pleasure, praise, or other rewards, is a value that permeates classical music education. The attitude requires musicians to possess a strong enough sense of their imagined future to invest in that future. As Beverley Skeggs notes, investment in a particular future requires imagining a future self that is valued by society and therefore is worth investing in.[41] If the imagined future is precarious or uncertain—more likely for those from less secure class positions—then investing in it makes less sense. It is notable that all members of the "bright futures" group were identified as hailing from professional middle-class and upper-middle class families, but tended not to have strong class identification, instead seeing themselves as 'normal'. They *were* normal relative to the circles in which they moved: their parents were lawyers, academics, vicars, teachers, research scientists, architects, or entrepreneurs, who ran their own companies. Some of these young people had seriously considered pursuing a career in music, often following the intense emotional experience of attending residential youth music courses, such as with the National Youth Orchestra (NYO).

However, everyone in this group had eventually made the 'difficult decision' (Fred) not to study music at a tertiary level. This choice had clearly involved much soul-searching for this participant, who eventually decided to study Business at a prestigious university. Fred described this preference as 'personal', but it is telling that retaining his securely middle-class position would be more likely if he pursued Business rather than Music at university; he followed the path that reproduced his class position. The affective experience of playing classical music had threatened to derail this, but in the end class identity prevailed. Nevertheless, Fred was able to convert his experiences into classed resources. At the time of his interview (between his first and second years of university), he was founding a business with a friend he had met in the NYO. His musical contacts had 'set me up hugely'. Fred's friend, Jack, who was now studying History and wanted to go into Politics, agreed that 'the social side [of music] will always be important.' One of the key assets of the middle classes is their social capital: the wide social networks they use to share knowledge, such as to find employment or the best schools.[42] For Fred, Jack, and others with "bright futures", classical music had provided them with networks of other middle-class professionals on which they would be able to draw in the future.

For violinist Alice, as for Fred, the decision not to study Music at university was difficult. Playing classical music had already paid high dividends:

Alice had obtained a music scholarship to a private school, which she believed had led to better exam results than would have been achievable in the state sector; as a result, she had been accepted by a university she perceived as better. Rewards such as these were already being reaped by many of these young people—little wonder that they agonised over whether to follow a career in music. And yet, none of the "bright futures" group appeared to regret their decision not to follow this path. Fred predicted that he would find an orchestral career boring if he had to do it for too long. Other interviewees suggested they were not prepared to put in the amount of work they knew would be necessary. For this group, learning classical music was part and parcel of the habitual practices of people in their class position. Rewards existed in the form of social networks, international travel, and access to grand and prestigious spaces such as the Royal Albert Hall, but these were similar to the types of experiences this group would accrue anyway.[43] Learning music had not made a transformative difference to their lives in the way it had for those from the new middle-class group, who found that classical music introduced them to an entirely different social scene.[44]

The second, much smaller group we shall brand "masters of the musical universe", comprising musicians from professional and upper-middle class backgrounds. By contrast with the "bright futures" group, these "masters" *had* decided to become professional musicians, but only because they had been promised a high status within the classical music world through winning awards, gaining entry onto highly selective music programmes, and encouragement from high-status teachers or mentors. At 16, Toby had already been singled out as a future "master", being selected while still at school to start a Music degree at the junior conservatoire programme he attended. With his sights set on a classical music career, he was on the way towards a high status in the musical world, perhaps as a composer, his chief interest. This group also included two young conductors, Adam and Will (both in their twenties), who had already secured positions of authority with relative ease. Adam had studied Music at Oxbridge and described how:

> When I got towards the end of university . . . I looked back at the competitions I'd won and positions I was being given over other people, and I thought: "This is something that's worth putting all my energy into pursuing professionally." I'm aware that by the time I reach thirty, I could not have made it . . . and then if it doesn't work, I can convert to Law and "sell my soul", you know . . . There are lots of things that I could earn some money doing.

Like Adam, other "masters" believed they had options for alternative careers if they did not attain their musical goals. It is significant that this group were exclusively male. As Scharff found, men disproportionately hold positions of power in classical music in the UK: for example, just 1.4% of conductors working in the UK are female.[45] The ease with which Adam,

Will, and Toby occupied positions of prestige, and expected to continue to do so, shows that this identity is already formed by the mid-to-late teens, and that class as well as gender plays a part in making this role seem natural to these young men.

The study's third group is the "humble and hard working", comprising musicians from lower-middle-class families, as well as some of the young women from established middle-class backgrounds. Such young people passionately wanted to make a career out of music, predominantly aiming to become either orchestral players or opera singers. They did not expect or desire to occupy positions of power within the industry. Not only had they internalised the identity of being a classical musician; they had also invested their whole lives in it. This was an exciting prospect for them. Ellie, for example, described how her career plans involved continual learning and improving (hence 'hard-working'):

> I'd love to be in an orchestra, to be at the back of an orchestra and be told what to do. Because I feel a lot of the time I'm always at the front and I already know what to do. I want to learn . . . I don't want to be a leader, I don't have any aspirations [like] that—earning money or being the soloist or whatever—just having the sense that I'm learning constantly.

Ellie had lower ambitions than the "masters", but her identity as a musician was total. All of her friends, her housemates, and her boyfriend were musicians. Music was her world: 'I never feel like I'm missing out on the rest of life because . . . I've got music . . . We're in our own little world. I have no awareness of what's happening outside this world.' Furthermore, with only two exceptions out of 15, every "humble and hardworking" participant was adamant that they wanted to be a classical musician, even if they also played other types of music, such as jazz, folk, or music theatre. Many members of the same group also cited experience of youth music, such as performing with the NYO, as a decisive moment in their decision to pursue a career in music. The intensive sociability of the residential courses, the close friendships they formed, and the powerful emotional experience of playing orchestral music combined to create a set of circumstances that convincingly positioned music as a fulfilling and rewarding career, despite the sacrifices it would entail.[46]

While most of the study's participants fitted clearly into one of these three categories, some of their trajectories were still unclear at the end of the research. Jenny, for example, resisted easy categorisation: her mother had been adamant that Jenny would be a professional musician and had worked hard to ensure her daughter attended a specialist music secondary school. Jenny left the school at 16, having found it stressful and difficult, and decided not to go to music college, being unconvinced that she would make the grade as a professional musician. To her delight, however,

Jenny subsequently discovered she had the grades needed to accept a place at Oxford to study Music. Jenny's mother had tried to guide her towards a "humble and hard-working" path, but Jenny rejected this, instead moving into the "bright futures" group.

How Class and Gender Shape Young Musicians' Pathways

The study's three groups demonstrate how gender and class position shaped the imagined and chosen futures of its young participants. Musicians with "bright futures" would often seriously consider becoming a professional musician. Their intensive social and emotional experiences of classical music during their youth threatened to derail the reproduction of their class position, but all members of the group eventually decided against this career path except for those who were promised positions as "masters of the musical universe". Instead, "bright future" youth musicians embarked on prestigious management training schemes, postgraduate law courses, or other routes that helped uphold social status. Among the established middle-class group, gender was crucial in influencing career aspirations: many of the young women who came from professional middle-class families went on to study Music at tertiary level, but young men from similar backgrounds would not. Jack, for example, had a "bright future"; his sister, Ellie, was "humble and hardworking". This difference needs to be understood in light of the argument that British music conservatoires and exam boards in the nineteenth century functioned in part as institutions to credentialise respectable middle-class femininity.[47] This historical reading as to why more women than men studied at music conservatoires remains relevant today, for performing classical music is still a much more socially acceptable pathway for middle-class young women than it is for young men.

What can we learn from the present study's data about class inequalities in the classical music industry more widely? First, an obvious point: in this study, young people's identities and aspirations were formed before entering and during higher education. Participation in youth music courses and ensembles during teenage years appeared to exert a strong influence on young people's decision-making and a formative effect on their identities. The powerful effect of ensemble participation for young classical musicians suggests that the social scene of youth classical music is an important site for addressing inequalities (such as gender-based) between those involved. Second, class inequalities are very heavily gendered. As discussed elsewhere, the classical music scene is revealing of the normative gender identities of the established middle class, and there is evidence that classical music can exacerbate existing gender inequalities.[48] To some extent, however, the normative practices of classical music may simply be reflecting and reproducing modes of femininity that are valued within the established middle class.[49] These two factors clearly reinforce each other, in that classical music today represents a 'respectable' form of middle-class femininity that fits closely with the gender ideals of this group.[50]

Third, different forms of inequality based on social, cultural, and economic resources intersected within this scene. The study yielded many examples of classical music's potential to compound already existing inequalities, from educational scholarships, through extensive networking among the established middle class, to learning the bodily and social confidence that studies show is required to enter many elite professions.[51] However, musicians entering the youth classical music scene from outside the professional or upper middle class had to make a heavy investment not only of time but also in reinventing their identity to be able to fit into this new social world. This prospect appears to appeal to young people from working class or new middle class groups who desire to move away from where they grew up, socially and geographically. Classical music offers a means of escape; notably, such geographical mobility is typically required in order to train and work in the creative industries, including classical music.[52] However, the psychological costs of taking on a new social class identity can be high, and as a performance discipline where insecurities become magnified, classical music can exacerbate such difficulties.[53] These factors, coupled with often low financial reward, make classical music a highly uncertain form of capital in which to invest.

Surprisingly, all of the new middle-class and working-class participants were keen to pursue careers as classical musicians—a finding that returns us to the role of pleasure and fulfilment in classical music and its potential disruption of Bourdieu's model. For example, "humble and hard-working" musicians, who were all female and/or new middle class or working class, described their wish to pursue a career in classical music in terms of its intrinsic rewards. For female singers among this group, this aspiration was partly because of the powerful physical experience of opera-singing. This suggests that while pleasure and fulfilment need to be taken into account when analysing young classical musicians' aspirations, an affective dimension of musical experience worked to entrench gender and class inequalities, rather than to work against them.

§

This chapter's tripartite typology has shown how class and gender are highly formative in determining young musicians' pathways. Classical music, an uncertain form of capital, confers very clear, tangible benefits on some musicians, but for others hard work and economic investment do not necessarily add to existing capital. In a sense, then, classical music practice does work as cultural capital in the essence of Bourdieu's formulation: it is formed out of the culture that the middle classes *obtain anyway* in the course of their day-to-day lives, but which other groups in society must work to acquire. For musicians from working-class and new middle-class backgrounds, classical music can work as a mechanism for social mobility, but this requires a heavy investment, socially, materially, and emotionally.

In the context of these aspirations, this chapter has also examined decision-making affecting how young people self-select into the classical music scene. Factors involved in this decision-making include school-based music provision and participation,[54] how class and parenting interact to discourage or encourage children to take up classical music,[55] and how children's social identity, including gender and class, interacts with social stigma to affect participation and retention rates in classical music.[56] Indeed, for many of the present study's young musicians, classical music's social scene was judged to be equally or more important than musical participation itself. Some young musicians, then, happily embrace the scene's "sociable geek" identity, whereas this identity is less easy to inhabit for others, such as working-class university students, who, as Reay, Crozier, and James found, fitted in socially by avoiding the label of 'the clever one or the swot' in a student learning culture defined by 'laid-back' attitudes.[57]

To understand social inequalities around classical music fully is to understand the ways in which it carries cultural capital. The scene's social and aesthetic aspects must be analysed together, as this chapter has done by relating the pleasure and fulfilment of playing classical music with young musicians' decision-making. However, the aesthetic demands of classical music affect its social structures and inequalities in more profound ways. Musical as well as social, the boundaries around classical music and its professional entry points are policed by those who have invested in social status through classical music, such as examiners, parents, and critics.[58] Aesthetically, classical music enacts this boundary-drawing by requiring years, more often decades, of practice to become musically proficient—demands that exclude anyone unable or unwilling to make this long-term investment. This means that while gender equality may improve, classical music in the UK is likely to remain a profession mainly populated by the middle classes.

Notes

1. Vaizey's speech to the Association of British Orchestras (ABO) is quoted in Vanessa Thorpe, 'Ed Vaizey: "No Excuse" for Lack of Diversity in British Orchestras', *The Guardian* (23 January 2016), www.theguardian.com/music/2016/jan/23/ed-vaizey-no-excuse-for-lack-of-diversity-in-british-orchestras (accessed 30 January 2016).
2. See Kim Allen, Josie Quinn, Sumi Hollingworth, and Anthea Rose, 'Becoming Employable Students and "Ideal" Creative Workers: Exclusion and Inequality in Higher Education Work Placements', *British Journal of Sociology of Education*, 34/3 (2013), 431–52; Mark Banks and Kate Oakley, 'The Dance Goes on Forever? Art Schools, Class and UK Higher Education', *International Journal of Cultural Policy*, 22/1 (2015), 1–17; Dave O'Brien, Daniel Laurison, Andrew Miles, and Sam Friedman, 'Are the Creative Industries Meritocratic? An Analysis of the 2014 British Labour Force Survey', *Cultural Trends*, 25/2 (2016),

116–31; Stephanie Taylor and Karen Littleton, *Contemporary Identities of Creativity and Creative Work* (Farnham: Ashgate, 2012).

3. O'Brien, Laurison, Miles, and Friedman, 'Are the Creative Industries Meritocratic?', 117.
4. Christina Scharff, *Equality and Diversity in the Classical Music Profession* (King's College London, 2015), http://blogs.kcl.ac.uk/young-female-and-entre preneurial/files/2014/02/Equality-and-Diversity-in-the-Classical-Music-Profess ion.pdf (accessed 2 April 2015).
5. This decision is taken partly to redress a lack of attention to explanations of class inequality in classical music production, and partly due to a theoretical premise that gender identities are always formed in relation to class position and cannot be analysed separately from class. For further discussion of gender and middle-class identities in classical music, see Anna Bull, 'Gendering the Middle Classes: The Construction of Conductors' Authority in Youth Classical Music Groups', *The Sociological Review*, 64 (2016), 855–71.
6. See, for example, Ivan Hewett, 'Music Education: A Middle-Class Preserve?', *The Telegraph* (11 June 2014), www.telegraph.co.uk/culture/music/music-news/10891882/Music-education-a-middle-class-preserve.html (accessed 12 April 2017); Frances Richens, 'Classical Music Becoming Middle Class, Committee Hears', *Arts Professional* (9 September 2016), www.artsprofessional. co.uk/news/classical-music-becoming-middle-class-committee-hears (accessed 12 April 2017).
7. See David Cannadine, *Class in Britain* (3rd edn; London: Penguin, 2000); Beverley Skeggs, 'Class, Culture and Morality: Legacies and Logics in the Space for Identification', in *The SAGE Handbook of Identities*, ed. Margaret Wetherell and Chandra Talpade Mohanty (London: Sage, 2010), 339–59.
8. See Kate Pickett and Richard Wilkinson, *The Spirit Level: Why Equality Is Better for Everyone* (London: Penguin, 2010), 20–30.
9. See, for example, Pierre Bourdieu, *Distinction: A Social Critique of the Judgement of Taste*, trans. Richard Nice (Cambridge, MA: Harvard University Press, 1984); Michèle Lamont, *Money, Morals and Manners: The Culture of the French and American Upper-Middle Class* (Chicago: University of Chicago Press, 1992); Beverley Skeggs, *Formations of Class and Gender: Becoming Respectable* (London: Sage, 1997); Tony Bennett, Mike Savage, Elizabeth Silva, Alan Warde, Modesto Gayo-Cal, and David Wright, *Culture, Class, Distinction* (New York: Routledge, 2009).
10. Pierre Bourdieu. 'The Forms of Capital', in *Handbook of Theory of Research for the Sociology of Education*, ed. John Richardson (New York: Greenwood Press, 1986), 241–58.
11. Bourdieu. 'The Forms of Capital', 48–51.
12. Carol Vincent, Nicola Rollock, Stephen Ball, and David Gillborn, 'Raising Middle-Class Black Children: Parenting Priorities, Actions and Strategies', *Sociology*, 47/3 (2012), 429.
13. Vincent, Rollock, Ball, and Gillborn, 'Raising Middle-Class Black Children', 429.
14. Vincent, Rollock, Ball, and Gillborn, 'Raising Middle-Class Black Children', 435.
15. See Bennett, Savage, Silva, Warde, Gayo-Cal, and Wright, *Culture, Class, Distinction*, 93. Mari Yoshihara reaches a similar conclusion in *Musicians From a Different Shore: Asians and Asian Americans in Classical Music* (Philadelphia: Temple University Press, 2007), 147.
16. For example, one young woman in this study found the authoritarian tactics of some choral conductors to be humiliating and unpleasant, but the pleasure of choral singing led her to acquiesce to this form of social organisation. See Bull,

'Gendering the Middle Classes'. See also Antoine Hennion, 'Music Lovers: Taste as Performance', *Theory, Culture & Society*, 18/5 (October 2001), 1–22.

17. See Yoshihara, *Musicians From a Different Shore*, 149.
18. See Musicians' Union, *The Working Musician* (2012), www.musiciansunion. org.uk/Files/Reports/Industry/The-Working-Musician-report.aspx, 5. (accessed 9 December 2016).
19. Studies relevant to this chapter include: Geoffrey Baker, *El Sistema: Orchestrating Venezuela's Youth* (Oxford: Oxford University Press, 2014); Clare Hall, *Voices of Distinction: Choirboys' Narratives of Music, Masculinity and the Middle-Class* (Ph.D. diss., Monash University, 2011); Henry Kingsbury, *Music, Talent, and Performance: A Conservatory Cultural System* (Philadelphia: Temple University Press, 1988); Lisa McCormick, *Performing Civility: International Competitions in Classical Music* (Cambridge: Cambridge University Press, 2015); Christina Scharff, *Gender, Subjectivity, and Cultural Work: The Classical Music Profession* (London: Routledge, 2018); Yoshihara, *Musicians From a Different Shore*.
20. See Hall, 'Voices of Distinction'; Scharff, *Gender, Subjectivity, and Cultural Work*; Yoshihara, *Musicians From a Different Shore*.
21. Scharff, *Gender, Subjectivity, and Cultural Work*.
22. See Mike Savage, 'The Musical Field', *Cultural Trends*, 15/2–3 (2006), 169. This article draws on data from the Cultural Capital and Social Exclusion study, which involved 25 focus groups with 143 participants, leading onto a nationally representative interviewer-administered survey of 1,564 participants, as well as ethnic boost sample of 227, and following this, qualitative interviews with 45 participants. For a full discussion of the study methods, see Bennett, Savage, Silva, Warde, Gayo-Cal, and Wright, *Culture, Class, Distinction*, 260–78.
23. Bennett, Savage, Silva, Warde, Gayo-Cal, and Wright, *Culture, Class, Distinction*, 82–4.
24. These descriptions use market research categories to analyse class. A, B, and C1 roughly correlate with middle class; C2, D, and E roughly correlate with working class. For further discussion, see Rosemary Crompton, *Class and Stratification* (3rd edn; Cambridge: Polity, 2015).
25. Simon Hume and Emma Wells, *ABRSM: Making Music* (London: Associated Board of the Royal Schools of Music, 2014), also available at http://gb.abrsm. org/de/making-music/# (accessed 23 March 2015). The study involved responses from 1,726 children and 1,255 adults learning music, weighted to a nationally representative profile on age and gender in line with statistics obtained from the Office of National Statistics, as well as data from 4,491 teachers.
26. See David Wright, *The Associated Board of the Royal Schools of Music: A Social and Cultural History* (Woodbridge: Boydell & Brewer, 2013), 226.
27. Hume and Wells, *ABRSM: Making Music*, 18–19.
28. Georgina Born and Kyle Devine, 'Music Technology, Gender, and Class: Digitization, Educational and Social Change in Britain', *Twentieth-Century Music*, 12/2 (2015), 135–72. This study draws on data from UCAS (the Universities and Colleges Admission Service) from 12 institutions, between them hosting 38 degrees, for six demographic variables over a period of five years (2007/08 to 2011/12). The authors found that 90% of students on music technology degrees were male between these years, and that 50% came from the lowest three quintiles of higher education participation areas of the UK. Other measures of class found similar patterns. 'Traditional' music degrees had a gender balance of 55% female to 45% male and admit a greater proportion of students from POLAR quintiles 4 and 5, i.e. those regions most likely to participate in higher education and showing greatest relative advantage.
29. Department for Business, Innovation and Skills, 'Pupils on Free School Meals Attending Music Colleges. A Freedom of Information Request to Department

for Business, Innovation and Skills' (31 July 2013), www.whatdotheyknow. com/request/pupils_on_free_school_meals_atte#incoming-414358 (accessed 11 November 2014).

30. I draw here on unpublished research ('Analysis of Demographic Background of UK Music Students') conducted in 2014 by Christina Scharff, Patricia Kokot and John Blamey.

31. Born and Devine, 'Music Technology, Gender, and Class', 153.

32. Born and Devine, 'Music Technology, Gender, and Class', 146.

33. This century has seen a growing interest in such transitions. See, for example, Susan Hallam, Andrea Creech, Ioulia Papageorgi, and Lynne Rogers, *Local Authority Music Services Provision (2007) for Key Stages 1 and 2* (London: Institute of Education, 2007); Susan Hallam and Vanessa Prince, *Research into Instrumental Music Services* (London: Institute of Education, 2000); Alexandra Lamont, David J. Hargreaves, Nigel A. Marshall, and Mark Tarrant, 'Young People's Music In and Out of School', *British Journal of Music Education*, 20/3 (2003), 229–41; Lynne Rogers and Susan Hallam, 'Music Services', in *Music Education in the 21st Century in the United Kingdom. Achievements, Analysis and Aspirations Rogers*, ed. Susan Hallam and Andrea Creech (London: Institute of Education, 2010), 279–94.

34. Participants in these groups were aged between 12 and early 20s, but interviewees were all 16 or over due to ethics considerations. All interviews were audio-recorded and transcribed verbatim with permission.

35. See David Lockwood, 'Introduction: Marking Out the Middle Class(es)', in *Social Change and the Middle Classes*, ed. Tim Butler and Michael Savage (London: UCL Press, 1995), 1–14; Diane Reay, Gill Crozier, and David James, *White Middle Class Identities and Urban Schooling* (Basingstoke: Palgrave Macmillan, 2011).

36. See Rob Moore, *Basil Bernstein: The Thinker and the Field* (New York: Routledge, 2013) 167–8.

37. James Barlow, Peter Dickens, Tony Fielding, and Mike Savage, *Property, Bureaucracy and Culture: Middle Class Formation in Contemporary Britain* (London: Routledge, 1995), 127.

38. See Reay, Crozier, and James, *White Middle Class Identities and Urban Schooling*, 28–31.

39. Reay, Crozier, and James identify three vertical middle-class fractions among their research participants based on historic class location: first, first-generation middle-class, i.e. those from aspiring working-class backgrounds who were the first in their families to have a professional occupation; second, second-generation middle-class, i.e. children of first-generation middle-class parents; third, the established middle class, who, for the most part, had attended private schools as well as university and whose own parents and grandparents often enjoyed such opportunities, including at elite universities. The authors note that 'in such families there were often clear markers of wealth and positions of power, status and influence'. Reay, Crozier, and James, *White Middle Class Identities and Urban Schooling*, 28–9. For my study, I have amended these labels to new, professional, and upper middle class to better reflect participants' subjective labels of their class position. The working-class participant in my research was therefore identified as such on the basis of his parents' occupations and education levels and his own education.

40. Since almost all participants were white, the study does not attempt to scrutinise racial inequalities. Yoshihara and Scharff's findings about discrimination and low representation among classical musicians from ethnic minority groups suggest that this factor warrants further attention. See Yoshihara, *Musicians from a Different Shore*, 4, 131–65, 190; Scharff, *Equality and Diversity in the Classical Music Profession*, 13, 17.

41. See Beverley Skeggs, *Class, Self, Culture* (London: Routledge, 2003), 46.
42. See Stephen J. Ball and Carol Vincent, ' "I Heard It on the Grapevine": "Hot" Knowledge and School Choice', *British Journal of Sociology of Education*, 19/3 (1998), 377–400.
43. See, for example, Phillip Kirby, *Leading People 2016* (The Sutton Trust, 2016), www.suttontrust.com/researcharchive/leading-people-2016/ (accessed 8 September 2016); Paul Wakeling and Mike Savage, 'Entry to Elite Positions and the Stratification of Higher Education in Britain', *The Sociological Review*, 63/2 (2015), 290–320.
44. I discuss this issue further in *The Musical Body: How Gender and Class Are Reproduced Among Young People Playing Classical Music in England* (Ph.D. diss., Goldsmiths, University of London, 2015), 125–51.
45. Scharff, *Equality and Diversity in the Classical Music Profession*, 13.
46. This argument leads into a wider set of debates around the creative industries, whereby the pleasure and fulfilment of cultural work is presented by cultural workers as one of the key motivating factors for individuals to enter these professions, and which provide a rationale for the precarious nature of work in this sector. See, for example, Angela McRobbie, *Be Creative: Making a Living in the New Culture Industries* (Cambridge: Polity, 2015).
47. See Bull, *The Musical Body*.
48. See Bull, 'Gendering the Middle Classes'.
49. See, for example, Claire Maxwell and Peter Aggleton, 'Agentic Practice and Privileging Orientations among Privately Educated Young Women', *The Sociological Review*, 62/4 (August 2014), 800–20.
50. Anna Bull, 'El Sistema as a Bourgeois Social Project: Class, Gender, and Victorian Values', *Action, Criticism & Theory for Music Education*, 15/1 (January 2016), 136.
51. See, for example, Louise Ashley, Jo Duberley, Hilary Sommerlad, and Dora Scholarios, *Non-Educational Barriers to the Elite Profession Evaluation* (Social Mobility & Child Poverty Commission, 2015), www.gov.uk/government/news/study-into-non-educational-barriers-to-top-jobs-published (accessed 6 November 2015); Social Mobility Commission, *Socio-Economic Diversity in Life Sciences and Investment Banking*, www.gov.uk/government/publications/socio-economic-diversity-in-life-sciences-and-investment-banking (accessed 26 September 2016); Lauren A. Rivera, *Pedigree: How Elite Students Get Elite Jobs* (rev. edn; Princeton: Princeton University Press, 2016).
52. See Alessandra Faggian, Roberta Comunian, Sarah Jewell, and Ursula Kelly, 'Bohemian Graduates in the UK: Disciplines and Location Determinants of Creative Careers', *Regional Studies*, 47/2 (April, 2013), 183; Caitriona Noonan, 'Professional Mobilities in the Creative Industries: The Role of "Place" for Young People Aspiring for a Creative Career', *Cultural Trends*, 24/4 (September, 2015), 299–309.
53. Sam Friedman, 'Habitus Clivé and the Emotional Imprint of Social Mobility', *The Sociological Review*, 64/1 (February 2016), 129–47.
54. See note 33. See also Shirley Cleave and Karen Dust, *A Sound Start: The Schools' Instrumental Music Service* (Windsor: NFER-Nelson, 1989).
55. See, for example, Hall, 'Voices of Distinction'; Sarah Irwin and Sharon Elley, 'Concerted Cultivation? Parenting Values, Education and Class Diversity', *Sociology*, 45/3 (June 2011), 480–95; Nicola Rollock, David Gillborn, Carol Vincent, and Stephen J. Ball, *The Colour of Class: The Educational Strategies of the Black Middle Classes* (London: Routledge, 2015); Valerie Walkerdine, Helen Lucey, and June Melody, *Growing Up Girl: Psychosocial Explorations of Gender and Class* (New York: New York University Press, 2001).

56. See, for example, Louise Archer, Sumi Hollingworth, and Anna Halsall, ' "University's Not for Me—I'm a Nike Person": Urban, Working-Class Young People's Negotiations of "Style", Identity and Educational Engagement', *Sociology*, 41/2 (April, 2007), 219–37; Becky Francis, Barbara Read, and Christine Skelton, *The Identities and Practices of High Achieving Pupils: Negotiating Achievement and Peer Cultures* (London: Bloomsbury, 2012).

57. Diane Reay, Gill Crozier, and John Clayton, ' "Fitting In" or "Standing Out": Working-Class Students in UK Higher Education', *British Educational Research Journal*, 36/1 (February 2010), 117.

58. See Daniel Leech-Wilkinson, 'Classical Music as Enforced Utopia', *Arts and Humanities in Higher Education*, 15/3–4 (July 2016), 325–36.

7 Inequalities in the Classical Music Industry

The Role of Subjectivity in Constructions of the "Ideal" Classical Musician

Christina Scharff

Inequalities in the cultural and creative industries have come on the agenda in recent years. Academic research and debates in the media and the cultural sector have highlighted the lack of diversity in the cultural workforce. In line with these developments, several reports have mapped existing inequalities in the classical music industry.[1] Such analyses have documented a range of patterns, including the middle-class culture of classical music practice, the under-representation of female musicians and musicians from working-class and/or black and minority ethnic backgrounds, and vertical segregation (referring to the over- or under-representation of particular groups in positions of power) as well as horizontal segregation (relating to the concentration of particular groups in specific sectors of the classical music industry).[2] Equally important, research has also analysed some of the gendered and racialised norms that circumscribe performance,[3] and drawn attention to issues of sexual harassment.[4]

A wide range of explanations for the persistence of inequalities in the classical music profession has been uncovered. Research on the lack of diversity in the cultural and creative industries has demonstrated that informal recruitment practices disadvantage women, black and minority ethnic workers, as well as individuals from working-class or lower middle-class backgrounds.[5] Higher education also seems to play a part in perpetuating inequalities in these industries,[6] which, in the classical music industry, can be extended to primary and secondary education.[7] Similarly, the issue of parenting is frequently raised in such debates, especially in relation to mothering.[8] As I explore in detail in this chapter, parenting has to be approached from a feminist angle, which takes into account the reality that women continue to act as primary caregivers, while avoiding reaffirming the link between women and childcare.[9]

Most pertinent to the arguments presented in this chapter, recent research has begun to explore the role of subjectivity in inequalities in the cultural and creative industries. This body of work has highlighted the link between perceptions of the ideal worker subjectivity and ongoing inequalities.[10]

Subjectivity is a complex term that has been approached in different ways.[11] In the contexts discussed here, it refers to the kinds of selves that are required to count as a "creative", "artist", or classical musician. In her research on screenwriting, for example, Bridget Conor has identified the ideal subject positions for the screenwriter, such as the pioneer, egotist or fighter, and demonstrated how these masculine figures point to 'gendered understandings of heroic, individual creativity.'[12] Indeed, prevailing notions of creativity are gendered. As Alison L. Bain remarks: 'In contemporary Western mythology, the artist is understood to be male.'[13] This myth risks marginalising women from creative processes and roles.[14]

This chapter takes as its starting point analyses of the role of subjectivity in inequalities in the classical music profession, looking in particular at classed, gendered and racialised constructions of the "ideal" classical musician. After a brief overview of the research methods underpinning the analysis presented here, the first analytical section hones in on the importance of networking to succeed in the classical music profession. More specifically, it draws on interviews to ask whether the networked and networking classical musician is a middle-class subject. Section two returns to the issue of gender and parenting to demonstrate how having children is often portrayed as "difficult" or "tough". While practical considerations such as working hours contribute to a sense that working in classical music is difficult to combine with having a family, my analysis shows that female musicians face particular dilemmas when deliberating whether, and when, to have children. Crucially, these dilemmas go beyond practical considerations and play out in the realm of subjectivity, most notably through the tensions that emerge from constructions of ideal musicians as emotionally invested, which seem to leave little space for additional commitments. Having traced some of the ways in which class and gender intersect with the ideal worker subjectivity in the context of the classical music industry, the final section explores racialised constructions of musicians. In particular, it critiques portrayals of East Asian players as "robotic" and "technical",[15] demonstrating that these constructions are indicative of a racial hierarchy where Western classical music continues to be associated with whiteness. These portrayals of East Asian players are not only derogatory, but also represent such musicians as unmusical. Subjectivity, then, intersects with race, class and gender in complex ways. Crucially, it is not my intention to provide a deterministic analysis, but to deepen our understanding of inequalities in the classical music profession.

The data presented here is part of a larger project on the classical music profession, exploring contemporary issues such as the subjective experiences of precarious work, how urban contexts affect work in the cultural and creative industries, and ways in which musicians negotiate inequalities.[16] The study focused on the experiences of female musicians to document their previously under-researched working lives and was largely based on sixty-four semi-structured in-depth interviews. Research participants were based in London (n=32) and Berlin (n=32) to explore how artistic lives are experienced in different urban contexts. Most participants were in their late twenties or early thirties at the time of interview (2012–13). The sample consisted of musicians who played a range of instruments, as well as singers, conductors, opera directors and composers. Reflecting the under-representation of working-class and black and minority ethnic players in the classical music profession, the sample was overwhelmingly white and middle class. Forty-four musicians in the sample identified as middle class, seven as working class, and two as lower middle class. Eleven were not sure how to describe their socio-economic background, which resonates with broader arguments that popular awareness of class seems to wane.[17] Fifty-six described their racial background as white, four as mixed raced, two as East Asian, one as black and one as Asian. The research was conducted following research ethics guidelines and analysed by using discourse analysis in order to identify recurring discursive patterns arising from what participants said.[18] Interviews were conducted in German and English, and all translations from German into English are my own.

Networking: A Classed Practice?

Many participants pointed out that networking was a key component of working as a classical musician. According to Carolyn, networking was really important: 'I do see that as part of our job, I don't think you can really get away from that, and I do think the whole networking thing is really important.' Isabella also felt that networking was crucial to succeeding in the industry: 'In the current climate with everybody wanting stuff and what is happening with economics, it is a lot of competition. Besides being an amazing musician, you have to be a clever networker.' June echoed these sentiments when she stated that 'self-promotion, networking . . . it's just huge. I'd say if you are a good entrepreneur, and a good self-promoter, it would almost go to 80% of your success.' Freelancers in particular pointed out that they found all of their work through networking. Stefanie, for example, said that networking might not be so important if

> you are just looking for an orchestra job . . . but for something like the life that I would like, absolutely. That's how I would get work. Meeting people and having a website, which I am currently working on, being good at talking to people at intermissions and after shows.

Such statements resonate with wider research on work in the cultural and creative industries, which has demonstrated that recruitment is often based on 'personal networks'.[19] As Conor, Rosalind Gill and Stephanie Taylor have argued: ' "word-of mouth", reputation-based decisions [are] by far the most common way of securing or distributing work."[20]

However, as several studies on the cultural sector have shown, informal recruitment practices disadvantage women as well as professionals from black and minority ethnic and working-class backgrounds.[21] According to Irena Grugulis and Dimitrinka Stoyanova's study on networking in the UK film and television industry, a key element of disadvantage is the quality of a network's resources and its related potential to lead to quality jobs; indeed, 'white, male, middle-class informants were far more likely to enjoy networks which could provide access to quality work.'[22] Other studies have foregrounded the importance of confidence and "know-how" in networking, highlighting their reliance on types of social and cultural capital that are unevenly distributed along classed lines, and which therefore disadvantage students and workers from less privileged socio-economic backgrounds.[23]

How, then, do research participants' class backgrounds affect their perceived ability to network? Isabella was particularly outspoken about the intersections between her class background and her negative feelings towards networking:

> I hate it. I mean, you see, I come from a middle-class, lower middle-class family. My parents are educated, but they do not have much money. So of course I was taught how to behave. But if you do not do it when you are a kid, it becomes hard for you, what to say, how to do it.

Crucially, Isabella did not find it impossible to network. Instead, she emphasised that she had learned how to do it when she moved to London:

> But then I moved to London and you meet quite a few people like this, because London is full of people like this, high-class, a lot of money, not only, but you meet a lot of these people at concerts . . . You learn to get accustomed; you learn they love music, so you have to rely on that. You're the thing they are interested in. I love art so I know some things about painting, but I don't know everything, because I wasn't accustomed to it as a kid, because I come from a very small place, but because of this you just learn. You become like a kid who is twenty who is like "oh my God!", and that is it. Just be yourself and be nice and listen a lot and smiling a lot and they are really lovely people.

By pointing out that most of the people she had to network with were 'high-class', Isabella highlights class differences between herself and the people she meets in the context of her work. Resonating with her prior statement, she emphasises that she did not mix with 'high-class' people as part of her upbringing. She 'wasn't accustomed to it as a kid'. Nevertheless, she claims that she learned how to do the necessary small talk, thus presenting herself as someone who is able to overcome barriers.

Similar to Isabella, June linked her difficulties with networking to her 'upbringing'. Describing her parents as 'working-class type', she later spoke about her reluctance to network:

I think from my upbringing and from the way my culture is, it's very hard for me networking, and doing all that. Which is extremely important. Well, it's not important but it's lucrative. If you can work the room after the show, you can then secure yourself some work for a very long time.

As discussed elsewhere,[24] June was one of a few participants who did not come from a middle-class family and who linked some of her struggles of navigating the classical music profession to her working-class background. For example, she spoke about her parents' unfamiliarity with Western classical music and their concerns about her not getting a 'real job'. June, then, explicitly oriented to the importance of class background (and, implicitly, to class differences) in her interview.

Statements by Isabella, June and also Angela suggest that class background plays a role in how classical musicians negotiate networking. Angela described her family as 'not very well situated' and remarked that she knew very little about the classical music industry when she started as a student. Several participants in Germany endorsed the idea of networking with conservatoire teachers prior to auditions, typically by arranging and paying for a "consultation" lesson. Angela was not aware of this practice and 'naively' went to the auditions:

So, today I'd advise everybody to do that [networking with conservatoire teachers] beforehand. I mean, simply for the reason, I mean, I don't think it's great, really . . . I don't think it's good, but if everybody does it and you are the only one, yes, from the negative background with no contacts who goes there, and you are as good as somebody who, for example, has such a contact, then it's always the case that the other person will probably get it [a place].

Angela describes class backgrounds like hers as a 'negative background with no contacts', casting it in a negative light, but also foregrounding the role that having contacts plays in gaining access to conservatoires. Class background thus intersects with networking not only in terms of feeling comfortable around 'high-class' people (Isabella), but also in relation to the kinds of contacts one may or may not have (Angela), and whether one finds it 'hard' to network (June).

Crucial to this chapter's wider argument on the role of subjectivity in the context of inequalities in the classical music profession, the successfully networked and networking individual seems to be from a middle-class background. Participants who felt comfortable networking were *all* middle class. As Carolyn further remarked: 'I enjoy meeting people. I'm a really bubbly person, so I'm very happy to talk to people after a concert and that kind of thing.' Annegret likewise described networking as something that happens to her quite 'automatically' and that she does not do 'consciously'. More broadly, many participants displayed intimate knowledge of how to network successfully in the profession, for example, by highlighting the importance of avoiding 'cold calling' (Nora), i.e. approaching people one has not yet established a relationship with, drawing attention to appropriate codes of conduct by cautioning against 'pushy' behaviour (Jane), or stating it was useful to remember details about colleagues' personal and professional lives (Esther). Aligned with such matters of networking etiquette, there was also policing of musicians who overdo it. Stefanie, for example, stated:

> I have seen people who do the networking thing and it just totally turns me off, because . . . they are way too desperate about it. I don't think you have to do that. I think you can be genuinely interested and because of that meet people and have musical relationships come out of that. I don't think it's necessary to be so desperate, like plastering yourself all over somebody, like "Here is my business card!"

The middle-class participants' detailed descriptions of the ins and outs of networking, as well as their rather confident attitude towards it, contrast with the difficulties that some of the working-class or lower middle-class research participants voiced. Significantly, this did not mean that participants from less privileged socio-economic backgrounds were unable to engage in networking. As demonstrated, Isabella, for example, emphasised that she had acquired the necessary know-how.

The perceived ability to be a successful networker also intersects with national background. Non-native speakers highlighted difficulties in making phone calls to promote one's work (Kira) or stated that they found it 'tiring' to socialise over drinks after a concert (Esmeralda): 'Especially for me, when I'm tired to speak in English, sometimes it's more hard. So it's awful, you don't know what you are saying anymore.' Equally important, several participants highlighted the gendered dynamics of networking and, more specifically, concerns about self-promotion. Female musicians have to negotiate a range of gendered challenges when engaging in self-promotion, including accusations of lacking modesty, fears of not being taken seriously as an artist, and reservations about "selling yourself" in a wider, sexualised context.[25] Indeed, Isabella's statement and her reference to being 'nice', to smile a lot, and to listen can be read as pointing to some of the gendered dimensions of networking. Consequently, class background is not the only factor that affects musicians' perceived ability to network; it also intersects with gender and national background.

"Difficult and Tough": Parenting in the Classical Music Profession

An issue that is commonly raised—especially in public debates about gender inequalities in the cultural sector—is parenting. Specifically, it is often argued that women are under-represented in the cultural industries because of difficulties of combining such creative work with raising children.[26] From a feminist perspective, however, these perhaps well-intended explanations for the persistence of gender inequalities pose a dilemma:

> On the one hand, one needs to recognize the continued reality that caring for children is largely undertaken by women, yet on the other, by doing so, one risks re-cementing the relationship between women and children and perpetuating the very gender inequality one wants to critique.[27]

With this in mind, the issue of parenting in the context of the classical music profession can be approached from a slightly different perspective. Drawing on Natalie Wreyford's research on constructions of the 'committed, creative worker' and the ways in which this perpetuates gender inequalities around parenting,[28] the next section will explore how participants discussed parenting.

According to Wreyford's research on the British film industry, the ideal creative worker is portrayed, and constructed, as someone who is driven and committed, which in turn 'functions to exclude anyone with other responsibilities or demands on their time.'[29] Given ongoing portrayals of women as primary caregivers, this construction is not gender-neutral but affects female, creative workers in several ways. They are perceived, for example, as potential mothers, whether or not they want to have children.[30] This may affect hiring decisions, where it may be presented as more 'rational' to hire a man because he would be less likely to take any time off for paternity leave.[31] Most important to the present argument, constructions of the driven and committed creative worker as free from caring responsibilities mean that female classical musicians have to engage in a range of negotiations when considering having children. These negotiations are not limited to navigating the practical and very real constraints of juggling having a career and a family, particularly in a freelance environment where entitlement to maternity benefits is rare. Arguably, they go deeper, in that they also seem to involve identity work whereby female musicians have to reconcile seemingly incompatible pursuits, such as being 'other-oriented', with the selfish 'immersion which is essential to the creative process.'[32] As we shall see, this dilemma is faced not only by musicians who are mothers, but also by those contemplating whether they would like to have children.

When questioned on their views about having children as a classical musician, around a third of participants portrayed it as 'really difficult' (Alice, Amanda and Isabella) or 'a problem' (Jana). Similarly, Christine remarked:

> For me, it's not necessarily something that I think I want to do . . . but it is difficult, because you think "if I did change my mind, how would I do that, you know, without having that regular income?" Well, secure

income . . . But at the moment I am thinking it is not something that I'd want to do, so for me it is not so bad. But for people who do, and especially for people who want children young, if they want to be a composer or a musician, it's really, really tough.

Echoing these sentiments, Holly, a composer, stated:

As a woman, it's hard, especially if you want to have a family. I have absolutely no idea how that works. Because I would love to have a family one day, but . . . genuinely, I don't know how that would work. What do you do with the children when you are writing? Where do they go? I don't know. It's baffling.

Esmeralda, who has a daughter, also described being a female musician with a child as 'tough':

It's tough, it's really tough. Because sometimes when they call you for a gig and you really wanna do it, the babysitter is not always available. Now I've got more help, but I mean it is tough, it is awfully tough, really.

In all of these statements, having children is portrayed as 'tough'.

This is not to suggest that having children as a classical musician is impossible. Like Esmeralda, several research participants already had children and described how they managed to juggle childcare with the demands of being a musician. Another participant, Janine (who had had a child at the comparably young age of 25), explained that her rationale was to do it 'now, when I can take a break, when my career hasn't built up too much.' Michaela, by contrast, emphasised that she had a supportive partner who 'has my back and that's how I can do it all.' And participants sometimes referred to the intersections between income and parenting, for example, by emphasising the need to earn well in order to afford high-quality, flexible childcare (e.g. Alice and Ricarda).

However, this portrayal of having children as difficult and tough was pronounced. In addition to the reasons mentioned above, participants—with or without children—pointed to: the unsocial hours musicians must work and the lack of childcare provision during such hours; the lack of maternity benefits, especially for freelancers; and the importance of regular practice to remain able to compete professionally. Some participants portrayed freelancing as amenable to balancing a career with having children, mainly due to the flexibility it provides. Conversely, other participants, and most notably those who were already mothers, drew attention to the challenge of combining freelance work, typically unpredictable in nature, with raising a family. Their accounts resonate with existing research, which demonstrates that female, creative workers who work flexibly struggle to carve out the time and space to combine creative work with domestic and caring responsibilities.[33]

The role that constructions of the ideal worker subjectivity play in perpetuating inequalities is also highlighted by tensions between mothering and emotional investment in work—an issue raised by several participants. As Stephanie Taylor and Karen Littleton have shown: 'If your work and your personal relationships require the same *kind* of commitment and emotional input, then, logically, there will be extra difficulty combining them.'[34] This tension came to the fore in various statements made by participants who did not yet have children:

AMANDA: I just kind of feel I'm doing something I love, so I don't need [to have children] . . . at the moment . . . I can see how it would be really difficult if I wanted a family.

ISABELLA: I don't think I could give enough attention to a kid compared with the attention I want to give to my violin and to the person I love. I don't know if there is enough space.

JANE: We are both very happy, we love our careers and we love each other, and being together and stuff. We love life at the moment and [having children] would be such a big change.

CHRISTINA: And do you think you'd feel differently if, say, you had a job with maternity leave?

JANE: I think if I really loved the job as passionately as I do now, it would still be an issue.

Notably, these tensions were rarely cast in terms of practical considerations around childcare, but in terms of emotional capacity: Amanda, Isabella and Jane each express their passion for their work and highlight how this would conflict with caring for a child. Their accounts suggest that the fully committed, classical musician is emotionally invested in their work. The necessary commitment thus exceeds practical considerations (such as availability to play at particular times) and also plays out in the realm of subjectivity. Crucially, this conflict is heightened for female creative workers, who face another tension between the selfishness demanded by creative work and 'long-established gendered positionings of women as other-oriented, attending to the needs of others and heeding their preferences.'[35] As Isabella put it succinctly, she does not know whether 'there is enough space' to focus on her violin and her partner, as well as a child. Having children, then, is not just a matter of external constraints and considerations, but also raises issues that reach into the realm of subjectivity and the internal conflicts that arise from a woman, a creative, and a caregiver.

Of Robots and Race: Constructions of Musicality

Having traced some of the connections between class, gender and subjectivity, I will now focus on racialised constructions of classical musicians.

As Taru Leppänen has reminded us, 'Western classical music is in many ways connected with Whiteness, despite the rarity of explicit expressions of race and ethnicity in connection to the culture of this musical form.'[36] Indeed, the majority of research participants disavowed racial inequalities in the classical music profession. While some participants openly discussed the lack of racial diversity among musicians, most interviewees disarticulated racial inequalities. As discussed in detailed elsewhere,[37] participants used a range of rhetorical devices to disavow persisting racial hierarchies. As an illustration, three musicians from a black and minority ethnic background denied having experienced any form of discrimination personally, while seven white participants portrayed the classical music scene as inclusive, using a range of terms such as 'international' (Linda), a 'melting pot' (June), 'very open' (Emilia) and a world in which there is 'one from each nation' (Sophie). Sometimes, these assertions were followed by a list of the countries represented, which were overwhelmingly white/European. References to the classical music world's openness and internationalism figured as cover terms, brushing aside existing racial inequalities. Given the composition of the sample with fifty-six white and eight black and minority ethnic participants, it is notable that white privilege remained unacknowledged, which represented yet another way in which racial inequalities remained unaccounted for.

Listening to participants, I did, however, notice some implicit, racial hierarchies. Several participants described East Asian players as 'technical' or 'robotic'—and therefore, by extension, unmusical. For example, in the context of recordings becoming more 'clinical', with fewer audible mistakes, Isabella stated:

> You listen to the recordings right now and there is just a clinical perfection because we try all the time to clean everything up . . . like, you know, those Japanese, or whatever, those robots that play violin. What is the point of that? We know a computer can play this, but you can't make people cry after this and in the end the music is about the drive of emotions, and if you can't drive the emotions but you just say that you can play very fast. . . .

Isabella's portrayal echoes 'widespread opinions that essentialise Asian musicians as technicians', where 'Asians have the technique, Westerners have the heart, the soul. The image of Asians as automatons, robots without souls, appears frequently in the Western imagination.'[38] Isabella's view dehumanises Japanese players, comparing them to machines, while 'those Japanese, or whatever' seems to subsume musicians from other East Asian countries under this generalising, othering expression.

These stereotyping notions are meaningful because they construct East Asian players as less musical, implying that technical ability is achieved and conveyed at the expense of communicating emotions through performance. Indeed, as Grace Wang has demonstrated, East Asian players are frequently constructed as hardworking and disciplined, which either appears 'to evacuate them of creativity and feeling',[39] or is regarded 'as a substitute for real artistry.'[40] 'Musical' and 'artistic' performance, however, is constructed as key to successful musicianship:

> Since the romantic period, classical music has embraced the idea that music must spring from the musician's self. Although a good violinist has to be trained in the right place by the right teachers, excellent musical performance can only occur when it springs from the musician's inspiration.[41]

Leppänen's research on how East Asian performers are evaluated in music competitions has demonstrated that they are often seen as less musical.[42] Portrayals of East Asian musicians as 'robotic' thus affect their recognition as musicians. Of course, there are nevertheless several celebrated East Asian soloists, and Mari Yoshihara's ethnography of Asian and Asian-American musicians has demonstrated the complex ways in which such musicians navigate their racial and musical identities in the classical music world.[43]

The persistence of racialised hierarchies in relation to who qualifies as musical, artistic and creative also came to the fore elsewhere. Annabel mentioned female, Japanese students coming to Germany to finesse their ability to express themselves emotionally through their music. Discussing her conservatoire music teacher, she stated that he

> almost only had Japanese women, almost only women, almost only Japanese women. . . . and their playing was incredibly virtuoso, and they come having completed their training, and then come to Europe to "learn the heart", that's the cliché, or the vocation, or the feeling. Because everything else they can already do.

Kira, a Japanese participant, employed a similar rationale to explain her move to Germany to complete another degree:

> I have always wanted to go somewhere, to Europe, mainly. Because, well, yes, the music, that I play, is from Europe . . . . Comes from Europe, right. And I simply wanted to live somewhere in Europe to feel everything at close range. I mean, people in Japan are also well informed. I mean, classical music is very popular there . . . but very technical. It's a bit superficial, I think. Because, it's, well, it's transplanted culture. So it doesn't have any roots [in Japan]. And yes, I somehow wanted to explore the roots and, yes, go back to the original, so to speak.

By telling me that she wanted to go to Germany to 'explore the roots' of Western classical music, portraying the Western classical music culture in Japan as 'technical', and expressing her desire to 'feel everything at close range', Kira

reiterates many of the discourses common to depictions of East Asia's relationship with Western classical music. As I have pointed out, these discourses
position East Asian players as potentially lacking in musicality, and thus artistry and creativity. They also imply that Western classical music is merely
"on loan" to East Asians. As Mina Yang has observed: 'Although Asians
have been playing Western art music for over a century, and playing it well,
the essentialist idea that this music by natural right belongs to Europeans—
is on loan to Asians on an interim basis—prevails.'[44] The deployment of
Western classical music in East Asia has a long and complex history.[45] While
Kira draws attention to the popularity of Western classical music in Japan,
her claim that it is a 'transplanted culture' contributes to a sense that East
Asian players are one step removed from the genre and its traditions.

East Asian musicians are not alone in being "othered" by racialised discourses. Kim had attended the junior department of a London conservatoire
as a child and remembered how her and her mother's opinions were not
taken seriously:

> We were not taken so seriously, because they always said 'Oh, but your
> family doesn't know anything about music.' And also, I think, because
> I am half-Indian and half-English, and this idea of pedigree, or Western
> culture, so they felt 'Well, how should you know?' Or I think they used
> to say to my mum: 'How should you know this person is better or not,
> since you are not a musician and you are not from a Western culture?'

This memory points to further ways in which Western classical music as
a genre is racialised and associated with European descent and whiteness.
Indeed, Kim had to deal with a range of racial prejudices since childhood:

> You know, even just working in an orchestra, you can experience
> prejudice—how people interact with you. Just, you know, from your
> name and things like that. And also, I don't know, it might be, because
> I'm sort of a fiery player. That's sometimes put down to my ethnic origin.

Linking 'fiery' playing to ethnicity in this manner suggests an association of
whiteness and Western classical music that positions differently racialised
subjects in various ways. While it would seem to portray East Asians as less
musical, musicians from other (in this case, mixed-race) backgrounds may
be positioned as almost excessively expressive. As such, this analysis is a
starting point for wider research on the interplay of race, subjectivity and
Western classical music.

Equally important, racialised discourses also intersect with other axes of
differentiation, such as gender. Female East Asian players are often sexualised.[46] Commenting on orchestral players' behaviour while on tour, one
participant, Ricarda, observed: 'But you do just see these older guys kind
of disappearing off upstairs with two [East] Asian girls on tour. And you're

like: "Wow! Do you still do that? Like, what century are you in?"' While Ricarda is clearly critical of such behaviour, her reference to 'two [East] Asian girls' is notable. Arguably, East Asian women are set apart from white women in this statement and are presented in a particularly sexualised way. In keeping with the preceding analysis, which highlighted some of the inter-sections between class, gender, race and subjectivity, it is clear that racialised constructions of East Asian players also cut across gendered discourses.

Conclusion

This chapter has attempted to shed light on some of the less visible pro-cesses that may account for ongoing gender, class and racial inequalities in the classical music profession. More specifically, it has traced some of the intersections between class, gender, race and subjectivity in constructions of the "ideal" classical musician. The kinds of subjectivities required to net-work appear to be closely aligned with middle-class culture, making it more difficult, albeit not impossible, for musicians from working-class or lower middle-class backgrounds to engage in the practice. Similarly, my analysis of research participants' thoughts about parenting has demonstrated that the emotional investment associated with being a musician may conflict with additional emotional commitments. Crucially, some research participants had children, demonstrating that having a family and a career in the classi-cal music industry is not incompatible. By analysing participants' thoughts about having children, I sought to foreground the perceived tensions between the emotional commitments required, both to be a musician and to be a par-ent. As such, my analysis demonstrated that the question of having children surpasses practical considerations; it also raises issues around one's identity as a committed musician. Last but not least, the chapter critiqued represen-tations of East Asian players as 'technical' and 'robotic' to highlight how some constructions of musicality are racialised implicitly as white, thereby affecting claims surrounding musicality. Such racialised constructions do not mean that players from black and minority ethnic backgrounds find it impossible to succeed in the classical music industry. But by exploring the ways in which class, gender and race play out in the context of subjectivity and creative work, my additional focus on subjectivity strives to add to our understanding of inequalities in the classical music profession and to illumi-nate some of the "deeper" ways in which these play out.

Notes

1. See Natalie Bleicher, *New Music Commissioning in the UK: Equality and Diversity in New Music Commissioning* (British Academy of Songwrit-ers, Composers & Authors, 2016), https://basca.org.uk/newsletter/BASCA_ Music-Commissioning.pdf; Christina Scharff, *Equality and Diversity in the Classical Music Profession* (London: King's College London, 2015), http://blogs.kcl.ac.uk/young-female-and-entrepreneurial/files/2014/02/

Equality-and-Diversity-in-the-Classical-Music-Profession.pdf; and Women In Music's annual BBC Proms surveys, www.womeninmusic.org.uk/proms-survey. htm.

2. See Arts Council England, *Equality and Diversity Within the Arts and Cultural Sector in England* (London: Arts Council England, 2014), www.artscouncil. org.uk/media/uploads/Equality_and_diversity_within_the_arts_and_cultural_ sector_in_England.pdf; Georgina Born and Kyle Devine, 'Music Technology, Gender, and Class: Digitization, Educational and Social Change in Britain', *Twentieth-Century Music*, 12/2 (2015), 135–72; Anna Bull, *The Musical Body: How Gender and Class are Reproduced Among Young People Playing Classical Music in England* (Ph.D. diss.; Goldsmiths, University of London, 2015); Philippe Coulangeon, Hyacinthe Ravet and Ionela Roharik, 'Gender Differentiated Effect of Time in Performing Arts Professions: Musicians, Actors and Dancers in Contemporary France', *Poetics*, 33/5 (2005), 369–87; William Osborne and Abbie Conant, A Survey of Women Orchestral Players in Major UK Orchestras as of March 1, 2010 (2010), www.osborne-conant.org/orch-uk.htm; Mari Yoshihara, *Musicians From a Different Shore: Asians and Asian Americans in Classical Music* (Philadelphia: Temple University Press, 2007).

3. See Brydie-Leigh Bartleet, 'Women Conductors on the Orchestral Podium: Pedagogical and Professional Implications', *College Music Symposium*, 48 (2008), 31–51; Taru Leppänen, 'The West and the Rest of Classical Music: Asian Musicians in the Finnish Media Coverage of the 1995 Jean Sibelius Violin Competition', *European Journal of Cultural Studies*, 18/1 (2014), 1–16; Lisa McCormick, 'Higher, Faster, Louder: Representations of the International Music Competition', *Cultural Sociology*, 3/1 (2009), 5–30; Grace Wang, 'Interlopers in the Realm of High Culture: "Music Moms" and the Performance of Asian and Asian American Identities', *American Quarterly*, 61/4 (2009), 881–903; Mina Yang, 'East Meets West in the Concert Hall: Asians and Classical Music in the Century of Imperialism, Post-colonialism, and Multiculturalism', *Asian Music*, 38/1 (2007), 1–30.

4. See Elizabeth Gould, 'Disorientations of Desire: Music Education Queer', in *Music Education for Changing Times: Guiding Visions for Practice*, ed. Thomas R. Regelski and Terry Gates (London: Springer, 2009), 59–71; Roberta Lamb, 'The Possibilities of/for Feminist Music Criticism in Music Education', *British Journal of Music Education*, 10/3 (1993), 169–80.

5. See Doris R. Eikhof and Chris Warhurst, 'The Promised Land? Why Social Inequalities are Systemic in the Creative Industries', *Employee Relations*, 35/5 (2013), 495–508; Rosalind Gill, 'Cool, Creative and Egalitarian? Exploring Gender in Project-Based New Media Work in Europe', *Information, Communication & Society*, 5/1 (2002), 70–89; Ashika Thanki and Steve Jefferys, 'Who are the Fairest? Ethnic Segmentation in London's Media Production', *Work Organisation, Labour & Globalisation*, 1/1 (2007), 108–18; Leung Wing-Fai, Rosalind Gill and Keith Randle, 'Getting In, Getting On, Getting Out? Women as Career Scramblers in the UK Film and Television Industries', in *Gender and Creative Labour*, ed. Bridget Conor, Rosalind Gill and Stephanie Taylor (Chichester: Wiley, 2015), 50–65.

6. See Kim Allen, Jocey Quinn, Sumi Hollingworth and Anthea Rose, 'Becoming Employable Students and 'Ideal' Creative Workers: Exclusion and Inequality in Higher Education Work Placements', *British Journal of Sociology of Education*, 34/3 (2013), 431–52; Penny Jane Burke and Jackie McManus, ' "Art for a Few": Exclusion and Misrecognition in Art and Design Higher Education Admissions', *National Arts Learning Network* (2009), http://blueprint-files.s3.amazonaws.com/1321362562-AFAF_finalcopy.pdf; Kate Oakley and Dave O'Brien, 'Learning to Labour Unequally: Understanding the Relationship

between Cultural Production, Cultural Consumption and Inequality', *Social Identities*, 22/5 (2016), 471–86.

7. See Bull, *The Musical Body*; Erin Johnson-Hill, 'Imperial Surveillance: The Origins of Power Formation in Victorian Music Education', paper presented at Classical Music: Critical Challenges, King's College London, 17 October 2014; Roe-Min Kok, 'Music for a Postcolonial Child: Theorizing Malaysian Memories', in *Musical Childhoods and the Cultures of Youth*, ed. Susan Boynton and Roe-Min Kok (Connecticut: Wesleyan University Press, 2006), 89–104.

8. For example, Skillset, *Women in the Creative Media Industries* (2010), www.ewawomen.com/uploads/files/surveyskillset.pdf.

9. See Wing-Fai, Gill and Randle, 'Getting In, Getting On, Getting Out?'.

10. See Allen, Quinn, Hollingworth and Rose, 'Becoming Employable Students and 'Ideal' Creative Workers'; Bridget Conor, *Screenwriting: Creative Labour and Professional Practice* (London: Routledge, 2014); Rosalind Gill, 'Unspeakable Inequalities: Post Feminism, Entrepreneurial Subjectivity, and the Repudiation of Sexism Among Cultural Workers', *Social Politics: International Studies in Gender, State and Society*, 21/4 (2014), 509–28; Stephanie Taylor and Karen Littleton, *Contemporary Identities of Creativity and Creative Work* (Farnham: Ashgate, 2012); Natalie Wreyford, *The Gendered Contexts of Screenwriting Work: Socialized Recruitment and Judgments of Taste and Talent in the UK Film Industry* (Ph.D. diss.; King's College London, 2015).

11. See Henrietta Moore, 'Subjectivity', in *Gender: The Key Concepts*, ed. Mary Evans and Carolyn H. Williams (London: Routledge, 2013), 203–8.

12. Conor, *Screenwriting: Creative Labour and Professional Practice*, 121.

13. Alison L. Bain, 'Female Artistic Identity in Place: The Studio', *Social & Cultural Geography*, 5/2 (2004), 172.

14. See David Hesmondhalgh and Sarah Baker, 'Sex, Gender and Work Segregation in the Cultural Industries', in *Gender and Creative Labour*, ed. Bridget Conor, Rosalind Gill and Sarah Taylor (Chichester: Wiley, 2015), 23–36; Sarah Proctor-Thomson, 'Feminist Futures of Cultural Work: Creativity, Gender and Diversity in the Digital Media Sector', in *Theorizing Cultural Work: Labour, Continuity and Change in the Creative Industries*, ed. Mark Banks, Stephanie Taylor and Rosalind Gill (London: Routledge, 2013), 137–48.

15. Please note that I use British terminology by referring to East Asian musicians, whereas some of the works cited were published in the United States and so refer to 'Asian' musicians instead.

16. See Christina Scharff, *Gender, Subjectivity and Cultural Work: The Classical Music Profession* (London: Routledge, 2018).

17. See Tony Bennett, Mike Savage, Elizabeth Bortolaia Silva, Alan Warde, *Modesto Gayo-Cal and David Wright, Culture, Class, Distinction* (New York: Routledge, 2009), 2.

18. The approach taken in this chapter is similar to that taken by Stephanie Taylor and Karen Littleton; see Taylor and Littleton, *Contemporary Identities of Creativity and Creative Work*, 44–5.

19. Eikhof and Warhurst, 'The Promised Land?', 499.

20. Conor, Bridget, Rosalind Gill and Stephanie Taylor, 'Introduction: Gender and Creative Labour', in *Gender and Creative Labour*, 11.

21. See Gill, 'Cool, Creative and Egalitarian?; Irena Grugulis and Dimitrinka Stoyanova, 'Social Capital and Networks in Film and TV: Jobs for the Boys?', *Organization Studies*, 33/10 (2012), 1311–31; Keith Randle, Cynthia Forson and Moira Calveley, 'Towards a Bourdieusian Analysis of the Social Composition of the UK Film and Television Workforce', *Work, Employment & Society*, 29/4, (2015), 590–606; Thanki and Jefferys, 'Who Are the Fairest?; Wing-Fai,

Gill and Randle, 'Getting In, Getting On, Getting Out?'; Wreyford, *The Gendered Contexts of Screenwriting Work*.

22. Grugulis and Stoyanova, 'Social Capital and Networks in Film and TV', 1312.
23. See Allen, Quinn, Hollingworth and Rose, 'Becoming Employable Students and 'Ideal' Creative Workers'; and Randle, Forson and Calveley, 'Towards a Bourdieusian Analysis of the Social Composition of the UK Film and Television Workforce'.
24. See Anna Bull and Christina Scharff, ' "McDonalds Music" Versus "Serious Music": How Production and Consumption Practices Help to Reproduce Class Inequality in the Classical Music Profession', *Cultural Sociology*, 11/3 (2017), 283–301.
25. I explore these issues further in 'Blowing Your Own Trumpet: Exploring the Gendered Dynamics of Self-promotion in the Classical Music Profession', *The Sociological Review*, 63 (May 2015), 97–112.
26. See, for example, Skillset, *Women in the Creative Media Industries*.
27. Wing-Fai, Gill and Randle, 'Getting In, Getting On, Getting Out?', 59.
28. Wreyford, *The Gendered Contexts of Screenwriting Work*, 159.
29. Wreyford, *The Gendered Contexts of Screenwriting Work*, 100.
30. See Wreyford, *The Gendered Contexts of Screenwriting Work*, 59.
31. Wing-Fai, Gill and Randle, 'Getting In, Getting On, Getting Out?', 61.
32. Taylor and Littleton, *Contemporary Identities of Creativity and Creative Work*, 119.
33. See Bain, 'Female Artistic Identity in Place: The Studio'; Lisa Pohlman, 'Creativity, Gender and the Family: A Study of Creative Writers', *The Journal of Creative Behavior*, 30/18 (1996), 1–24; Wreyford, *The Gendered Contexts of Screenwriting Work*.
34. Taylor and Littleton, *Contemporary Identities of Creativity and Creative Work*, 117; authors' emphasis.
35. Stephanie Taylor, 'Negotiating Oppositions and Uncertainties: Gendered Conflicts in Creative Identity Work', *Feminism & Psychology*, 21/3 (2011), 368.
36. Leppänen, 'The West and the Rest of Classical Music', 1.
37. For more on this issue, see Scharff, *Gender, Subjectivity and Cultural Work*.
38. Yang, 'East Meets West in the Concert Hall', 14. See also note 15.
39. Wang, 'Interlopers in the Realm of High Culture', 887.
40. Yang, 'East Meets West in the Concert Hall', 13.
41. Leppänen, 'The West and the Rest of Classical Music', 10.
42. See Leppänen, 'The West and the Rest of Classical Music', 12.
43. See Yoshihara, *Musicians From a Different Shore*.
44. Yang, 'East Meets West in the Concert Hall', 16.
45. See, for example, Wang, 'Interlopers in the Realm of High Culture'; Yang, 'East Meets West in the Concert Hall'; Yoshihara, *Musicians From a Different Shore*.
46. See Yoshihara, *Musicians From a Different Shore*, 116.

8 Lifespan Perspective Theory and (Classical) Musicians' Careers

Dawn Bennett and Sophie Hennekam

Empirical research on musicians' work has begun to receive greater attention in recent years.[1] These studies show that music work is variously precarious, multi-genre, and internally driven, but there is little research that compares the work of classically-trained and other musicians. To enable such a comparison, there is a need to capture the dynamics of musicians' work across the career lifespan. This chapter draws on detailed empirical research that employed "lifespan" perspective theory—specifically, selection, optimization, and compensation (SOC) theory—to understand musicians' work in early, mid-, and late-career. The study was the first to consider musicians' work through the lifespan perspective, which emphasises that 'important changes occur during every period of development and that these changes must be interpreted in terms of the culture and context in which they occur.'[2] We highlight the complexities of creative work by reporting on the activities, career trajectories, opportunities, and constraints musicians face. We then critique employability by aligning the research data with broader empirical studies of graduate employability, defined as 'the ability to find, create and sustain work and learning across lengthening working lives and multiple work settings.'[3] We employ a subset of data from ten classically-trained musicians to enable comparison between the practice of classical and other musicians. Research on the characteristics of musicians' work has long been hindered by datasets that are insufficiently nuanced for finer analysis.

Lifespan development perspectives assume that patterns of change occur across a career, and that this involves multiple adaptive processes including acquisition, maintenance, transformation, and attrition.[4] As such, adaptation is a proactive process involving self-regulation, as individuals negotiate situations such as goal success or failure, or changes in environment and resources. SOC theory consists of three such adaptive strategies:

- *Selection*: the selection of goals and outcomes that align with existing resources and resource demands;
- *Optimisation*: the allocation of efforts and resources to optimise performance in the selected domains;
- *Compensation*: strategies to maintain a desired level of performance.

Individuals, then, are seen to align their existing resources and resource demands with these three strategies to facilitate effective functioning, adaptation, and development. Since *compensation* connotes adaptive strategies that respond to changes in industry and in individual needs and preferences, it is particularly important in music, where work is notoriously precarious and changeable; changes can occur at any age or career stage.

For the purposes of this study, a musician is defined as someone who works within music in one or more specialist roles.[5] Early-, mid-, and late-career are defined as having less than 10 years', 10–25 years', and more than 25 years' experience, respectively. The chapter draws on 108 case studies of musicians (of whom 10 were classically trained) involved in a broader, international study of the creative workforce.[6] Participants had practised as musicians for between three and 60 years, with most reporting between 20 and 30 years of experience. Participants from the Netherlands (74) were recruited through the country's principal creative industries trade union FNV-KIEM (response rate 11.9%); Australia has no comparable union, so its participants (34) were recruited through creative industries, networks and events, industry press, local media, and smaller trade unions.

Developed in 2009, the Creative Workforce Initiative (CWI) survey instrument employed in this study contains quantitative and qualitative elements with many open-ended questions,[7] and its structure and aims are fourfold: to paint a picture of creative work over time; to scrutinise the allocation of time; to chronicle workers' activities and modes of work; and to focus on education and professional learning. The survey also collated demographic information.[8] Our findings are presented and discussed in two main parts: firstly, using SOC theory to chart the concerns and adaptive strategies of musicians at different stages of their careers; then, secondly, focussing on classically-trained musicians to highlight similarities and differences in their practice. All responses are anonymised.

Early-Career Musicians

Figure 8.1 summarises the SOC strategies of early-career respondents. *Selection* strategy posits that decisions on career goals are predicated on people's resources and demands. For early-career musicians, selection centred on career goals and outcomes. In general, such musicians chose goals and

SOC strategy	Theme
Selection	Performance career goals dominate
Optimisation	Broadening career thinking to include non-performance roles
Compensation	A more flexible attitude towards non-performance roles

Figure 8.1 Early-Career Themes and Strategies

outcomes that would enable them to align their existing resources with their resource demands: what they expected to have in the future. Passion and talent were the dominant career drivers and performance careers were the primary career goal. Many musicians wrote about their long-term engagement with music and its impact on their career thinking. Most early careerists aspired to a performance career, which was positioned as superior to other career outcomes; a solo career was the pinnacle of success. Musicians positioned non-performance careers, such as teaching, as less desirable. For example:

> We all want a performing career, if possible even going solo. That's why you study music: to play in front of an audience. Becoming a teacher is the worst-case scenario, that's for the ones who don't make it. It's the last-choice option.

The music career hierarchy has been recognised by multiple scholars, who note the influence of early socialisation,[9] performance-focussed examination systems,[10] performance-based tertiary curricula,[11] and performance-based indicators of success.[12] This differs considerably from the motivations and priorities of pre-service music educators (music education students);[13] yet, the hierarchy dominated the thinking of early-career musicians.

Optimisation is the process of allocating efforts and resources to optimise performance in selected domains. Early-career musicians evidenced optimisations through their shifting career goals. This most often involved rethinking career success to incorporate careers beyond performance. Even where performance goals were met, musicians began to realise that few musicians practise solely in performance roles, even when this is financially viable. Rather, musicians explored multiple opportunities and often found meaningful work within a number of practice domains, such as teaching and management roles.

Compensation refers to the strategies employed to maintain a desired level of work-related performance. Realising that stable music careers in one organisation, sector, or industry are uncommon,[14] early-career musicians began to anticipate the need to take on multiple concurrent roles (and even multiple careers).[15] A new priority for the early careerists was the need to sustain and enhance their employability; they began to see that this would be a consistent feature of their careers. Experiencing "boundaryless" careers,[16] many early-career musicians began to explore why, how, and with whom they might find success:

> I do a bit of everything: composing, designing, developing [and] performing. Nowadays you need to use all the different talents you have. You cannot rely on one particular skill. I believe people have several careers in several domains, and that continuous learning and developing oneself is key to staying employable.

SOC strategy	Theme
Selection	Actions driven by changing career and personal goals
Optimisation	Skills and knowledge transferred to new contexts; new skills developed
Compensation	Undertaking multiple roles, including work in other sectors

Figure 8.2 Mid-Career Themes and Strategies

Although the early-career phase is particularly challenging for many musicians, many factors persist across the career lifespan. Mid- and late-career professionals, especially women, are increasingly likely to become less career-mobile, more likely to seek stable income,[17] and are more prone to injury.[18] These themes were evident in musicians' accounts of the mid-career phase, as discussed in the following section and summarised in Figure 8.2.

Mid-Career Musicians

Remarkably, almost all mid-career musicians emphasised that their careers had not unfolded as expected. This was attributed to the early-career dominance of narrowly defined performance ambitions. Musicians reflected that they had underestimated the fierce competition for performance work and had "naïvely" expected to secure performance-based careers. Mid-career musicians bemoaned how they had earlier emphasised creative activities at the cost of the commercial aspects of their practice. They had also underestimated the need to engage in teaching and administration. Mid-career musicians accepted that most musicians engage in multiple activities in order to make a living, and they began to focus more energy on finding a niche and promoting their business:

> As a freelancer, there is a lot of paperwork and those administrative tasks take a lot of time. Getting work is another issue: I'm constantly going to auditions, scanning the internet for opportunities, travelling to meet someone, which could possibly lead to some work in the future. All those activities distract from the real work!

For mid-career musicians, selection strategy is striking: by this phase of their career, 80% of musicians had changed their career goals at least once. These decisions were underpinned by resource and demand factors, including dissatisfaction with work, desire for a more stable income, insufficient opportunities to showcase their abilities, irregular working hours, and changing family circumstances. Mid-career musicians also mentioned geographic (re)location, inadequate self-promotional skills, and a desire for greater autonomy. A shift away from performance-centred goals also often led to a renewed early-career-type phase within the context of their established practice:

> I feel I'm now having a second career as a teacher. When I had children, my career aspirations shifted drastically. While I still feel the urge to be creative, I also have a strong motherly instinct and no longer work long and irregular hours. I wanted a predictable job that would provide stable income. Teaching met those criteria.

Participants described both positive and negative critical moments that had informed their career decisions and musical identities. In line with self-affirmation theory, positive experiences reassured musicians about their career choices and increased career efficacy and career capital.[19] Positive experiences also bolstered adaptability and self-integrity, and influenced more individual definitions of career success. Specific examples include praise from respected others, prizes, commissions, and work secured through reputation:

> Winning this competition functioned as a signal that my performance was being noticed and appreciated. It really helped me to believe in myself and pursue my career as a singer.

These explicit "appraisals" of work are known to strengthen intrinsic values such as self-efficacy and self-confidence,[20] and create reputational capital from which further work can be secured.[21] This is particularly important within industries such as music, where career success is rarely experienced linearly; for example, promotion within a firm.[22] Indeed, perceptions of career success often incorporate recognition and reputational capital (other-referent), intrinsic satisfaction (self-referent),[23] and a positive outlook for the future (also self-referent).[24]

As in the above example, self-referent behaviour typically includes an assessment of previous "selves" experienced in early career. Certain positive life changes, such as parenthood or buying a home, were raised because of their negative impacts on a career. Negative experiences such as poor health, physical injury, reduced funding, and insufficient work (viewed as other-referent) were also influential in the assessments of mid-careerists, and negative indicators, such as an unsuccessful audition, decreased musicians' self-efficacy and confidence:

> I'm unable to get used to the negative feedback and rejection during auditions. I know it's part of the job and I shouldn't care about it, but it does influence how I see myself, it does hurt. Rationally I know it does not mean much, but deep inside it makes me wonder a bit more whether I'm made to be a pianist.

Unable to align their career choice (music) and resource demands, some mid-career musicians responded by selecting an alternative career path. Other musicians adopted a self-narrative in which 'a commercially compromised self is refurbished as a rebellious artist self.'[25] This was seen in the reshaping of a portfolio of work to include previously unconsidered roles. Despite negative experiences, musicians' accounts emphasised the role of their passion or "calling"[26] in withstanding rejections and barriers.

Consistent with the optimisation strategies of early-career musicians, the need to remain employable featured strongly in the accounts of mid-careerists. While some mid-career musicians planned to leave music, others began to employ an SOC strategy to reorientate their careers. Mid-careerists added new skills and capacities as required, but they also began to emphasise new applications of their skills in artistry, teaching, teamwork, social media, problem-solving, marketing, communication, management, adaptability, and administration:

> I have the impression that it's less and less about being creative. Technical skills, improvisation, it doesn't seem to be enough . . . Things are changing in [such] a way that I'm wondering whether I shouldn't look for a job where I can simply use my existing skills, [avoiding] the constant need for up-skilling.

Or, as another mid-career respondent remarked:

> It's all about selling what you have and being creative with it . . . I think it's about understanding what you have and using this to go forward in your career.

As a strategy to offset decline in order to maintain the desired level of career performance, compensation was important to mid-career musicians, who frequently emphasised concerns about income:

> I'm mixing many activities as opportunities come my way. I basically say yes to anything, and I have a very irregular schedule and workload. While I try to do a maximum of jobs that somehow relate to music, it's unfortunately not always possible. I take what I can get.

Mid-career optimisation, then, included a broadening of career horizons and, relatedly, the acknowledgement of other skills. It therefore also involved a process of rethinking one's very identity and place, musically speaking:

> A career that is exclusively performing is not feasible for me. While I found that difficult to accept in the beginning, I now see that I have

other qualities . . . I'm now using my different qualities instead of focussing on becoming a well-known musician.

The musicians' determination to remain in music was a striking feature of both optimisation and compensation strategies, and this could be read as a self-affirming response to career threats and challenges. However, mid-career narratives reveal a deeper identity struggle in which aesthetic and economic selves can become separated,[27] and in which extrinsic or other-referent indicators are denied in favour of the artistic self-narrative.[28] For example:

> Maybe I'm not the talented violinist I've always thought I was. I have talent, but there are thousands of others who may have more talent than me. In order to make a living, I've started to provide private courses for adults and children at their homes. It's not what I had in mind, but it provides a stable income and I do feel valued for what I do. I think a mix of teaching and sometimes some performances is a good mix for me.

To see how such thinking continues to colour a musician's career, we turn to SOC strategies reported by late-career musicians (see Figure 8.3).

Late-Career Musicians

Research has shown how older workers often seek to prolong their use of existing skills rather than learn new ones.[29] So it was with late-career musicians, who employed selection strategies that focussed on their areas of strength: their career capital.

> I have all this life experience, I'm motivated and I have a lot to give. Please just trust me and I'll give my 100%. Let me do what I'm good at.

Whereas mid-career musicians employed multiple skills, late-career musicians reported an even greater range. The latter placed greater emphasis on

SOC strategy	Theme
Selection	A desire to use and extend existing skills rather than develop new ones
Optimisation	Greater focus on the transferability of existing skills and knowledge
Compensation	A broader portfolio, often including self-employment; moving towards physically less challenging roles

Figure 8.3 Late-Career Themes and Strategies

their experience, particularly the transfer of skills and experience outside music or in entrepreneurial roles.

> Instead of focussing on what I don't have, I'm emphasising what I do have in terms of experience and competencies. If you're a little creative, you can turn your weaknesses into strengths and argue that your existing competencies and qualities can be used differently in the context of being an entrepreneur. It's all about formulating it in a coherent way.

In a similarly optimising manner, another late-career participant remarked:

> One strength I have, and that's based on my age or career stage, is that I have had time to build up a solid network: a broad one that is not just made of musicians, but also directors, editors, programmers, composers, teachers, etc. Such a broad overview or network of people working in music-related professions helps to set up something different now. Business is about word-of-mouth—getting known—and I already have a solid base.

Yet, late-career musicians found themselves unable to transition from positions that are difficult to maintain once physical abilities have decreased and health risks grown.[30] These reports included musicians in full-time performance roles, for whom there were no alternative roles within their organisations. Two compensation strategies were cited as a way to overcome reduced energy, declining physical fitness, or diminishing performance skills. Employed by musicians working within an organisation, the first strategy was to request a physically less challenging position; for orchestral musicians, this is rarely possible. In line with previous research,[31] a second, more common strategy was for musicians to transition into self-employed work and to outsource or reduce aspects of their practice.

Earlier studies also confirm that self-employment is especially prevalent at the mid- and late-career stages, including in music.[32] In this chapter's study, some older musicians felt forced into self-employment:

> Let's make this clear: self-employment is not a choice. It's a way for me to stay active in the workforce. It's the *only* way to stay active, as recruiters seem to believe that creativity declines with age.

Late-career musicians, then, identified myriad challenges, including less financial stability, a reliance on network-based recruitment practices, long working hours, and age discrimination. Ameliorating these challenges required selection, optimisation and compensation strategies to be employed, often concurrently. The use of reputational career capital reflected the constant troubling of identity, which is a typical feature of fluid career paths. Late-career musicians' sense of self can be experienced as unsettled, threatened, or socially invalidated. Moreover, musicians' sense of self is often separated into component parts, with each component part negotiated differently in order to retain the whole.

Classically-Trained Musicians as a Subset of the Sample

The aim of this section is to ascertain how the practice of the study's 10 classically-trained respondents differed from that of the other respondents. We seek not to generalise but to present patterns of similarity and difference that might inform future studies. The first question our survey respondents answered was how they would describe themselves as an artist. Nine of the classical musicians (90%) defined themselves as "musicians", as did 98 (89%) of the other respondents. Notably, however, none of the classically-trained musicians differentiated themselves as "classical" musicians. Because of this, we refer to them here as classically-trained musicians. For clarity, and acknowledging that many musicians might include classical music in their work, the remaining musicians are described as "other" musicians.

Half of each cohort identified as musicians in some contexts and not in others, and "passion" was the main career driver for 90% of the classically-trained musicians, compared with 71% for the other musicians. Across both cohorts, 80% of musicians aspired to continue their music careers, one-fifth described themselves as unsure, and career goals had changed, on average, 2.2 times. Only 40% of classically-trained musicians (and 43% of the other musicians) aspired to work exclusively in the creative industries. On average, all musicians, classically trained or otherwise, undertook 20%–25% of their work outside the creative industries: the most common roles were teaching, charitable work, or working with minority groups in the community. This was also reflected in the respective levels of unpaid work: 42% of classically-trained musicians' total work, 39% for other musicians.

Most musicians had completed formal university-level education. There were no differences between the educational levels of classically-trained and other musicians; however, classically-trained musicians were more satisfied with their education, rating it 9.3 out of 10, compared with 7.2 overall. All musicians offered similar suggestions for improvement, including a stronger focus on running a small business and greater exposure to the practice of being a musician. The dominant skillset was identified for all musicians as performance, problem-solving and communication, small business and marketing, social media, teaching, teamwork, and adaptability. While both cohorts held an average of two different roles, there were distinct differences between their respective allocations of time. Classically-trained musicians reported working more hours in music-related activities (40–49 hours per week, compared with 30–39 hours), were six times less likely to work in the community sector, and 20% more likely to work in commercial or not-for-profit sectors. Both cohorts aspired to have more work in not-for-profit settings, indicating the value they placed on their existing work with and in the community.

Teaching and performance work were major sources of income for the musicians, but to a different extent. Teaching was a source of revenue for 60% of the classically-trained musicians and for 37% of the musicians in other genres; performance was a source of income for 64% of musicians overall, and sales of work provided income for 20%. Other income sources across the 108 musicians, all genres taken together, included royalties and copyright income, répétiteur and accompaniment work, directing, producing, and writing. None of the classical musicians were unemployed, unlike 21% of other musicians. Furthermore, only 20% of the classically-trained musicians worked part-time, compared with 44% of the other musicians. These figures align with access to social supports: over twice the percentage of classical musicians (50% compared with 24%) had access to a retirement scheme and health insurance. Classically-trained musicians also reported better access to life and/or disability insurance, albeit at low numbers: 30% compared with 12%. Hardly any musicians had access to career counselling.

Better access to supports suggests that more classically-trained musicians have traditional employer relationships, albeit on a project-by-project basis. They also considered themselves better equipped to sustain their incomes during periods of economic downturn, suggesting higher levels of social capital as implied in the networks, discussed in the next paragraph. This was borne out in the data: of the classically-trained musicians, 70% reported increased income over the past 12 months. This was the case for only 23% of the other musicians, of whom almost half (48%) reported a decrease. Of the 20% of classically-trained musicians who reported a decrease in income, all had been able to replace that income from another source. This is striking, as only 30% of the other musicians had been able to replace lost income. The classically-trained musicians attributed their sustainability to reputation, skills development, networked forms of work, incremental salary increases, and more hours of work.

A further indication of employment type concerns its location. Classically-trained musicians were 20% less likely to work primarily from home and 25% more likely to work at an employer's premises, such as a concert venue or recording studio. The other musicians reported a range of work sites, including studios, theatres, schools, public places, cafés, and restaurants. Networked forms of work were crucial: all classically-trained musicians reported obtaining work through networks, and 83% often used networks to find work. This stands in stark contrast with the remainder/non-classically-trained musicians, of whom only 31% often used networks. Another difference was that all classically-trained musicians gained work through professional associations, which featured for only 49% of the other musicians. Both musician cohorts used online networks to promote products and/or services: Facebook was used most often (by 75% of the classically-trained musicians), followed by personal websites.

Conclusions

Employing lifespan perspective theory, this chapter revealed early-career musicians to be focussed on performance goals and outcomes, which they hoped would align their available resources and resource demands. Even at this stage of their careers, musicians began to optimise their potential by rethinking career success in terms other than performance. By mid-career, musicians reported that their initial performance focus and lack of career awareness had limited their ability to maximise their potential. 85% of mid-career musicians had changed their career goals at least once. They frequently emphasised declining income, and they compensated for this by leaving music or adopting multiple roles and new skills within and beyond music. By late career, musicians employed selection strategies that enabled them to apply their broad skills and experience to roles within and outside music. Often entrepreneurial and featuring self-employment, these roles were most often the result of an enforced transition.

This chapter makes two interrelated contributions to theory. The first relates to previous SOC studies, which have tended towards cross-sectional designs. Recent studies acknowledge that workers' use of SOC strategies can fluctuate over time.[33] While longitudinal data would be ideal to test this hypothesis, we simulated a lifespan perspective using a retrospectively longitudinal approach to look back in time within individual accounts and to analyse snapshots of practice at different career phases. The robustness of this approach was assured by triangulating survey data with the findings of previous studies in which we had focussed on specific career phases.[34] The findings illustrate the potential for SOC theory studies to create meaningful, retrospective lifespan perspectives. The interplay of the three SOC strategies is believed to maximise resources and positive outcomes, such as goal accomplishment and well-being. Our data confirms that the use of strategies fluctuates over time, and that strategies are frequently used in combination. Our second contribution relates to the negotiation of identity. Musicians' career decisions and identities were self-affirming in terms of career success, adaptability, and self-integrity, yet musicians also experienced significant identity struggles. Similarly, the tendency to hold multiple concurrent roles was shown to be a functional career challenge to mobility and, indeed, psychologically. Working both within and outside the creative industries can result in multiple conflicting or incompatible identities, sometimes closely related to the artistic practice but at other times in entirely different domains.[35] Our findings suggest that emphasising connections between multiple identities could lead to better psychological outcomes.

On this basis, individuals may benefit from emphasising the interdependence of different activities, creating a meta-identity to which all identities can relate. Since many musicians simultaneously experience elements of early-, mid-, and late-career as their roles change, their SOC strategies may be similarly non-sequential. Indeed, musicians did not typically seek to resolve their incompatible identities or to tackle their psychological stress. Behaviour instead tended towards Nic Beech et al.'s concept of per-petuated self-questioning identity work,[36] in which such tensions form a career-long and arguably fundamental aspect of the musician's identity. This reality aligns with Christina Scharff's commentary that competition can be self-directed and part of the entrepreneurial mindset.[37] We contend that self-questioning identity work is fundamental to musicians' practice and their sense of self, promoting a non-linear aesthetic and economic decision-making predicated on the non-sequential use of SOC strategies. That musicians may not seek to resolve these tensions surely has signifi-cant implications for how we might rethink career preparation and sup-port in this area.

Notes

1. See, for example: Thomas A. Cummins-Russell and Norma M. Rantisi, 'Net-works and Place in Montreal's Independent Music Industry', *The Canadian Geographer*, 56/1 (February 2012), 80–97; Robert Freeman, *The Crisis of Clas-sical Music in America: Lessons from a Life in the Education of Musicians* (Lanham, MD: Rowman & Littlefield, 2014); and Leslie M. Meier. 'Popular Music Making and Promotional Work Inside the "New" Music Industry', in *The Routledge Companion to the Cultural Industries*, ed. Kate Oakley and Jus-tin O'Connor (Abingdon: Routledge, 2015), 402–12.
2. Denise Boyd and Helen Bee, *Lifespan Development* (7th edn; London: Pearson, 2015), 4.
3. Dawn Bennett, 'Developing Employability in Higher Education Music', *Arts and Humanities in Higher Education*, 15/3–4 (July 2016), 410.
4. For more on SOC theory, see: Paul B. Baltes and Margaret M. Baltes, 'Psycho-logical Perspectives on Successful Aging: The Model of Selective Optimization With Compensation', in *Successful Aging: Perspectives From the Behavioral Sciences*, ed. Paul. B. Baltes and Margaret M. Baltes (New York: Cambridge University Press, 1990), 1–34; and Boris B. Baltes and Marcus W. Dickson, 'Using Life-Span Models in Industrial-Organizational Psychology: The Theory of Selective Optimization With Compensation', *Applied Developmental Sci-ence*, 5/1 (June 2001), 51–62.
5. See also Dawn Bennett, *Understanding the Classical Music Profession: The Past, the Present and Strategies for the Future* (Abingdon: Ashgate, 2008), Chapter 8.
6. The Creative Workforce Initiative (CWI) is run from Curtin University, Aus-tralia: see http://ccat-lab.org/creative-workforce-initiative/.
7. The CWI survey instrument is summarised in Dawn Bennett, Jane Coffey, Scott Fitzgerald, Peter Petocz, and Al Rainnie, 'Beyond the Creative: Understanding the Intersection of Specialist and Embedded Work for Creatives in Metropolitan Perth', in *Creative Work Beyond the Creative Industries: Innovation, Employ-ment, and Education*, ed. Greg Hearn, Ruth Bridgstock, Ben Goldsmith, and Jess Rodgers (Cheltenham: Edward Elgar, 2014), 158–74.
8. Closed questions were analysed using the Statistical Package for the Social Sci-ences (SPSS) quantitative software, version 24. Open questions were analysed using content analysis, which enabled the systematic and replicable compres-sion of text into fewer content categories alongside inspection of the data for recurrent instances. Frequency counting was used as appropriate. SOC theory was employed to analyse how music workers negotiate their allocation of time and skills, skills deficits, and modes of work. Both authors were involved in the analysis, coding multiple cases, and crosschecking to ensure validity.

9. See Richard Colwell and Hildegard Froehlich, *Sociology for Music Teachers: Perspectives for Practice* (London: Pearson Education, 2007), 78–99.
10. See Paul Evans and Gary McPherson, 'Identity and Practice: The Motivational Benefits of a Long-Term Musical Identity', *Psychology of Music*, 43/3 (January 2015), 407–22.
11. See Janet Mills, 'Working in Music: Becoming a Performer-Teacher', *Music Education Research*, 6/3 (2004), 245–61.
12. See Margaret Schmidt and Jelani Canser, 'Clearing the Fog: Constructing Shared Stories of a Novice Teacher's Journey', *Research Studies in Music Education*, 27/2 (December, 2006), 55–68.
13. See Kelly Parkes and Brett D. Jones, 'Motivational Constructs Influencing Undergraduate Students' Choices to Become Classroom Music Teachers or Music Performers', *Journal of Research in Music Education*, 60/1 (February 2012), 101–23.
14. See Yehuda Baruch, 'Transforming Careers: From Linear to Multidirectional Career Paths: Organizational and Individual Perspectives', Career Development International, 9/1 (2004), 58–73.
15. See Sophie Hennekam, 'Dealing with Multiple Incompatible Work-Related Identities: The Case of Artists', *Personnel Review*, 46/5 (2017), 970–87.
16. See Lillian T. Eby, Marcus Butts, and Angie Lockwood, 'Predictors of Success in the Era of the Boundaryless Career', *Journal of Organizational Behavior*, 24/6 (August 2003), 689–708.
17. Gendered aspects of career decision making are explored by multiple scholars. See, for example, Elizabeth F. Cabrera's study reported as 'Opting Out and Opting In: Understanding the Complexities of Women's Career Transitions', *Career Development International*, 12/3 (2007), 218–37.
18. Raymond M. Delbert, June Hart Romeo, and Karoline V. Kumke give an excellent overview of injury and illness among classically-trained musicians in 'A Pilot Study of Occupational Injury and Illness Experienced by Classical Musicians', *Workplace Health & Safety*, 60/1 (January 2012), 19–24.
19. See, for example, Claude M. Steele, 'The Psychology of Self-Affirmation: Sustaining the Integrity of the Self', *Advances in Experimental Social Psychology*, 21 (1988), 261–302.
20. See Sophie Hennekam and Olivier Herrbach, 'HRM Practices and Low Occupational Status Older Workers', *Employee Relations*, 35/3 (2013), 339–55.
21. See Dawn Bennett and Pamela Burnard, 'Human Capital Career Creativities for Creative Industries Work: Lessons Underpinned by Bourdieu's Tools for Thinking', in *Higher Education and the Creative Economy: Beyond the Campus*, ed. Roberta Comunian and Abigail Gilmore (London: Routledge, 2016), 123–42.
22. See Michael B. Arthur, Svetlana N. Khapova, and Celeste P. Wilderom, 'Career Success in a Boundaryless Career World', *Journal of Organizational Behavior*, 26/2 (March 2005), 177–202.
23. See Thomas W. H. Ng, Lillian T. Eby, Kelly L. Sorensen, and Daniel C. Feldman, 'Predictors of Objective and Subjective Career Success: A Meta-Analysis', *Personnel Psychology*, 58/2 (May 2005), 367–408.
24. Nicky Dries, Roland Pepermans, and Olivier Carlier define and illustrate these categories in 'Career Success: Constructing a Multidimensional Model', *Journal of Vocational Behavior*, 73/2 (October 2008), 254–67.
25. Nic Beech, Charlotte Gilmore, Paul Hibbert, and Sierk Ybema, 'Identity-in-the-Work and Musicians' Struggles: The Production of Self-Questioning Identity Work', *Work, Employment and Society*, 30/3 (June 2016), 509.
26. Silviya Svejenova discusses calling in relation to resilience in ' "The Path with the Heart": Creating the Authentic Career', *Journal of Management Studies*, 42/5 (July 2005), 947–74.

27. Complex identity work among creatives is also discussed in Manto Gotsi, Constantine Andriopoulos, Marianne W. Lewis, and Amy E. Ingram, 'Managing Creatives: Paradoxal Approaches to Identity Regulation', *Human Relations*, 63/6 (February 2010), 781–805.

28. Self-alienisation is discussed by Jana Costas and Peter Fleming, 'Beyond Dis-Identification: A Discursive Approach to Self-Alienation in Contemporary Organizations', *Human Relations*, 63/3 (March 2009), 353–78.

29. For more information on older workers and learning preferences, see Ruth Kanfer and Phillip L. Ackerman, 'Aging, Adult Development, and Work Motivation', *Academy of Management Review*, 29/3 (July 2004), 440–58.

30. This finding has also been identified in other sectors. See, for example, Dirk Buyens, Hans Van Dijk, Thomas Dewilde, and Ans De Vos, 'The Aging Workforce: Perceptions of Career Ending', *Journal of Managerial Psychology*, 24/2 (2009), 102–17.

31. Sophie Hennekam has also identified the prevalence of self-employed work among creative industries workers. See, for example, 'Challenges of Older Self-Employed Workers in Creative Industries: The Case of the Netherlands', *Management Decision*, 53/4 (2015), 876–91; and Daniel C. Feldman and Mark C. Bolino, 'Career Patterns of the Self-Employed: Career Motivations and Career Outcomes', *Journal of Small Business Management*, 38/3 (July 2000), 53–67.

32. See Feldman and Bolino, 'Career Patterns of the Self-Employed', 53–67; and Dana Mietzner and Martin Kamprath, 'A Competence Portfolio for Professionals in the Creative Industries', *Creativity and Innovation Management*, 22/3 (March 2013), 280–94.

33. See Hannes Zacher, Felicia Chan, Arnold B. Bakker, and Evangelia Demerouti, 'Selection, Optimization, and Compensation Strategies: Interactive Effects on Daily Work Engagement', *Journal of Vocational Behavior*, 87 (April, 2015), 101–7.

34. Sophie Hennekam and Dawn Bennett, 'Involuntary Career Transition and Identity Within the Artist Population', *Personnel Review*, 45/6 (2016), 1114–31.

35. See, for example, Nick Rabkin, 'Teaching Artists: A Century of Tradition and a Commitment to Change', *Work and Occupations*, 40/4 (October 2013), 506–13.

36. Beech, Gilmore, Hibbert, and Ybema, 'Identity-in-the-Work and Musicians' Struggles: The Production of Self-Questioning Identity Work', 518.

37. See Christina Scharff. 'The Psychic Life of Neoliberalism: Mapping the Contours of Entrepreneurial Subjectivity', *Theory, Culture & Society*, 33/6 (July 2015), 107–22.

9 Reimagining Classical Music Performing Organisations for the Digital Age

Brian Kavanagh

This chapter considers how classical music performing organisations, particularly orchestras and opera companies, are changing in response to digital technologies and shifting stakeholder expectations. Both types of change can be framed by what certain theorists call institutional logics—that is, the mechanisms, practices, beliefs, and values that define the boundaries of institutional fields. Such logics shift over time, often because of radical technological change that "disrupts" established practices and behaviours within industrial sectors. The classical music industry, then, is a prime example for analysis of changing logics and innovations. Drawing on field data generated from a series of interviews conducted at ten leading classical music performing organisations, including the London Symphony Orchestra, Detroit Symphony Orchestra, Berlin Philharmonic, and Glyndebourne Opera, this chapter scrutinises how such organisations are responding to the opportunities and challenges of digital technologies, and how this interaction is affecting their practices and principles.

Sparked by the emergence of new technologies and the distribution of music as a digital good online, the music industry has experienced substantive shocks that have transformed its structure significantly. Innovations in audio- and video-streaming, and in mobile networking have irrevocably altered patterns of artistic, commercial, and social exchange between producers and consumers of music. In the classical sector, for example, certain orchestras that once relied on record labels to produce and distribute recordings are now taking ownership of their recorded output by developing their own digital production capabilities, or by taking advantage of new distribution channels such as iTunes and Amazon. Similarly, consumers of classical music can now purchase recordings in multiple formats, including traditional ("physical") formats such as the CD and Super Audio CD (SACD), and downloadable formats such as MP3, FLAC, and DSD.[1] Consumers also enjoy access to performances on platforms such as YouTube and Vimeo. Meanwhile, social media services such as Facebook and Twitter are influencing marketing strategies across classical music, by facilitating a more direct relationship with audiences.

To scrutinise these myriad shifts in the context of institutional logics, let us first consider the term further. Roger Friedland and Robert R. Alford originally defined institutional logics as 'supraorganisational patterns of human activity by which individuals and organisations produce and reproduce their material subsistence and organise time and space.'[2] They also highlighted key institutions that are guided by distinct institutional logics, namely the capitalist market, the bureaucratic state, democracy, the nuclear family, and Christianity. Patricia H. Thornton and William Ocasio revised this scheme, identifying six further fields: the market, the corporation, professions, the state, the family, and religions.[3] Subsequently, Royston Greenwood and Roy Suddaby rethought the concept, defining institutional logics as 'the taken-for-granted practices and beliefs, often encoded in laws that specify the boundaries of a field, its rules of membership, and forms of its communities.'[4] Institutional logics, then, define the boundaries of institutional fields and inform the actions of organisations operating in them.

In classical music, such logics, non-static by nature, define intrinsic elements such as music copyright law, inter- and intra-organisational dependencies (for example, among orchestras, record labels, arts funding organisations, audiences, patrons, and corporate sponsors), practices associated with music performance, the perceived value of classical music, and the production, distribution, and consumption of music recordings. Mary Ann Glynn and Michael Lounsbury investigated shifts in the sector's aesthetic and market logics, focussing on the Atlanta Symphony Orchestra at a time when it was confronted by declining patronage, government support, and audience numbers.[5] The orchestra's response involved drawing on 'more "mainstream" or "pop" interpretations of classical music', leading to a blurring of aesthetic and market logics.[6] That is, the orchestra reacted to environmental pressures by popularising its repertoire—"dumbing down", some might argue—to appeal to a broader audience. This immediately shows institutional logics to be non-static and exemplifies how commercial market logics can threaten the sanctity of aesthetic logics. This case exposes a connection between shifting logics and field decline; the following section considers how technological innovation across the genre compels logic shifts and related changes in music-industry practices.

The Impact of Technology on Classical Music

As Julian Johnson has suggested, classical music is 'often distinguished by its apparent lack of connection with technology . . . [yet] since most people now encounter classical music primarily in recorded form, its presence is thoroughly mediated by contemporary technology.'[7] In fact, classical music is an institutional setting in which technologies old (e.g. musical instruments) and new co-exist. Indeed, the genre has a rich history of technological innovation, and composers have typically been swift to respond to the latest technologies: Handel employed the glockenspiel in his oratorio *Saul* (1738) following its invention in the late seventeenth century;[8] Tchaikovsky was quick to incorporate the newly invented celesta in his famous *Nutcracker Suite* (1892) following its appearance in 1886; twentieth-century composers such as Bohuslav Martinů, Olivier Messiaen, and Edgar Varèse explored early electronic instruments such as the theremin and the ondes martenot, both of which appeared in the late 1920s. In the post-war period, new and increasingly compact circuitry aided the invention of the synthesiser, and more recently composers have used computers in their work: Karlheinz Stockhausen and Pierre Schaeffer famously established specialised studios for experimentation in the area, such that so-called electroacoustic music is now an important subgenre of contemporary music. Composers, then, have long embraced such innovation, contrary to any notion that classical music is antithetical to technological change.

Gradual developments, mechanical or digital, have also had a tremendous impact on performers, ensembles, and audiences. This has largely centred on aesthetic logics (that is, the aesthetic basis for artistic creation), informing the choices and judgements that composers, performers, and audiences make. But technology also helps establish markets for classical music, particularly for printed sheet music, audio recordings, and video content. At the same time, the market logics that define the sector are principally constructed around the live music event: musicians are contracted to perform concerts, audiences pay an admission fee, and musicians receive remuneration. Patrons of the arts and its funding bodies contribute to the annual income of classical music organisations and commission composers to write new music. Additionally, the sale of sheet music, which emerged in the nineteenth century, has developed into an important market that continues to stimulate music-making, particularly among amateur musicians. Indeed, the sheet music publishing business was the sector's largest market force until it was disrupted by the invention of audio recording, playback devices and vinyl records in the twentieth century, and the related emergence of markets for recorded music. This phenomenon was the most significant shift in the industry's market logics in modern times, at least until the advent of MP3 technology in the early 1990s.

The recorded music industry has itself undergone a series of transformations following technological innovation, which has had both a disruptive and sustaining impact on its markets. The market for vinyl records, for example, was disrupted by the commercial launch of the CD in 1982. The new format was disruptive to manufacturers of vinyl records and record players (turntables), but sustained copyright holders, producers, and distributors by boosting sales of recordings.[9] As Stephen Witt observes: 'In the late 1990s on the strength of the CD boom, the recording industry enjoyed the most profitable years in its history.'[10] Yet, sales of classical music recordings *declined* in the 1990s, prompting record labels such as EMI and Decca to reduce their long-term commitment to classical artists. Labels also began to focus on what Norman Lebrecht described, perhaps unfairly, as 'freak hits', a reference to the tendency of record labels to focus on artists and repertoire they felt could be marketed to mass audiences: 'Nigel Kennedy one year, Spanish monks the next . . . [C]ompilation discs designed to be played while driving a car, making love or weeding the garden.'[11]

The emergence of MP3s and related advances in online and mobile technologies would disrupt the industry still further. In keeping with disruptive innovation theory,[12] the MP3 was initially of poor quality,[13] but soon became a realistic alternative to physical recordings. Indeed, the MP3, coupled with software developments such as Napster,[14] inspired digital distribution via unauthorised peer-to-peer (P2P) file-sharing and the transformation of the principal consumer process long associated with music consumption.[15] The MP3, then, disrupted established patterns of artistic, social, and commercial exchange between producers and consumers of music. The economic consequence was a gradual reduction in recording opportunities for artists and music ensembles: 'By the end of 2004 the future of the recording music industry looked dire. Compact disc sales were down yet again. EMI, burdened with debt, was hurtling toward receivership.'[16]

Digital innovation has similarly redefined the logics underpinning the traditional broadcasting sector: radio, television, and, in particular, the production and distribution of video content. The availability of relatively inexpensive broadcast-quality digital video cameras and video-editing software (in some cases, freeware) means that musicians and ensembles can now self-produce such content. Meanwhile, the Internet provides opportunities to distribute content to audiences more directly, circumventing traditional channels—albeit with limited potential to monetise these outlets when consumers can access so much cultural content for free. This restriction complicates the task of developing a commercial strategy to produce and distribute music online.[17] Nevertheless, classical music ensembles have redefined their relationship with audiences, navigating a space between traditional concepts of what a classical music ensemble is (they continue to perform traditional repertoire live) and visions of what they might become in the digital space. The following section, then, considers how orchestras and opera companies are developing modern digital strategies, acquiring new capabilities and introducing new practices.

Digital Innovations, Shifting Logics

Many workers in the classical music sector appreciate the paradox digital technology presents. As Paul Hughes (General Manager, BBC Symphony Orchestra and BBC Singers) remarks, digital technology offers the opportunity to 'develop more direct relationships with audiences by making music available to more people in more ways, and in more formats, than could ever have been imagined twenty years ago.'[18] Yet, digital technology is also disruptive to how ensembles produce and distribute the music they record, and to how audiences discover and access such content. Anne Parsons (President, Detroit Symphony Orchestra) accepts that once-dominant logics are shifting and outlines the need for orchestras to respond accordingly:

> Everything that is going on today challenges dominant logic in the [classical music] field. We play in these great halls with perfect acoustics and we charge money, and we appeal to a certain segment of society. That's the dominant logic and today it's upside down. Technology is one of the reasons it's upside down. Now, people don't want to be closed, they want to be open; they don't want music to be expensive, they want it to be free. The live performance and the concept of the digital product are one and the same but [require] different delivery systems. Musicians are dedicated to live performance, as they should be, but if you are in the business that we are in you must be focused on the audience. New audiences have moved to technology, so to ignore that or to fight it is at your peril.[19]

In considering the shift from analogue to digital technologies, Elizabeth Scott (former Chief Media and Digital Officer, Lincoln Center for the Performing Arts, New York) suggests that classical music organisations need to ask themselves 'why would they do anything digitally before they seek to innovate in the [digital] arena?'[20] Scott highlights a tension between what she calls the 'promise of digital' and what non-profit classical music organisations can realistically achieve by developing and implementing digital strategies:

> The great promise of digital technology and platforms for classical music institutions is the ability to deliver on what is so often core to the mission of those institutions [around] access, whether that access is educational, informative, or breaking down barriers that are cost related. So, the promise of these platforms is tremendous but the question is: what's realistic?[21]

Realising this promise requires classical music performing organisations to think and act differently, but the barriers they encounter can include resource constraints, the rigidities of established practices and routine, and cognitive framing such as resistance from staff, unionisation, and concerns around digital rights management control. It is immensely difficult to balance and exercise control across these areas.

A further challenge is to reconcile new logics with mission aims and the changing expectations of internal (musicians) and external (audiences, funders) stakeholders. For example, classical music audiences still expect to be able to buy new recordings, and in a greater range of formats, yet orchestras receive fewer recording opportunities from record labels.[22] Recordings continue to play an important role in advancing the mission of classical music organisations,[23] serving to enhance their status and legitimacy within the classical music field and the broader cultural sector: they represent critical resources to attract donations, grants, and, indeed, audiences. Therefore, a dilemma for these organisations is to maintain their relationship with audiences and other stakeholders through recordings by developing new strategies, capabilities, and practices.

To address such issues, the London Symphony Orchestra (LSO) established in 2000 the first orchestra-owned record label: LSO Live. The orchestra made its first recording in 1913 and has since featured on over 5,000 releases. However, according to Chaz Jenkins (former Head of LSO Live), the LSO had become 'highly dependent on relationships with record companies' for the production and distribution of its recordings in the pre-digital recording era, such that the orchestra 'practically lived in Abbey Road Studios in London and recording work represented a very important source of income for [its] musicians.'[24] As the recorded music industry began to fragment in the early part of this century, the LSO became frustrated by what Jenkins describes as 'the increasing tendency of the major record labels to look at the short term rather than the long term,' a tendency Jenkins feels was contrary to the orchestra's stated aims—to make the music the LSO performs available to the greatest number of people.[25] At the same time, the orchestra understood that 'audio recordings would continue to play an important role in reaching new audiences' and that it had a commitment to a global audience who expected new LSO recordings: 'Suddenly, technology made it possible for an orchestra to set up its own record label and to market itself globally in ways that were absolutely impossible years ago.'[26]

Through LSO Live, the orchestra took ownership of audio production and distribution processes that were once the sole preserve of record labels. To establish LSO Live, management negotiated a profit-share arrangement with their musicians. Rather than receive a fee for recording sessions, or royalties from the resulting products, musicians became shareholders of the recordings, sharing in profits accrued from their physical or online sales and downloads.[27] The LSO, a self-governing organisation, retains ownership of the label, its recordings, and thus their intellectual property rights (IPR).[28] The LSO also maintains complete artistic control, notably in relation to the repertoire it records and its collaborative guest artists (conductors and soloists). The orchestra also controls all stages of the production and distribution process.

The benefits of this model have led other orchestras to adopt similar strategies. Following the LSO's lead, the Amsterdam-based Royal Concertgebouw Orchestra (RCO) founded its own record label (RCO Live, f. 2004). David Bazen (Business Administrator, RCO) states:

> It had become clear to the Concertgebouw that launching a record label was a good solution to digital disruption. Instead of recording music yourself and delivering it to, say, EMI, and then hoping that they might do something with it, by doing it yourself at least you are in control.[29]

More recent successors to LSO Live's model include the Seattle Symphony Orchestra's (SSO) record label, Seattle Symphony Media, and the Berlin Philharmonic's Berliner Philharmoniker Recordings (both f. 2014).

The diffusion of this "in-house" model signals the emergence of new logics to define how orchestras produce and distribute audio recordings, allowing them to continue to connect audiences, through audio recordings, with the live music event. It also marks an obvious shift in control, from record labels to orchestras. When the LSO announced LSO Live in 2000, it apparently drew 'dismissive even hostile comments from record company executives unhappy that one of the world's finest orchestras should take control of its discographic destiny.'[30] By developing the first orchestra-owned record label, the LSO occupied a "space" within a changing institutional environment by adopting aspects of a declining recorded industry model—the production and distribution of CDs—while serving physical and digital markets.

The New York City–based Metropolitan Opera, commonly referred to as "The Met", has also been a pioneer in the sector. It was the first classical music organisation to video-broadcast successfully when it introduced Opera in Cinema (f. 2006). The initiative harnessed innovations in digital cinema projection and satellite distribution, and reimagined the relationship between opera and its audiences. As Scott attests:

> One of the outstanding successes in the digital media space has been the Metropolitan Opera's speed of scale of growth and success with its democratised $20 ticket offerings of its opera product in cinemas.[31]

The success of Opera in Cinema prompted other high-profile opera companies, such as Glyndebourne Opera, the Royal Opera House, and the Vienna State Opera, to broadcast their own live performances into cinemas. This further diffusion suggests that opera—a narrative-driven genre with an attractive, visual element—is well suited to the medium. Orchestras, however, face a greater challenge to convince audiences to experience their (typically instrumental) music in cinemas, as evidenced by the Los Angeles Philharmonic Orchestra cancelling its series of planned live broadcasts in cinemas across the United States in 2012 due to poor ticket sales.[32]

Nevertheless, other orchestras have developed alternative broadcasting strategies to engage audiences more directly: the Berlin Philharmonic launched its innovative Digital Concert Hall in 2008. This first bespoke online platform for video-streaming classical music concerts is a subscription service that allows users to experience all of the orchestra's performances live from its resident concert hall (Berlin's Philharmonie) in high-definition audio and video through a website, TV, or mobile app.[33] The orchestra performs each concert programme three times in the Philharmonie, broadcasting the final performance live online. Following post-production editing, a final version of the concert is placed in an online archive. Subscribers can choose from a range of "tiered" ticketing options—weekly, monthly, or annually—which in addition to providing access to live concert broadcasts, gives users access to an archive that includes hundreds of concert performances, documentary films, interviews with musicians and composers, and a range of educational content.

The Digital Concert Hall extends the orchestra's historical engagement with new technology,[34] and seeks to meet the modern expectations of its audience, who, as Tobias Möller (Marketing and Communications Director, Berlin Philharmonic) observes, 'expect the orchestra to be at the cutting edge of the latest technology . . . [Our audience is] "quality conscious" and expect the organisation to deliver a [technological] service that reflects the quality that the orchestra delivers artistically.'[35] Although the Digital Concert Hall represents an important feature of the orchestra's identity, it is still obliged to engage with other platforms within the broader digital ecosystem. YouTube and Facebook support the Digital Concert Hall by providing direct marketing channels to its potential users. Indeed, YouTube allows the organisation to reach far greater audiences than the Digital Concert Hall.[36] However, as Möller says, the Digital Concert Hall serves a distinct role, allowing the organisation to 'curate and present content in a hand-tailored environment . . . It is a place where people feel the Berliner Philharmoniker is the host.'[37] By developing its own digital platform, the orchestra has also created a new revenue stream for its musicians and guest artists—an accomplishment it cannot expect to match on third-party platforms.

The Digital Concert Hall, however, was expensive to found; its ongoing maintenance is made possible only with the support of Deutsche Bank. Most classical music organisations lack such resources or brand visibility, or simply have different needs and expectations, and so must develop alternative strategies. In 2011, the Detroit Symphony Orchestra (DSO) launched Live from Orchestra Hall—a video-streaming service that webcasts performances from its resident Orchestra Hall. The start of the decade found the orchestra trying to rebuild its brand and reputation following one of the worst labour stoppages in modern orchestral history.[38] According to Parsons, one of the few positives to emerge from the dispute was to impel the orchestra to 'embrace technology and other activities that fall under the umbrella of accessibility.'[39] Indeed, one of the core aims of Live from Orchestra Hall is to make the DSO 'the most accessible orchestra in the world.'[40] To this end, the DSO live-broadcasts all of its concerts from Orchestra Hall (approximately twenty per season) for free via an official website and mobile app.[41]

The DSO's aspiration reflects a philosophy that classical music should be available to everyone. Accessibility, indeed, is a pressing concern for all classical music organisations as they adapt to an increasingly multicultural, technocratic society, and to concerns about declining audiences and reduced funding. The digital space can surely help break down commonly perceived barriers to classical music, which, as an institutional field, has often epitomised the thorny concept of "high" art but is now motivated to be more democratic and accessible.[42] The immediacy of video, then, is unsurprisingly key to many contemporary strategies, despite the needs and expectations of audiences and other stakeholders varying tremendously across the sector. For example, the SSO uses video content to promote the orchestra online to a largely local audience, with no call for a bespoke web-streaming platform. The Met, on the other hand, has developed web-streaming subscription services (complementing Opera in Cinema), as has the Vienna State Opera. Glyndebourne Opera pursued a different strategy, partnering with the Guardian Media Group in 2001 to broadcast six operas online for free, and again in 2017 with *The Telegraph* newspaper to broadcast three operas online and in cinemas across the United Kingdom and Ireland.

Such variety signals the absence of a dominant logic, pointing to uncertainty and, perhaps, to scepticism regarding the tangible *value* of the new medium to classical music organisations. The question must be asked: Do audiences want to experience classical music on an electronic device, when a fundamental part of what makes classical music so special is hearing it live in a concert hall and sharing in that experience in a social space? To echo Scott's question, why should classical music performing organisations adapt digital technology at all? Elena Dubinets (Vice President of Artistic Planning, SSO) is convinced they must:

> The world is changing and you cannot imagine any function of the world without technology anymore, and it's the same with orchestras. If we haven't yet changed, then we must change. Technology must become an integral part of what we do . . . We must begin to absorb everything around us.[43]

The crux is that to follow Dubinets's lead, classical music organisations must manage internal organisational change as old business models, from media agreements and marketing strategies to workers' rights, are disrupted. Union regulations have long been extremely important to orchestral life, but the protection of musicians' rights is coming under pressure because of digital technologies. Managers of the New York Philharmonic (NYP), for example, are engaged in ongoing negotiations with the American Federation of Musicians to realign relations between management and NYP musicians in the face of digital disruption. In the context of developing a digital audio recording strategy, Bill Thomas (Vice-President and COO, NYP) emphasises the continuing costs involved in creating new recordings under existing union rules, and that the organisation 'still has to pay musicians [for recording sessions] on top of their regular salary to release products . . . making recording difficult and cost-prohibitive.'[44]

The implication is that expectations must be realigned. Should musicians still expect upfront payment for recording work as they did in the past, when record labels funded recording sessions and related musician fees? To circumvent the costs associated with the traditional recording business model—not only musicians' fees, but also the resources required to produce and distribute physical products—NYP managers established an integrated media agreement with musicians, allowing the orchestra to release 'a lot of audio products through iTunes and other digital outlets . . . very inexpensively' because musicians agree to a revenue share in lieu of an upfront recording fee.[45] Given the model's departure from historic norms, it relies on goodwill and flexibility on the part of musicians and their unions. While the integrated media agreement does not offer the NYP the kind of flexibility that self-governing orchestras such as the LSO or Berlin Philharmonic enjoy, the orchestra recognises that 'without it, and the exposure it affords the orchestra, there is no market.'[46] This case shows that unless managers can reach new digital media agreements with musicians, organisations such as the NYP risk being left behind. As Thomas concludes:

> Because digital technology is constantly changing, orchestras need to be able to respond quickly . . . [which calls for] new levels of flexibility so orchestras can do innovative projects that do not require potentially long and protracted negotiations with musicians and with musicians' unions.[47]

In other words, to realign expectations within classical music performing organisations is to reflect the digital environment in which they now operate.

§

Digital innovation presents classical music performing organisations with a series of contradictions and dilemmas. Although the digital space may seem antithetical to traditional classical music culture, orchestras and opera companies must adopt digital technology in response to shifts in the logics that define their industry, otherwise they risk being (further) marginalised in an increasingly techno-literate society. Online and mobile technologies are simultaneously disruptive (for example, to the social and economic arrangements surrounding intellectual property) *and* sustaining (allowing more direct engagement with audiences). Orchestras and opera companies are therefore questioning their traditional practices, inspiring new, purposeful actions and strategies to respond to and influence these logics. The perspective of institutional logics can help us to understand how digital innovations present challenges to classical music performing organisations, but also offer exciting opportunities for the industry to redefine itself. Put another way, digital technology can prompt us, and the industry itself, to rethink identity by challenging the *collective* perception of classical music, how classical music performing organisations see themselves (internal identity), and how others view them (external identity). The latter is surely critical to the industry's long-term fortunes and, more pertinently, to whether the great 'promise of digital' can be realised.

Notes

1. Guided by the research of Karlheinz Brandenburg (on music compression) and Dieter Seitzer (on the transfer of music over a phone line), the Fraunhofer Institute for Integrated Circuits developed MP3 technology in the late 1980s and early 1990s. The first commercial MP3 player did not appear until 1998; the following year marked the first time a record company (SubPop) distributed music tracks in the format. Free Lossless Audio Codec (FLAC) is similar to MP3 but "lossless": audio is compressed without reducing sound quality. Direct-Stream Digital (DSD) is a high-resolution format used by Sony and Philips for their system of digitally recreating audible signals for the SACD.
2. Roger Friedland and Robert R. Alford, 'Bringing Society Back in: Symbols, Practices, and Institutional Contradiction', in *The New Institutionalism in Organisational Analysis*, ed. Walter W. Powell and Paul. J. DiMaggio (Chicago: University of Chicago Press, 1991), 243.
3. Patricia H. Thornton and William Ocasio, 'Institutional Logics and the Historical Contingency of Power in Organisations: Executive Succession in the Higher Education Publishing Industry, 1958–1990', *The American Journal of Sociology*, 105/3 (1999), 805.
4. Royston Greenwood and Roy Suddaby, 'Institutional Entrepreneurship in Mature Fields: The Big Five Accounting Firms', *Academy of Management Journal*, 49/1 (2006), 28.
5. See Mary Ann Glynn and Michael Lounsbury, 'From the Critics' Corner: Logic Blending, Discursive Change and Authenticity in a Cultural Production System', *Journal of Management Studies*, 42/5 (2005), 1031–55.
6. Glynn and Lounsbury use 'market logics' to refer to 'broader notions of self-interest and profit-motive that animate commercially driven action,' and 'aesthetic logics' to refer to 'notions of artistry that animate and inform the integrity of the classical canon and its musical genres.' Glynn and Lounsbury, 'From the Critics' Corner', 1037.
7. Julian Johnson, *Who Needs Classical Music?* (New York: Oxford University Press: 2002), 92.
8. In fact, the glockenspiel can be traced to the fourteenth century, but such versions of the instrument consisted of bells, which were replaced by bars in the late seventeenth century.
9. Recording Industry Association of America (RIAA) figures show that in the United States, for example, recorded music sales peaked in 1999 ($14.59bn, compared with 1983's $3.79bn); CD sales specifically peaked in 2000 (942.5m). See www.riaa.com/u-s-sales-database/ (accessed 19 July 2017).
10. Stephen Witt, *How Music Got Free: What Happens When an Entire Generation Commits the Same Crime?* (London: Bodley Head, 2015), 79–80.
11. Norman Lebrecht, *Who Killed Classical Music? Maestros, Managers, and Corporate Politics* (London: Citadel Press, 1997), 219.
12. Clayton M. Christensen and Joseph L. Bower suggest that a disruptive technology 'typically present[s] a different package of performance attributes—ones that, at least at the outset, are not valued by existing customers.' However, 'the performance attributes that existing customers do value improve at such a rapid rate that the new technology can later invade those established markets.' Christensen and Bower, 'Disruptive Technologies Catching the Wave', *Harvard Business Review*, 73/1 (January–February 1995), 44.

13. The quality of an MP3 file is largely determined by the bitrate of an encoded piece of audio and the quality of the encoder algorithm used to create the file. Bitrate determines the number of kilobits per second (kps) of audio and therefore the quality of the resulting sound. Early encoders sampled audio content at 128kps, however with greater bandwidth availability and larger hard drives, bitrates of up to 320kps are now common.

14. Boasting 80 million registered users at its peak, Napster was found to be in violation of music publishers' copyright and was closed by court order in July 2001. It nevertheless signalled a fundamental shift in the logics that define how music is distributed and consumed.

15. For a more detailed account of the impact of digital technology on music consumption patterns, see Luca Molteni and Andrea Ordanini, 'Consumption Patterns, Digital Technology and Music Downloading', *Long Range Planning*, 36 (2003), 389–406.

16. Witt, *How Music Got Free*, 189.

17. As Lawrence Lessig observes, 'the network doesn't discriminate between the sharing of copyrighted and non-copyrighted content.' Lawrence Lessig, *Free Culture: How Big Media Uses Technology and the Law to Lock Down Culture and Control Creativity* (New York: Penguin, 2004), 18; also available at www.free-culture.cc/freeculture.pdf.

18. Paul Hughes, interview with the author, 8 July 2011.

19. Anne Parsons, interview with the author, 1 February 2014.

20. Elizabeth Scott, interview with the author, 5 May 2014.

21. Scott, interview with the author.

22. See Witt, *How Music Got Free*, 83–5, 189.

23. Many orchestras still adhere to similar forms of non-profit governance and exist to advance complementary mission aims that, broadly speaking, are intended to preserve and promote the classical music canon. Although the raison d'être of orchestras is to perform live, they engage in complementary activities in support of their core mission, including radio broadcasts and audio recordings.

24. Chaz Jenkins, interview with the author, 4 August 4 2011.

25. In common with other non-profit organisations, the London Symphony Orchestra has a mission statement, the latest version of which emphasises this aim: see https://alwaysmoving.lso.co.uk/our-vision/london-symphony-orchestra (accessed 29 May 2017).

26. Jenkins, interview with the author.

27. Conductors and soloists also share in profits accrued.

28. In the pre-digital era, the LSO were contracted to record for major record labels such as EMI, who retained the rights to those recordings.

29. David Bazen, interview with the author, 14 October 2011.

30. This is the LSO's own account: https://lso.co.uk/orchestra/history/recordings.html (accessed 27 June 2017).

31. Elizabeth Scott, interview with the author, 5 May 2014.

32. See David Ng, 'L.A. Philharmonic Kills Series of Live Broadcasts to Cinemas' [8 October 2012], *Los Angeles Times*, http://articles.latimes.com/2012/oct/08/entertainment/la-et-cm-los-angeles-philharmonic-live-canceled20121009 (accessed 27 July 2017).

33. The orchestra has developed a dedicated website (www.digitalconcerthall.com) and apps, enabling users to access content on Smart TVs, mobile devices, and streaming devices such as Amazon Fire TV and Apple TV.

34. Under the direction of Herbert von Karajan (Principal Conductor between 1955 and 1989), the Berlin Philharmonic was acutely aware of the power of audio and video broadcasting technologies to enhance its reputation. The orchestra was also an early adopter of digital innovation, making the first-ever test pressing of a CD in 1979—a recording of Richard Strauss's *Eine Alpensinfonie*.

35. Tobias Möller, interview with the author, 9 November 2011.
36. According to an official press release (3 May 2017), the Digital Concert Hall has approximately 30,000 ticket-buying users; the orchestra's YouTube channel (www.youtube.com/user/BerlinPhil) attracts millions of viewers.
37. Möller, interview with the author, 20 June 2017.
38. The dispute prompted DSO musicians to strike for six months from October 2010, cancelling almost an entire concert season. Concerts resumed in April 2011 with a weekend of free concerts.
39. Anne Parsons, interview with the author, 7 May 2014.
40. Parsons, 7 May 2014.
41. See www.dso.org/live.aspx (accessed 10 August 2017).
42. For an historical account of the institutionalisation of high culture, see Paul J. DiMaggio, 'Cultural Entrepreneurship in Nineteenth-Century Boston', in *Nonprofit Enterprise in the Arts: Studies in Mission and Constraint*, ed. Paul J. DiMaggio (New York: Oxford University Press, 1986), 41–61. DiMaggio suggests, for example, that the founding of the Museum of Fine Arts in Boston (1870) and the Boston Symphony Orchestra (1881) provided a framework 'for the definition of high art' and for its 'segregation from popular forms' (49).
43. Elena Dubinets, interview with the author, 15 May 2014.
44. Bill Thomas, interview with the author, 5 June 2014.
45. Thomas, interview with the author, 5 June 2014.
46. Vince Ford (Vice President, Digital and Strategic Initiatives, New York Philharmonic), interview with the author, 5 June 2014.
47. Thomas, interview with the author, 19 July 2017.

Part III

Challenges and Debates

10 Is Classical Music a Living or Heritage Art Form?

Susanna Eastburn

'Why do we call this music classical, as if it's dead?'[1] This question, asked during a panel discussion at Classical:NEXT in 2014, has stayed with me. When I think about classical music, I often reflect on the derivation of the word 'classical': from the Latin *classis*, a rank or division of Roman people—in fact, not too distant from the modern use of 'class' to denote societal strata. Around the time of the sixteenth and seventeenth centuries, 'classical' also took on the meaning of "timeless", with a particular relationship to what was perceived as the pinnacle of European culture, the Greco-Roman era. Associated with the word today, therefore, are connotations of clear hierarchies, of value judgements that are somehow objective and fixed across time, and of a principally Eurocentric view of culture. Even when considering contemporary "modern classics", the implication is of acceptance into a revered canon of Great Work within a circumscribed tradition.

Of course, being 'classical' is not automatically the same thing as being 'dead', as the mischievously provocative questioner at the head of this chapter implies. However, a living art form must have the creation of new work at its heart. The baked-in associations and formal clarity of classical music can be problematic, to put it mildly, when it comes to contemporary music, and in particular how it is treated by the wider classical music sector. A healthy, resilient, living art form in the twenty-first century needs to embrace "mess". It must recognise the decisive shifts happening in the wider world brought about by, among other things, the digital revolution, as well as the upswelling of historically marginalised perspectives, such as those of women, minorities, and people from lower socio-economic backgrounds. This can be achieved through a constant, challenging, and creative discourse with the traditions of the past, but, above all, it needs a wholehearted critical engagement with new music and its creators.[2]

A great joy of working at Sound and Music is the daily opportunity it provides to talk with composers and artists. When I joined the organisation as Chief Executive in late 2012,[3] the growth of an energetic, DIY, often composer-led scene was instantly noticeable. Composers and artists around the country, particularly those in the earlier part of their professional career, were putting on their own events, festivals, and series, and often in unconventional spaces such as clubs, tunnels, post-industrial spaces, churches, or car parks. (There are, of course, venerable antecedents, such as the Aldeburgh and St Magnus Festivals founded by Benjamin Britten and Peter Maxwell Davies respectively, the ensembles of composers such as Cornelius Cardew, Gavin Bryars, Michael Nyman, and Roger Redgate, and, more recently, the trailblazing Camberwell Composers' Collective.) The programming of this new generation is bold and eclectic, often drawing in other art forms and uninhibitedly mixing musical genres. Presentation is informal and intimate—although with brilliant performers—and can allow audiences to move around and explore the space, bringing their drinks with them. Such events often attract a different sort of audience: not necessarily new music aficionados, but a culturally curious crowd, connecting on social media, and spreading the word about their experience.

Talking to the impressive people behind these events, I was curious to discover more about *why* they were putting themselves through the ordeal—immense work, stress, financial risk—that organising your own event entails. Being a freelance composer is already freighted with uncertainty, so why were they adding to this pressure? The reasons given were remarkably consistent: they had strong views on the programming of new music, and strong views about the audience's experience of new music. They also believed that opportunities to create new work were otherwise limited and that the criteria that had to be met in order to allow such opportunities were often opaque. These factors motivated a strong desire to generate composing and performance opportunities for themselves and for their like-minded peers.

Recognising and responding to this trend, Sound and Music created the "Composer-Curator" programme in 2013.[4] Still unique, the programme is explicitly aimed at composers who curate and organise new music series, events and festivals, putting resources, decision-making, and control back into their hands through a mix of financial and other bespoke support, including marketing, fundraising, and the chance to meet peers on the programme. The results have included ensemble performances,[5] festivals, a tour of historical Scottish venues, a radio show, and a British tour of two new works of verbatim music theatre.[6] The scheme has profoundly changed us as an organisation: we have learned that putting composers at the centre of an activity allows them to thrive—not just as composers in the conventional sense, but in how they think about the ways in which audiences hear and experience live music. This encompasses both the physical environment and the audio-visual journey that centres on the experience of the work, rather than its genre.

Curation itself, then, may be viewed as an extended form of composition, as the resulting originality of the Composer-Curator projects—and indeed the many other artist-led projects around the UK and elsewhere—attests. Enabled to proceed on their own terms, composers are encouraged to develop a distinctive curatorial voice, and to be active participants in a flourishing, alternative creative scene. Sound and Music has also learned that the best people to describe the experience of new music, and to communicate those descriptions authentically to audiences, are often composers themselves. Armed with these observations, those of us today who believe in new music's value as an adventurous, challenging, living form of cultural expression have a tremendous opportunity to allow it to take its position confidently alongside other art forms, such as literature or contemporary visual art, where new work and its creators are central to public understanding and interaction.

Stacked against this is the risk that the larger classical music institutions—the orchestras, opera houses, venues, festivals, and so forth—will resist the need to change; that classical music will become a heritage art form, expending its energies and resources on showcasing classics of the past, with new music becoming a dislocated niche, misunderstood, derided, or simply ignored. To glimpse below the line of any online article about new music is to realise that some people would regard this as the best possible outcome! Yet, thankfully, the unlikely duo of public policy (which expects new work to be created, but is often hazy about what that entails),[7] and inspiring champions in the form of individual conductors, artists, administrators, and, of course, composers themselves, means that new music retains its foothold in institutional programming.

Even so, we have to ask, "at what cost?" Consciously or otherwise, new music too often suffers from a lack of confidence in its intrinsic interest and value, and in the audience's capacity to engage with and appreciate complicated new things. I have heard more than one programmer of a leading arts institution remark that too much new work will alienate their core audience. This fear can translate into apologetic programming, classic examples being a new work slipped in before the interval, with a well-known symphony as a "reward" afterwards; or the free 6 p.m. performance, perhaps in a public space with poor lighting and acoustics. Instead programming should consider works as *music* and as bold imaginative statements that speak to our times.

The marketing of new music can also be very off-putting to an inexpert potential audience member, relying on selling concerts on the basis of the names of performers or composers of whom a non-specialist audience may well not have heard. (Not confined to new music, this industry phenomenon can make an attendee feel inferior, excluded, or unwelcome before they even arrive at the performance.) There can also be a tendency to deploy technical or off-putting jargon, or, conversely, relentless hyperbole, describing everything and everyone as "exciting" or "ground-breaking". Why not simply try to suggest what it may be like to be in that place, at that time, with other people, listening to something together?

The classical music industry generally lacks the imagination and courage to programme more diverse voices, from the present day and the past. Happily, there are examples of larger organisations thinking intelligently and with flair about these dilemmas. The Southbank Centre's year-long "The Rest Is Noise" festival (2013) explored the soundtrack of the twentieth century and showed it was possible to programme (over an extended period) music often considered difficult, helping an engaged, curious, and gratifyingly large audience to discover and be enriched by a world with which it had previously been largely unfamiliar.[8] (Of course, the series was not, and did not set out to be, a festival of new music.) In Glasgow with the BBC Scottish Symphony Orchestra and in other cities around the world, Ilan Volkov's Tectonics Festival has also blazed a trail with its bold, imaginative commissioning and programming.

Organisations other than Sound and Music have also begun to respond to the dynamic, artist-led new music scene: the BBC Proms has experimented with leaving London's Royal Albert Hall and broadcasting from other venues, including the Peckham car park where the Multi-Story Orchestra present their work.[9] Prestigious funded ensembles and festivals around the country are similarly putting on events and performing in unconventional spaces: pubs, warehouses, tunnels, theatres, churches, and festivals. While such approaches inject a note of freshness into the classical music scene and help broaden audiences for new music, they also lead me to lingering concerns about power, resources, and gatekeeping. Larger organisations receiving core public funding clearly enjoy greater security (and, relatedly, the ability to plan ahead more easily) than the DIY scene; yet they admire how fresh and dynamic that scene is, with its exciting new venues and curious, diverse, youthful audiences. In a partnership or collaboration with artist-led work, the large established institutions have the upper hand: a relationship of power and patronage is inevitably retained—unless, that is, a systematic and sustained approach to giving away control, decision-making, resources, choices, and communication is adopted every step of the way.

This matter of decision-making and control, and how it is structured, leads me back to the title question of this chapter: Is classical music a heritage or living art form? In the main, the large and powerful orchestras, opera houses, venues, and festivals of classical music are still structured according to a post–Industrial Revolution paradigm: a hierarchical approach to organising time, people, and money in order to maximise efficiency and productivity and to streamline accountability and decision-making. In an age where resources, competition, and expectations collide and pile pressure on arts institutions, this mode of organisation is, superficially at least, easy to defend. However, it does not reflect contemporary reality—specifically a digital revolution that has led to a more closely networked society, yet one that is also dispersed and plural in its perspectives.

Increasingly, the organisations that thrive are those that recognise and harness this reality and build it into their structures—to aggressively expand their business (Facebook, Alphabet), to pursue more obvious public good (microfinance initiatives such as Bangladesh's Grameen Bank), or to fulfil some purpose in between (Innocent, Brewdog). In the arts sector, the messy interplay of diverse perspectives, user engagement, and data insight is still in its infancy, but in the creative industries at large it has led to the success of organisations as varied as Buzzfeed, YouTube, and HBO, with whom arts organisations are directly competing for audience attention and loyalty. (Incidentally, if you fear audiences' ability to engage with long and complex forms, then try talking to a fan of *Game of Thrones*.)

The majority of classical music organisations are still structured around the artistic and financial decisions of a handful of very senior people, who are in no sense diverse when considered as a group. The inherent problem with this situation is illustrated sharply by the British Association of Song-writers, Composers & Authors (BASCA), whose 2016 research showed that 72% of commissions are granted not transparently but through the direct choice of Artistic Directors.[10] Artistic Directors—I write as someone who has held such a role—are typically honourable, open-minded, and culturally curious, but they inevitably hold subjective views about different composers and their music. This amounts to judgement and taste—both incredibly important qualities in creating distinctive, engaging programmes—but I think the similar backgrounds of the individuals involved can only narrow the field in terms of who and what is heard.

In this traditional, hierarchical system, the flow of resources directly mirrors how power is held and decisions are made. What would it be like for an organisation to give up some of this power, to hand over more resources as well as artistic and financial decision-making directly to artists? With Sound and Music's Composer-Curator programme, we have found this to be a joyful and liberating experience. We provide an agreed level of resources and support, as well as a regular sounding board, but otherwise the Composer-Curators are in full control of what they want to programme, where it happens, how they describe it. The programme is unbelievably varied, happens in every region in the UK, and draws in many voices that are new to us. We could never create such an interesting or diverse programme on our own. To take a further example: the PRS for Music Foundation's Composers' Fund gives composers with a strong track record funding at pivotal stages in their career, so that they can pursue their own artistic interests.[11] This direct funding addresses the power imbalance, frees composers to pursue projects that are most important to them, and gives them more cards to play when negotiating with potential commissioners.

What, then, does the future hold? Sadly, if the status quo is maintained, it is easy to picture a doomsday scenario in which classical music appears hopelessly outdated and irrelevant, increasingly distant from the diverse realities of British society today. Serious questions about its public remit are already being asked. In its 2015 report 'Enriching Britain: Culture, Creativity, and Growth', The Warwick Commission found that between 2012 and 2015 the wealthiest, best educated, and least ethnically diverse 8% of the population accounted for 44% of attendances to live music, benefitting from £94 per head of Arts Council music funding.[12] Those of us who feel passionately about classical music understand that this is untenable, that this art form *can* attract and connect with new people, but only when its behaviours become more open, diverse, and contemporary; in short, less exclusive. If we take the time to listen and reflect, then we can observe composers and artists are creating amazing work and showing us the way forward. It is incumbent on those of us in positions of leadership to take the time to encourage necessary change and evolution, to willingly give up control and resources, and to enable more voices to be heard. Diversity of perspectives and backgrounds brings a sense of freshness and encourages discovery, renewal, and spontaneity; it challenges off-putting expectations; and it allows many more people to find ways into this art form we love.

Notes

1. Question posed at the Classical:NEXT conference, Vienna, May 2014. Founded in 2012, Classical:NEXT has established itself as Europe's leading classical music industry forum.
2. A word on definitions: throughout this article the term "new music" is used to mean 'adventurous, original, recently-created music or sound, in any genre' and "composer" to mean 'somebody who creates that'.
3. Sound and Music is the national charity for new music in the United Kingdom. Its mission is to maximise the opportunities for people to create and enjoy new music. Its work includes composer and artist development, partnerships with a range of other organisations, audience development, touring, information and advice, network building, and education. It champions new music and the work of British composers and artists, and seeks to ensure that they are at the heart of cultural life and enjoyed by many.
4. See www.soundandmusic.org/projects/welcome-composer-curator.
5. For further details, see www.soundandmusic.org/projects/composer-curator-past-projects (accessed 11 September 2017).
6. In verbatim theatre the creator(s) interview individuals about a specific topic and then use the interviewees' actual words to construct the text/libretto.
7. For example, Arts Council England's strategy has a strong focus on innovative work, creative artists, and diversity. See Arts Council England, *Great Art and Culture for Everyone: 10-Year Strategic Framework, 2010–2020* (2nd edn; Arts Council England, 2013), and especially its 2016 progress report in which 'Goal 1: Artistic Excellence' is discussed: www.artscouncil.org.uk/sites/default/files/download-file/Great-art-and-culture-for-everyone_Much-done-many-challenges-remain_15–2–16.pdf (accessed 11 November 2017).
8. Named after American critic Alex Ross's hugely successful book, the festival achieved this through weekends of talks, debates, and films and a chronological series of concerts. For further details, see www.southbankcentre.co.uk/whats-on/festivals-series/rest-noise.
9. The Multi-Story Orchestra (f. 2011) regularly presents concerts at Bold Tendencies, a disused car park in South London. For further information, see www.multi-story.org.uk/about.
10. See Natalie Bleicher, *New Music Commissioning in the UK: Equality and Diversity in New Music Commissioning*, https://basca.org.uk/newsletter/

BASCA_Music-Commissioning.pdf (British Academy of Songwriters, Composers & Authors, 2016).

11. See PRS Foundation, "Composers' Fund", http://prsfoundation.com/funding-support/funding-music-creators/next-steps/the-composers-fund/

12. See Warwick Commission, 'Enriching Britain: Culture, Creativity and Growth', https://www2.warwick.ac.uk/research/warwickcommission/futureculture/finalreport/warwick_commission_report_2015.pdf (University of Warwick, 2015), 33.

11 Dancing to Another Tune

Classical Music in Nightclubs and Other Non-Traditional Venues

Julia Haferkorn

> The large purpose-built concert hall is essentially a nineteenth-century invention.[1]

In the United Kingdom today, performances of classical music in non-traditional venues are widespread. Recent examples include a string quartet concert in the depths of a Lake District slate mine, chamber music in a grungy Camden pop venue, and an orchestral performance in the loading bay of the Royal Albert Hall; in Scotland, the East Neuk Festival boasts that all of its concerts occur in venues 'not originally designed as a concert hall'; while the BBC Proms feature an orchestral performance in a South London municipal car park for the second year running.[2] The phenomenon is by no means exclusive to the UK. In Toronto you could hear Beethoven's Fifth Symphony in a dilapidated power plant; in Berlin Radialsystem V, a pump station-turned-arts centre, regularly presents classical music; in Texas, a string quartet offers works by Ravel and Grieg in a cave; and, in southern France, the classical music festival Musique à la Ferme (Music on the Farm) celebrates its tenth anniversary.[3] To some observers, such performances are the 'new normality';[4] and discourse on the topic is growing, involving the musicians themselves, arts organisations, and social commentators.[5]

How and why did this trend emerge? Since the concert hall building boom of the late nineteenth century,[6] performances of orchestral and chamber music have typically taken place in purpose-built locations. And while the emergence of experimental music in the mid twentieth century prompted some performances to move into non-traditional venues,[7] concerts featuring works from the classical canon generally stayed put in the concert hall. Change only began in the early 2000s, when, in different countries and independently of one another, the founders of two ground-breaking club nights decided to present classical music in non-traditional venues, such as nightclubs and bars, as a *marketing strategy*, that is to reach a new and younger audience.

Following a trial phase in Hamburg, "Yellow Lounge" held its first 'classical club night' at Cookies, one of Berlin's most popular nightclub, in May 2003.[8] Ten months later, "Nonclassical" chose Cargo, a trendy club in a disused East London railway yard, for its first event. The two series emerged from very different backgrounds: Yellow Lounge was founded by a working group within the classical music department of Universal Music Group (UMG), the world's largest music corporation.[9] Nonclassical, on the other hand, was founded by the composer Gabriel Prokofiev (grandson of Sergei), whose background in electronic music had inspired him to set up Nonstop, a small experimental dance music label. Despite the founders' differences in size and, by extension, financial resources, the motivations for setting up the concert series were remarkably similar— both aimed to attract a younger audience to classical music and both had concluded that the genre's traditional presentation was insufficient for that purpose. Christian Kellersmann, then General Manager, Classical Music, recalls:

> At the start of my employment . . . at Universal stood a central question: how do we reach a new, young audience? None of my friends or pop colleagues listened to classical music. This was less because of the music itself but rather because of its image: dusty, conservative, morose . . . For us, the freshness, the sexiness, the spontaneity, the modern presentation was missing in the classical world. We wanted to listen to the music with our friends. But the way into the concert hall was not an option for them (yet).[10]

Prokofiev expresses very similar sentiments:

> I felt strongly that my classical stuff would appeal to my peer group, but when it was performed in the traditional classical setting most of the audience would be twice my age. There's nothing wrong with that, but it seemed a shame that my friends weren't there. That was a big motivator in getting Nonclassical going: thinking you've got to present classical music like other music.[11]

Presenting classical music 'like other music' meant adopting elements from the pop music sector, such as musicians communicating directly with the audience, DJs playing music—classical or otherwise—before and after the live performance, and using venues that were frequented by young attendees. Following on from positive press responses and, more importantly, numerous enthusiastic concertgoers, both series flourished. Yellow Lounge and Nonclassical established monthly events in their "home" cities and also presented their concepts in other European countries. Both projects, then, were influential forerunners and have had a noticeable impact on the industry. One further organisation, founded some years later, also contributed to the development of presenting classical music in new venues and less formal formats: the chamber music series "Classical Revolution" held their debut event in San Francisco's Revolution Café in September 2006 and went on to inspire musicians in the United States and Europe to set up their own series in bars, bookshops, and art houses.[12]

Indeed, the number of classical music concerts in non-traditional venues worldwide today is too great to chronicle here; instead, this chapter will focus on British (and particularly London-based) developments. To that

---

Nonclassical (2004–)

Nonclassical is a club night and record label, founded in 2004 by composer Gabriel Prokofiev. It runs monthly 'classical club nights' at The Victoria Dalston in East London as well as larger one-off events, such as the orchestral 'Rise of the Machines' concerts in industrial spaces, exploring the impact of machines on classical music. On its website, Nonclassical describes its activities as 'breaking out of the constraints of the traditional concert hall.' Nonclassical nights predominantly feature new compositions and contemporary-classical works.
www.nonclassical.co.uk

The Night Shift (2006–)

The Night Shift is a concert series run by the Orchestra of the Age of Enlightenment (OAE), an ensemble that performs classical music on period instruments. The series regularly presents classical music performances in non-traditional venues: in 2017, such venues included the Old Queen's Head (a Victorian pub in North London), the CLF Art Café (a warehouse space in South London), and the Camden Assembly (a historic indie music venue). Repertoire is typically chosen from the classical canon.
www.oae.co.uk/subsite/the-night-shift

London Contemporary Orchestra (2008–)

Founded by Artistic Directors Hugh Brunt and Robert Ames, the London Contemporary Orchestra (LCO) uses a range of non-traditional venues. In 2013, LCO's "Imagined Occasions" series saw the orchestra play site-specific works in the abandoned Aldwych underground station, while a more recent concert took place in Printworks, a new music and arts venue in East London that was previously home to the printing presses of the *Metro* and *Evening Standard* newspapers. As its name suggests, the orchestra performs contemporary works.
www.lcorchestra.co.uk

Figure 11.1 Fact File on Organisations Using Non-Traditional Venues

Limelight at the 100 Club (2009–13)

Limelight was a classical music concert series that took place at one of London's oldest rock venues, the 100 Club, on 100 Oxford Street. It was founded in 2009 by Emily Robbins (née Freeman) and Milly Olykan, who at that time both worked as artist managers at IMG Artists. The series featured a range of well-known classical music performers, including violinist Nicola Benedetti, soprano Danielle de Niese, and pianist Leif Ove Andsnes. The series had the strapline 'classical music in a rock 'n' roll setting'.

Yellow Lounge London (2011–13)

Yellow Lounge is a concert series that presents classical music performances primarily in nightclubs. Originating in Berlin (f. 2003), Yellow Lounge was created by Universal Music Group, and concerts predominantly feature high-profile classical music performers signed to the (UMG-owned) Deutsche Grammophon label. Yellow Lounge concerts were presented in London in 2011–13, in venues such as the Old Vic Tunnels and the historic nightclub Fabric.
www.yellowlounge.co.uk

The Multi-Story Orchestra (2011–)

The Multi-Story Orchestra was founded in 2011 to perform Igor Stravinsky's *The Rite of Spring* at Bold Tendencies car park in Peckham, South London. The orchestra is run by joint Artistic Directors, composer Kate Whitley and conductor Christopher Stark. In addition to performances in the Peckham and other car parks, the orchestra tours schools, performing in assembly halls and playgrounds.
www.multi-story.org.uk

The Little Orchestra (2014–)

The Little Orchestra was founded by conductor Nicholas Little and his brother Kim with the specific aim of breaking down barriers to classical music by presenting concerts in less formal settings. One of their regular performance locations is Oval Space, a multi-purpose venue overlooking the decommissioned Bethnal Green gasholders in East London, which also presents rave nights. The orchestra's strapline is 'great classical music in an unclassical setting'.
www.thelittleorchestra.com

Figure 11.1 (Continued)

end, Figure 11.1 outlines seven prominent organisations and initiatives. The chapter draws on interviews with representatives of six of these (inactive since 2013, Yellow Lounge London is the exception). It also considers how classical music concert practice in non-traditional venues differs from that of traditional venues and offers reasons why such non-traditional events are consistently successful in attracting younger audiences.[13] Finally, the chapter examines the impact such concerts have had, and continues to have, on the classical music sector as a whole.

'Physical Sites Create Particular Atmospheres'[14]

Physical surroundings have a powerful, immediate, and distinct impact on the people who visit them. Imagine entering a hospital ward at night, compared to walking into a Central London pub. Environmental psychologists show how the design of a physical place not only influences the mental state of those in the space, but also that it shapes their attitudes and behaviours.[15] Still the most common location for classical music concerts, a purpose-built concert hall "sends" clear signals about expected behaviour: fixed seating in rows discourages social interaction in the auditorium; the grandeur of the building is imposing; and the physical division between the raised stage and the auditorium makes clear that no interaction between audience and performer is expected. Indeed, Christopher Small describes how entering a concert hall results in new attenders 'lowering their voices, muting their gestures, looking around them, [and] bearing themselves in general more formally'.[16] His observation is supported by a recent study by Lucy Dearn and Stephanie Pitts, who examined how 40 young people responded to a chamber music concert and found that participants were concerned about whether they were welcome and how they should behave in the traditional concert setting.[17]

Linked intrinsically to the physical site of the concert hall, the concert "rituals" of classical music performance tend to grant attenders a passive role, expecting them to remain silent, motionless, and seated (derided by some as the "sit-and-stare" model).[18] This leads to the question, what happens when the performance is relocated to a different type of venue? Kate Whitley and Christopher Stark of the Multi-Story Orchestra argue that:

> By escaping the spaces that classical music normally inhabits it becomes possible to escape from its traditional associations, and [to] potentially attract audiences who might find those associations—but not the music—alienating.[19]

For Whitley, the neutrality of a Peckham car park, the orchestra's home venue, was particularly attractive, for it could be used as a 'blank canvas'.[20] No space, however, is entirely free from connotation, and the choice of location for a classical music concert can be a powerful statement. Some organisers consciously use the distinctly different connotations raised by an alternative venue to recontextualise the music they programme. Prokofiev's starting point for his first Nonclassical events, for example, was to choose venues that were in no way associated with the 'elite' values attached to classical music:

> I wanted [the venue] to be the last place where you'd ever imagine seeing a classical ensemble. It was a rebellious thing to do and it was this idea of 'why can't these posh instruments, these old-fashioned museum things, actually be in a gritty club?' It makes it much more exciting. Somewhere that felt gritty and grimy and had attitude and felt like a venue where anything could happen. I didn't want anywhere too glitzy [or] shiny, because then it almost comes back into the elitist field of classical music.[21]

Claiming gritty and grimy venues 'where anything could happen' for a musical purpose is reminiscent of the rave movement of the late 1980s and early 1990s. In fact, the similarities between spaces then used for raves and now for classical concerts are striking, as Sivan Lewis' description of rave venues shows: 'The derelict locations—warehouses, car parks, railway arches—with their dusty floors and industrial ambience, offer only crumbling walls, a loud sound system, and the potential for anything to happen.'[22]

Taking classical music out of the concert hall and into industrial spaces and nightclubs is a self-assertive, even rebellious, act. It represents the next generation striving to "claim" music for themselves and distancing it (and themselves) from the traditional classical sector. With the exception of Yellow Lounge, the founders of all organisations discussed in this chapter were in their twenties or early thirties when they started out. Indeed, several of them, including the founders of the Little Orchestra and the London Contemporary Orchestra (LCO), stress that they do not even see themselves, or their organisations, as part of the classical music industry. Similarly, Emily Robbins (neé Freeman), who co-founded the "Limelight" series at the 100 Club, was aware of and enjoyed the presentational contrast of her concert series:

> [The 100 Club, one of London's oldest rock venues] gave us that fabulous strapline 'putting classical music in a rock 'n' roll setting.' So [it was] a historical club where The Rolling Stones and The Beatles had played over the years, and we thought that was quite cool. At the time we went in, there was still graffiti in the dressing rooms of all the bands that had played there. And you've got [acclaimed opera singer] Danielle de Niese coming in her finery and singing on the stage there, so that was a nice juxtaposition for us.[23]

As John Connell and Chris Gibson have argued, physical sites create particular atmospheres, and the use of space can lend credibility to an event.[24]

By presenting classical music in venues that are run down or lack splendour, an entry barrier can be removed for those who might be deterred or intimidated by a more traditional concert hall.

Practical Implications

Beyond atmosphere, the physical realities of using a space not designed as a place for listening to acoustic music warrant attention. Sound conditions, for example, are often less than ideal. Reverberation times vary greatly between venues, and noise entering from the external environment can be problematic. Some observers find this a distinct drawback:

> I mean, playing in Peckham car park [the home venue of the Multi-Story Orchestra], acoustically, is a nightmare; it's opened up to the elements, there's a train-line going along, so it's a very different playing experience to playing in the Wigmore Hall.[25]

Many attenders, however, value what they call a 'connection to the real world', as Whitley describes:

> [Any negative reaction] is always countered by someone at the performance that says, 'Oh, I absolutely loved it, and it was so magical when the train went by. It really seemed to fit with the music and it made me feel like it was part of the real world.' [Any sound from the trains] gives it a real-world context and setting, instead of experiencing it in isolation. It makes you feel like part of the world as it goes on.[26]

Organisers take a range of approaches to managing acoustics in non-traditional venues: some use light amplification to counter any sound problems the performance might face (Limelight, Nonclassical, Yellow Lounge, and the Night Shift); others choose non-traditional venues whose acoustics happen to be very well-suited to non-amplified instrumental music (The Little Orchestra at Oval Space); while others match specific works to the acoustics of specific venues (LCO), as Co-Artistic Director Robert Ames explains:

> It's about being sensitive to the music. If you put on a really quiet piece by [Morton] Feldman and you're going to do it in a warehouse that's surrounded by traffic, then obviously that won't work, no matter how cool the warehouse is. But if you put on a work by Feldman in an insulated, amazing, clean gallery space, where people can go on a pilgrimage to listen to twelve hours of Feldman in complete silence, then that's going to work pretty well.[27]

Organisers must also consider that most non-traditional venues, such as nightclubs and industrial spaces, lack fixed seating or, indeed, any seating at all. Some of the organisers use this as an opportunity, hiring seating and creating arrangements to promote greater sociability. For the Little Orchestra's concert, for example, attenders have the option to book a 'two-person comfy sofa' (Figure 11.2). At the 100 Club, Limelight likewise arranged atmospheric seating on round tables covered with white tablecloths and decorated with tea lights.

Other organisers take the view that seating is neither necessary nor appropriate for their type of event; in fact, some argue that having the audience stand plays an important role in the concert experience, further distinguishing the atmosphere from that of a concert hall and giving attenders the freedom to move. John Holmes of the "Night Shift" explains:

> We don't want everyone to be sitting down: it's supposed to be a gig. Otherwise you recreate the atmosphere at a concert hall. Also, it's harder to move around and to get to the bar when people are sitting down.[28]

Prokofiev agrees that seating can lure concertgoers to slip back into the traditional format, at risk of losing openness. He insists that having the audience stand is crucial to Nonclassical's success, for it replicates how attenders engage with visual art:

> If you're standing and you can go to the bar you have that autonomy that you have in an art gallery. In a gallery you're in charge and can just go to the next room if you like. No one is forcing you to look at a work,

Figure 11.2 The Little Orchestra Perform Barber's Violin Concerto at Oval Space, London, September 2016

(photograph: Annabel Staff)

and no one is telling you "this is good" or "this is bad", and if you're interested, you stay. As soon as you have that autonomy I think you pay more attention and your mind opens up more because you're in control. On the most basic level, if you are standing, you are free to leave.[29]

While the practical realities of performing in non-traditional venues can be challenging, they also open up choices of how to present a concert that are not always available in the traditional concert hall.

'Presenting Classical as if It Were Rock'[30]

Due to the growth of the live music industry over the past two decades,[31] the majority of young people under the age of 35 are familiar with popular music concert practices. Several organisations are openly adopting those practices, with Nonclassical asserting that 'the success of the night partly stems from the fact that it presents classical as if it were rock or electronic music.'[32] In practical terms, this approach manifests itself in several ways. Rather than adopt the standard classical concert format of two halves of 45–60 minutes of music with an interval in between, the programme is presented in 'sets' (see, for example, Figure 11.3) which are typically shorter and provide more or longer breaks that allow attenders to visit the bar or socialise. Often, more than one artist appears, performing at different times during the evening. Artists for the Limelight series were also announced as 'headline' and 'support', in keeping with popular music practice,[33] and, as Holmes underlines, such events are deliberately referred to as gigs, not concerts.

Another important distinction is that latecomers are admitted at any time, contrary to the traditional practice whereby entry is denied once a performance has begun. The time advertised is not the concert's start time, as would be customary, but the bar opening time, with the performance beginning 30, 60, or even 90 minutes later.[34] Many such concert series also begin later in the evening than traditional concerts; the Night Shift takes its name from this idea, with events typically starting at 8.30 p.m., an hour after doors open (see Figure 11.3). Nonclassical, Yellow Lounge London, and others feature DJs before and after the live performance—another common practice at popular music concerts. Musicians at non-traditional venues also usually perform in casual dress, mirroring the majority of the audience rather than donning the type of formal attire (suits or dinner jackets for men; evening dresses for women) associated with classical, and particularly orchestral, music.

A final comparison concerns visual presentation. Several organisers use coloured lighting for their concerts, or project on a wall images or close-ups of musicians performing. Yellow Lounge, for example, makes VJs (video jockeys) an integral part of its events. As arts consultant Alan Brown observes, lighting and special effects are a vital part of larger-scale popular music concerts, and anybody having attended one would bring a heightened

SET LIST

7.30PM	DOORS	
8.30PM	**SET 1**	
	PUNTO	Section from Horn Quartet No. 1
	MOZART	Section from Duo for Violin & Viola in G Major
	CIRRI	Section from Duo for Violin & Cello
9.30PM	**SET 2**	
	KUNZ	Section from Horn Quartet No. 3
	SCHUBERT	String trio in Bb
	FUCHS	Section from Horn Quartet No. 3

KATI DEBRETZENI violin
JOHN CROCKATT viola
JONATHAN BYERS cello
ROGER MONTGOMERY horn

THENIGHTSHIFT.CO.UK    OAENIGHTSHIFT

Figure 11.3 A Typical "Night Shift" Set List
(image: Orchestra of the Age of Enlightenment)

expectation for visual stimulation with them to a classical music concert.[35] Indeed, borrowing concert practices from popular music can be a powerful tool, especially to connect with young people. Dearn and Pitts show how a group of classical concertgoers under the age of 25 drew heavily on 'the vast learning that they bring from their own musical worlds', using predominantly popular music-related knowledge as their point of reference.[36]

Socialising or Listening?

By giving the audience time and space to socialise before, after, and even during performances, organisers of classical music concerts in non-traditional venues acknowledge there is more to attending a concert than just listening to music. Several authors have discussed the social aspect of concert-going: Pitts describes 'the close relationship between social and musical enjoyment that is at the heart of concert attendance';[37] Nicholas Cook likewise states that a concert is conceived as 'a social occasion rather than a music delivery system';[38] but, as Leon Botstein argues, anonymity within the audience has become the norm at many classical music events in traditional halls.[39] The contrast with, say, the Little Orchestra, who emphasise the social side of their concerts, could not be greater: 'We've designed a night out that is social, relaxed, intimate and fun . . . Arrive and enjoy some drinks with friends, and maybe make some new ones.' As Prokofiev says, events in non-traditional venues aspire to be 'a choice for a musical night out.'[40]

Such organisers therefore recognise that many attenders of classical concerts seek the same benefits—relaxation, entertainment, and an opportunity to socialise—that any other leisure activity would provide.[41] This seems to contradict traditional and still dominant perceptions that audiences primarily attend classical music concerts to be intellectually stimulated through "high" art or because of a desire to learn something. It also prompts several questions: Is the music, which is seemingly the prime focus in a traditional concert hall, just a by-product of the non-traditional event? And does it matter what the audience's motivation is to attend, be it to relax, socialise, or be intellectual stimulated or educated? In the case of the LCO, Ames feels that his audiences attend for social *and* musical reasons and that these motivations are equally valid: 'If people come for the social experience I hope they are inspired by the music. If they come simply for the music I hope they have a good social experience.'[42] Holmes agrees:

> There is nothing wrong with the social experience being the primary motivation: we're not trying to trick them into experiencing some high art! It's about integrating classical music into someone's night out. It's structured so they can fit dinner, drinks around it, or go out clubbing afterwards (not that I think that actually happens very often) . . . It's an even more special moment for performers when it's clear that the

audience is not expecting to enjoy the music, or when they have no expectations of the music but then they do enjoy it.'[43]

Increased social activity has further practical implications. While the purpose-built concert hall has enforceable, segregated spaces for listening (the auditorium) and socialising (the foyer), part of the appeal of many concerts at non-traditional venues is that the bar, a focal point for socialising, is in the same location as the performance and that attenders are welcome to have a drink with them while they listen. This means, however, that noises from glasses clinking and bottles being opened might be heard during the performance. The concern might be that musicians must now 'earn silence',[44] or that such background noise either devalues the music or fails to give it due respect and attention. Prokofiev feels that low level noise is a small price to pay:

> It's unavoidable that you sometimes get a little disturbance but I think it's definitely worth that sacrifice. The problem is that, otherwise, you go down a slippery slope of this kind of "silence is sacred", "this is a religious experience" type of concert thing, when as soon as someone just moves or says sometime a few people turn around, look daggers at them and shush. In our events we want to make it and keep it relaxed. We don't want it to have this uptight stuffiness, this tension that you can get quite easily . . . People can come and go with their drink.[45]

In practice, such practical problems are minor, and all organisers agree that their audience are largely attentive and "self-regulating". Robbins explains that while Limelight audiences were encouraged to move around, they tended to wait to visit the bar until a piece had finished.[46] Prokofiev agrees, explaining how 'it's kind of natural, as in when the music is good and . . . demands silence, everyone knows and then when someone's loud it's a case of just being rude. So, it's quite subtle, but it seems to work by itself.' Similarly, violinist Maggie Faultless (OAE) has summarised her experience of performing for Night Shift concerts:

> You might think that the informality of these venues would create a casual relationship with the music—I'm often asked if pub venues means it's noisy, but not a bit of it (the clank of a few glasses from the bar aside). In fact we've found that there seems to be an enhanced degree of listening as people are much more directly involved in the music making, and this intense listening creates the atmosphere of the performance.[47]

It is precisely the informality that makes performances in non-traditional venues unique and particularly welcoming to new attenders. To revert to a traditional format would be to destroy what makes the events unique. By redefining the "listening situation", the spectrum of what is acceptable in terms of etiquette and behaviours at classical music concerts is changing.

Several organisers consciously try to create a listening environment with which attenders *choose* to engage, as Whitley explains:

> Although people are free to wander, get a drink from the bar, take a look at the view, or hang around at the back of the crowd and dip in and out of watching the performance if they like, the set-up is designed to create a focused listening environment.[48]

Ames pursues a similar theme:

> We [the LCO] create a situation whereby we use lighting, programme certain types of music, and amplify music sometimes, in a way that creates a really "big" listening experience in those spaces. So although we give people the freedom to walk out, or go to the bar if they want to, we try and create situations where actually really listening to the music quite intensely is the ideal situation. But we don't force it.[49]

To examine this balance between socialising and listening, it is important to consider that concertgoers are not necessarily motivated to attend because they wish to experience the greatest possible sound quality. The coughing and shuffling of the most dedicated audiences make for an authentic listening experience, but not one as "clean" as a high-quality audio recording heard at home.[50] The reasons for attending a classical concert are many, and the music itself can be experienced in a number of ways. As Cook asks:

> What kind of rational cost-benefit calculation might lead people to go to a concert? The answer, clearly, has to do with the things that are not delivered by even the highest-quality headphones.[51]

Moreover, to Prokofiev, all levels of engagement with the music are acceptable, after all 'people are listening when they are standing by the bar . . . and are taking it in. [That's] still a valid experience.'[52]

From Presentational to Participatory

Thomas Turino distinguishes between 'participatory' performances, where there is no distinction between artist and audience (for example, a church congregation singing hymns), and 'presentational' performances, where one group provides music for another (for example, musicians for their audience).[53] Turino also proclaims European classical music concerts—in traditional concert halls—as perhaps the most pronounced form of presentational performance, where the audience sits still in silent contemplation while the music is being played, only to comment on it through applause after a piece has been completed.[54]

Contrast this with Bonita Kolb, an arts marketing specialist, who finds that 'people are no longer willing to defer to authority . . . [for] they want control of their own destiny [and] are impatient with passive experiences.'[55] As a result, she argues, audiences want to participate actively in leisure activities, rather than observe idly.

If this is true (or, indeed, desired by concert organisers), how can performances of classical music grant audiences a more active role? Looking first at the artist-audience relationship, performances of classical music in non-traditional venues typically reduce the physical distance between the groups. In stark contrast to the raised stages and fixed seating typical of traditional halls, Figures 11.2 and 11.4 show just how close the audience, whether standing or sitting, can be to the performers at non-traditional venues. Removing such physical barriers may not necessarily grant audiences a more active role, but it alters the hierarchy between musicians and the audience, putting them on a more equal footing. The close proximity also encourages concertgoers to talk with musicians after the performance and to get a closer look at scores and instruments.

The Little Orchestra acknowledges that this proximity and engagement are central to its mission, as it promises:

> An hour of beautiful music, delivered in an intimate, atmospheric space, where you can almost reach out and touch the orchestra. Each piece will be introduced by Nicholas [Little, the orchestra's founder], the conductor, to help you find a way in, if you need it.[56]

This closeness can benefit performers, too. Robbins explains that Limelight's similar intimacy was key to persuading classical music "stars" to appear during the series, while Holmes also notes how musicians are interested in and feel able to respond individually, being physically closer to the audience than usual. In a similar vein, Faultless elaborates:

> [The Night Shift] is about empowerment. Audiences want to have a bit more ownership of what they're listening to. The best performances involve a three-way relationship—the music (i.e. what's on the page), the audience and the performers. The performers react not only to the written notes but to each other and, most importantly, to the audience. But all too often in today's concerts, the third part of that equation is forgotten. Often when we're performing you can't even see beyond the first couple of rows, let alone to the back of a thousand-seat concert hall.[57]

Figure 11.4 Nonclassical Club Night at the Royal Opera House, London,
September 2015

(photograph: Royal Opera House/Sim Canetty-Clarke)

This ethos unites each of the organisations this chapter surveys: contrary
to traditional classical music concert practice, performers usually introduce themselves or the works to be performed either before the concert or
between works.[58] Such direct communication makes audience members feel

acknowledged and develops 'a valued sense of performer-audience rapport', as Melanie Dobson describes in her study on new audiences for classical music.[59]

Social media is enabling a further kind of audience participation. Lucy Bennet acknowledges how social media has not only allowed concertgoers 'to find and connect with each other, but also to tweet and text concert set lists, photos and other information as they happen.'[60] At Night Shift events, the audience is encouraged to communicate with organisers and each other in this manner, and the number of such interactions—tweets, Instagram posts, and so forth—peaks when performers, rather than members of the administrative team, invite them.[61] Engaging with audiences through social media can also occur in the lead up to the concert, providing potential concertgoers with information about the event and gaining their trust as an organisation. Ames explains:

> That's the joy of social media: having connections with the audience . . . You build a narrative around the concert before it's even started. So you can start introducing them to pieces [and] snippets of music behind the scenes . . . and can let people know what they're going to get, or what they're getting into, before they come. You build trust with the audience whereby they trust you to present them with something that's going to inspire them.[62]

In turn, prospective attenders can voice their opinion on aspects of the concert, expressing likes and dislikes, and potentially shaping future events.

The Multi-Story Orchestra is the only organisation (of this chapter) that makes audience participation an explicit part of their concerts. The orchestra's innovative activities intensify attenders' experience of the music itself and enable direct attender/performer engagement prior to the performance (see Figure 11.5). Whitley describes how its "Living Programme Note" initiative works:

> "Living Programme Note" performances are where we split the orchestra into smaller groups of six or seven who are then spread around the car park, and the audience is free to wander around to meet and chat with them . . . The musicians play bits of the piece and create participatory things for the audience to do: for [Mozart's] Jupiter Symphony's sarabande movement [II.] they were teaching the audience the difference between a waltz and a sarabande and getting them all . . . to sing, to clap to its rhythms, or learn a dance. So, [that's] the first 45 minutes [before the "proper" performance]. Then, everybody congregates in the orchestral space and there's a "warmth" from the audience right away, just like when they clap, when the orchestra sits and starts. Everyone is so engaged already.[63]

While social media is available to any organisation and musicians can address the audience regardless of the type of venue, the flexible use of

Figure 11.5 The Multi-Story Orchestra Perform a "Living Programme Note" on Beethoven's Sixth Symphony in Bold Tendencies Car Park, Peckham, London, July 2016

(photograph: Nigel Rumsey)

space is a specific advantage of non-traditional venues, allowing organisers to engineer close physical proximity between performers and audience and, if desired, use the space for specific participation activities.

Concerts in Non-Traditional Venues and the Classical Music Market

No studies have sought to establish the share that events in non-traditional venues enjoy in the wider classical music market; however, the active series discussed in this chapter regularly sell out, which indicates substantial interest.[64] Additionally, the common view, supported by data collected by several organisations, suggests that non-traditional venues are more successful (than traditional halls) in attracting a younger audience to classical music, and an audience that is *new* to the genre. A 2015 survey conducted at Non-classical's "Minimalism Night" (held at East London nightclub XOYO) found that 89% of the 350 attenders were aged 35 or under, and that 58% of attenders did not regularly attend classical concerts.[65] Data published in 2013 showed that 85% of the Night Shift's regular audience was aged 35 or under, with 15%–20% overall new to classical music.[66] A 2016 survey by the Multi-Story Orchestra found that 52% of its concertgoers were aged 35 or under, and that 55% attended classical music events once a year or less.[67] The LCO performed to a total audience of over 12,400 in 2016/17 and supplied information about their social media following: 61% of their 6,800 Facebook followers and 66% of their 7,000 Twitter followers were aged 35 or under.[68]

These surveys, while modest in scale, indicate the tremendous potential of non-traditional venues and events to increase attendance of classical music concerts, particularly among young people. After attending a Nonclassical concert, American critic Greg Sandow wrote:

> The mainstream institutions are missing a lot. They're missing poten-tially large ticket sales and the artistic and cultural opportunity of a lifetime—a chance to join with the newest, most powerful force in the art they claim to represent, and to connect classical music with a new generation of smart younger people.[69]

How, then, might these institutions tap into this new audience? Some tra-ditional concert venues have responded by exploring spaces within their building not originally designed for live performances. An early example was the 2011 "Harmonic Series" at London's Southbank Centre, conceived and curated by cellist Oliver Coates, and 'designed to bring unexpected sounds to unexpected corners of the Royal Festival Hall.'[70] Elsewhere in London, the Barbican Centre hosts "Sound Unbound", a biannual festival of sixty concerts in 'an unusual range of venues' that gives audiences the opportunity 'for informal and close-up interactions' with performers.[71] Ste-phen Pritchard describes this ambitious event:

> For the price of a colourful wristband, 3,000 people—54% of whom . . . were new to the venue—savoured a vast musical tasting menu, served up informally over a weekend in short sessions across the entire centre, in foyers and on outdoor terraces, in halls and performing spaces.[72]

Other large institutions have collaborated with some of the organisations this chapter has chronicled: the Royal Opera House gave Nonclassical free rein over its 750-capacity Paul Hamlyn Hall, an event that quickly sold out (Figure 11.4); the BBC Proms in 2016 and 2017 featured Multi-Story Orchestra concerts—in its original car park rather than at the Royal Albert Hall; and the LCO performed at The Tanks at Tate Modern in 2017, also as part of the BBC Proms.[73]

Such institutions are attracted to new sales, of course, but this is inex-tricable from the audience's age range and their newness to the art form. Arts Council England's mission statement, 'great art and culture for every-one',[74] strongly implies that it expects every organisation it funds to strive for diversity. National Portfolio Organisations (that is, those organisations

Arts Council England regularly funds) looking to widen their reach might do well to try out a new venue, collaborate with existing organisations, or adopt some of the innovations examined in this chapter. At the same time, the risk of alienating existing audiences is real (socialising during concerts, for example, might be at odds with the expectations of a long-standing subscription concert attender) and warrants careful thought about which, if any, practices established organisations might wish to adopt. Looking ahead, it is perhaps necessary for larger organisations to cater for various markets, satisfying the needs of an established audience as well as those of potential new audiences interested in less formal formats and new settings. This strategy is still rarely adopted, although there are exceptions, including the London Symphony Orchestra presenting "Open Air Classics", which sees the orchestra relocate from its usual Barbican and St Luke's venues once a year to perform open-air in Trafalgar Square.

Fears will need to be alleviated if non-traditional venues and events are perceived to threaten the traditional model of classical concert-giving: both models can, and surely must, be concurrent. However, performing classical music in non-traditional venues is not "easy money". Classical music performance typically involves rehearsing challenging works with multiple instrumentalists—an expensive process regardless of venue—and most of the organisations described in this chapter do not survive financially through ticket income alone: Nonclassical, the Multi-Story Orchestra, and the LCO have received grants through Arts Council England's Grants for the Arts scheme, and other public grants; the OAE finances the Night Shift through a variety of sources, including crowdfunding, donor support, and Arts Council England core funding; and the Little Orchestra collaborates with private donors. The founders of Limelight at the 100 Club were able to trade on their wide network of contacts within the classical music industry. The series featured some of classical music's most successful artists, who agreed to be paid "expenses only" either because of their fascination with the new format, to garner press interest, to promote an album, or a combination of these factors. Robbins acknowledges this to be an unsustainable business model and explains that, in part, the series folded because of the amount of time that would have been required to obtain sponsorship.[75] Yellow Lounge London likewise featured prominent musicians, but these were all affiliated to UMG, who, according to Kellersmann, covered their costs—a funding model possible for large-scale corporations but out-of-reach for an arts organisation.[76]

Conclusion: Lasting Change?

After almost fifteen years of classical music concerts in non-traditional venues, the idea has had a marked and varied influence on the sector; it is also an irreversible trend organisers are determined to, and believe will, broaden.

Robbins suggests that well-known classical musicians, such as those who performed at Limelight, and the next generations of concertgoers, administrators, and managers, will entrench this change:

> If Nicola Benedetti [who performed at Limelight in 2009] decided that . . . before or after she played in [any] classical venue, she'd say a few words—that would have an impact. I think you are already seeing that more and more . . . And when younger people go into the management or directorship of orchestras[,] they're [now] questioning all of those assumptions [about concert-giving, so] there is a natural shift to "move with the times". The struggle [before] was that you had people who were never even *questioning* [but] just allowing a very old-fashioned format to continue.[77]

The normalisation of new, more relaxed formats has indeed relied on—and will continue to rely on—young composers and musicians being accustomed to different types of classical concerts, and having the confidence and support to stage events in a similar vein. As we have seen, this process need not put classical concerts in non-traditional venues and their associated practices (e.g. audience participation, freedom to move, shorter "sets", later starts to concerts) in a second "tier" of concert-giving; they can be an artistic equal to more traditional events. Whitley agrees:

> Multi-Story's biggest impact in terms of the rest of the sector is doing something . . . designed to engage audiences, but, artistically, [being] treated no differently . . . It's not an outreach event [or] part of the education programme; it's in the main Aldeburgh Festival [a June 2017 performance in an Ipswich multi-storey car park] and, similarly, the Prom is part of the Proms and recorded by [BBC] Radio 3, as the other Proms were . . . There are often education programmes designed to engage people, and "core" artistic work designed to do something artistically, "purely". I don't think these things necessarily need to be separate.[78]

This means that an important part of facilitating change will be to emphasise to concertgoers, critics, and the public that, while the lens through which it is viewed is different, the *content* of the concert—the music itself—is still central. Brown is sanguine about this prospect:

> Fear of the unknown will gradually lose its grip as more and more musicians, managers, board members and concert-goers come to understand that it is not necessary to sacrifice artistic quality in order to make classical music concerts a little more interesting and appealing to a twenty-first-century audience.[79]

In the meantime, the next steps for research of this scene will be to scrutinise its audience's size and make-up in further detail. Such data would provide proper benchmarks to test success, to drive further innovations, and to strengthen the case of the organisations themselves when they seek funding. Similarly, research is needed to determine if attendance translates into longer-term engagement with classical music, such as exploring other works through recordings or attending other live events. Such work might help organisations reconsider concert spaces; for while acoustics are traditionally the first consideration when building a new hall, non-traditional events would suggest that the space's flexibility, in terms of both audience-performer engagement and the potential to alter layout, may be just as significant to classical music's future. As Cook has argued, classical music 'continues to make sense when played in the innumerable ways that are made possible by [a] multiplicity of available performance parameters.'[80] If presenting Mozart in a car park or Bach in a nightclub allows classical music to be introduced to, and enjoyed by, a wider audience, then such concerts will only benefit the genre, and its sector, as a whole.

Notes

1. Christopher Small, *Musicking: The Meanings of Performing and Listening* (Middletown: Wesleyan University Press, 1998), 21.
2. The Modulus Quartet performed new compositions in a slate mine in Honister, Yorkshire, on 6 May 2017; the Orchestra of the Age of Enlightenment performed works from the classical canon at the Camden Assembly, London, on 23 May 2017; London Contemporary Orchestra performed works by Steve Reich, Johnny Greenwood, and others in the loading bay of the Royal Albert Hall on 4 March 2017; venues at the East Neuk Festival included church halls and cafes; the Multi-Story Orchestra performed works by Bach, John Adams, and Kate Whitley at Bold Tendencies car park in Peckham, London, on 26 August 2017. For further details of these events, see: http://honister.com/modulus-quartet-6th-may-2017/; http://camdenassembly.com/events/the-night-shift/; www.lcorchestra.co.uk/events/royal-albert-hall/; www.eastneukfestival.com/venues/; www.bbc.co.uk/events/epc5q9 (all accessed 21 July 2017).
3. The Toronto Symphony Orchestra performed Beethoven's Fifth Symphony at the Hearn Generating Station, Toronto, on 21 June 2016; the Mahler Chamber Orchestra performed works by Beethoven, Bach, Haydn, Cage, and others at Radial System V on 21 May 2016; the Axiom Quartet performed works by Grieg, Ravel, Bernstein, and others in a cave in Boerne, Texas, on 5 September 2015. For further details, see: http://nationalpost.com/entertainment/music/can-classical-music-reach-a-new-audience-through-unlikely-venues/wcm/ad9cc17e-83ce-4c52-aab9-a38c6335bf7a; www.radialsystem.de/rebrush/en/rs-radialsystem-v-einleitungstext.php; www.visitboerne.org/calendar/concert-cave-axiom-quartet; https://musiquealaferme.com/language/en/home (all accessed 22 July 2017).
4. Tim Rutherford-Johnson, quoted in Thom Andrewes and Dimitri Djuric, *We Break Strings: The Alternative Classical Scene in London* (London: Hackney Classical Press, 2014), 71.
5. See, for example: Berlotti Buitoni Trust, 'Is the Concert Hall the Only Place?' [2015], www.youtube.com/watch?v=FefcZzAIGLA; and Tom Hodge, 'Musical

Places in Unusual Spaces', *Huffington Post* (29 September 2014), www.huff
ingtonpost.co.uk/tom-hodge/classical-music-venues_b_5875526.html (both
accessed 22 July 2017).

6. Examples of concert halls built during this period include Musikverein (Vienna,
1870), the Royal Albert Hall (London, 1871), Carnegie Hall (New York, 1891),
and Wigmore Hall (London, 1899).

7. Yoko Ono, for example, hosted concerts in her loft in New York City, in collaboration with composer La Monte Young in the early 1960s. For a comprehensive history of "alternative" venues, see Sarah May Robinson, *Chamber Music
in Alternative Venues in the 21st Century U.S.: Investigating the Effect of New
Venues on Concert Culture, Programming and the Business of Classical Music*
(DMus diss.; University of South Carolina, 2013), 4–35.

8. See Christian Kellersmann, 'Der Frack ist bitte an der Garderobe abzugeben'
(19 August 2013), http://christiankellersmann.de/der-frack-ist-bitte-an-der-
garderobe-abzugeben/ (accessed 22 July 2017).

9. Along with Sony Music Entertainment and Warner Music Group (WMG), UMG
is one of the three "majors", which between them account for over two-thirds
of global record label revenue (68.7% in 2016). See www.musicbusinessworld-
wide.com/global-market-shares-2016-sony-and-warner-gain-on-universal-as-
indies-rule/ (accessed 22 July 2017).

10. Kellersmann, 'Der Frack ist bitte an der Garderobe abzugeben'; translation by
the author.

11. Gabriel Prokofiev, quoted in Jessica Duchen, 'Gabriel Prokofiev on the BBC's
Ten Pieces, Nonclassical, and a New Carnival of the Animals', *The Independent*
(24 June 2015), www.independent.co.uk/arts-entertainment/classical/features/
gabriel-prokofiev-on-the-bbcs-ten-pieces-nonclassical-and-a-new-carnival-of-
the-animals-10340546.html (accessed 22 July 2017).

12. The chamber music series "Classical Revolution" was founded by Charith
Premawardhana. See Alberta Barnes's interview with Charith Premawardhana
for further details: http://blog.sharmusic.com/blog/bid/83997/Interview-with-
Charith-Premawardhana-Founder-of-Classical-Revolution (accessed 22 July
2017).

13. The organisations' own surveys use a threshold of under 35 years of age to
define 'young audiences'.

14. John Connell and Chris Gibson, *Sound Tracks: Popular Music Identity and
Place* (London: Routledge, 2003), 204.

15. See, for example, Sally Augustin, *Place Advantage: Applied Psychology for Interior Architecture* (Chichester: Wiley, 2009), 1.

16. Small, *Musicking*, 23.

17. See Lucy K. Dearn and Stephanie E. Pitts, '(Un)popular Music and Young Audiences: Exploring the Classical Chamber Music Concert from the Perspective of
Young Adult Listeners', *Journal of Popular Music Education*, 1/1 (March 2017),
58.

18. See, for example, Igor Toronyi-Lalic, 'Imagined Occasions', *The Arts Desk* (28
May 2013), www.lcorchestra.co.uk/reviews/imagined-occasions-3/ (accessed 23
July 2017).

19. Kate Whitley and Christopher Stark, 'Orchestral Manoeuvres in the Car Park',
The Guardian (20 June 2014), www.theguardian.com/music/musicblog/2014/
jun/20/peckham-car-park-multi-story-orchestra-sibelius (accessed 23 July
2017).

20. Whitley, quoted in Andrewes and Djuric, *We Break Strings*, 70.

21. Gabriel Prokofiev, interview with the author, 27 June 2017.

22. Sivan Lewin [1997], quoted in Connell and Gibson, *Sound Tracks*, 205.

23. Emily Robbins, interview with the author, 27 June 2017.

24. See Connell and Gibson, *Sound Tracks*, 204.
25. Tim Rutherford-Johnson, quoted in Andrewes and Djuric, *We Break Strings*, 71.
26. Kate Whitley, interview with the author, 3 August 2017.
27. Robert Ames, interview with the author, 12 July 2017.
28. John Holmes, interview with the author, 20 June 2017.
29. Prokofiev, interview.
30. 'Nonclassical: About Us', www.nonclassical.co.uk (accessed 29 July 2017).
31. The substantial growth in the wider live music industry is well documented. See, for example, Peter Tschmuck, *The Economics of Music* (Newcastle-upon-Tyne: Agenda, 2017), 34.
32. 'Nonclassical: About Us', www.nonclassical.co.uk (accessed 29 July 2017).
33. Robbins, interview.
34. Alternatively, two start times are advertised: "doors open" and "concert start".
35. See Alan Brown, 'Smart Concerts: Orchestras in the Age of Edutainment [12 January 2004]', https://knightfoundation.org/reports/magic-music-issues-brief-5-smart-concerts-orchestr (accessed 29 July 2017).
36. Dearn and Pitts, '(Un)popular Music and Young Audiences', 58.
37. Stephanie E. Pitts, 'What Makes an Audience? Investigating the Roles and Experiences of Listeners at a Chamber Music Festival', *Music & Letters*, 86/2 (May 2005), 269.
38. Nicholas Cook, *Beyond the Score: Music as Performance* (Oxford: Oxford University Press, 2013), 398.
39. See Leon Botstein, 'Music of a Century: Museum Culture and the Politics of Subsidy', in *The Cambridge History of Twentieth Century Music*, ed. Nicholas Cook and Anthony Pople (Cambridge: Cambridge University Press, 2004), 41.
40. Prokofiev, interview.
41. See Bonita M. Kolb, *Marketing for Cultural Organizations: New Strategies for Attracting Audiences* (3rd edn; Abingdon: Routledge, 2013), 72.
42. Ames, interview.
43. Holmes, interview.
44. Oliver Coates, quoted in Andrewes and Djuric, *We Break Strings*, 68.
45. Prokofiev, interview.
46. Robbins, interview.
47. Maggie Faultless, 'Purcell and a Pint: Welcome to a New Kind of Classical Concert', *The Guardian* (6 February 2012), www.theguardian.com/music/musicblog/2012/feb/06/classical-music-in-a-pub (accessed 30 July 2017).
48. Whitley and Stark, 'Orchestral Manoeuvres in the Car Park'.
49. Ames, interview.
50. Admittedly, while the vast majority of works in the classical music canon are available in recorded form, this is not the case with contemporary music in the classical tradition.
51. Cook, *Beyond the Score*, 395.
52. Prokofiev, interview.
53. Thomas Turino, *Music as Social Life: The Politics of Participation* (Chicago: University of Chicago Press, 2008), 26/51.
54. Turino, *Music as Social Life*, 52.
55. Kolb, *Marketing for Cultural Organizations*, 47.
56. From The Deal section of the Little Orchestra website, http://thelittleorchestra.com/#thedealrow (accessed 29 July 2017).
57. Faultless, 'Purcell and a Pint'.
58. The level of direct communication with the audience varies between organisations. While direct communication is an all-important part of concerts by the Little Orchestra, the LCO usually only interacts directly with its audience at smaller and more intimate concerts.

59. Melissa C. Dobson, 'New Audiences for Classical Music: The Experiences of Non-Attenders at Live Orchestral Concerts', *Journal of New Music Research*, 39/3 (2010), 111.

60. Lucy Bennet, 'Texting and Tweeting at Live Music Concerts: Flow, Fandom and Connecting With Other Audiences through Mobile Phone Technology', in *Coughing and Clapping: Investigating Audience Experience*, ed. Karen Burland and Stephanie Pitts (Aldershot: Ashgate, 2014), 89.

61. Holmes, interview.

62. Ames, interview.

63. Whitley, interview.

64. Recent sold-out concerts include: The Little Orchestra performing Beethoven's "Eroica" Symphony at Oval Space (capacity 200) on 4–5 May 2017; The Multi-Story Orchestra performing Mozart's "Jupiter" Symphony at Bold Tendencies car park in Peckham (cap. 600) on 17–18 June 2017; and the LCO performing a new work by composer Catherine Lamb in The Tanks at Tate Modern (cap. 350) on 6 September 2017.

65. The unpublished survey was provided to the author by Nonclassical.

66. See Culture Hive, *Case Study—The Night Shift: Orchestra of the Age of Enlightenment* (2013), http://culturehive.co.uk/wp-content/uploads/2013/05/Case-study-OAE-The-Night-Shift.pdf (accessed 21 July 2017).

67. The unpublished survey was provided to the author by the Multi-Story Orchestra.

68. The figures were provided to the author by LCO. They must be seen in the context of social media being more popular among younger generations.

69. Greg Sandow, 'A Young, Hip, Classical Crowd', *The Wall Street Journal* (28 March 2009), www.wsj.com/articles/SB123819267920260779 (accessed 29 June 2017).

70. See Jessica Duchen, 'The Cellist Who Wants to Shake up London with a Classical Mystery Tour', *The Independent* (21 January 2011), www.independent.co.uk/arts-entertainment/classical/features/the-cellist-who-wants-to-shake-up-london-with-a-classical-mystery-tour-2190095.html (accessed 29 July 2017).

71. See, for example, www.barbican.org.uk/full-line-up-announced-for-sound-unbound-the-barbican-classical-weekender-29–30-april-2017 (accessed 29 July 2017).

72. Stephen Pritchard, 'Sound Unbound', *The Observer* (7 May 2017), www.theguardian.com/music/2017/may/07/sound-unbound-barbican-review-andras-schiff-wigmore-hall?CMP=share_btn_link (accessed 1 December 2017).

73. Previously used to store oil, The Tanks are large circular spaces in the foundations of the former power station.

74. Arts Council England, 'Our Mission and Strategy', www.artscouncil.org.uk/about-us/our-mission-and-strategy (accessed 30 July 2017).

75. Information about funding was provided to the author in the interviews with Prokofiev, Whitley, Ames, Little, Holmes, and Robbins.

76. Kellersmann, 'Der Frack ist bitte an der Garderobe abzugeben'.

77. Robbins, interview; emphasis Robbins's.

78. Whitley, interview.

79. Brown, 'Smart Concerts', 16.

80. Cook, *Beyond the Score*, 400.

12 Curating Classical Music

Towards a Synergetic Concert Dramaturgy

Masa Spaan, trans. Brendan Monaghan

In her essay 'Concert Etiquette: The New Rules', Gillian Moore recalls a fellow concertgoer censuring her during a performance at London's Royal Festival Hall with the words: 'You were moving your head up and down during the music. You need to learn to behave in concerts, or stay at home!'[1] Given Moore's role as Director of Music at the Southbank Centre (of which the Royal Festival Hall is the largest hall), this anecdote illuminates all too well the intractable nature of concert etiquette, and how it still governs most classical concert-going. To explore this further is to observe several broader norms, for example: repertoire presented according to standard patterns (e.g. overture—solo concerto—interval—symphony); musicians wearing neat, black "uniform", entering and exiting the stage in a formal, prescribed manner; the physical separation of on-stage musicians and seated audience; and concertgoers expected to understand when to applaud. These practices are dominant, customary, and were famously theorised by Christopher Small as a 'concert ritual'.[2] To subsequent sociologists, such as Cas Smithuijsen, the rigidity of such conventions transforms the concert experience into a 'regime'.[3]

Such traditions are also historical, being associated with nineteenth-century ideals of profundity, depth of knowledge, and musical meaning. To apply concentrated effort to fathom, say, symphonic structure is to understand and experience the music in a "pure" form—a mode of listening that, according to these historical principles, only the concert-giving ritual can mediate. Indeed, drawing on the powerful and related principles of formalism and musical autonomy,[4] such principles still hold sway over much of today's classical concert practice. In the twentieth century, sporadic attempts were made to "informalise" concert etiquette, especially for the performance of contemporary music. Yet, even the most "alternative" concerts of the mid-to-late twentieth century, for example, Pierre Boulez's "rug" concerts (1973–75/77)—a series held in New York's Philharmonic Hall for which seating was replaced by cushions and rugs—did not alter the concert 'ritual' fundamentally.

As Moore's experience illustrates, the longevity of traditional concert practices can have negative consequences: had a first-time attender been scolded in such a manner, they would surely have been deterred from visiting again. Traditionalists—if we might describe Moore's accuser as such—surely represent the (usually silent) majority of most classical music audiences. However, there are signs of change, as many classical concertgoers bring with them new expectations and tastes; that is, they have a looser affinity with established concert rituals or are prompted to rethink their assumptions.[5] With various degrees of success, individuals and organisations are experimenting with ways to modernise the classical concert. One broad change is in the perceived role of music programmers, who are increasingly redefined as 'curators'.[6] A feature of this new type of classical music programming is to curate concerts through storytelling and other tailor-made concepts, emulating approaches more common in the visual arts (a genre from which, of course, the term 'curator' is derived).

The tendency leads us to ask how the revitalisation of classical music concerts should be carried out, and why the issue is so urgent now, in the twenty-first century. In Alessandro Baricco's remarkable collection of essays, *I barbari* (*The Barbarians*), the philosopher and musician hypothesises that a profound change, a mutation no less, is taking place in contemporary culture.[7] Baricco examines how information technology is altering the way we experience the world and its arts, and also charts how programme makers can shape their programmes and curate art today. This chapter examines how Baricco's ideas lay the foundations for methods—including my own—to revitalise classical music programming.

I barbari, Mutating Cultures, and Classical Music

Although *I barbari*'s title laments a perceived decline in contemporary civilisation, Baricco central speculation is optimistic: that we are currently witnessing a paradigm shift, from which a fundamentally new civilisation will emerge. Belonging to a new wave of post-postmodern thinkers, Baricco argues for new forms of signification, meaning, and value, in which "vertical" ideals of depth and profundity are joined by "horizontal" modes, galvanised by ever-broader networks and rapid technological change. In a similar vein, sociology and communication science have taught us how digital communication is redefining our behaviours, societies, and relationships.[8] Baricco, indeed, characterises as 'constellations' the ways in which certain technological innovations—the obvious example would be Google—are changing our knowledge, experiences, and our understanding of those concepts. 'Barbarians' alter their (and our) civilisation's domains to create 'systems of passage',[9] a term Baricco uses to describe the intersections between different worlds. The hope that this Information Age (as it is sometimes described) will herald a new, more democratised sensibility among people is key, given its potential to modernise language and to increase the range of audiences for the arts.

The potential implications for classical music are clear and far-reaching. As we have already seen, the genre operates against the backdrop of dominant traditions; it is therefore a prime candidate to be one such 'mutated' domain.[10] We can couple this fact with another: that because we Googling beings increasingly experience "horizontal" sensation of associations, sequences, differences, and intersections, it is incumbent upon programmers, or "curators", to find and speak a more common language in this new world.[11] A further factor, then, is that with endless hours of music available online, instantly and often for free, people from all backgrounds are (theoretically) able to broaden their musical horizons with great ease. More work will be needed to examine how such "omnivorous" listeners experience classical music.[12] In practice, however, Baricco's principles and their extension—from "horizontal" connections, through new modes and languages, to wider and newer audiences—are *already* underpinning modern approaches to concert programming. Indeed, this chapter draws on several interviews with the creative figureheads of several prominent classical music organisations, including Holland Festival, Huddersfield Contemporary Music Festival (HMCF), Lincoln Center for the Performing Arts (New York), Music on Main (Vancouver), Muziekgebouw aan 't IJ (Amsterdam), the Royal Concertgebouw Orchestra, and the Southbank Centre.[13] While the histories and frequencies of the events these organisations promote and host vary, they each strive to innovate and, relatedly, to discover new ways to retain, diversify, and engage new audiences.

A strategy common to each interviewed programmer is to exploit interconnections between classical music and other genres, disciplines, and related themes. Moore, for example, described how the Southbank Centre's Ether Festival focussed on unexpected parallels between modern developments in classical music and other genres, such as experimental, dance, and popular music. Consequently, the festival featured the work the composer/ visual artist Christian Marclay in 2012, and two years earlier highlighted the debt contemporary electronic music owes the twentieth-century classical composer Edgar Varèse. A second strategy is to pursue themes that reflect the "spirit" of a particular period of time. The Royal Concertgebouw Orchestra's "AAA" series ("Actueel, Avontuurlijk, Aangrijpend") chooses as its starting point a topical issue upon which to foster dialogue between twentieth- and twenty-first-century classical music and other disciplines. The series, whose title means 'topical, adventurous, moving', is thematic and interdisciplinary, and it nurtures "mini-festival" collaborations between Amsterdam institutions.[14] In 2014, 'Privacy' was one such topic; its artistic manifestation was musical intimacy, for example, as found in Shostakovich's autobiographical string quartets. Artists, filmmakers, and social commentators responded to this programme by contributing their own imagery in parallel programmes.

Strikingly common to all interviewees, a third strategy concerned ways in which programmers must consider and manage a number of extra-musical factors, for example, location and audience interaction: Graham McKenzie (Artistic Director, HCMF) described often using spaces that are unconventional but which suit the music, taking audiences out of their comfort zone and into different listening zones; Jon Nakagawa (Director of Contemporary Programming, White Light Festival, New York) recalled exploiting unusual venues and alternative set-ups to optimise the intimacy of the concert experience; and David Pay (Artistic Director, Music on Main) stressed the significance of interaction and conversations between the musicians and concertgoers during and after concerts. Pay's analogy was a homely welcome: relaxed, intimate, but also sociable.

Interviewees also generally endorsed the value of supplementary activities and materials, such as programme notes, pre-concert talks, parallel programmes, and community involvement, but they explicitly cautioned against using unimaginatively academic, technical, or archaic language. This does not mean communication cannot be detailed; the point is to provide context in a common, accessible way. Pay went a step further by abandoning programme notes altogether, as he sought to avoid imposing interpretations on concertgoers or to colour the dialogue he hoped to foster. Such an initiative points towards another theme: audience reach. Programmers were unequivocal that artistic quality and the need to engage and attract audiences were compatible endeavours: the Ether Festival's programme around Varèse proved to Moore that drawing substantive parallels between contemporary classical music and other genres could attract new audiences; the "AAA" series was designed to encourage audience to "trickle" between art forms under its interdisciplinary umbrella; and Nakagawa and another interviewee, Maarten van Boven (Artistic Director, Muziekgebouw aan 't IJ), both declared their laudable aim to achieve crossover—between core and peripheral programmes and between dance, theatre, and music audiences respectively.

To create vibrant formats that are (perceived to be) relevant to concertgoers' lives was a common ambition of the interviewees. To view their beliefs and activities in the context of Baricco's arguments is to reveal further commonalities, especially on the artistic or social connections they each raised, and on their shared ambition, as we can theorise it, to transform the concert into a deliberately shaped ensemble of synergetic "ingredients". In line with Baricco, this outlook need not be interpreted as defeatist, as though it somehow dilutes the autonomy or historicism of the musical experience. Rather, it is a progressive model that can, and does, inspire and revitalise personal practice—as the rest of this chapter explores.

Towards a Synergetic Concert Dramaturgy

Programming for various companies, venues, and festivals has allowed me many opportunities to experiment.[15] Although each of these organisations has its own history, interests, and operational complexities, my most urgent, overriding aim has been to enliven and renew classical music. The scale on which programmers can, and must, innovate has to be weighed carefully on each occasion, but what I call *synergetic concert dramaturgy*—drawing on Baricco to strive beyond traditional, "ritualistic" barriers—offers me the greatest hope for the future. This method is significant on two levels: individually, to help develop customised concert programmes; and to guide venues and festivals as they develop concepts for their annual activities. The following section examines three such examples, of which the first and third are from my own practice; the second is cited because it exhibits a comparable, and inspirational, way of working.

The first example is a programme created in 2016 for the South Netherlands Philharmonic as part of its "Spicy Classics" series aimed at students and young professionals (Figure 12.1). The basic idea was to present a programme featuring Mozart's Piano Concerto No. 17 in G major, K. 453 in a non-traditional format, starting from the general theme of "elegance"—a quality widely attached to Mozart's music. The Dutch pianist Daria van den Bercken performed not only as a soloist, giving a beautiful rendition of the concerto, but also spoke about her interpretative decisions and even interviewed concertgoers after the concert. Hosted by Van den Bercken and her Keys to Music Foundation, attenders also experienced various manifestations of "elegance", including music by Francis Poulenc, Jean-Philippe Rameau, and specially interwoven new works Dutch-American composer David Dramm; another unusual innovation was that Mozart's concerto, epitomising elegance, framed the programme, with the opening movement heard towards the beginning of the concert and the remaining

Figure 12.1 "Spicy Classics", Timmerfabriek, Maastricht, 12 October 2016
(photograph: Jean-Pierre Geusens)

movements performed together at the end.[16] Exhibitions and concerts in similar spaces were later arranged, juxtaposing further reflections on the same theme by architects, engineers, philosophers, and politics students, among others.

At the beginning of the concert, attenders were led to their seats by a procession of performing musicians, smoothening the progression from exhibition to concert. Complementing the event's theme and aims, Rosabel Huguet's lighting and choreography were also important because the chamber pieces were performed in different places around the performance space.[17] What appeared tremendously complicated on paper was subtler and balanced in practice; always paramount, the music was nevertheless given a "horizontally" associative context. Extramusical context was intended to provide a gateway to the music for new, young, omnivorous attenders—a mode of programming that recalls Baricco's idea of striving for quality but tailoring it to the intended audience. This event's synergies, then, were explicitly thematic, customisable, and put the choice and order of repertoire at their heart. Such details, of course, are common to much classical music programming, but synergetic concert dramaturgy is set apart by further considerations and determinants: collaborations with musicians who are willing, committed participants and able to communicate openly; substantive links to other genres, disciplines, or themes; the nature and potential of the venue; and, relatedly, the ways in which performances can be staged and/or choreographed. Not all of these characteristics must be employed or present in the final event, but each must be considered.

Similar approaches characterise the presentation of the *Human Requiem* programme by the Rundfunkchor Berlin (dir. Simon Halsey), originally a 2012 coproduction with Sasha Waltz & Guests at Radialsystem V in Berlin. This award-winning programme took as its starting point Johannes Brahms's *Ein deutsches Requiem*, op. 45—the orchestral accompaniment was rearranged for four-hand piano by Phillip Moll—but adapted its universal message to find currency with the tumultuous politics of today. To achieve this, director Jochen Sandig developed a "human" requiem to amplify the idea that Brahms wrote his *Requiem* not to comfort the deceased, as such, but for those left behind—an interpretation given credence by Brahms's selection of biblical texts and his own letters.[18] Sandig crafted a directed, choreographed programme in which Halsey and the singers moved about the audience as various scenes were acted out in a continuously changing soundscape:

> The division between the spaces for stage and audience is dissolved, the listening public no longer sit[s] in front of the sound but instead right in the middle of it, creating a new set of interrelationships between the text, the actual bodies of performers and listeners, the space and the sound . . . Sandig has realised his dream to create a choreographic "physicalisation" of Brahms's *Ein deutsches Requiem*.[19]

Figure 12.2a Neo-Fanfare 9x13 perform "Morendo" at Wonderfeel Festival, 23 July 2016[20]

(photograph: Foppe Schut)

Figure 12.2b Neo-Fanfare 9x13 perform "Morendo" at Wonderfeel Festival, 23 July 2016[21]

(photograph: Foppe Schut)

Incredibly intimate, moving, and popular, the event is still touring, having been revived in Paris, Athens, Hong Kong, Brussels (notably, in the aftermath of the 2015 terrorist attacks), the US, and, indeed, Berlin.

We have chronicled two ways in which synergetic programming practice can be used to develop individual concert programmes. Such dramaturgical connections can also guide and inspire venues and festivals as they plan or rethink their annual series or festival programmes. A third example, then, is the Wonderfeel Festival (f. 2015), a three-day outdoor festival held annually in 's-Graveland, a remarkable, 25-hectare estate (Schaep en Burgh) close to Amsterdam.[22] The festival was established to allow audiences to escape from the natural course of their daily lives and to experience classical music in nature, far removed from both the city and the genre's usual concert-going conventions (Figure 12.2a and 12.2b). This idea permeates the festival, from its bucolic location and informal atmosphere, to its organic food and beautiful concert tents:

> [Festivalgoers] will find six Wonderfeel stages, a mini-stroll from each other. The stages meet everyone's tastes: from Mozart to Steve Reich, from Vivaldi to Arvo Pärt with hints towards jazz, world and pop music. Listen to world-class musicians easy and relaxed on a bench, on a beanbag under the trees, or on a blanket on the grass: the young and upcoming as well as the established. There are hotdogs and beer, bouillabaisse and rosé. Movies, stories and craft [activities] for children . . . 250 musicians, 100 concerts, music documentaries, lectures, children's activities, [and] food trucks.[23]

More importantly, then, the festival is truly synergetic, aims to provoke curiosity about classical music-making, and looks to attract a broad generational range of festivalgoers. Concerts and other activities are also curated in themed tents (Figure 12.3) including the "Unheard" podium, which looks to unearth obscure or new music from all eras, including our own, and to stage other innovative performances: "Hush" was one such programme, featuring Dutch soprano Nora Fischer singing songs of Claudio Monteverdi, John Dowland, and Henry Purcell in a more contemporary, "singer-songwriterly" way, as Fischer explains:

> One of [my] long awaited dreams [was] the redefinition of early music songs. This period has provided songs with an incredible beauty that are extremely close to the pop music of today, only with a performance practice that is usually far away from the ears of this generation . . . stripped of mannerisms, sung in a lower key, and performed in the purest version: simple, timeless and intensely beautiful. Sometimes groovy and soulful, sometimes silent and soul-piercing. Approached with the creativity of songwriters in the twenty-first century.[24]

Figure 12.3 Wonderfeel Festival, Tent Village, 2016
(photograph: Foppe Schut)

Wonderfeel's other podia and tents—"White Label" (borrowing the term from the record industry), "Orphanage of the Classical Hits", "Barn", "Solo", "Village" (used for children's programming), and "The Field" at the festival's entrance—are scheduled in parallel across the three days, encouraging festivalgoers to navigate their own route through the event. Taken together, the festival's programming and design are designed to take attenders on an adventurous voyage through a carefully curated range of classical music concerts. The results have been impressive: sold-out events and a diverse audience, with a significant proportion of attenders new to classical music.[25]

The potential is not only real; it is being realised. Programmes that accord with synergetic concert dramaturgy generate new formats, recontextualise classical music, and attract new fans to the genre. It lessens the potential stigma associated with needing to be educated in, or familiar with, the traditional conventions of concert-going; it also grants an outlet to existing concertgoers who are "omnivorous" or simply keen to have, and appreciate, new experiences. The conscious, programmatic act of selecting and designing each of a concert's ingredients—particular musicians (or groups of musicians), their programme, lighting, choreography, extramusical prospects, and so forth—opens a system of passages (to adopt Baricco's term). As a guiding concept, then, synergetic concert dramaturgy is a catalyst to reflect on current classical music practice, to innovate and think forward, and to make that practice more relevant to contemporary audiences. As renowned opera intendant Gerard Mortier argues: 'Real tradition isn't consolidated, it consolidates. Tradition doesn't mean we have to hold to the rules that are fixed in the past, but enables us to invent new rules to design the future.'[26]

Notes

1. See Gillian Moore, 'Concert Etiquette: The New Rules' (16 September 2015), http://freyahellier.com/gillian-moore (accessed 23 January 2017).
2. Christopher Small, *Musicking: The Meanings of Performing and Listening* (Middletown: Wesleyan University Press, 1998), 94ff.
3. Cas Smithuijsen, *Stilte! Het ontstaan van concertetiquette* (Amsterdam: Podium, 2001), 129.
4. Nineteenth-century aesthetician Eduard Hanslick's ideas are summarised in Mark Evan Bonds, 'Aesthetic Amputations: Absolute Music and the Deleted Endings of Hanslick's Vom Musikalisch-Schönen', *19th-Century Music*, 36/1 (2012), 3–23.
5. The field of research in these areas is young but growing quickly. See, for example: Bonita M. Kolb, 'The Effect of Generational Change on Classical Music Concert Attendance and Orchestras' Responses in the UK and US', *Cultural Trends*, 11/41 (2001), 1–35; Melissa C. Dobson, 'New Audiences for Classical Music: The Experiences of Non-attenders at Live Orchestral Concerts', *Journal of New Music Research*, 39/3 (2010), 111–24; and Garry Crawford, Victoria Gosling, Gaynor Bagnall, and Ben Light, 'An Orchestral Audience: Classical Music and Continued Patterns of Distinction', *Cultural Sociology*, 8/4 (2014), 483–500. Scrutinised in Chapter 11 of this volume, the rise of concerts held in non-traditional venues is a notable twenty-first-century example whereby concertgoers are encouraged to experience and enjoy classical music differently.
6. Various institutions and publications have begun to speak of music programmers' more 'curatorial' role. See, for example: the Institute for Curatorial Practice in Performance at Wesleyan University, Middletown, Connecticut, United States (www.wesleyan.edu/icpp/index.html); and Johan Idema, *Present! Rethinking Live Classical Music* (Amsterdam: Muziek Centrum Nederland, 2012).
7. See Alessandro Baricco, *The Barbarians: An Essay on the Mutation of Culture* [2006], trans. Stephen Sartarelli (New York: Rizzoli, 2014).
8. See, for example, Jan van Dijk, *The Network Society* (3rd edn; London: Sage, 2012).
9. Baricco. Barbarians, 73ff.
10. A few musicologists have also appreciated that, as a genre, classical music has not just been evolving in recent times, but has become highly mutable. See, for example, Adam Krims, 'Marxism, Urban Geography and Classical Recording: An Alternative to Cultural Studies', *Music Analysis*, 20/3 (October 2001), 355ff.
11. See Baricco, *Barbarians*, 61.
12. In a cultural context, sociologist Richard A. Peterson coined the term 'omnivore' to refer to consumers' increased breadth of cultural taste. See Richard A. Peterson, 'Understanding Audience Segmentation: From Elite and Mass to Omnivore and Univore', *Poetics*, 21/4 (1992), 243–58.

13. Semi-structured, the interviews interrogated programmers on their artistic strategies, then examined Baricco's ideas in that light: see Masa Spaan, *Hier komen de Barbaren! Innovations in Concert Practices* (MA diss.; ArtEZ University of the Arts, Arnhem, 2013).

14. I acknowledge the assistance of Hans Ferwerda, the festival's Project Coordinator.

15. Among others, these organisations include Rotterdam Philharmonic Orchestra, South Netherlands Philharmonic, Concertgebouw de Vereeniging, and the Wonderfeel Festival.

16. A short film capturing the event's various aims is available at https://vimeo.com/211469105 (accessed 15 November 2017). The full programme was: Dramm: *Walking Through Rameau* (premiere) ("procession"); Rameau, 'Prelude' from Act 5 of *Les Boréades* (to start concert); Dramm: Transition to Mozart; Mozart: Piano Concerto No. 17 (I. Allegro, with new cadenza by Dramm); Francis Poulenc: Flute Sonata (I. Allegretto malincolico); Dramm: *7am Menuet* for Piano and Chamber Ensemble (premiere); Rameau: 'Musette' from Act 3 of *Les fêtes de Hébé*; Rameau: 'Contredanse' from Act 1 of *Les Boréades*; Mozart: Piano Concerto No. 17 (II. Andante and III. Allegretto—Presto, with new cadenza by Dramm). After the first concert in Maastricht (12 October 2016), "Spicy Classics" visited Eindhoven (Klokgebouw, 14 October 2016) and Ittervoort (Adams Percussion Factory, 15 October 2016).

17. Huguet is renowned for her work in Berlin, especially for Radialsystem V and for dance company Sasha Waltz & Guests.

18. Although a Catholic requiem mass is indeed sung for the souls of the deceased, Brahms chose for his Requiem biblical texts that focus on comforting the living. See Michael Musgrave, *Brahms: A German Requiem* (Cambridge: Cambridge University Press, 1996), 21.

19. Quoted from Rundfunkchor Berlin's description of the event: www.rundfunkchor-berlin.de/projekt/human-requiem; a short film of the performance is also available: www.youtube.com/watch?v=zZXL6JHAijo (both accessed 15 November 2017).

20. See Neo-Fanfare 9x13, "Morendo", also www.9x13.nl/morendo-2016 (accessed 12 December 2017).

21. See Neo-Fanfare 9x13, "Morendo", also www.9x13.nl/morendo-2016 (accessed 12 December 2017).

22. "Wonderfeel" (www.wonderfeel.nl) is not a Dutch word, but one coined to describe and brand the festival. Attenders can purchase day tickets or a three-day pass.

23. Wonderfeel, www.wonderfeel.nl/home/ (accessed 15 November 2017).

24. Quoted from Fischer's website: http://norafischer.com/#page/projects. The programme takes its name from Purcell's 'Hush, no more' (from The Fairy Queen, Z.629), whose interpretation by Fischer and guitarist Marnix Dorrestein (a.k.a. IX) can be viewed at www.youtube.com/watch?v=l3MwiZu0q28 (both accessed 15 November 2017).

25. This is substantiated by audience surveys, conducted annually. 'First-time attenders', as they were defined, comprised 8% and 7.8% of attenders in 2016 and 2017 respectively.

26. Gerard Mortier, *Dramaturgie van een passie*, trans. Jan Vandenhouwe (Antwerp: De Bezige Bij, 2014), 72; quote trans. Masa Spaan.

13 Talking About Classical Music
Radio as Public Musicology

Chris Dromey

In the spacious, public foyer of London's Southbank Centre (Europe's largest arts centre), a wall-sized advert trails the concerts of the venue's four resident orchestras with the slogan 'a classical music season exclusively for pretty much everyone.'[1] Orthodox marketing practice might well blanche at the use of 'exclusively' to describe classical music. Inclusivity and accessibility are the contemporary watchwords of a musical genre long dogged by cultural stereotypes, particularly surrounding (middle) class and (old) age. But the slogan's deliberate oxymoron is surely self-aware and provocative, aiming to stop readers in their tracks, to play on classical music's image problem, and ultimately, of course, to attract concertgoers. More broadly, then, the slogan underlines the importance of language to how classical music is perceived today, and the sensitivities that influence and regulate that association. As a marketing ploy, 'exclusively' here is both an invitation—the music these orchestras produce is for *you*, dear reader—and a qualified reminder of classical music's elite credentials. Potential concertgoers are invited to imagine a special or premier event, not one that is cliquish or exclusory.

How such language frames classical music is the central theme of this chapter. Language is used in myriad ways to contextualise and set expectations about classical music, but many such forms currently slip under musicology's radar, despite being essential to how the genre is perceived: from programme notes, liner notes, and reviews that steer audiences' experiences, to "bluffer's" guides and the efforts of marketers to promote and demystify classical music. Consider also the rise of social media, society's keen appropriation of classical music,[2] and oral media such as podcasts and radio, and the work required to understand how perceptions of classical music are shaped in the broadest sense becomes clear. To appreciate this argument is also to begin to make the case for *public musicology*, a bidirectional process that recognises and attaches greater significance to public-musicological artefacts (such as liner notes and radio) and considers how musicology can make music relevant and useful in the public sphere.

This nascent field is particularly pertinent to classical music, with its grand history and exclusive image. This chapter focuses on one of the most public forms of musicology to classify and critique how BBC Radio 3 and Classic FM speak about the music they broadcast. To survey the types and range of language they use is to reveal not only how the genre is portrayed on the radio today, but also the assumptions about what classical music is, and what it is supposed or presumed to do. In turn, the chapter will offer an account of how Radio 3 and Classic FM fulfil different but overlapping roles in today's classical music industry. Figures show that these stations reach 1.89 and 5.36 million listeners per quarter respectively, making radio by far the most popular way in which people access classical music.[3] Radio is therefore a meaningful way to critique the dilemmas—crises, as some commentators would have it—classical music faces.

Indeed, radio itself, and particularly Classic FM, has been criticised heavily over the years, as we shall see. Such views are historically engrained, but how credible or true are they today? Might radio, in fact, be less a symptom of certain parts of classical music's supposed malaise, and more a cure? Admittedly, examining radio as a conduit for musical understanding and enjoyment is challenging: the complete task would be as much philosophical and linguistic as cultural and musicological. This chapter is intended to be a midpoint that builds on recent musicology and sociology on both radio and the state of classical music, and which looks ahead to consider how public musicology might respond to the modern realities of classical music. A study of the vocabulary Radio 3 and Classic FM use to characterise classical music is therefore framed by two field-scoping sections: on public musicology itself and, first, on the intense debates that encircle the genre today.

Crisis? Which Crisis?

Classical music animates deep feelings among its advocates. Each week seems to be marked by a new think piece, blog, or interview ruminating on the genre's relevance and purpose in the twenty-first century. Social media is often the accelerant of such debates, which traverse territories old and new, from the perennial concerns of engaging audiences and arresting perceived decline, to more specific flashpoints contesting, for example, the significance of music notation or contemporary changes in music education.[4] Taken together, such issues become existential. Most members of the classical music industry (including performers and composers), and most fans of the music itself, will surely have pondered how the genre should navigate its way through an unforgiving but revolutionary digital era, or how to achieve the future-proofing goal of retaining, growing, and diversifying its practitioners and audiences. As the Southbank Centre's slogan tacitly implies, many people regard classical music as a relic: stuffy, elitist (pejoratively so), and out of touch with societies that are increasingly pluralist.

Efforts to make classical music more accessible by embracing digital technology or informality in presentation, including those described elsewhere in this volume, are exciting but often controversial. They can even run the risk of entrenching opinion or reifying stereotypes: witness Classic FM, said to 'remove the guts of classical music, transforming it into a kind of fragrant security blanket', a quote to which we shall return.[5] Many such debates have long troubled classical music but today come with a fresh face, as industry, education, and academia struggle to adjust to the modern realities of society, economics, and policy-making. Significantly, these debates are also typically divergent, for academia and industry rarely collaborate; with admirable exceptions, the relationship is mutually ridden with suspicion. Meanwhile, disciplines within academia are often isolated from one another, despite notionally overlapping as they each strive to preserve or scrutinise classical musical culture. For the purposes of this chapter, then, we can make sense of existing research in these areas by recognising that it possesses three main strands: work that has sought to defend classical music by describing its intrinsic aesthetic, historical, and cultural values; a more socio-musicological strand that focuses on classical music's contemporary practices, with special regard for the inherent imbalances of its organisational, systemic, and societal structures; and, finally, on the relationship between classical music and radio itself.

The first strand comprises a body of opinion that generally accedes to the idea of a genre in crisis. Julian Johnson, for example, diagnoses a widespread 'legitimation crisis' and decries the 'devaluation' of classical music, an argument that goes on to implicate the role of the market and popular music in relativising musical taste.[6] Joshua Fineberg expresses concern about the 'downward homogenizing of taste toward the lowest common denominator',[7] but progressively challenges audiences to free themselves from 'a single listening style' and to shun the 'cult of celebrity'.[8] Lamenting how 'elitism and esotericism [are] too often associated' with classical music,[9] Lawrence Kramer has pursued a similar theme, although he would presumably welcome how some ensembles and promoters have responded to his call for a less formal, more interactive mode of presentation, aping the successes of the visitor-friendly museums he acclaims.[10]

Even so, the central question, or problem, regarding the extent of the public's engagement with and understanding of classical music remains, making Kramer's contribution to the debate the most pessimistic:

> Caught out by a formidable rival [popular music] on one hand and a loss of participants on the other, classical music lost part of its emotional transparency as the [twentieth] century progressed. Music that once seemed utterly available now seemed to harbor secrets . . . The culture of classical music came to seem, not without justice, mandarin and out of touch, ripe for obsolescence.[11]

This first strand of research has a strong sense of didacticism, advocating and valorising attentive (as opposed to passive) listening. By extension, it suggests how classical music is supposed to be heard, regarded, and defined—because from this perspective, the three are inextricable. To focus on classical music's structures, textures, or 'formal-coherence' as a means of recapturing 'emotional transparency' is to help defend the genre itself because these musical characteristics are implied, with some justification, to be the least straightforward to comprehend and appreciate.[12] The more contentious question is whether this challenge makes such characteristics somehow superior in themselves or peculiar to classical music. If the power or meaning of a symphony, say, resides in its movement-spanning teleology, as it often does, then it is natural to seek to defend classical music by championing a nuanced understanding of structure. Such arguments, indeed, belong to a grand music-aesthetic tradition.[13]

At the same time, a truth rarely admitted is that certain classical genres have either attained, or always enjoyed, primacy over others, being valued more highly in culture or by musicologists. The two dominant examples, the symphony and opera, are both historically important "received" genres that were fundamental to how harmony and structure evolved—musical elements that, in turn, gave rise to the analytical concept of harmonic structure. Therefore, the histories of how classical music has been written, valued, and heard are highly persuasive and closely linked. But they do not necessarily account for or correspond with other forms of classical music (much less other musical genres), or with different modes of listening and understanding. The two oppositions set up to underlie many defences of classical music, namely passive/attentive listening and popular/classical music, are extremely useful to pedagogy and aesthetics, but they are not true dichotomies. Popular musicology (or popular music studies), still a relatively young discipline, is littered with analyses of that genre's textural, structural, and harmonic diversity, while great swathes of classical music has the 'immediacy' Johnson envies in popular music.[14]

More fundamentally, many musical genres refuse to fall neatly into either category, particularly so-called hybrid forms that garner much airplay and dominate the classical charts. Radio, similarly, is a prime example of how the role of listening in this debate warrants a more rounded perspective. To be an attentive listener is not necessarily to be knowledgeably or consistently so, and in a society in which music is more available than ever to hear, to be passive much of the time is simply inevitable. Even in a classical concert setting, where usually audiences are aurally and literally confined, we typically provide programme notes, acknowledging that concertgoers may "tune out" to read them during the performance. Yet, this pragmatic notion of an attentive-passive spectrum feels almost heretical in the context of classical music, so potent are ideas, perceived or real, about the "correct" ways to understand, enjoy, and value such music.

On the periphery of the same debate lies our second strand, for some authors have begun to process these ambiguities and to chart a way forward. Adams Krims, for example, sought not to prioritise, or hierarchise, listening styles, but endorsed a 'historicising, rather than moralising, narrative' to frame classical music, adding that ' "classical" has mutated.'[15] By acknowledging how classical music has 'always involved a merging of older cultural practices with contemporary conditions',[16] Krims was less fatalistic than many scholars. Perhaps the closest parallel here is with Ruth Levitt and Ruth Rennie's adage that 'those who speak of a "crisis" in classical music are really describing the irrevocable demise of old, familiar attitudes, expectations and ways of working.'[17] Studies belonging to this second strand of research range from investigating how diversely audiences feel about and interact with classical music, to asking why access to, and success within, classical music can remain stubbornly limited by personal factors such as class, age, and gender. The latter field is growing quickly to try to address such inequities through scholarship, activism, and collaboration.[18] The former, meanwhile, has typically centred on audiences, for example, young, first-time concertgoers (the holy grail for forward-looking promoters) to prove that lacking knowledge and experience of classical music, including concert-going etiquette and lexical understanding, is generally correlated to lower levels of enjoyment.[19]

Superficially, the finding may seem obvious, but authors Lucy Dearn and Stephanie Pitts draw an important further connection by describing how attenders with 'existing classical music knowledge and vocabulary . . . *comply* with those expectations [i.e. surrounding musical enjoyment].'[20] In a similar vein, Elizabeth Hellmuth Margulis has showed how participants in an experiment to test musical enjoyment 'preferred excerpts [of various Beethoven quartets] that were preceded by no description' and that 'when [programme note-like] text of a structural or dramatic nature prefaced an excerpt, participants reported enjoying the music less.'[21] Again, the power of discourses surrounding classical music—to 'comply', 'moralise', or intimidate—is seen to be emotionally strong. Hellmuth Margulis's tentative proposal to explain her finding, that some listeners may prefer to be 'swept away by the music, without explicit information of its constituent elements . . . [for] such awareness may interfere with their enjoyment', need not be an argument for blissful ignorance, or trigger complaints about "dumbing down".[22] On the contrary, this type of listening is extremely common, does not yield to a simple choice between active or passive, attentive or inattentive, and reveals that languages associated with classical music can be unwittingly exclusory. These wider truths are, or should be, as important to defenders of classical music as they are to critics of its systemic structures.

The third area of debate to chronicle is that of radio, a medium that spends several hours each day discussing and describing classical music, but which has also has attracted much criticism because of this mediating role. BBC Radio 3 (f. 1946) and its younger rival Classic FM (f. 1992) devote the greatest daily amount of airplay to classical music in the United Kingdom. The definition is admittedly a little unwieldy, for Classic FM proudly calls itself the country's 'only 100% classical music radio station',[23] which highlights Radio 3's extra coverage of folk, jazz, and other non-classical music (as well as literature, philosophy, and other cultural forms). Nevertheless, the stations' histories and identities invite comparison. Radio 3 is a public service broadcaster whose launch, as the Third Programme, was described by the then Director-General of the BBC as 'directed to an audience that is not of one class but that is perceptive and intelligent.'[24] Related to the earlier establishment of the BBC itself,[25] this ethos continues to colour perceptions of Radio 3. Positioning the station as a dominant arbiter of taste, the aim morphed all too easily into other value-laden beliefs claimed for it, for example, that 'the whole point about Radio 3 was that it was aloof.'[26]

However it is characterised, Radio 3's ethos also calls for special and periodic justification, particularly when views on public subsidy are polarised. Owned by British media company Global, Classic FM would appear to encounter fewer such dangers, yet this commercial status has itself proved controversial. As Luke Howard observed a few years after Classic FM's launch, the station quickly became associated with "crossover" classical music, in particular because it aided the commercial success of Henryk Górecki's Third Symphony (1976, also known as *Symphony of Sorrowful Songs*).[27] Still a poorly defined genre, so-called classical crossover has attracted criticism, albeit not always fairly: Górecki's symphony contains 'no element of genre-mixing or pandering to a pop audience' and is crossover only insofar as it "crossed over" to the non-classical charts (on the British album charts, it peaked at #6 in February 1993).[28] Howard's quote, indeed, discloses this loaded meaning ('pandering'); again, the fear is that classical music will be trivialised, misappropriated, or both. But whether we recognise classical crossover musically or commercially, another fact stands out: that it predates Classic FM. When the genre's modern history is written, it will surely trace its origins to the 1960s and its heyday to the late 1970s and early 1980s.[29]

Criticism of Classic FM stems from a deeper fear, typified by Richard Barbrook's complaint (made in the context of the station applying for a broadcasting licence) that 'in the tenth year of [Margaret] Thatcher, classical music has been transformed from a spiritual experience into a format for attracting old and richer listeners.'[30] This argument, in turn, belongs to something of a radio-sceptic tradition in classical music: Arnold Schoenberg railed against radio's 'boundless surfeit' of music;[31] and it is small step to extend to radio Michael Chanan's perceptive description of the 'aesthetic antimony' of classical music and television.[32] Anyone who has strained to hear classical music on the go will understand how radio can be inimical to the genre's 'special kind of solace'.[33] This issue applies equally to Radio 3 and Classic FM, yet notice how the arguments we have chronicled so far *also* describe, characterise, and implicitly limit classical music, assuming it to be either 'aloof', 'spiritual', 'special', or 'solacing'. Even Schoenberg's pithy phrase betrays a fear of being unable to contain and, by extension, preserve the boundaries of classical music. This language is a form of cultural exceptionalism we will revisit; to rely on it is to underline its significance. The perceived problems of broadcasting classical music, be it radio stations' contrasting styles or the medium itself, only make these areas more fruitful to explore. Scrutiny of the relationship between classical music, radio, and language is overdue.

The Study

Appendix 1 chronicles the vocabulary that Radio 3 and Classic FM employ to contextualise the music they broadcast. Its "day in the life" survey encompasses every piece of verbal and accompanying online commentary heard or available to read on a random day in 2017. No single day of radio broadcast is truly typical, of course, and the fact that the selected day, March 1, was also Ash Wednesday and St David's Day explains and inflates the daily use of adjectives such as 'penitential', 'appropriate', or 'special', and also accounts for the broadcast of certain pieces of music associated with Lent (i.e. Carlo Gesualdo's *Miserere* and Francis Poulenc's *Tristis est anima mea* on Radio 3; no such repertoire specifically attached to Ash Wednesday was heard on Classic FM) and with Wales (James James's 'Land of my Fathers', Karl Jenkins's *Over the Stone* and 'In paradisum' from the *Requiem*, and the traditional 'Men of Harlech' on Classic FM; William Mathias's *Serenade* and live performances by the Welsh ensemble 9Bach on Radio 3). Because the combined number of instances of highlighted vocabulary used across the day totals 906, these annual events do not distort the survey significantly. On the contrary, they usefully highlight how, through their choice of repertoire, the stations chose to mark these occasions in their own way.

Relatedly, Radio 3's schedule on the day in question included one of its twice-weekly live religious services (3.30 p.m.–4.30 p.m., curtailing "Afternoon on 3"). This was the second of three omissions from Appendix 1: the others were the repeat of Donald Macleod's "Composer of the Week [Beethoven]" (6.30 p.m.–7.30 p.m., first heard at midday) and Dr Simon Rennie's non-musical "The Essay: [Anthony] Burgess at 100" (10.45 p.m.–11 p.m.). Appendix 1 otherwise chronicles 24 hours of coverage on each station, from Sam Pittis's overnight programme (1 a.m.–6 a.m.) to Margherita Taylor's "Smooth Classics" (10 p.m.–1 a.m.) on Classic FM, and from Catriona Young's "Through the Night" (12.30 a.m.–6.30

a.m.) to the Max Reinhardt-presented "Late Junction" (11 p.m.–12.30 a.m.) on Radio 3. That Taylor's "Smooth Classics" was the second such titled programme of the day after John Brunning's "Smooth Classics at 7" (the third hour of "Classic FM Drive") points to one of the principal reasons for why Classic FM is so successful—and so polarising. The starkest contrast in the stations' use of language is in their respective use of 'relax', 'soothe', 'unwind', and their derivatives: thirty such instances on Classic FM; none on Radio 3. The comparison excludes the related use of 'smooth', repeated often as a pre-recorded link reminding listeners of the programmes' titles; the closest equivalent to 'smooth' on Radio 3 was Sean Rafferty's colourful description of alternative folk group 9Bach as 'mellifluous'.

At the same time, these thirty instances are atypical insofar as they do not usually describe individual pieces of music, instead tending to focus on the listener, and specifically the connection between the "persuading" presenter and the "bidden" listener: 'Light the fire and relax . . .'; 'I'll guarantee to keep you relaxed. . . '; ' . . . sublime, relaxing music, designed to ease away the stresses and strains of the day.' The "Smooth Classics" themselves are mostly slow in tempo, strings-led, memorable (that is, melodically repetitive), or a combination of the three, for example, Ralph Vaughan Williams's *Fantasia on a Theme of Thomas Tallis*, Pyotr Ilyich Tchaikovsky's cello *Nocturne*, the slow movement from Alessandro Marcello's Oboe Concerto, and Robert Parsons's *Ave Maria*. 'Smooth' literally, and figuratively, promises no "bumps" or "bitterness".[34] Compiled and aired in this way, these pieces of music become part of a wider Classic FM canon that, superficially at least, puts the listener in charge and unapologetically eschews challenging or unpopular repertoire. As Darren Henley (Classic FM's Managing Director) says: 'We play very little of Schoenberg's music on Classic FM because our listeners tell us they don't like it.'[35]

Indeed, the station's musically and presentationally 'friendly, accessible style' surely accounts for its wide listenership.[36] This style has also prompted reactions that range from reasonable and objective, for example, that the station often 'present[s] classical music as an adjunct to functional activities [e.g. driving, relaxing]',[37] to more contentious and aesthetically loaded remarks, for example, that its 'muzak has become a powerful source of cultural corruption',[38] that it increases the 'threat of narcosis',[39] and, to complete our earlier description of the station, that:

> Classic FM forensically removes the guts of classical music, transforming it into a kind of fragrant security blanket, rips great pieces of music out of context and history, and utilises presenters oozing with courtesy who are like dentists, soothingly telling you that there will be no pain, and everything will be all right.[40]

This excoriating opinion from Paul Morley, a self-described recent convert to classical music (if not to Classic FM), is given succour by the type of vocabulary listed so far, which is generic in itself and generalising in its prevalence. Yet, radio—any radio—mediates and recontextualises the music it broadcasts, and the passage of time causes classical music—any music—to be repurposed, appropriated, and reinterpreted. These truths sustain any living musical genre. To single out Classic FM for removing classical music from its 'context' is illogical, unproven, and points to a subsequent truth that criticism of the station's alleged mischaracterisation or stereotyping of classical music is itself stereotypical.[41]

Similarly, it is telling that criticisms of Classic FM are often paired with fears that it is a corruptive influence on Radio 3. It is natural that these stations should be compared, but perspectives that are dismissive, overprotective, or, worse, supercilious tend either to betray a narrow ideology or simply preach to the choir. Paul Driver's longer argument, for example, is that the 'aural medium of radio poses a much smaller threat of narcosis [compared with television], but Classic FM is doing its best to make up the odds; while the patness and have-nice-day-ness [sic] of pop . . . have been infiltrating Radio 3.'[42] Although old, such arguments recur: they resurfaced in the early 2010s as Radio 3 began to implement the BBC's cost-saving plan (*Delivering Quality First*, 2011) by broadcasting fewer orchestral and live lunchtime concerts, recording less contemporary music, and devoting more on-air time to interacting with listeners.[43] From the opposite perspective, Classic FM even joined the debate, criticising Radio 3 for allegedly aping its commercial competitor.[44]

To return to Appendix 1, a more objective analysis might observe that *both* stations aired *Fantasia on a Theme by Thomas Tallis* (Radio 3, in fact, programmed it twice) in order to compare Brunning's solitary 'glorious' on Classic FM with Young's explanation of musical "recycling" or Tom Redmond's lengthier discussion of the music's effect and historic significance. A fairer approach recognises that Redmond was speaking in the context of a live concert, so his oral programme note is more, if not perfectly, comparable to Jane Jones's evening "Full Works Concert" on Classic FM. (Most of the latter "concerts" consist of studio recordings.) More carefully, we can tally 479 instances of descriptive or analytical language on Classic FM on the day in question, contextualising the music they broadcast by using 170 different words. In turn, we can describe how each station's lexicon falls into different categories to compare them in greater detail. Compared with Classic FM, Radio 3 featured fewer instances of such language (422) but employed over a hundred *more* unique words (272). We can therefore expect the stations' most commonly used words, their frequency, and their implications to be significantly varied.

It proves so. 'Great', coupled with 'greatest' or 'greatness', was heard thrice as often on Classic FM (24 vs. 8), typically to describe the music itself,

its performers, or its interpretation, and once to explain how Italian composer Nino Rota was 'inspired by great women' during a look ahead to International Women's Day. The next most common terms were 'lovely' (and
its derivatives, used 18 times on Classic FM, 4 times on Radio 3), 'wonder-
ful' (15 vs. 6), 'favourite(s)' (14 vs. 3), 'classical' (12 vs. 0, excluding the
ubiquitous 'classic'), 'new' (11 vs. 6, allowing 'world-exclusive', 'premiere',
and 'debut'), and 'dedicate' or 'dedication' (10 vs. 0). The statistical con-
trasts here are particularly stark because Classic FM's presentational style
has a strong self-promotional and chart-led tendency. 'Favourite' is often
used self-reflexively (' . . . the UK's favourite classical music station. . . ') or
to mark a piece of music said to be the 'favourite' of a particular presenter,
celebrity, or performer. A similar personality-based approach explains how
'dedication' is used typically by or for the listeners, rather than to explain
a piece's original dedication, and a greater contrast still (16 vs. 0) is revealed by collating Classic FM's day-long references to it annual "Hall of
Fame", for example, 'championing', 'promoting', 'voting', 'your choice',
and 'countdown'.[45]

This language, seemingly democratic and engaging, also inspires criticisms of Classic FM 'presenting classical music as if it were pop . . . rank[ing]
pieces into charts'.[46] It is true that an inevitable feature (or flaw) of the model
is its circularity: the voted-for "classics" dominate the charts, which feed
into future playlists, ergo the cycle continues. Radio 3 has no such explicitly commercial or hierarchical (that is, chart-led) equivalent to Classic FM,
and makes fewer repetitions of the descriptive language it employs. Its most
common terms have already been listed above, save for 'beautiful'/'beauty'
(8 times, vs. Classic FM's 9), 'celebrate' and its derivatives (6 per station),
'brilliant', 'fine'/'finest' (both 5 each), and 'youthful'/'student work' (4 times;
nil for Classic FM). Radio 3 shares with Classic FM a natural tendency to
promote the music it broadcasts but places greater emphasis on the *quality*
of its output, affirming classical music's historicism or, implicitly at least, its
superiority through language such as 'ancestry', 'award-winning', 'genius',
'intellectual', 'luminaries', 'peerless', and 'revered' (12 instances in total)
to describe figures such as Arturo Toscanini, Edward Elgar, Gerald Finzi,
Beethoven, Mozart, and Tchaikovsky.

Classic FM employed none of these particular valorising terms, instead
describing performers, composers, or their music as 'expert', 'famous', 'celebrity', 'leading', and 'legend'/'legendary', and doing so (for these more generic words) as often as Radio 3 (8 instances in total). Such a self-validating
vocabulary endorses and, by extension, defends classical music, although to
reflect on the findings of Dearn, Pitts, and Hellmuth Margulis, whether this
emphasis helps or hinders (or engages or alienates) is open to question. It
also represents what musicology recognises as *canonising* language, a category that was particularly noticeable on Radio 3 in two further ways. The
positive, affirmatory set of terms 'benchmark', 'distinguished', 'enduring',

'harbinger', 'historic', 'iconic', 'important', 'instrumental' (as in 'instrumental to'), and other sideways references to canonicism, for example, 'cornerstone of the repertoire' and 'High Church [of string-writing]', were heard only on Radio 3 (14 instances in total).

Classic FM employed an alternative set of similar terms: the more colloquial, if still canonising, 'prodigy', 'masterpiece', and 'masterly', together with 'appropriate', 'suitable', and 'proper'—usually to suggest music "hitting the spot", and again therefore focussing on a listener experience presumed, and guided, to be emotionally satisfying (12 instances in total). A stereotyping subset of this same category, which either described composers as 'mad', or discussing their 'mania', or branded them or their music 'obsessive', 'madcap', or 'unhinged', was specific to Radio 3 (6 times in total). Unsurprisingly, perhaps, Beethoven attracted half of these comments, his role as a founder of Romanticism still entwined with a "tortured genius" ideal we are increasingly likely today to see as a damaging correlation of creativity and illness.

The next category of language is distinguishable because it can be viewed as a discrete set of synonyms for classical music itself: words specific to Radio 3 such as 'life-affirming', 'metaphysical', 'humanistic', 'spirituality [of the music]', 'magic'/'magical', 'mystical', 'stellar', 'utopia', and further references to its otherworldliness, for example, 'beyond reality' and 'another planet' (13 occasions, if we count 'High Church' again). Classic FM used none of these oratorical flourishes, although it shared with Radio 3 comparable references to 'heavenly'/'celestial', 'sublime', and 'pure' (5 occasions each in total). Collectively, these terms distance classical music from the "everyday". The presentation of classical music as timeless, exemplary, or sublime is not new—philosophers and aestheticians have long admired and perpetuated its intangibility (or incorporeality)—and this category is conceptually connected to that of quality and canonisation.

At the same time, these terms point us towards a more technical category because they encroach on an aesthetic tradition that has often taken inspiration from the exceptionalism bestowed on classical music by describing it as, or simply having faith in it being, 'sublime' or 'transcendental'. This category still endorses the genre but employs language such as 'luminous', 'clean', 'colour', 'atmospheric', 'energy'/'energise'/'invigorating', 'flavour', 'dreamy', and '[musically] economical' (12 occasions on Radio 3, with 'moody' and 'brooding' the only comparable terms on Classic FM) to communicate or "translate" the music's design or effect for listeners. More specialist still are descriptions of certain works as 'chromatic', 'contrapuntal', 'cyclical', 'develop[ing]' (as in musical 'development'), '[musical] dialogue', 'dissection', 'interwoven [texture]', '[musical] recycling', 'atonal', and an allusion to Mozart's genre-hopping referentiality (11 occasions on Radio 3). Such language is also generally less metaphorical and abstract than our previous set's 'colour' and 'luminous',[47] but the paradox is that as this new language nudges listeners towards a more tangible, analytical perspective on classical music, it undeniably becomes more arcane and puzzling to anyone without a basic grounding in music theory.

Classic FM, indeed, employed none of these terms—an important distinction that takes the study in two further directions. The first is to consider how the stations cover news or subjects that encompass the single-word descriptors classified so far but go further by dwelling on certain historical, topical, or analytical themes. Radio 3 featured twice as many such instances as Classic FM on the day in question.[48] Radio 3, for example, discussed: the gender gap in classical music composition, airing guest Odaline de la Martinez's 'Song of the Rider' from *Canciones*; the structure and genre of Elgar's *Introduction and Allegro*; antiphony, texture, and referentiality in *Fantasia on a Theme by Thomas Tallis*; and a critic's musicologically interesting verdict on Ryan Wigglesworth's 'old-fashioned atonality' in his new opera *The Winter's Tale*. Among other subjects, Classic FM hailed Carris Jones, the first full-time female chorister to be appointed in St Paul's Cathedral's long history, chronicled Luigi Boccherini's life and career, and introduced listeners to British conductor-arranger John Wilson.

A final category of language we can identify focuses on how the stations "ready" their listeners; or, how each station approaches the idea that listening to classical music can require listeners to develop knowledge, exert effort, or at least keep an open mind. Neither station ventures into this contentious area often, perhaps shying away from a potentially off-putting tone, but their presentation is very different when they do. On Radio 3, language such as 'baffling', 'brace yourself', 'complex', 'connoisseurs', 'contemporary' (implied to be 'progressivist'), 'difficult'/'challenging'/'tricky', 'enigmatic', 'intense', and 'investigation' (as in 'investigative') was heard 17 times. We could add to this category terms such as 'authentic', 'heartfelt', and 'real [music]' (7 instances), for while these value-laden adjectives, in truth, serve multiple purposes, a stark contrast with Classic FM is clear. Save for a single 'intense' (to describe Enya), the commercial station shared none of these terms with Radio 3. If we seek a Classic FM equivalent to Radio 3's admission that classical music can 'baffle', 'challenge', and so forth, we find irreverent mentions of 'boffins', 'pinch yourself', and *'hors d'oeuvre'*, or mood-lightening puns such as: '[Next,] a bit of "Power" Grainger. . . ' (a play on children's TV series *Power Rangers* to introduce music by Percy Grainger); 'The only way is Elgar . . ." (a pun on British "structured reality" series *The Only Way Is Essex*); and ". . . The Great Gate of Chicken Kiev . . .", trailing the best-known movement from Modest Mussorgsky's *Pictures at an Exhibition*.

Again, while frivolities such as these can be (harshly) adjudged to trivialise classical music, the more fundamental conclusion concerns how Classic FM sees the genre, or rather what it implies and prescribes its modern-day purpose to be: popular and, by definition, memorable, or at least accessible. "Up next, your 'first-cup-of-coffee-in-the-office piece' "; positive, *relatable* language abounds. Nevertheless, the argument that Radio 3 and Classic FM represent 'opposing positions' is surely too black and white.[49] The vocabulary they employ suggests that their characterisation of classical music does differ in two main ways, although both are contentious: Classic FM places greater emphasis on its listeners and their experience of the music; Radio 3's presentational style and format generally lend themselves to greater understanding of the music it broadcasts, insofar as its vocabulary is wider and more analytical. Yet, musical understanding is not a singular concept. One definition of it (of many) is synonymous with the qualities—particularly accessibility and memorability—we can ascribe to Classic FM. Indeed, the station's boundless positivity is a less ambiguous third distinction. The commercial incentive of this outlook has its pitfalls. Rejecting *un*popular composers is easier than rehabilitating their reputations or justifying their music. But it also permits a sanguine vision of classical music that is 'continuing to reinvent itself and to thrive',[50] and it invites listeners to join the special, open club of classical music, 'exclusively for pretty much for everyone.'

Postscript: Radio as Public Musicology

The operational contradictions of classical music are not unique to Classic FM. Radio 3, the Southbank Centre, and all mindful classical music organisations grapple with the risks, tensions, and paradoxes this chapter has encountered: a genre that is both "heritage" and alive; the over-optimistic outlook that risks complacency; the embattled or despairing position that understates the genre's modern problems or exaggerates claims for its universality; the language, even that which prizes understanding, that can alienate; and a genre often characterised, and valorised, as sublimely mystical and otherworldly, but which to survive must be functional and relatable to the everyday. The temptation to consider music configurationally, such as discussing how its elements complete patterns that characterise the whole, is analytically valuable and often revelatory. This form of musical understanding is also the most difficult, is neglected as a result, and belongs to a formalist tradition that explains both Morley's caustic comments and Driver's rose-tinted lament for an iteration of Radio 3 that was once 'concerned with no one in particular, only the subject matter itself.'[51] In other words, it can too easily appear conservative, arcane, or simply off-putting. It is also one of several forms of musical understanding and enjoyment. Describing what music signifies, the emotions it inheres and inspires, the conditions that caused it to be, and more practical forms such as performance, also deserve recognition, however they are manifested.

Just as classical music's challenges should not be viewed in isolation from one another, forms of musical understanding interrelate. Scrutiny of these assumptions is surely central to the future of classical music. Charles Henry Purday, a pioneer of the modern concert programme note, wrote in 1836 that

> an important advantage would accrue to art and society in general, if some means were adopted to render musical performances as intellectual as they are sensual . . . The public are not to be blamed for taking little interest in what they do not understand . . . Consequently, performances, if listened to at all, are heard with indifference.[52]

While these distinctions belong to a world without radio or programme notes, it is some comfort to recognise that entangled talk of disengagement, lack of understanding, and the vocabulary of classical music is far from new. Purday's intrepidity led to the prevalence of programme note writing, albeit inconstantly styled as "prologue", "analytical", or "synoptical" notes. It is worth asking how such a public-musicological spirit could be rekindled in the twenty-first century.[53] Public musicology today would, and should, look different to its nineteenth- and even twentieth-century iterations; today's dilemmas concern *identity* (of classical music organisations, and of the evolution of classical music itself) as much as *access*, an industry buzzword since the late twentieth century. Moreover, this chapter's definition of public musicology as a bidirectional process is intended to imply not only that musicology should pay greater attention to public-musicological artefacts (as resources for study and as means of communication), but also that music, the classical music industry, and musicology itself would benefit from closer cooperation.

In some respects, the foundations are strong. Connections between industry and musicology already include outreach programmes, blogs,[54] pre-concert talks, new innovations in concert-giving described elsewhere in this volume,[55] a blossoming branch of musicology occasionally prefixed by "applied",[56] and, of course, radio—each area sustaining or improving classical music's relationship with the public. Such connections, however, are typically sporadic and loose, and classical music does not yet rival other subjects' more explicitly public modes of presentation. History, for example, has a well-understood strand of "public history", especially in North America.[57] Science, too, enjoys a high profile, aided by its Professors for Public Understanding and its comparably great exposure on television and social media. University-paired YouTube channels such as Numberphile make special effort to communicate mathematical discoveries to the public. (Classical music fans will recognise the stereotypes that beset public understanding of Mathematics: esoteric, irrelevant to everyday life, notated with indecipherable symbols.)[58]

A largely untapped resource in musicology, radio occupies a unique position because it is such a potent form of public musicology itself. If public musicology is to be understood and pursued broadly (which, by definition, it must), then it should recognise and engage not only performers and composers, but also concert programmers, museum and archive curators, publishers, local historians, activists, those who collaborate and bridge disciplines (e.g. music export or tourism, music therapy, music supervisors), and, conceivably, any administrator or manager working in the classical music industry. Radio stations and musicologists do not currently look to reflect this professional and artistic breadth in their activities. Relatedly, it is striking that compared with classical music, disciplines such as History and Mathematics *relish* their perpetual search for new discoveries, theories, and interpretations, and seem to enjoy a less angst-ridden balance between subjectivity and objectivity as a result.

There are innumerable ways in which public musicology could follow suit, whether on the radio, in the concert hall, or in academia: giving a public platform to a new iteration of activist-musicology that is invigorating online debate (for example, the excellent www.musictheoryexamplesby-women.com); broadcasting rehearsals to disclose how performances, and musical works themselves, are crafted;[59] acknowledging and appreciating classical music's inherent interconnections to other musical genres, film, and pursuits such as sport; not shying away from, being embarrassed by, or even attacking the genre's multivalency as an art form; and striving to debunk or at least understand the many clichés that cloud understanding of certain composers or styles (Schoenberg, for example, where arch-modernist memories of his accomplishments have had a marginalising and distorting effect).[60] Without public awareness and understanding, the influence of classical music is similarly undermined. Where classical music is hamstrung by the difficulties of describing or analysing it, introspective or objectivising approaches can too easily take the form of censure or self-pity. Instead, to guide public musicology and modernise perceptions of classical music, let us appreciate that many of classical music's "answers" remain up for grabs, being both available and to be decided; that this contradiction is one of many, for the characterisation of classical music can be difficult, diverse, but fascinating for it; and that whether motivated socially or musically, scholarship is confronting the artistic and professional realities of classical music and racing to catch up.

Appendix 1 Keyword Survey of Verbal and Online Commentary, BBC Radio 3 and Classic FM, 1 March 2017

Terms	BBC Radio 3	Classic FM	Context	Programme
Admired/ admirable		1	"… a composer [Korngold] greatly admired by Nicola Benedetti …"	John Suchet, 9 a.m.–1 p.m.
	1		Wigglesworth, *The Winter's Tale* (trail for May broadcast, quoting reviewer)	Petroc Trelawny, 6.30 a.m.–9 a.m.
Adventure/ adventurous	1		"… for adventurous listeners …" ("Late Junction")	Website
			"… musical adventure …" (Gerald Scarfe interview)	Rob Cowan, 9 a.m.–12 p.m.
Amazing		1	Richard Harvey, 'Cantilena', *Concerto Antico*	Margherita Taylor, 10 p.m.–1 a.m.
	2		9Bach, 'Ifan'	Sean Rafferty, 4.30 p.m.–7.30 p.m.
			Baluji Shrivastav, 'Dhun Bhairvi'	Max Reinhardt, 11 p.m.–12.30 a.m.
Ambience	1		"… environmental ambience …" (Devonanon, 'Oslo')	Max Reinhardt, 11 p.m.–12.30 a.m.
Analysis (stylistic or historical)	12		"Finally, here was a piece of English music." (Anon., 'Sumer is icumen in'); "… old-fashioned atonality …" (Wigglesworth, *The Winter's Tale*—trail for May broadbast, quoting reviewer); "… more Cuban …than Mexican [in origin]." (Joplin, *Solace: A Mexican Serenade*)	Petroc Trelawny, 6.30 a.m.–9 a.m.
			"… transitional period… [in the] dawning world of opera …" (Monteverdi, *Madrigali Guerrieri et amoroso*)	Rob Cowan, 9 a.m.–12 p.m.
			"… nifty bit of rhythm-changing …" (Skempton, *Moving On*); "… conservative Viennese listeners might not have appreciated …" (Beethoven, 'Pathétique' Sonata); "… bridge between J.S. and Haydn …" (C.P.E. Bach);	John Toal, 1 p.m.–2 p.m.

		Reference to cyclically "linked movements" (Messiaen, *Les Offrandes oubliées*); "...love of romanticism..." (Sviridov, *Miniature Triptych*)	Verity Sharp, 2 p.m.–3.30 p.m.
		On structure and genre ("essentially a concerto grosso") of Elgar, *Introduction and Allegro*; on structure, "counterpoint... [and] interwoven" texture of Tippett, *Divertimento on Sellinger's Round*; on antiphony, tonality/modality, texture and referentiality of Vaughan Williams, *Fantasia on a Theme by Thomas Tallis*	Tom Redmond, 7.30 p.m.–10 p.m.
Ancestry	1	"...cosmopolitan ancestry..." (Finzi, Clarinet Concerto)	Tom Redmond, 7.30 p.m.–10 p.m.
Anguished	2	On Beethoven's music ("Composer of the Week")	Website
		On Beethoven's music ("Composer of the Week")	Donald Macleod, 12 p.m.–1 p.m.
Anian	1	9Bach, interview, defining their musical "...vibe [or] 'connection', ..."	Sean Rafferty, 4.30 p.m.–7.30 p.m.
Anniversary/ birthdays	7	"...flurry of birthdays..."	Sam Pittis, 1 a.m.–6 a.m.
		Chopin's birthday; "...year of legends..."	Tim Lihoreau, 6 a.m.–9 a.m.
		Chopin's birthday (*Grande valse brillante*)	John Suchet, 9 a.m.–1 p.m.
		"...flurry of birthdays..."; Armstrong, 'Glasgow Theme', *Love Actually* (quoting listener); festivities and competition to mark Classic FM's birthday	Anne-Marie Minhall, 1 p.m.–5 p.m.
	4	On 100 years of Jazz; "Happy birthday, Jazz." (both retweets)	Twitter
		"...big anniversary..." (Debussy, 'La cathédrale engloutie', *Préludes*); Couperin, arr. Adès, *Les baricades mistérieuses*	Sean Rafferty, 4.30 p.m.–7.30 p.m.

(Continued)

Appendix 1 (Continued)

Terms	BBC Radio 3	Classic FM	Context	Programme
Appropriate (and synonyms)		14	"...perfect blend of night-time music..."; "..."; "...perfect music to ease you into the night on "Smooth Classics"..."	Twitter
			Jenkins, 'Agnus Dei', *The Armed Man: A Mass for Peace*; "...perfect midweek music..."	Sam Pittis, 1 a.m.–6 a.m.
			Re. "Early Toast"; "...really "Haydn" the spot"; "...something which might hit the spot..."; "...hitting the proper St David's Day music..."; "...perfect start to the midweek spot..." (Satie); "...perfect start to the midweek..." (J.S. Bach, Orchestral Suite No. 1)	Tim Lihoreau, 6 a.m.–9 a.m.
			Mendelssohn, *Fingal's Cave*; "...music to match every day or every month..."; "...musical perfection..." (Tchaikovsky, 'Miniature Overture', *Nutcracker Suite*)	John Suchet, 9 a.m.–1 p.m.
			"...how [the] afternoon should sound..." (Beethoven, Symphony No. 6, 3rd–5th movts)	Anne-Marie Minhall, 1 p.m.–5 p.m.
	3		"...perfect music as spring beckons..." (Dvořák, *Carnival Overture*)	Rob Cowan, 9 a.m.–12 p.m.
			On "Late Junction"	Twitter
			"...perfection..."	Sean Rafferty, 4.30 p.m.–7.30 p.m.
Atmospheric	4	1	Grieg, 'Solveig's Song', *Peer Gynt* (quoting listener)	Anne-Marie Minhall, 1 p.m.–5 p.m.
			"...his most atmospheric music..." (trail for Sibelius, *Radio 3 In Concert*) (x 2)	Petroc Trelawny, 6.30 a.m.–9 a.m.
			"...bringing atmosphere into music-making..." (Perianes, interviewed); Trad., 'Breuddwyd y Bardd', perf. 9Bach	Sean Rafferty, 4.30 p.m.–7.30 p.m.
Authentic/ authenticity	3		"...authentic performance..." (Mozart, *Sonata for Piano Four-Hands*); on Stravinsky (interviewing Gerald Scarfe)	Rob Cowan, 9 a.m.–12 p.m.
			Perianes on performance	Sean Rafferty, 4.30 p.m.–7.30 p.m.

Word			Examples	Presenter, time
Award-winning	3		"...award-winning musicians..." (C.P.E. Bach, Trio in A minor)	John Toal, 1 p.m.–2 p.m.
			9Bach (trail for "In Tune")	Verity Sharp, 2 p.m.–3.30 p.m.
			Beto Villares, 'Quincas'	Max Reinhardt, 11 p.m.–12.30 a.m.
Awesome		1	Quoting listener (on Enya, 'May It Be', *Lord of the Rings*, perf. 2CELLOS, arranger not announced)	John Suchet, 9 a.m.–1 p.m.
Baffling	1		"[Beethoven's music] must've baffled those who first heard it." ("Composer of the Week")	Donald Macleod, 12 p.m.–1 p.m.
Beautiful/beauty	8	9	Puccini, *La bohème*; trail for upcoming music; Strauss Jr, *The Blue Danube*	Sam Pittis, 1 a.m.–6 a.m.
			Borodin, String Quartet No. 1 (3rd movt); Korngold, 'Marietta's Lied'; Hampshire countryside, plugging Grange Festival; Gershwin, Piano Concerto; Field, Piano Concerto (2nd movt)	John Suchet, 9 a.m.–1 p.m.
			Butterworth, *The Banks of Green Willow* "...searingly beautiful..." (retweet on Gesualdo, *Miserere*)	Anne-Marie Minhall, 1 p.m.–5 p.m. Twitter
			"...glancing beauty..." (Wigglesworth, *The Winter's Tale*, trail for May broadbast, quoting reviewer); "...one of the most beautiful products in all French music." (Ravel, *Daphnis et Chloé*, quoting Stravinsky)	Petroc Trelawny, 6.30 a.m.–9 a.m.
			Mozart, *Sonata for Piano Four-Hands*; Beethoven, 'Pathétique' Sonata "...a beautiful resilient emotional sanctuary: a little corner of utopia..." (quoting review of new DR Koncerthuset); "...shimmeringly beautiful..." (trail for "In Tune")	Rob Cowan, 9 a.m.–12 p.m. John Toal, 1 p.m.–2 p.m. Verity Sharp, 2 p.m.–3.30 p.m.
			"...incandescent beauty..." (Caldara, Sinfonia in C major, 1st movt)	Sean Rafferty, 4.30 p.m.–7.30 p.m.

(*Continued*)

Appendix 1 (Continued)

Terms	BBC Radio 3	Classic FM	Context	Programme
Benchmark	1		"... new [performance] benchmark ..." (Javier Perianes interview)	Sean Rafferty, 4.30 p.m.–7.30 p.m.
Best		9	"... the best classical music ..."; "... the very best ..."; "... the best ..."	Website
			Trail for upcoming music	Tim Lihoreau, 6 a.m.–9 a.m.
			Mozart, Overture to *Don Giovanni*	John Suchet, 9 a.m.–1 p.m.
			"... nothing but the very best classical music ..."	Anne-Marie Minhall, 1 p.m.–5 p.m.
			Trad., 'Men of Harlech'; Brahms, Symphony No. 3 (complete)	Jane Jones, 8 p.m.–10 p.m.
			"Best Of" John Barry (plugging concert)	Margherita Taylor, 10 p.m.–1 a.m.
Beyond reality (as in otherworldly)	1		"... best ever sounds ..." (retweet)	Twitter
	2		"... beyond reality ..." (interview with Gerald Scarfe)	Rob Cowan, 9 a.m.–12 p.m.
			On Beethoven "transport[ing] the [string quartet] to another planet."	Donald Macleod, 12 p.m.–1 p.m.
Big/biggest		5	"... big music today ..."; Copland, *Fanfare for the Common Man*	Tim Lihoreau, 6 a.m.–9 a.m.
			"... biggest survey of classical music in the world"; Tchaikovsky	John Suchet, 9 a.m.–1 p.m.
			"... big piece ..." (E. Bernstein)	John Brunning, 5 p.m.–8 p.m.
Bleak	1		Mussorgsky, *Songs and Dances of Death*	Verity Sharp, 2 p.m.–3.30 p.m.
Blissful		8	"... blissfully soothing music ..."; Jenkins, 'Laudamus te'; Gloria (quoting listener); Tchaikovsky, Nocturne; Schubert, 'Auf dem Wasser'; Delius, *On Hearing the First Cuckoo in Spring*; Parsons, *Ave Maria*; Albinoni, *Adagio* (Giazotto not mentioned); Svendsen, Symphony No. 1 (2nd movt)	Margherita Taylor, 10 p.m.–1 a.m.

Term		Description	Presenter/Time
Blustery	1	Mendelssohn, *Fingal's Cave*	John Suchet, 9 a.m.–1 p.m.
Boffins	1	Re. "Hall of Fame"	Sam Pittis, 1 a.m.–6 a.m.
Boost	2	"… give you a boost on the first day of Lent."; "… [music to] give you a boost …" (Handel, 'Largo', *Xerxes*)	Sam Pittis, 1 a.m.–6 a.m.
Bouncing	1	"… bouncing along nicely …" (C.P.E. Bach, Cello Concerto)	Sam Pittis, 1 a.m.–6 a.m.
Brace yourself	1	Trailing "Late Junction"	Twitter
Bravo/ congratulations	3	"Bravo to the triangle player." (Albéniz, *Tango*) Congratulating "first full-time female chorister to be appointed in the 1000-year history of St Paul's Cathedral."	Tim Lihoreau, 6 a.m.–9 a.m. Anne-Marie Minhall, 1 p.m.–5 p.m.
Breathless	1	"Congratulations to the conductor …" (Brahms, Symphony No. 3, complete)	Jane Jones, 8 p.m.–10 p.m.
		"… leaves you breathless …" (Beethoven, Symphony No. 3)	John Suchet, 9 a.m.–1 p.m.
Breathtaking	1	2CELLOS	Twitter
Brightest	1	"… brightest … British composing talent …" (Classic FM-run composition competition for U25s)	John Suchet, 9 a.m.–1 p.m.
Brilliant	5	"… brilliant playing …" (Schubert); trail for upcoming music; Holst	Sam Pittis, 1 a.m.–6 a.m.
		Beethoven, Symphony No. 3 (1st movt)	John Suchet, 9 a.m.–1 p.m.
		Rossini, praising musicians	John Brunning, 5 p.m.–8 p.m.
	5	Ginastera, *Danzas Argentinas*; Mozart, *Sonata for Piano Four-Hands*; quiz, quoting listener	Rob Cowan, 9 a.m.–12 p.m.
		Mendelssohn, *Octet*, 4th movt	Sean Rafferty, 4.30 p.m.–7.30 p.m.
		Tippett, *Divertimento on Sellinger's Round*	Tom Redmond, 7.30 p.m.–10 p.m.
Brooding		Beethoven	Sam Pittis, 1 a.m.–6 a.m.
Bucolic	1	Dvořák, Symphony No. 8 (complete)	Verity Sharp, 2 p.m.–3.30 p.m.

(*Continued*)

Appendix 1 (Continued)

Terms	BBC Radio 3	Classic FM	Context	Programme
Burst		3	"... a quick burst . . ." (Charpentier); "... burst of Spanish guitar . . ."	Sam Pittis, 1 a.m.–6 a.m.
	2		"... burst onto the scene . . ." (Enya, 'May It Be', Lord of the Rings)	John Suchet, 9 a.m.–1 p.m.
			"... bursts of energy . . ." (Beethoven, 'Pathétique' Sonata)	John Toal, 1 p.m.–2 p.m.
			"... burst into glorious colour . . ." (Trad., 'Trafeiliais y Byd', perf. 9Bach)	Sean Rafferty, 4.30 p.m.–7.30 p.m.
Calm		3	"... altogether calmer commute . . ." (trail)	John Suchet, 9 a.m.–1 p.m.
			"... the music is going to be calm and relaxed all the way."; "... soundtrack to a calm evening. . .)	John Brunning, 5 p.m.–8 p.m.
	2		G. Williams, *Calm Sea in Summer*; trail for BBC4's "Symphony of Physics"	Petroc Trelawny, 6.30 a.m.–9 a.m.
Canon	1		Skempton, *Moving On*	John Toal, 1 p.m.–2 p.m.
Carefree	1		"... carefree conclusion . . ." (Finzi, Clarinet Concerto)	Tom Redmond, 7.30 p.m.–10 p.m.
Celebratory/ celebrate		6	"Vaguely celebratory, isn't it?" (Elgar, *Pomp and Circumstance*, March No. 4)	Tim Lihoreau, 6 a.m.–9 a.m.
			Trail for afternoon schedule (x 2); James, 'Land of my Fathers'	John Suchet, 9 a.m.–1 p.m.
			Handel, Organ Concerto ('Cuckoo and the Nightingale'); Vaughan Williams, *Wasps Overture*	Anne-Marie Minhall, 1 p.m.–5 p.m.
	6		"... celebrating local music legends . . ." (on BBC Music Day); "... bacchanalian dance of celebration at the end . . ." (Ravel, Suite No. 2, *Daphnis et Chloé*)	Petroc Trelawny, 6.30 a.m.–9 a.m.

Category		Quote	Presenter
		"... worth celebrating ..." (Dvořák, *Carnival Overture*); Gesualdo, *Miserere*; "... celebrate Toscanini's ..." (Glinka, *Jota aragonesa*)	Rob Cowan, 9 a.m.–12 p.m.
		"... proper celebration ... of Welsh music." Trad., 'Trafeiliais y Byd', perf. 9Bach	Sean Rafferty, 4.30 p.m.–7.30 p.m.
Celebrity	1	On Beethoven ("Composer of the Week")	Donald Macleod, 12 p.m.–1 p.m.
Challenging	1	"technically challenging ..." (Beethoven, *Große Fuge*)	John Toal, 1 p.m.–2 p.m.
Championing (incl. references to voting, countdown, listener choice)	16	"Hall of Fame" (Mendelssohn, *Concerto for Two Pianos*); re. "Hall of Fame"; Brahms, Symphony No. 1 (3rd movt); Jenkins, 'Agnus Dei' from *The Armed Man: A Mass for Peace*	Sam Pittis, 1 a.m.–6 a.m.
		"... 2017 countdown ..."; "... it's your choice, so ..."; "... voting is open ..."; "... biggest survey of classical music in the world ..."; "... a composer [J.S. Bach] well-represented in the Top 300 [of Classic FM's "Hall of Fame"]."; "... a composer [Beethoven] with more entries than any other in the Top 300."; Korngold, 'Marietta's Lied'; "You are in charge of the music ..." ("Classic FM Requests")	John Suchet, 9 a.m.–1 p.m.
		"... [Sibelius's] second-highest performer in the "Hall of Fame" ..."; "... [It's] going in the right direction [up the charts]." (Sibelius, *Karelia Suite*, 3rd movt)	Anne-Marie Minhall, 1 p.m.–5 p.m.
		"... hope he's going to do very well in this year's "Hall of Fame" ..." (Elgar)	Margherita Taylor, 10 p.m.–1 a.m.
Chromatic	1	Skempton, *Moving On*	John Toal, 1 p.m.–2 p.m.

(*Continued*)

Terms	BBC Radio 3	Classic FM	Context	Programme
Classic		2	"... favourite classics ..." "What a classic this is." (E. Bernstein)	Twitter John Brunning, 5 p.m.–8 p.m.
Classical		12	"... the UK's favourite classical music station."; "... great classical music ..." (x 3); "... finest classical music on offer ..."	Twitter
			"... the best classical music ..."; "... great classical music [from] the Land of Song [Wales]."	Website
			"... favourite classical music ..." (Boccherini)	Sam Pittis, 1 a.m.–6 a.m.
			"... biggest survey of classical music in the world ..."; "... [2CELLOS] showed [with their arrangement of Michael Jackson's 'Smooth Criminal'] that the cello could do a lot more than classical music." (Enya, 'May It Be' from Lord of the Rings—perf. 2CELLOS, arranger not announced)	John Suchet, 9 a.m.–1 p.m.
			"... nothing but the very best classical music ..." "... three hours of ... relaxing classical music ..." (website)	Margherita Taylor, 10 p.m.–1 a.m.
Clean	1		"... clean sound world ..." (Musician on Vaughan Williams, *Fantasia on a Theme by Thomas Tallis*)	Tom Redmond, 7.30 p.m.–10 p.m.
Colour	2		"... burst into glorious colour ..." (Trad., 'Trafeiliais y Byd'; perf. 9Bach)	Sean Rafferty, 4.30 p.m.–7.30 p.m.
			"... warm romantic colour ..." (Finzi, Clarinet Concerto)	Tom Redmond, 7.30 p.m.–10 p.m.

Keyword	Count	Content	Presenter / Time
Committed		On Owain Arwel Hughes	Jane Jones, 8 p.m.–10 p.m.
Company	1	"... keep you company in the early hours ..."	Twitter
	3	"... keeps you company all through the night ..."	Website
Complex		"... '[Classic FM is my] constant companion.' ..." (quoting listener)	Anne-Marie Minhall, 1 p.m.–5 p.m.
	3	"... remarkably complex soundscape ..." (retweet)	Twitter
		"... complex man ..." (on Beethoven, "Composer of the Week")	Website
		Beethoven, Große Fuge	
Composer's lives or interests		On Boccherini's life and career	John Toal, 1 p.m.–2 p.m.
	4	Plug for presenter's talk on Mozart, the Man Revealed	Tim Lihoreau, 6 a.m.–9 a.m.
		Vaughan Williams a "huge fan of listening to the radio"	John Suchet, 9 a.m.–1 p.m.
		On Dvořák's "big break... [his] benefactor ... and unpublished [works]."	Anne-Marie Minhall, 1 p.m.–5 p.m.
	2	On "teacher-pupil relationship" (Bridge, Spring Song)	Margherita Taylor, 10 p.m.–1 a.m.
			Petroc Trelawny, 6.30 a.m.–9 a.m.
Connoisseurs	1	"Composer of the Week" (Beethoven)	Donald Macleod, 12 p.m.–1 p.m.
Console	1	Quoting Beethoven ("Composer of the Week")	Donald Macleod, 12 p.m.–1 p.m.
Contemporary		"... console yourself ..." (Czerny)	Sam Pittis, 1 a.m.–6 a.m.
	1	"... contemporary forever ..." (Beethoven, Große Fuge, quoting Stravinsky)	John Toal, 1 p.m.–2 p.m.
Contrast		Beethoven, 'Pathétique' Sonata	John Toal, 1 p.m.–2 p.m.
	3	Elgar, In the South (Alassio) (quoting Elgar)	Rob Cowan, 9 a.m.–12 p.m.
		Mussorgsky, Songs and Dances of Death (its contrast with Dvořák)	Verity Sharp, 2 p.m.–3.30 p.m.

(Continued)

Appendix 1 (Continued)

Terms	BBC Radio 3	Classic FM	Context	Programme
Contrite	1		Lotti, *Miserere*	Sean Rafferty, 4.30 p.m.–7.30 p.m.
Controversial	1		On Johnny Cash's Cherokee concept album ("Late Junction")	Twitter
Cornerstone (and implied references to canonic)	3		"... cornerstones of [the] repertoire ..." (Handel, Concerto Grosso in F major); ... [repertoire] dominated by Britten)	Rob Cowan, 9 a.m.–12 p.m.
			"... magnificent summation ..." (Beethoven, "Composer of the Week")	Donald Macleod, 12 p.m.–1 p.m.
Cosmopolitan	1		"... cosmopolitan ancestry ..." (Finzi, Clarinet Concerto)	Tom Redmond, 7.30 p.m.–10 p.m.
Cosy		1	Horner, *Braveheart* (composer not announced)	Sam Pittis, 1 a.m.–6 a.m.
Contrapuntal	1		Tippett, *Divertimento on Sellinger's Round*	Tom Redmond, 7.30 p.m.–10 p.m.
Countryside	1		"... stroll through the Viennese countryside ..." (Beethoven, Symphony No. 6, 3rd–5th movts)	Anne-Marie Minhall, 1 p.m.–5 p.m.
Cracking	1		Ravel, Suite No. 2, *Daphnis et Chloé*	Petroc Trelawny, 6.30 a.m.–9 a.m.
Crying (references to)	3		Brahms, Tragic Overture ("weeps", quoting Brahms)	Petroc Trelawny, 6.30 a.m.–9 a.m.
			"... three-ply moment ..." (9Bach, 'Ifan')	Sean Rafferty, 4.30 p.m.–7.30 p.m.
			"... [leaves me] in tears, really ..." (Performer on Vaughan Williams, *The Lark Ascending*)	Tom Redmond, 7.30 p.m.–10 p.m.
Curated	1		On "Geometry of Now" festival ("Late Junction")	Website
Dance/dancing		3	Lehar, *Gold and Silver Waltz*	Sam Pittis, 1 a.m.–6 a.m.
			"... [makes you want to] do a pirouette ..." (Tchaikovsky, 'Waltz of the Flowers' from *The Nutcracker Suite*)	Anne-Marie Minhall, 1 p.m.–5 p.m.
			"... to dance ... Push back the furniture, eh?" (Monti, *Csárdás*)	John Brunning, 5 p.m.–8 p.m.
	4		"... bacchanalian dance ..." (Ravel, Suite No. 2, *Daphnis et Chloé*)	Petroc Trelawny, 6.30 a.m.–9 a.m.

Dazzling	1	Ginastera, *Danzas Argentinas* (x 2) "... joyously dancing ..." (Beethoven, "Composer of the Week")	Rob Cowan, 9 a.m.–12 p.m. Donald Macleod, 12 p.m.–1 p.m.
Dedicate/ dedication	10	Pierné, *Scherzo-Caprice* Dedicating music to listener; Puccini, *La bohème*; Mozart, 'Gran Partita' Serenade; Handel, 'Largo' from *Xerxes* Rota, 'Love Theme' from *Romeo and Juliet* Borodin, String Quartet No. 1 (3rd movt) Tchaikovsky, 'Waltz of the Flowers' from *The Nutcracker Suite*; Zimmer, Theme from *Pirates of the Caribbean*; Verdi, Prelude to Act I of *La Traviata*	Sean Rafferty, 4.30 p.m.–7.30 p.m. Sam Pittis, 1 a.m.–6 a.m. Tim Lihoreau, 6 a.m.–9 a.m. John Suchet, 9 a.m.–1 p.m. Anne-Marie Minhall, 1 p.m.–5 p.m.
Deep	1	"... inspired by great women ..." (Nino Rota viz. International Women's Day) "... deep listening ..." (quoting Oliveros—trail for "The Listening Service")	Margherita Taylor, 10 p.m.–1 a.m. Rob Cowan, 9 a.m.–12 p.m.
Delicate	1	Delius, *Summer Night on the River*	Jane Jones, 8 p.m.–10 p.m.
Delicious	2	"... deliciously relaxing music ..." (trail) Delius, *On Hearing the First Cuckoo in Spring* "... deliciously unhinged ..." (Dennehy, *Junk Box Fraud*)	John Brunning, 5 p.m.–8 p.m. Margherita Taylor, 10 p.m.–1 a.m. Max Reinhardt, 11 p.m.–12.30am
Delight/delightful	2	Handel, 'Ombra mai fu' Trad., 'Men of Harlech'	Margherita Taylor, 10 p.m.–1 a.m. Jane Jones, 8 p.m.–10 p.m.
Deserve/deserving	1	"Early Toast"	Tim Lihoreau, 6 a.m.–9 a.m.
Develop[ment]	1	Beethoven, 'Pathétique' Sonata	John Toal, 1 p.m.–2 p.m.
Devour	1	Retweet	Twitter
Dialogue (musical)	1	Handel, Concerto Grosso in F major	Rob Cowan, 9 a.m.–12 p.m.

(Continued)

Appendix 1 (Continued)

Terms	BBC Radio 3	Classic FM	Context	Programme
Different		2	"Different, isn't it?" (Brahms, 'How lovely are thy dwellings' from *A German Requiem*, perf. Accentus—arranger not announced); "... something very different [coming up] ..."	Anne-Marie Minhall, 1 p.m.–5 p.m.
	1		"... very different ..." (Liszt, *Die Lorelei*)	Rob Cowan, 9 a.m.–12 p.m.
Difficult		1	"... music [that was] difficult to follow ..." (On page-turning for a Wigmore Hall recital)	John Suchet, 9 a.m.–1 p.m.
	3		"... devil of a fugue ..." (Elgar, *Introduction and Allegro*); Finzi, Clarinet Concerto; "... difficult to listen to [originally] ..." (Vaughan Williams, *Fantasia on a Theme by Thomas Tallis*)	Tom Redmond, 7.30 p.m.–10 p.m.
Direct	1		On "directness" of Beethoven's music ("Composer of the Week")	Donald Macleod, 12 p.m.–1 p.m.
Discover/ discovery		2	"New discoveries ..."	Twitter
			"... rediscovering and rearranging from musicals ..." (on John Wilson)	John Suchet, 9 a.m.–1 p.m.
	1		"Find out ..." (trail for "The Listening Service")	Rob Cowan, 9 a.m.–12 p.m.
Disorderly	1		On Beethoven's circumstances and personality ("Composer of the Week")	Donald Macleod, 12 p.m.–1 p.m.
Dissection	1		On texture and structure of Tippett, *Divertimento on Sellinger's Round*	Tom Redmond, 7.30 p.m.–10 p.m.
Distinctive	1		"... instantly recognisable, distinctive music of Karl Jenkins." (*Over the Stone*)	Jane Jones, 8 p.m.–10 p.m.
Distinguished	1		On composers (interview with Gerald Scarfe)	Website
Dramatic/drama		2	"... [something] dramatic [coming up] ..."; "You just know there's going to be drama." (Mozart, Overture to *Don Giovanni*)	John Suchet, 9 a.m.–1 p.m.

	2	"…real drama…"; "…least visually dramatic [opera]…" (both Handel, *Tamerlano*, complete)	Catriona Young, 12.30 a.m.–6.30am
Dreamy	1	Beethoven, 'Pathétique' Sonata	John Toal, 1 p.m.–2 p.m.
Driven	1	Trad., 'Breuddwyd y Bardd', perf. 9Bach	Sean Rafferty, 4.30 p.m.–7.30 p.m.
		Beethoven, Symphony No. 3 (1st movt)	John Suchet, 9 a.m.–1 p.m.
Easy		"…easier [music] to follow…" (Field, Piano Concerto, 2nd movt)	John Suchet, 9 a.m.–1 p.m.
Eccentric	2	Interview with Gerald Scarfe	Rob Cowan, 9 a.m.–12 p.m.
		On Beethoven's "eccentric" habits ("Composer of the Week")	Donald Macleod, 12 p.m.–1 p.m.
Eclectic	2	Retweet	Twitter
		Trail for upcoming music	
Economy (musical)	1	On the "economy" of Beethoven's music ("Composer of the Week")	Catriona Young, 12.30 a.m.–6.30am
			Donald Macleod, 12 p.m.–1 p.m.
Emotional	1	"…always so emotional…" (trail for upcoming music)	John Suchet, 9 a.m.–1 p.m.
		Monteverdi, *Madrigali Guerrieri et amoroso*	Rob Cowan, 9 a.m.–12 p.m.
	2	"…a beautiful resilient emotional sanctuary: a little corner of utopia…" (quoting review of new DR Koncerthuset)	Verity Sharp, 2 p.m.–3.30 p.m.
Enchanting	1	Vaughan Williams, *The Lark Ascending*	Tom Redmond, 7.30 p.m.–10 p.m.
Energy (and synonyms)	4	"…the music…to get you going…"	Website
		"…an 11 a.m. pick-me-up…"	Twitter
		"…invigorating…" (Handel, Concerto Grosso in F major)	Rob Cowan, 9 a.m.–12 p.m.
		"…full of rude energy…" (on Beethoven, seemingly quoting John Russell, c.1821)	Donald Macleod, 12 p.m.–1 p.m.
		"…bursts of energy…" (Beethoven, 'Pathétique' Sonata)	John Toal, 1 p.m.–2 p.m.
Engaging	1	S.C. Dussek, Sonata in C minor	Rob Cowan, 9 a.m.–12 p.m.

(Continued)

Terms	BBC Radio 3	Classic FM	Context	Programme
Enigmatic	1		Beethoven, Große Fuge	John Toal, 1 p.m.–2 p.m.
Enjoyment/ enjoying		4	Trail for upcoming music	Sam Pittis, 1 a.m.–6 a.m.
			Tchaikovsky, 'Miniature Overture' from *The Nutcracker Suite*	John Suchet, 9 a.m.–1 p.m.
			Dubra, *Ave Maria 1* (quoting listener); Parsons, *Ave Maria*	Margherita Taylor, 10 p.m.–1 a.m.
	2		Dvořák, Symphony No. 8 (complete)	Verity Sharp, 2 p.m.–3.30 p.m.
			On Ryoko Akama/Boris Shershenkov collab. for Moscow's "Geometry of Now" festival	Max Reinhardt, 11 p.m.–12.30am
Enlighten	1		"...please enlighten ..." (Mendelssohn, *Frühlingslied*)	Sean Rafferty, 4.30 p.m.–7.30 p.m.
Entertain/ entertainment	2		"...music to intrigue, surprise and entertain."	Twitter
			"entertainments" (G.B. Sammartini, Concerto in F major)	Petroc Trelawny, 6.30 a.m.–9 a.m.
Enthusiasm		1	On Owain Arwel Hughes	Jane Jones, 8 p.m.–10 p.m.
Enticing		1	Telemann, Flute Sonata in G major	Catriona Young, 12.30 a.m.–6.30am
Escape		1	"...to escape with 'Smooth Classics'..."	John Brunning, 5 p.m.–8 p.m.
Evocative		3	"...here to evoke the spirit of the night." (Chopin, Nocturne in D flat major)	John Brunning, 5 p.m.–8 p.m.
			Smetana, 'Vltava' arr. for harp (arr. unannounced); Delius, *Summer Night on the River*	Jane Jones, 8 p.m.–10 p.m.
Excellent	1		Mussorgsky, *Songs and Dances of Death*	Verity Sharp, 2 p.m.–3.30 p.m.
			"...excellent new recording..." (Mozart)	John Brunning, 5 p.m.–8 p.m.
Exceptional	2	1	On Beethoven ("Composer of the Week")	Donald Macleod, 12 p.m.–1 p.m.
			"...promises to be exceptional ..." (Debussy, 'La cathédrale engloutie', *Préludes*)	Sean Rafferty, 4.30 p.m.–7.30 p.m.

Word	No.	Example	Presenter, time
Exciting	1	"… exciting new …"	Twitter
	2	Beethoven, 'Pathétique' Sonata (on pianist)	John Toal, 1 p.m.–2 p.m.
		"… exciting new generation of female composers …" (interviewing Vanessa Reed and Odaline de la Martinez)	Sean Rafferty, 4.30 p.m.–7.30 p.m.
Exhilarating	2	"… heart is racing …" (retweet)	Twitter
		Dvořák, Symphony No. 8 (complete)	Verity Sharp, 2 p.m.–3.30 p.m.
Experimental	1	"… experimental performance …" (Moscow's "Geometry of Now" festival)	Max Reinhardt, 11 p.m.–12.30am
Expert	1	"… expert German violin concerto …" (Beethoven)	Sam Pittis, 1 a.m.–6 a.m.
Expressive	1	Tchaikovsky, Pezzo capriccioso	Rob Cowan, 9 a.m.–12 p.m.
Exquisite	2	Mozart, Sonata for Piano Four-Hands	Rob Cowan, 9 a.m.–12 p.m.
		Korngold, 'Marietta's Lied'	John Suchet, 9 a.m.–1 p.m.
Exploratory	1	On John Barry-themed concerto	Margherita Taylor, 10 p.m.–1 a.m.
		Trail for upcoming music	Max Reinhardt, 11 p.m.–12.30am
Extraordinary	2	Trail for upcoming music	John Brunning, 5 p.m.–8 p.m.
		"… extraordinary playing … extraordinarily vibrant …" (Tippett, Divertimento on Sellinger's Round)	Tom Redmond, 7.30 p.m.–10 p.m.
Extravagant	1	"… extravagance of English riches …" (Vaughan Williams, The Lark Ascending)	Tom Redmond, 7.30 p.m.–10 p.m.
Fabulous	9	"… fabulous finale …" (Beethoven, Violin Concerto); trail for upcoming music	Sam Pittis, 1 a.m.–6 a.m.
		Respighi, The Birds ('Prelude'—Pasquini not credited); Bruch, Violin Concerto (finale); trail for upcoming music	Tim Lihoreau, 6 a.m.–9 a.m.
		"… fabulously named …" (Vaughan Williams, Wasps Overture)	Anne-Marie Minhall, 1 p.m.–5 p.m.
		Bernstein, 'Waltz', Divertimento; on new tearooms at Elgar's birthplace	Margherita Taylor, 10 p.m.–1 a.m.

(Continued)

Terms	BBC Radio 3	Classic FM	Context	Programme
Famous	2	3	"... one of his most famous pieces ..." (Bruch); "... one of the most famous pieces of all time." (trail for upcoming music) Elmer Bernstein "... more famous than J.S. [Bach] ..." (C.P.E. Bach, Trio in A minor) "... [one of Wales'] most famous musical sons." (Mathias)	Sam Pittis, 1 a.m.–6 a.m. John Brunning, 5 p.m.–8 p.m. John Toal, 1 p.m.–2 p.m. Petroc Trelawny, 6.30 a.m.–9 a.m.
Fan		1	Vaughan Williams a "huge fan of listening to the radio."	Anne-Marie Minhall, 1 p.m.–5 p.m.
Fantastic		2	Trail for upcoming music; "... fantastic, fantastic ..." (Boccherini)	Sam Pittis, 1 a.m.–6 a.m.
Favourite/ favourites		14	"... the UK's favourite classical music station."; "... favourite relaxing music ..."; "... favourite classics ..." "... Wales's favourite living composer ..." (Jenkins); "... favourite classical music ..." (Boccherini) Advert for "Hall of Fame Hour" "... your guaranteed favourite ..." "... favourite instrument [cello] ..."; "... a favourite of our very own SPs ..." (Mussorgsky, 'The Great Gate of Kiev'); "... wedding favourite ..." (Stanley, Trumpet Voluntary); "... one of J.K. Rowling's favourite pieces of music ..." (Tchaikovsky, Violin Concerto, finale)	Twitter Sam Pittis, 1 a.m.–6 a.m. Tim Lihoreau, 6 a.m.–9 a.m. John Suchet, 9 a.m.–1 p.m. Anne-Marie Minhall, 1 p.m.–5 p.m.

Term	No.	Description	Presenter / Time
		"... [presenter's] favourite French composer [unspecified—Fauré and Bizet heard after break] ..."	John Brunning, 5 p.m.–8 p.m.
	3	German, *Welsh Rhapsody*	Jane Jones, 8 p.m.–10 p.m.
		"... my favourite composer." (Elgar)	Margherita Taylor, 10 p.m.–1 a.m.
		On composers (Gerald Scarfe interview)	Website
		"... favourite work [of presenter's] ..." (Handel, Concerto Grosso in F major); quiz; quoting listener	Rob Cowan, 9 a.m.–12 a.m.
Filigree	1	Tippett, *Divertimento on Sellinger's Round*	Tom Redmond, 7.30 p.m.–10 p.m.
Film/cinematic	4	Silvestri, *Back to the Future*	Sam Pittis, 1 a.m.–6 a.m.
		"... founder of film music ..." (Korngold)	John Suchet, 9 a.m.–1 p.m.
		"... movie man himself ..." (J. Williams)	Anne-Marie Minhall, 1 p.m.–5 p.m.
		Richard Harvey, 'Cantilena', *Concerto Antico*	Margherita Taylor, 10 p.m.–1 a.m.
	2	Quiz on "Which film or TV show used this classical piece?" ("Essential Classics")	Twitter
		"... joyous cinematic celebration ..." (Beto Villares, 'Quincas')	Max Reinhardt, 11 p.m.–12.30am
Fine/finest	5	"... finest classical music on offer ..."	Twitter
		Handel, 'Air' from *Water Music*; "... fine start ..." (Sibelius, *Karelia Suite*, 3rd movt)	Anne-Marie Minhall, 1 p.m.–5 p.m.
		Rossini	John Brunning, 5 p.m.–8 p.m.
		Smetana, 'Vltava' (arranger for harp not announced)	Jane Jones, 8 p.m.–10 p.m.
	5	On amateur orchestras; "fine performer" (Joplin, *Solace*); G.B. Sammartini, Concerto in F major	Petroc Trelawny, 6.30 a.m.–9 a.m.
Flavour	1	Stravinsky, *Ebony Concerto*; Liszt, *Die Lorelei*	Rob Cowan, 9 a.m.–12 p.m.
		"... Italian flavour ..." (Elgar, *In the South (Alassio)*)	Rob Cowan, 9 a.m.–12 p.m.

(Continued)

Terms	BBC Radio 3	Classic FM	Context	Programme
Flowery		1	Tchaikovsky, 'Waltz of the Flowers', *The Nutcracker Suite*	Anne-Marie Minhall, 1 p.m.–5 p.m.
Fluidity	1		"…natural fluidity [of the clarinet] …" (Finzi, Clarinet Concerto)	Tom Redmond, 7.30 p.m.–10 p.m.
Folk	3	2	Canteloube; Holst / Mussorgsky, *Songs and Dances of Death* / 9Bach's "Celtic" sound / Baluji Shrivastav, 'Dhun Bhairvi'	Sam Pittis, 1 a.m.–6 a.m. / Verity Sharp, 2 p.m.–3.30 p.m. / Sean Rafferty, 4.30 p.m.–7.30 p.m. / Max Reinhardt, 11 p.m.–12.30am
Forget	1		"… forget the ups and downs of the working day …"	John Brunning, 5 p.m.–8 p.m.
Freedom	1		Monteverdi, *Madrigali Guerrieri et amoroso*	Rob Cowan, 9 a.m.–12 p.m.
Fresh	1		Davis, *Frontiers* (1st movt)	John Suchet, 9 a.m.–1 p.m.
Founder		1	"… founder of film music …" (Korngold)	John Suchet, 9 a.m.–1 p.m.
Frolicsome	1		Moeran, 'Spring, the sweet Spring', *Songs of Springtime*	Sean Rafferty, 4.30 p.m.–7.30 p.m.
Furious	1		"…wild and furious dance …" (Ginastera, *Danzas Argentinas*)	Rob Cowan, 9 a.m.–12 p.m.
Future/futuristic		2	Silvestri, *Back to the Future* / "…looking to the future, as we have always done …" (U25 composition competition) / "…futuristic …" (Sviridov, *Miniature Triptych*)	Sam Pittis, 1 a.m.–6 a.m. / Anne-Marie Minhall, 1 p.m.–5 p.m.
Gem/jewel	1	4	"…giant gem …" (Schubert, Symphony No. 1, 1st movt); "… [coming up] a jewel, a gem, from the violin repertoire …" (Mendelssohn) / "… little gem …" (Bach, 'Jesu, joy…'); Spohr, Symphony No. 6 / "…archive gem …"	Verity Sharp, 2 p.m.–3.30 p.m. / Anne-Marie Minhall, 1 p.m.–5 p.m. / Margherita Taylor, 10 p.m.–1 a.m.
	2			Twitter

		"... youthful gem ... " (Mendelssohn, *Octet*, 4th movt)	Sean Rafferty, 4.30 p.m.–7.30 p.m.
Genius	1	On Beethoven ("Composer of the Week")	Donald Macleod, 12 p.m.–1 p.m.
Gentle	2	"... [the music has a] gentleness ... " (Brahms, 'How lovely are thy dwellings')	John Suchet, 9 a.m.–1 p.m.
		Tchaikovsky, *Nocturne*	Margherita Taylor, 10 p.m.–1 a.m.
		Kreisler, *Berceuse romantique*	Catriona Young, 12.30 a.m.–6.30am
Giant	1	"... giant gem ... " (Schubert, Symphony No. 1, 1st movt)	Anne-Marie Minhall, 1 p.m.–5 p.m.
Glorious	3	"... glorious sound of the cello ... "; Enya, 'May It Be', *Lord of the Rings*	John Suchet, 9 a.m.–1 p.m.
		Vaughan Williams, *Fantasia on a Theme of Thomas Tallis*	John Brunning, 5 p.m.–8 p.m.
Retweet	3		Twitter
		Dvořák, Symphony No. 8 (complete)	Verity Sharp, 2 p.m.–3.30 p.m.
		"... burst into glorious colour ... " (Trad., 'Trafeiliais y Byd', perf. 9Bach)	Sean Rafferty, 4.30 p.m.–7.30 p.m.
Going strong (as in enduring)	1	"... still going strong ... " (Vaughan Williams, *Wasps Overture*)	Anne-Marie Minhall, 1 p.m.–5 p.m.
Good/goodies	4	"... doubly good work ... " (Czerny)	Sam Pittis, 1 a.m.–6 a.m.
		J. Williams, Theme from *Superman*; Jenkins, *Palladio*	Tim Lihoreau, 6 a.m.–9 a.m.
		Enya, 'May It Be' from *Lord of the Rings*—perf. 2CELLOS, arranger not announced (quoting Elton John)	John Suchet, 9 a.m.–1 p.m.
		Bach, Cantata 140	Petroc Trelawny, 6.30 a.m.–9 a.m.
Gorgeous	1	"... lots of gorgeous music ... " (trail for day ahead)	Sam Pittis, 1 a.m.–6 a.m.
	4	Enya, 'May It Be' from *Lord of the Rings*—perf. 2CELLOS, arranger not announced	John Suchet, 9 a.m.–1 p.m.
		Bernstein, 'Waltz', *Divertimento*; Albinoni, *Adagio* (Giazotto not mentioned)	Margherita Taylor, 10 p.m.–1 a.m.

(Continued)

Appendix 1 (Continued)

Terms	BBC Radio 3	Classic FM	Context	Programme
Great/greatest/ greatness		24	"... pulling no punches when it comes to great music."; "... great classical music [from] the Land of Song [Wales]."; "... world's greatest music ..."	Website
			"... great classical music ..." (x 3); "... morning of great music ..."	Twitter
			"Great music ..." (Boccherini); "Great guests ..."; "... the great and the good ..."	Sam Pittis, 1 a.m.–6 a.m.
			"... possibly the greatest living composer [from Wales] ..." (Jenkins)	Tim Lihoreau, 6 a.m.–9 a.m.
			Beethoven, Symphony No. 3 (1st movt); Rameau, Dance of the Savages; "... great recording ..." (Elgar, Violin Concerto, finale); Verdi, 'Va, pensiero' from Nabucco	John Suchet, 9 a.m.–1 p.m.
			"... great form ..." (Vengerov performing Mendelssohn); "great choir" (Trad., 'Men of Harlech', quoting listener); Mozart, 'Soave sia il vento' (announced in Eng.), Così fan tutte	Anne-Marie Minhall, 1 p.m.–5 p.m.
			"... the great man's music ..." (Bach, Prelude No. 1); "... great music ..." (Elgar); Beethoven, Symphony No. 8; "... world's greatest music ..."	John Brunning, 5 p.m.–8 p.m.
			"... inspired by great women ..." (Nino Rota viz. International Women's Day); on Daniel Barenboim	Margherita Taylor, 10 p.m.–1 a.m.
	8		Bach, Cantata 140	Petroc Trelawny, 6.30 a.m.–9 a.m.
			Tchaikovsky, Pezzo capriccioso; on conductor (Dvořák, Carnival Overture); Monteverdi, Madrigali Guerrieri et amoroso; "... great technical facility ..." (Mozart, Sonata for Piano Duet in F major)	Rob Cowan, 9 a.m.–12 p.m.

Keyword	Count	Quote	Presenter / Source
		On Beethoven ("Composer of the Week") Beethoven, *Große Fuge* "...[the] gravity of great music..." (Perianes interview)	Donald Macleod, 12 p.m.–1 p.m. / John Toal, 1 p.m.–2 p.m. / Sean Rafferty, 4.30 p.m.–7.30 p.m.
Guarantee	4	"I guarantee you're going to love it [unspecified new release]."; "...piece I guarantee you'll never have heard before..."; "...your guaranteed favourite..."	John Suchet, 9 a.m.–1 p.m.
		"I'll guarantee to keep you relaxed." (Chopin, Nocturne in D flat major)	John Brunning, 5 p.m.–8 p.m.
Guide	1	"Let @SamPittis guide you..."	Twitter
Happiness (and synonyms)	3	"...wake up with a smile." (Marcello, Oboe Concerto)	Tim Lihoreau, 6 a.m.–9 a.m.
		"Here's a piece you might want to have a bit of a giggle to." (Nevin, 'Narcissus' from *Water Scenes*)	John Suchet, 9 a.m.–1 p.m.
		"happily relaxing" (Parsons, Ave Maria, quoting listener)	Margherita Taylor, 10 p.m.–1 a.m.
	3	Brahms, *Tragic Overture* (quoting Brahms)	Petroc Trelawny, 6.30 a.m.–9 a.m.
		On audience's "smiles" (Elgar, *Introduction and Allegro*); "...so many smiles on stage..." (Finzi, Clarinet Concerto)	Tom Redmond, 7.30 p.m.–10 p.m.
Harbinger	1	"...a harbinger of things to come..." (Beethoven, "Composer of the Week")	Donald Macleod, 12 p.m.–1 p.m.
Heartfelt	3	On Beethoven ("Composer of the Week")	Website
		On Beethoven ("Composer of the Week")	Donald Macleod, 12 p.m.–1 p.m.
		"...soul music...[sung] from the heart..." (9Bach, 'Ifan')	Sean Rafferty, 4.30 p.m.–7.30 p.m.

(Continued)

Appendix 1 (Continued)

Terms	BBC Radio 3	Classic FM	Context	Programme
Heavenly/celestial	2	2	"... heavenly portrait ..." (Holst); Quoting Schumann on Schubert; Trail for upcoming music (O'Regan); Smyth, *Overture to The Boatswain's Mate*	Sam Pittis, 1 a.m.–6 a.m.; Anne-Marie Minhall, 1 p.m.–5 p.m.; Sean Rafferty, 4.30 p.m.–7.30 p.m.
Heavy	1		"... heavy bass ..." (Trad, 'Breuddwyd y Bardd', perf. 9Bach)	John Toal, 1 p.m.–2 p.m.
Helter-skelter	1		Beethoven, 'Pathétique' Sonata	Tom Redmond, 7.30 p.m.–10 p.m.
"High Church"	1		... [the] "High Church" of string writing ... (Vaughan Williams, *Fantasia on a Theme by Thomas Tallis*)	
High-octane	1		Mendelssohn, *Octet* (4th movt)	Sean Rafferty, 4.30 p.m.–7.30 p.m.
Highlights		1	Plugging Grange Festival	John Suchet, 9 a.m.–1 p.m.
Hilarious	2		Smyth, Overture to *The Boatswain's Mate* (x 2)	Sean Rafferty, 4.30 p.m.–7.30 p.m.
Homage	2		Mendelssohn, *Frühlingslied*; Couperin, arr. Adès, *Les baricades mistérieuses*	Sean Rafferty, 4.30 p.m.–7.30 p.m.
Hors d'oeuvre		1	Schubert	
Huge	1		Beethoven, *Große Fuge*	John Brunning, 5 p.m.–8 p.m.
Humanistic	1		In context of words elevating music "higher" (Tarik O'Regan, interviewed)	John Toal, 1 p.m.–2 p.m.
Iconic	1		Debussy, 'La cathédrale engloutie', *Préludes*	Sean Rafferty, 4.30 p.m.–7.30 p.m.
Idyllic	1		Vaughan Williams, *The Lark Ascending*	Sean Rafferty, 4.30 p.m.–7.30 p.m.
Imagine/imaginary	3		"... Nielsen's imaginary journey ..." (trail for *Radio 3 In Concert*) (x 2); Trail for "The Listening Service"	Tom Redmond, 7.30 p.m.–10 p.m.; Petroc Trelawny, 6.30 a.m.–9 a.m.; Rob Cowan, 9 a.m.–12 p.m.
Immerse		1	"... music to immerse yourself in ..." (Delius, 'Walk to the Paradise Garden')	John Suchet, 9 a.m.–1 p.m.

Term	Count	Description	Presenter / Time
Important (and synonyms e.g. instrumental to)	4	Beethoven, 'Pathétique' Sonata; On working towards gender equality in the classical music industry; Elgar, *Introduction and Allegro*; Finzi, Clarinet Concerto	John Toal, 1 p.m.–2 p.m.; Sean Rafferty, 4.30 p.m.–7.30 p.m.; Tom Redmond, 7.30 p.m.–10 p.m.
Impressive	1	"... doesn't have to be fast and furious to be impressive." (Enya, 'May It Be', *Lord of the Rings*)	John Suchet, 9 a.m.–1 p.m.
Incandescent	1	"... incandescent beauty . . . " (Caldara, Sinfonia in C major, 1st movt)	Sean Rafferty, 4.30 p.m.–7.30 p.m.
Incredible	1	On DR Koncerthuset's acoustics	Verity Sharp, 2 p.m.–3.30 p.m.
Indulge/ indulgence	2	"... indulge in music . . . " (unidentified Spanish guitar piece); Trail for upcoming music; "... indulgence of English music . . . "	Sam Pittis, 1 a.m.–6 a.m.; Tim Lihoreau, 6 a.m.–9 a.m.; Tom Redmond, 7.30 p.m.–10 p.m.
Infectious	1	Ginastera, *Danzas Argentinas* (x 2)	Rob Cowan, 9 a.m.–12 p.m.
Informed	1	On "Music in Time" feature	Twitter
Influence	2	Mozart, Clarinet Concerto (2nd movt); R. Strauss on Elgar, *In the South* (*Alessio*); Ginastera, *Danzas Argentinas*	John Suchet, 9 a.m.–1 p.m.; Rob Cowan, 9 a.m.–12 p.m.
Innocent	1	Wigglesworth, *The Winter's Tale* (trail for May broadbast, quoting reviewer)	Petroc Trelawny, 6.30 a.m.–9 a.m.
Innovations	1	"... early innovations in opera . . . " (on Monteverdi madrigals viz. opera)	Twitter

(Continued)

Appendix 1 (Continued)

Terms	BBC Radio 3	Classic FM	Context	Programme
Inspired/ inspirational (incl. commissioned)		13	"...music...inspired by the Land of Song [Wales]."	Website
			Jenkins, 'Agnus Dei', *The Armed Man: A Mass for Peace*; Beethoven	Sam Pittis, 1 a.m.–6 a.m.
			"Let the music this morning inspire you...."; Rameau, *Dance of the Savages*; trail for afternoon's schedule	John Suchet, 9 a.m.–1 p.m.
			Beethoven, Symphony No. 6 (3rd–5th movts)	Anne-Marie Minhall, 1 p.m.–5 p.m.
			German, *Welsh Rhapsody*; Trad., 'Men of Harlech'; "...commissioned by Prince Charles." (Jenkins, *Over the Stone*); on Brahms's Third Symphony being composed in a single summer	Jane Jones, 8 p.m.–10 p.m.
			"...inspired by great women..." (Nino Rota viz. International Women's Day); Armstrong, 'Balcony Scene', *Romeo and Juliet*	Margherita Taylor, 10 p.m.–1 a.m.
	5		Schumann, *Novelletten*	Catriona Young, 12.30 a.m.–6.30am
			G. Williams, *Calm Sea in Summer*	Petroc Trelawny, 6.30 a.m.–9 a.m.
			Messiaen, *Les Offrandes oubliées*	Verity Sharp, 2 p.m.–3.30 p.m.
			Perianes on performing Schubert	Sean Rafferty, 4.30 p.m.–7.30 p.m.
			On inspiration behind Tippett, *Divertimento on Sellinger's Round*	Tom Redmond, 7.30 p.m.–10 p.m.
Intellectual	2		Tchaikovsky, *Pezzo capriccioso*; Elgar, *In the South (Alessio)*	Rob Cowan, 9 a.m.–12 p.m.
Intense		1	Enya, 'May It Be' from *Lord of the Rings*—perf. 2CELLOS, arranger not announced	John Suchet, 9 a.m.–1 p.m.
	4		"...compressed intensity...." ("Composer of the Week", on Beethoven's music)	Website
			Elgar, *In the South (Alassio)*	Rob Cowan, 9 a.m.–12 p.m.

Keyword	No.	Description	Presenter, time
International Women's Day		"... compressed intensity . . ." ("Composer of the Week", on Beethoven's music); on Beethoven's rate of composition	Donald Macleod, 12 p.m.–1 p.m.
	1	"... inspired by great women . . ." (Nino Rota viz. International Women's Day	Margherita Taylor, 10 p.m.–1 a.m.
	3	Noting International Women's Day	Rob Cowan, 9 a.m.–12 p.m.
		On PRS's "Women Make Music" scheme (discussion with Vanessa Reed)	Sean Rafferty, 4.30 p.m.–7.30 p.m.
		Noting International Women's Day	James Jolly, 10 p.m.–11 p.m.
Interwoven	1	On "interwoven" texture of Tippett, Divertimento on Sellinger's Round	Tom Redmond, 7.30 p.m.–10 p.m.
Intriguing	2	"... music to intrigue, surprise and entertain."	Twitter
Intuitive	1	Skempton, Moving On	John Toal, 1 p.m.–2 p.m.
Inventive/ invented	3	Skempton, Moving On (quoting listener)	John Toal, 1 p.m.–2 p.m.
		Wigglesworth, The Winter's Tale (trail for May broadbast, quoting reviewer)	Petroc Trelawny, 6.30 a.m.–9 a.m.
		Couperin, arr. Adès, Les baricades mistérieuses	Sean Rafferty, 4.30 p.m.–7.30 p.m.
		"... invented instrument . . ." (Dessner, Music for Wood and Strings)	Max Reinhardt, 11 p.m.–12.30am
Investigation (musical)	1	On "Geometry of Now" festival ("Late Junction")	Website
Join in	1	"Be ready to join in . . ." (Trad., 'Men of Harlech')	Jane Jones, 8 p.m.–10 p.m.
Joy	1	J. Williams, Theme from Chariots of Fire	Anne-Marie Minhall, 1 p.m.–5 p.m.
	2	"... always a joy to hear . . ." (Holst, St Paul's Suite)	Rob Cowan, 9 a.m.–12 p.m.
		"... joyously dancing . . ." (Beethoven, "Composer of the Week")	Donald Macleod, 12 p.m.–1 p.m.
Kitchen sink	1	A piece that has everything, including the "kitchen sink" (Smyth, Overture to The Boatswain's Mate)	Sean Rafferty, 4.30 p.m.–7.30 p.m.

(Continued)

Terms	BBC Radio 3	Classic FM	Context	Programme
Knowledge		1	"... tunes we all know ..." (Rodgers, arr. Wilson, *Sound of Music*)	John Suchet, 9 a.m.–1 p.m.
Lament	3		Monteverdi, *Madrigali Guerrieri et amoroso* On Beethoven ("Composer of the Week") Violinist on Tippett, *Divertimento on Sellinger's Round*	Rob Cowan, 9 a.m.–12 p.m. Donald Macleod, 12 p.m.–1 p.m. Tom Redmond, 7.30 p.m.–10 p.m.
Languid		1	"... languid trumpet ..." (Gershwin, *Piano Concerto*)	John Suchet, 9 a.m.–1 p.m.
Leading		2	Dukas Owain Arwel Hughes a "leading Welsh conductor"	John Brunning, 5 p.m.–8 p.m. Jane Jones, 8 p.m.–10 p.m.
	2		"... leading composers ..." "... leading composer ..." (Tippett, *Divertimento on Sellinger's Round*)	Rob Cowan, 9 a.m.–12 p.m. Tom Redmond, 7.30 p.m.–10 p.m.
Legend/legendary	1	1	Jenkins, *Palladio* "... celebrating local music legends ..." (on BBC Music Day)	Tim Lihoreau, 6 a.m.–9 a.m. Petroc Trelawny, 6.30 a.m.–9 a.m.
Less well-known (as in obscure)	1		"... less well-known ..." (Sviridov, *Miniature Triptych*)	Verity Sharp, 2 p.m.–3.30 p.m.
Life-affirming	1		Dvořák, Symphony No. 8 (complete)	Verity Sharp, 2 p.m.–3.30 p.m.
Listen/listening	2		"... listen inwardly ..."; "... deep listening ..." (quoting Oliveros—both trail for "The Listening Service")	Rob Cowan, 9 a.m.–12 p.m.
Longing	1		Trad., 'Trafeiliais y Byd', perf. 9Bach	Sean Rafferty, 4.30 p.m.–7.30 p.m.

Term	n	Examples	Presenter and time
Lovely/love	18	Schubert; "... lovely playing ..." (Hubay, *Violin Concerto*, number not specified); "Just lovely." (Puccini, *La bohème*); Einaudi	Sam Pittis, 1 a.m.–6 a.m.
		"... rather lovely ..." ("Early Toast"); "... lovely arrangement ..." (Handel, 'Lascia ch'io pianga', *Rinaldo*); "Lovely to have you here."; "... lovely music for you all ..."; "... lovely arrangement ..." (Dvořák, 'New World' Symphony, arranged not announced); Da Falla, from *La vida breve*; "... [he] loved a sonata ..." (Soler, Sonata No. 84)	Tim Lihoreau, 6 a.m.–9 a.m.
		Brahms, 'How lovely are thy dwellings'; "I guarantee you're going to love it [unspecified new release]."; Debussy, *Clair de lune*; "... lovely combination [of guitar and violin] ..." (Granados, *Andaluza*); Delius, 'Walk to the Paradise Garden'; Verdi, 'Va, pensiero', *Nabucco*	John Suchet, 9 a.m.–1 p.m.
	4	"... really love ..." (Handel, quoting listener) Armstrong, 'Balcony Scene', *Romeo and Juliet*	Anne-Marie Minhall, 1 p.m.–5 p.m.
		"... loveliest arias ..." (looking ahead to "Composer of the Week")	Margherita Taylor, 10 p.m.–1 a.m.
			Rob Cowan, 9 a.m.–12 p.m.
		"... love of romanticism ..." (Sviridov, *Miniature Triptych*)	Verity Sharp, 2 p.m.–3.30 p.m.
		Welsh as a "lovely language" (9Bach, 'Ifan'); Dessner, *Music for Wood and Strings*	Sean Rafferty, 4.30 p.m.–7.30 p.m.
		On composers (interview with Gerald Scarfe)	Max Reinhardt, 11 p.m.–12.30am
			Website
Luminaries	1	Schubert, Piano Sonata, 2nd movt	Sean Rafferty, 4.30 p.m.–7.30 p.m.
Luminous	1	Beethoven, 'Pathétique' Sonata	John Toal, 1 p.m.–2 p.m.
Lyrical	1	Finzi: Clarinet Concerto	Tom Redmond, 7.30 p.m.–10 p.m.

(*Continued*)

Terms	BBC Radio 3	Classic FM	Context	Programme
Mad/madcap	3		"..."Was he mad?" ..." (Beethoven, "Composer of the Week")	Donald Macleod, 12 p.m.–1 p.m.
			"...madcap..." (Rossini, Overture to *La cambiale di matrimonio*)	Verity Sharp, 2 p.m.–3.30 p.m.
			"...queer mad fellow from Chelsea..." (quote on Vaughan Williams)	Tom Redmond, 7.30 p.m.–10 p.m.
Magic/magical	3		Trail for upcoming music; "...capturing magic..."; on Schubert (both interviewing Javier Perianes)	Sean Rafferty, 4.30 p.m.–7.30 p.m.
Magnificent	3		Retweet	Twitter
			"...magnificent summation..." (Beethoven, "Composer of the Week")	Donald Macleod, 12 p.m.–1 p.m.
			On Perianes's performance (Schubert, Piano Sonata, 2nd movt)	Sean Rafferty, 4.30 p.m.–7.30 p.m.
Mania	1		On Beethoven ("Composer of the Week")	Donald Macleod, 12 p.m.–1 p.m.
				Twitter
Masterpiece/masterly		3	"...masterpiece..." (Schubert)	John Brunning, 5 p.m.–8 p.m.
			"...masterly performance..." (Schubert)	Margherita Taylor, 10 p.m.–1 a.m.
			Parsons, Ave Maria	Margherita Taylor, 10 p.m.–1 a.m.
Meaning (musical)		1	On the meaning of Chopin's nocturnes, quoting Daniel Barenboim	Rob Cowan, 9 a.m.–12 p.m.
Meditation/meditative	2		"...sonic meditation..." (trail for "The Listening Service")	Sean Rafferty, 4.30 p.m.–7.30 p.m.
			O'Regan, *Three Motets from Sequence for St Wulfstan*	
Mellifluous	1		"...wonderfully mellifluous..." (9Bach)	Sean Rafferty, 4.30 p.m.–7.30 p.m.
Mellow		1	"...most mellow of instruments [cello]..."	John Suchet, 9 a.m.–1 p.m.
Melodious	1		Schubert, Piano Sonata (2nd movt)	Sean Rafferty, 4.30 p.m.–7.30 p.m.
Metaphysical	1		Javier Perianes on Schubert (interview)	Sean Rafferty, 4.30 p.m.–7.30 p.m.

Term		Description	Presenter/time
Misattributed	1	S.C. Dussek, Sonata in C minor	Rob Cowan, 9 a.m.–12 p.m.
Modern city (as in urban)	1	"... sonic incarnation of a modern city ..." (Dennehy, 'Junk Box Fraud')	Max Reinhardt, 11 p.m.–12.30am
Monumental	1	Schubert, Piano Sonata (2nd movt)	Sean Rafferty, 4.30 p.m.–7.30 p.m.
Mood/moody		Enya, 'May It Be', *Lord of the Rings*	John Suchet, 9 a.m.–1 p.m.
Moving	1	"... so moved by its performance ..." (Performer on Vaughan Williams, *The Lark Ascending*)	Tom Redmond, 7.30 p.m.–10 p.m.
Must-listen	1	"... must-must-listen (sic) ..." (Phamie Gow, 'London')	Anne-Marie Minhall, 1 p.m.–5 p.m.
Multi-disciplinary	2	On Moscow's "Geometry of Now" festival; "cross-platform documenter" (Jenny Berger Myhre, 'Speak Softly')	Max Reinhardt, 11 p.m.–12.30am
Mystical	1	"... mystical experience ..." (O'Regan (interview), *Three Motets from Sequence for St Wulfstan*)	Sean Rafferty, 4.30 p.m.–7.30 p.m.
Nice	6	"Nice, that, wasn't it?" (Spohr, *Clarinet Concerto*); "Nice, that, isn't it?" (*War Song*); "... bouncing along nicely ..." (C.P.E. Bach, Cello Concerto)	Sam Pittis, 1 a.m.–6 a.m.
		"... nice world-exclusive ..."; Cimarosa, Oboe Concerto (final movt)—arranger unannounced	John Suchet, 9 a.m.–1 p.m.
	3	On Scriabin	John Brunning, 5 p.m.–8 p.m.
		On Stravinsky (interviewing Gerald Scarfe)	Rob Cowan, 9 a.m.–12 p.m.
		Debussy, 'La cathédrale engloutie', *Préludes*; 9Bach, 'Ifan'	Sean Rafferty, 4.30 p.m.–7.30 p.m.
Nifty	1	"... nifty bit of rhythm-changing ..." (Skempton, *Moving On*)	John Toal, 1 p.m.–2 p.m.
Nightmare	1	"... on-stage nightmare ..." (On page-turning for a Wigmore Hall recital)	John Suchet, 9 a.m.–1 p.m.

(Continued)

Appendix 1 (Continued)

Terms	BBC Radio 3	Classic FM	Context	Programme
No-nonsense	1		Beethoven's music's "no-nonsense approach… without polite preamble… [getting] straight to the nitty-gritty."	Donald Macleod, 12 p.m.–1 p.m.
Nostalgic/nostalgia		1	"… romantic nostalgia …" Trad., 'Trafeiliais y Byd', perf. 9Bach	John Suchet, 9 a.m.–1 p.m. Sean Rafferty, 4.30 p.m.–7.30 p.m.
Obsessive	1		"… obsessive urge …" (on Beethoven, "Composer of the Week")	Donald Macleod, 12 p.m.–1 p.m.
Old-fashioned	1		"… old-fashioned atonality …" (Wigglesworth, *The Winter's Tale*—trail for May broadcast, quoting reviewer)	Petroc Trelawny, 6.30 a.m.–9 a.m.
Outstanding		2	"… [seeking] outstanding musical talent …" (U-25 composition competition) Trad. 'Men of Harlech'	Anne-Marie Minhall, 1 p.m.–5 p.m.
Natural	2		"… [success] requires maturity and humility and naturality (sic) …" (Perianes on performance) "… natural fluidity [of the clarinet] …" (Finzi, Clarinet Concerto)	Jane Jones, 8 p.m.–10 p.m. Sean Rafferty, 4.30 p.m.–7.30 p.m. Tom Redmond, 7.30 p.m.–10 p.m.
New (and synonyms, e.g. premiere, debut)		11	"… very special world premiere …"; "… brand new [festival] …" Trail for upcoming music Trail for upcoming music (x 2); Rameau, *Dance of the Savages*; Enya, 'May It Be', *Lord of the Rings*; "… piece I guarantee you'll never have heard before …" "… brand new music …" (U25 composition competition) "…excellent new recording …" (Mozart)	Twitter Sam Pittis, 1 a.m.–6 a.m. John Suchet, 9 a.m.–1 p.m. Anne-Marie Minhall, 1 p.m.–5 p.m. John Bruning, 5 p.m.–8 p.m.

		On harpist Catrin Finch stimulating "new repertoire"	Jane Jones, 8 p.m.–10 p.m.
	6	S.C. Dussek, Sonata in C minor; trail for upcoming world premiere; "... whole new worlds of sound ..." (trail for "The Listening Service")	Rob Cowan, 9 a.m.–12 p.m.
		O'Regan (interview viz. debut album)	Sean Rafferty, 4.30 p.m.–7.30 p.m.
		"...newly formed ..." (Elgar, *Introduction and Allegro*); on premiere of Tippett, *Divertimento on Sellinger's Round*	Tom Redmond, 7.30 p.m.–10 p.m.
Nomadic	1	On Beethoven ("Composer of the Week")	Donald Macleod, 12 p.m.–1 p.m.
Not bad	1	Mozart, *Requiem*	Sam Pittis, 1 a.m.–6 a.m.
Not sad	1	Beethoven, 'Pathétique' Sonata	John Toal, 1 p.m.–2 p.m.
Not weak	1	Beethoven, 'Pathétique' Sonata	John Toal, 1 p.m.–2 p.m.
One of a kind (as in unique)	1	"... unlike any other ..." (Boccherini)	Sam Pittis, 1 a.m.–6 a.m.
		"...one of a kind ..." (drawing comparison between Zappa and Burgess)	SR, 10.45 p.m.–11 p.m.
Outpouring (as in prolific)	1	"... outpouring of music ..." (Schubert)	Anne-Marie Minhall, 1 p.m.–5 p.m.
		"... music poured out of him ..." (Dvořák, Symphony No. 8, complete)	Verity Sharp, 2 p.m.–3.30 p.m.
Packed	1	"...packed programme ..."	Sam Pittis, 1 a.m.–6 a.m.
Passion/ passionate	2	Haydn, Symphony No. 103 (3rd movt)	John Brunning, 5 p.m.–8 p.m.
		Jenkins, *Over the Stone*	Jane Jones, 8 p.m.–10 p.m.
	3	On "Music in Time" feature	Website
		Handel, Concerto Grosso in F major; Monteverdi, *Madrigali Guerrieri et amoroso*	Rob Cowan, 9 a.m.–12 p.m.
Patriotic	1	Holst	Sam Pittis, 1 a.m.–6 a.m.
Peerless	2	Tchaikovsky, *Pezzo capriccioso*; on Toscanini	Rob Cowan, 9 a.m.–12 p.m.

(Continued)

Terms	BBC Radio 3	Classic FM	Context	Programme
Performance practice	1		"... too romantic is [to] interfere too much ... too classical is [to] interfere too little... [One must] approch [the] music like praying ..." (Perianes on performing Schubert)	Sean Rafferty, 4.30 p.m.–7.30 p.m.
Personification	1		Mussorgsky, *Songs and Dances of Death*	Verity Sharp, 2 p.m.–3.30 p.m.
Pinch yourself		1	"... pinch yourself ..."	Website
Pioneering	1		Berezovsky, 'Ne otverzhi mene' (announced in Eng.)	Catriona Young, 12.30 a.m.–6.30am
Politically incorrect		1	Rameau, *Dance of the Savages*	John Suchet, 9 a.m.–1 p.m.
Popularity/popularise (and close synonyms)	4	4	"... a composer [J.S. Bach] well-represented in the Top 300 [of Classic FM's "Hall of Fame"]."; "... [coming up], one of the best-known ...";"... former No. 1 ..." (Zimmer, *Theme from Pirates of the Caribbean*)	John Suchet, 9 a.m.–1 p.m.
			Jenkins, *Over the Stone*	Jane Jones, 8 p.m.–10 p.m.
			Berezovsky, 'Ne otverzhi mene' (announced in Eng.); Vaughan Williams bringing Tallis to a wider audience (Vaughan Williams, *Fantasia on a Theme by Thomas Tallis*)	Catriona Young, 12.30 a.m.–6.30am
			G.B. Sammartini, Concerto in F major	Petroc Trelawny, 6.30 a.m.–9 a.m.
			"... height of popularity ..." (Elgar, *Introduction and Allegro*)	
Political	1		Trad., 'Breuddwyd y Bardd', perf. 9Bach	Sean Rafferty, 4.30 p.m.–7.30 p.m.
Potential	1		"... exploits the full potential offered [by the duet] ..." (Mozart, *Sonata for Piano Duet* in F major)	Rob Cowan, 9 a.m.–12 p.m.

Category	No.	Example	Presenter, time
Power/powerful	1	"... powerhouse piece ..." (Mendelssohn, Violin Concerto, 1st movt)	Anne-Marie Minhall, 1 p.m.–5 p.m.
	3	Handel, *Tamerlano* (complete opera)	Catriona Young, 12.30 a.m.–6.30am
		Beethoven, 'Pathétique' Sonata	John Toal, 1 p.m.–2 p.m.
		"... height of musical powers ..." (Elgar, *Introduction and Allegro*)	Tom Redmond, 7.30 p.m.–10 p.m.
Praised	1	"... highly praised work ..." (Granados, 'Oriental', *Danzas españolas*)	Catriona Young, 12.30 a.m.–6.30am
Prodigious	1	Mendelssohn, *Concerto for Two Pianos*	Sam Pittis, 1 a.m.–6 a.m.
Psychology		Handel, *Tamerlano* (complete opera)	Catriona Young, 12.30 a.m.–6.30am
Puns or jokes	7	"... really Haydn the spot ..."; "... a bit of 'Power' [Percy] Grainger." (pun on children's TV series *Power Rangers*); "The only way is Elgar." (pun on UK 'reality' soap opera *The Only Way Is Essex*); "Michelle, ma belle ..." (snippet of Beatles lyric)	Tim Lihoreau, 6 a.m.–9 a.m.
		"... The Great Gate of Chicken Kiev ..."	Anne-Marie Minhall, 1 p.m.–5 p.m.
		"... we'll sail towards the "Full-Works Concert" with Puccini ..." (play on preceding Binge, *Sailing By*—a piece otherwise not announced); "... waxing rhapsodical with Rachmaninov next."	John Brunning, 5 p.m.–8 p.m.
Pure		Javier Perianes on Schubert (interview)	Sean Rafferty, 4.30 p.m.–7.30 p.m.
Quintessential	1	"... quintessentially English ..." (Elgar)	John Brunning, 5 p.m.–8 p.m.
		"... Handelian to the core ..." (Handel, Concerto Grosso in F major)	Rob Cowan, 9 a.m.–12 p.m.
Real	1	"... real music ..." (9Bach, 'Ifan')	Sean Rafferty, 4.30 p.m.–7.30 p.m.
Real name (as in reputation)	1	"[John Wilson has] made a real name for himself ..."	John Suchet, 9 a.m.–1 p.m.

(*Continued*)

Appendix 1 (Continued)

Terms	BBC Radio 3	Classic FM	Context	Programme
Recognisable		1	"... instantly recognisable, distinctive music of Karl Jenkins." (*Over the Stone*)	Jane Jones, 8 p.m.–10 p.m.
Recommend	1		Tchaikovsky, *Pezzo capriccioso*	Rob Cowan, 9 a.m.–12 p.m.
Recycling (musical)	2	1	Bach, Cantata 156 Vaughan Williams, *Fantasia on a Theme of Thomas Tallis*	Sam Pittis, 1 a.m.–6 a.m. Catriona Young, 12.30 a.m.–6.30am
Referential	1		Tippett, *Divertimento on Sellinger's Round* "... recalls [other genres] ..." (Mozart, *Sonata for Piano Duet in F major*)	Tom Redmond, 7.30 p.m.–10 p.m. Rob Cowan, 9 a.m.–12 p.m.
Reflective	1		Ginastera, *Danzas Argentinas*	Rob Cowan, 9 a.m.–12 p.m.
Regal	1	1	Handel, *Zadok the Priest* (opening section)	John Suchet, 9 a.m.–1 p.m.
Relax/relaxing		12	"Light the fire and relax . . ."; ". . . favourite relaxing music . . ."	Twitter
			". . . arrive relaxed wherever you're heading." (Marcello, Oboe Concerto)	Tim Lihoreau, 6 a.m.–9 a.m.
			"I'll guarantee to keep you relaxed." (Chopin, Nocturne in D flat major); ". . . the music is . . . calm and relaxed all the way."; ". . . deliciously relaxing music . . ."; ". . . sublime, relaxing music . . ."; ". . . relax into the evening . . ." ("Smooth Classics"); "sit back . . . relax." (trail)	John Brunning, 5 p.m.–8 p.m.
			"Unwind . . . with the world's most relaxing music." (trail)	Anne-Marie Minhall, 1 p.m.–5 p.m.
			". . . hour of relaxing, smooth classics."; ". . . [helps] to catch your breath at the busiest of days . . ." (Parsons, Ave Maria)	Margherita Taylor, 10 p.m.–1 a.m.
Remarkable	1		On Beethoven ("Composer of the Week")	Website

Keyword	Count	Music / context	Presenter and broadcast time
Respected	1	On Beethoven	Donald Macleod, 12 p.m.–1 p.m.
Revelatory	1	Vaughan Williams, *Fantasia on a Theme of Thomas Tallis*	Tom Redmond, 7.30 p.m.–10 p.m.
Revered	1	Mozart, *Sonata for Piano Four-Hands*	Website
Rival	1	"... rival [to Haydn] ..." (Pleyel, Flute Concerto)	Sam Pittis, 1 a.m.–6 a.m.
Romance/ romantic	6	Trail for upcoming music	Sam Pittis, 1 a.m.–6 a.m.
		R. Strauss, *Romanze*	Tim Lihoreau, 6 a.m.–9 a.m.
		"... romantic nostalgia ..."; Borodin, String Quartet No. 1 (3rd movt)	John Suchet, 9 a.m.–1 p.m.
		Armstrong, 'Glasgow Theme', *Love Actually* (quoting listener)	Anne-Marie Minhall, 1 p.m.–5 p.m.
		"... one can never have enough [romance]." (Beethoven, Romance No. 2)	Margherita Taylor, 10 p.m.–1 a.m.
Rousing	1	Berlioz, *Overture to Le Carnaval romain*	Catriona Young, 12.30 a.m.–6.30am
Sacred	1	Bryars, 'Section 5', *The Fifth Century*	Max Reinhardt, 11 p.m.–12.30am
Satirical	1	Vaughan Williams, *Wasps Overture*	Anne-Marie Minhall, 1 p.m.–5 p.m.
Seldom heard	1	"... seldom heard ..." (Tippett, *Divertimento on Sellinger's Round*)	Tom Redmond, 7.30 p.m.–10 p.m.
Sensitive	1	Delius, *Summer Night on the River*	Jane Jones, 8 p.m.–10 p.m.
Serenade	1	"... Elgar to serenade us ..." (Elgar, *Serenade for Strings*)	Margherita Taylor, 10 p.m.–1 a.m.
Serene	1	Mussorgsky, *Songs and Dances of Death*	Verity Sharp, 2 p.m.–3.30 p.m.
Serious	2	On Beethoven's music (x 2)	Donald Macleod, 12 p.m.–1 p.m.
		On Beethoven	Donald Macleod, 12 p.m.–1 p.m.
Shimmery/ shimmering	1	Smyth, *Overture to The Boatswain's Mate*	Sean Rafferty, 4.30 p.m.–7.30 p.m.
		Delius, *Summer Night on the River*	Jane Jones, 8 p.m.–10 p.m.
		"... shimmeringly beautiful ..." (trail for "In Tune")	Verity Sharp, 2 p.m.–3.30 p.m.
Short-lived [life]	2	Berezovsky, 'Ne otverzhi mene' (announced in Eng.); Arensky, 'Variations', Suite No. 3	Catriona Young, 12.30 a.m.–6.30am

(Continued)

Appendix 1 (Continued)

Terms	BBC Radio 3	Classic FM	Context	Programme
Simple	2		Beethoven ("Composer of the Week")	Donald Macleod, 12 p.m.–1 p.m.
			Beethoven, 'Pathétique' Sonata	John Toal, 1 p.m.–2 p.m.
Sleep		2	"Drift away every evening . . ."	John Brunning, 5 p.m.–8 p.m.
			"Drift away every evening . . ."	Margherita Taylor, 10 p.m.–1 a.m.
Slow	1		Beethoven, 'Pathétique' Sonata	John Toal, 1 p.m.–2 p.m.
Slow-motion	1		Skempton, *Moving On* (quoting listener)	John Toal, 1 p.m.–2 p.m.
Smooth (excl. frequent pre-recorded references to "Smooth Classics")		4	". . . perfect music to ease you into the night on 'Smooth Classics'. . ."	Twitter
			". . . smooth [sound] . . ." (Marcello, Oboe Concerto)	Tim Lihoreau, 6 a.m.–9 a.m.
			". . . smoothest sounds . . ." (website); ". . . soothing "Smooth Classics" . . ." (Thalberg, Piano Concerto, 2nd movt)	Margherita Taylor, 10 p.m.–1 a.m.
Snazzy	1		On new concert halls	Verity Sharp, 2 p.m.–3.30 p.m.
Soirée		1	Schubert	Sam Pittis, 1 a.m.–6 a.m.
Soothing		6	". . . soothing music . . ."	John Suchet, 9 a.m.–1 p.m.
			Tchaikovsky, *Nocturne*; Handel, 'Ombra mai fu'; ". . . blissfully soothing music . . ."; ". . . soothing Smooth Classic . . ." (Thalberg, Piano Concerto, 2nd movt); ". . . hour of relaxing, smooth classics."	Margherita Taylor, 10 p.m.–1 a.m.
Songlike	1		Finzi, Clarinet Concerto	Tom Redmond, 7.30 p.m.–10 p.m.
Soul	1		". . . soul music. . . [sung] from the heart . . ." (9Bach, 'Ifan')	Sean Rafferty, 4.30 p.m.–7.30 p.m.
Sparkling	1		Rossini, Overture to *La cambiale di matrimonio*	Verity Sharp, 2 p.m.–3.30 p.m.

			Twitter
Special	5	"... very special world premiere ..." Jenkins, *Palladio*	Tim Lihoreau, 6 a.m.–9 a.m.
		"... very special 'Full-Works Concert' ..."	Anne-Marie Minhall, 1 p.m.–5 p.m.
		"... very special programme [coming up]."; marking St David's Day	John Brunning, 5 p.m.–8 p.m.
	3	On Beethoven's relationships ("Composer of the Week")	Donald Macleod, 12 p.m.–1 p.m.
		"... very special composer ..." (interviewing Javier Perianes)	Sean Rafferty, 4.30 p.m.–7.30 p.m.
		"... [music you] really should be listening to ... something rather special." (Kel Assouf, 'Lab')	Max Reinhardt, 11 p.m.–12.30am
Spine-chilling Spirituality	1	Verdi, *Requiem* (at Grange Festival)	John Suchet, 9 a.m.–1 p.m.
	1	Vaughan Williams, *Fantasia on a Theme of Thomas Tallis*	Tom Redmond, 7.30 p.m.–10 p.m.
Spooky	1	"... spooky legend ..." (Debussy, 'La cathédrale engloutie', *Préludes*)	Sean Rafferty, 4.30 p.m.–7.30 p.m.
Spring/Spring-like	3	Davis, *Frontiers* (1st movt) J.S. Bach, Concerto for Violin and Oboe (first movt); Butterworth, *The Banks of Green Willow*	John Suchet, 9 a.m.–1 p.m. Anne-Marie Minhall, 1 p.m.–5 p.m.
	3	Mathias, *Serenade* "... perfect music as spring beckons ..." (Dvořák, *Carnival Overture*) Moeran, 'Spring, the Sweet Spring', *Songs of Springtime*	Petroc Trelawny, 6.30 a.m.–9 a.m. Rob Cowan, 9 a.m.–12 p.m. Sean Rafferty, 4.30 p.m.–7.30 p.m.
Stellar	1	"... stellar cast ..." (Rossini, Overture to *La cambiale di matrimonio*)	Verity Sharp, 2 p.m.–3.30 p.m.
Stormy	1	Beethoven	Sam Pittis, 1 a.m.–6 a.m.
Strange	1	"... strange nickname ..." (Schubert, 'Trout' Quintet)	Sam Pittis, 1 a.m.–6 a.m.

(*Continued*)

Appendix 1 (Continued)

Terms	BBC Radio 3	Classic FM	Context	Programme
Stressful	1		On page-turning for a Wigmore Hall recital	John Suchet, 9 a.m.–1 p.m.
Stripped-down [sound]	1		Trad., 'Breuddwyd y Bardd', perf. 9Bach	Sean Rafferty, 4.30 p.m.–7.30 p.m.
Stunning	1	3	Horner, *Braveheart* (composer not announced) Trail for upcoming music (new recording) F.H. Graf, Cello Concerto Ravel, Suite No. 2, *Daphnis et Chloé* (quoting listener)	Sam Pittis, 1 a.m.–6 a.m. John Suchet, 9 a.m.–1 p.m. Margherita Taylor, 10 p.m.–1 a.m. Petroc Trelawny, 6.30 a.m.–9 a.m.
Style/stylish	1	1	"... wrap March 1st up in style ..." Ginastera, *Danzas Argentinas*	Margherita Taylor, 10 p.m.–1 a.m. Rob Cowan, 9 a.m.–12 p.m.
Sublime	2	3	"... sublime, relaxing music ..." ("Smooth Classics") Korngold, 'Marietta's Lied' Dubra, Ave Maria 1 Purcell, *Prelude to The Fairy Queen Suite* Vaughan Williams, *Fantasia on a Theme by Thomas Tallis*	Website John Suchet, 9 a.m.–1 p.m. Margherita Taylor, 10 p.m.–1 a.m. Petroc Trelawny, 6.30 a.m.–9 a.m. Tom Redmond, 7.30 p.m.–10 p.m.
Successful	1		Brahms, Symphony No. 2	Sam Pittis, 1 a.m.–6 a.m.
Suppressive	1		"... violently suppressive ..." (Beethoven, "Composer of the Week")	Donald Macleod, 12 p.m.–1 p.m.
Surprise	1		"... music to intrigue, surprise and entertain."	Twitter
Talented	1	1	C.P.E. Bach, Trio in A minor Pleyel, Flute Concerto	John Toal, 1 p.m.–2 p.m. Sam Pittis, 1 a.m.–6 a.m.
Taught by/teacher		1	"... where he taught ..." (Holst, *St Paul's Suite*)	Rob Cowan, 9 a.m.–12 p.m.
Terrific	1		"... terrific on guitar ..." (Bach, Prelude No. 1—arranger not announced)	John Brunning, 5 p.m.–8 p.m.

Term		Description	Presenter, time
Test	1	"... test your knowledge [with a quiz] ..."	Rob Cowan, 9 a.m.–12 p.m.
Thrilling/thrilled	3	"... thrilling portrait ..." (trail for Sibelius, Radio 3 In Concert) (x 2)	Petroc Trelawny, 6.30 a.m.–9 a.m.
Throwaway	1	Clarinettist on performing Finzi "... throwaway pizzicato ..." (Elgar, Introduction and Allegro)	Tom Redmond, 7.30 p.m.–10 p.m. Tom Redmond, 7.30 p.m.–10 p.m.
Time-honoured	1	On the harp	Jane Jones, 8 p.m.–10 p.m.
Timeless	2	"... timeless recordings ..." (looking ahead to "Composer of the Week")	Rob Cowan, 9 a.m.–12 p.m.
Trailblazers	1	Vaughan Williams, The Lark Ascending 9Bach, 'Ifan'	Tom Redmond, 7.30 p.m.–10 p.m. Sean Rafferty, 4.30 p.m.–7.30 p.m.
Topical musical news or debate	2	Hailing the "first full-time female chorister to be appointed in the 1000-year history of St Paul's Cathedral."; On the station's composition competition for U25s	Anne-Marie Minhall, 1 p.m.–5 p.m.
	2	On gender gap in classical music composition (De la Martinez, 'Song of the Rider', Canciones)	Sean Rafferty, 4.30 p.m.–7.30 p.m.
		Sound is a "second-class citizen" in the art world (Mark Fell etc. on Moscow's "Geometry of Now" festival)	Max Reinhardt, 11 p.m.–12.30am
Tranquil	2	Chopin, Nocturne in D flat major; "... ideal soundtrack to a tranquil evening." ("Smooth Classics")	John Brunning, 5 p.m.–8 p.m.
Transcendental	1 1	Poulenc, Quatre motets (No. 1, quoting listener) Maleem Mahmoud Ghania, 'Peace in Essaouira (for Sonny Sharrock)' (feat. Pharoah Sanders)	Petroc Trelawny, 6.30 a.m.–9 a.m. Max Reinhardt, 11 p.m.–12.30am
Transparent	1	Wigglesworth, The Winter's Tale (trail for May broadcast, quoting reviewer)	Petroc Trelawny, 6.30 a.m.–9 a.m.
Treat	1	"... an absolute treat ..." (Finzi, Clarinet Concerto)	Tom Redmond, 7.30 p.m.–10 p.m.

(Continued)

Appendix 1 (Continued)

Terms	BBC Radio 3	Classic FM	Context	Programme
Tremendous			Sibelius, *Finlandia*	Sam Pittis, 1 a.m.–6 a.m.
Triumphant	1	1	"... triumphant coda ..." (Elgar, *Introduction and Allegro*)	Tom Redmond, 7.30 p.m.–10 p.m.
Trust	1		Trust between musicians (Finzi, Clarinet Concerto)	Tom Redmond, 7.30 p.m.–10 p.m.
Under-represented	1		On female composers (discussion with Vanessa Reed and Odaline de la Martinez)	Sean Rafferty, 4.30 p.m.–7.30 p.m.
Unhinged	1		"... deliciously unhinged ..." (Dennehy, 'Junk Box Fraud')	Max Reinhardt, 11 p.m.–12.30am
Uninterrupted	1	1	Dukas	John Brunning, 5 p.m.–8 p.m.
Unprecendented	1		Beethoven, *Große Fuge*	John Toal, 1 p.m.–2 p.m.
Unpredictable	1		"... notoriously unpredictable temperament ..." (Beethoven, "Composer of the Week")	Donald Macleod, 12 p.m.–1 p.m.
Unremitting	1	1	"... gosh, not a moment's pause ..." (J.S. Bach, Keyboard Concerto in E major, final movt)	John Suchet, 9 a.m.–1 p.m.
	1		Wigglesworth, *The Winter's Tale* (trail for May broadcast, quoting reviewer)	Petroc Trelawny, 6.30 a.m.–9 a.m.
Unusual/unfamiliar	1	1	"... unusual arrangement ..." (Brahms, 'How lovely are thy dwellings')	John Suchet, 9 a.m.–1 p.m.
	1		Tippett, *Divertimento on Sellinger's Round*	Tom Redmond, 7.30 p.m.–10 p.m.
Unwind/unwinding		10	"... [choice of music] designed to ease away the stresses and strains of the day." ("Smooth Classics")	Website
			Puccini, *La bohème*; "... if you're struggling to unwind ..." (Morricone, *La califfa*); trail for upcoming music	Sam Pittis, 1 a.m.–6 a.m.
			"... music to close your eyes to ..." (Delius, 'Walk to the Paradise Garden')	John Suchet, 9 a.m.–1 p.m.

Term	No.	Description	Presenter, time
Uplifting (and synonyms)	5	"Unwind … with the world's most relaxing music." (trail)	Anne-Marie Minhall, 1 p.m.–5 p.m.
		"… midweek wind-downs …"	John Brunning, 5 p.m.–8 p.m.
		Dubra, Ave Maria 1 (quoting listener); "helps with revision" (quoting listener); L. Bernstein, 'Waltz', Divertimento	Margherita Taylor, 10 p.m.–1 a.m.
		Trail for upcoming music	Sam Pittis, 1 a.m.–6 a.m.
		"… [put a] spring in the step …" (Rota, 'Love Theme', Romeo and Juliet); trail for upcoming music; "… if you know someone who needs a lift …"	Tim Lihoreau, 6 a.m.–9 a.m.
Utopia	1	"… music that lifts hearts and voices …" (Trad., 'Men of Harlech')	Jane Jones, 8 p.m.–10 p.m.
		"… a beautiful resilient emotional sanctuary: a little corner of utopia …" (quoting review of new DR Koncerthuset)	Verity Sharp, 2 p.m.–3.30 p.m.
Variety (musical)	4	"… mix of music …" (Mozart, Requiem); "… musical treasury…" (Brahms, Symphony No. 1)	Sam Pittis, 1 a.m.–6 a.m.
		Plug for presenter's book	Tim Lihoreau, 6 a.m.–9 a.m.
		"If it's musical variety you like, you're in the right place." (Strauss Jr, Persian March)	John Suchet, 9 a.m.–1 p.m.
		On Hockney's mixtape (interview with Scarfe)	Rob Cowan, 9 a.m.–12 p.m.
		"… variety inherent in [today's] programming …"	Verity Sharp, 2 p.m.–3.30 p.m.
Vibrant	2	O'Regan (interview), Three Motets from Sequence for St Wulfstan	Sean Rafferty, 4.30 p.m.–7.30 p.m.
		"… extraordinarily vibrant …" (Tippett, Divertimento on Sellinger's Round)	Tom Redmond, 7.30 p.m.–10 p.m.
Violent	1	"… violently suppressive …" (Beethoven, "Composer of the Week")	Donald Macleod, 12 p.m.–1 p.m.

(Continued)

Terms	BBC Radio 3	Classic FM	Context	Programme
Visceral	1		O'Regan (interview), 3 Motets from *Sequence for St Wulfstan*	Sean Rafferty, 4.30 p.m.–7.30 p.m.
Visionary		1	Owain Arwel Hughes	Jane Jones, 8 p.m.–10 p.m.
Warm		1	Horner, *Braveheart* (composer not announced)	Sam Pittis, 1 a.m.–6 a.m.
	1		"... warm romantic colour ..." (Finzi, Clarinet Concerto)	Tom Redmond, 7.30 p.m.–10 p.m.
Whet	1		"to whet our appetite [for the second half]." (Tallis, *Spem in alium*)	Tom Redmond, 7.30 p.m.–10 p.m.
Wild	1		"...wild and furious dance ..." (Ginastera, *Danzas Argentinas*)	Rob Cowan, 9 a.m.–12 p.m.
Win-win		1	"... win-win on Classic FM ..."	John Brunning, 5 p.m.–8 p.m.
Wonderful		15	"... night of wonderful music ..."; Mozart, *Requiem*; Charpentier; Smetana, *Overture*; "Such wonderful music ..." (Holst); "... wonderful music ..." (Nyman); Czerny	Sam Pittis, 1 a.m.–6 a.m.
			Bruch, *Double Concerto for Clarinet and Viola*; "... wonderful choice [by the listener] ..." (Verdi, Prelude to Act 1 of *La Traviata*)	Anne-Marie Minhall, 1 p.m.–5 p.m.
			Haydn, Symphony No. 103 (3rd movt)	John Brunning, 5 p.m.–8 p.m.
			Tchaikovsky, Nocturne; Dubra, Ave Maria 1; Mozart, Clarinet Concerto (2nd movt); Dvořák, 'Songs my mother taught me'	Margherita Taylor, 10 p.m.–1 a.m.
	6		"...wonderful voice ..."	Twitter
			Chopin, Mazurka in A minor	Petroc Trelawny, 6.30 a.m.–9 a.m.
			Tchaikovsky, *Pezzo capriccioso* (x 2); Ginastera, *Danzas Argentinas*	Rob Cowan, 9 a.m.–12 p.m.
			Finzi, Clarinet Concerto	Tom Redmond, 7.30 p.m.–10 p.m.

World music	1	On Catrin Finch's "collaborations with world music artists" (kora player Seckou Keita, for example, not mentioned)	Jane Jones, 8 p.m.–10 p.m.
Yay!	1	J.S. Bach, *Concerto for Violin and Oboe* (first movt)	Anne-Marie Minhall, 1 p.m.–5 p.m.
Youthful/student work	4	Messiaen, *Les Offrandes oubliées*; Rossini, Overture to *La cambiale di matrimonio*	Verity Sharp, 2 p.m.–3.30 p.m.
		"…youthful gem…" (Mendelssohn, *Octet*, 4th movt); Couperin, arr. Adès, *Les baricades mistérieuses*	Sean Rafferty, 4.30 p.m.–7.30 p.m.

Notes

1. The orchestras are the London Philharmonic, the Philharmonia, London Sinfonietta, and the Orchestra of the Age of Enlightenment.
2. In various forms and contexts, classical music is prevalent in society at large. Quite apart from the concert hall, consider its use in advertisements, new and "borrowed" film music, coffee shops, shopping malls, churches, and garden centres, and the popularity of classical "crossover" (further discussed later in this chapter). Tellingly, a grand catalogue (compiled and updated 1978–84) designed to help librarians and retailers identify classical works popularised by radio, television, advertisements, and films reached over 2,000 entries. See Phil Ranson, *"By Any Other Name": A Guide to the Popular Names and Nicknames of Classical Music, and to Theme Music in Films, Radio, Television and Broadcast Advertisements* (5th edn; Newcastle: Northern Library System, 1984).
3. These 2017 (Q1) figures are taken from www.rajar.co.uk/listening/quarterly_listening.php (accessed 21 June 2017).
4. See, for example: Alejandro L. Madrid, 'Diversity, Tokenism, Non-Canonical Musics, and the Crisis of the Humanities in U.S. Academia', *Journal of Music History Pedagogy*, 7/2 (2017), 124–9; Katy Wright, 'Teachers Blame EBacc for Decline in Music Student Numbers', *Music Teacher* (10 March 2017), www.rhinegold.co.uk/music_teacher/teachers-blame-ebacc-decline-music-student-numbers/ (accessed 20 March 2017), reporting on Ally Daubney and Duncan Mackrill, Changes in Secondary Music Curriculum Provision Over Time 2012–16 (11 November 2016), www.ism.org/images/files/Changes-in-Secondary-Music-Curriculum-Provision-Over-Time-Music-Mark-Conference.pdf and www.ism.org/professional-development/webinars/changes-in-secondary-music-provision (accessed 23 March 2017); Alan Davey, 'Don't Apologise for Classical Music's Complexity—That's Its Strength', *The Guardian* (8 May 2017), www.theguardian.com/music/2017/may/08/dont-apologise-for-classical-music-complexity-alan-davey-radio-3 (accessed 9 May 2017); and Ian Pace, 'Response to Charlotte C. Gill Article on Music and Notation', (30 March 2017) https://ianpace.wordpress.com/2017/03/30/response-to-charlotte-c-gill-article-on-music-and-notation-full-list-of-signatories/ (accessed 1 April 2017).
5. Paul Morley, 'An Outsider at the RPS Awards', *Sinfini Music* (24 May 2013), www.sinfinimusic.com/uk/features/series/paul-morley/paul-morley-on-the-rps-awards# (accessed 15 May 2015).
6. Julian Johnson, *Who Needs Classical Music? Cultural Choice and Musical Value* (Oxford: Oxford University Press, 2002), 3ff.
7. Joshua Fineberg, *Classical Music, Why Bother? Hearing the World of Contemporary Culture Through a Composer's Ears* (New York: Routledge, 2006), 21.
8. Fineberg, *Classical Music, Why Bother?*, 102, 51.
9. Lawrence Kramer, *Why Classical Music Still Matters* (Berkeley: University of California Press, 2009), 5.
10. See Kramer, *Why Classical Music Still Matters*, 13.
11. Kramer, *Why Classical Music Still Matters*, 15–16.
12. Fineberg, *Classical Music, Why Bother?*, 74.
13. I have written about this elsewhere. See Christopher Dromey, 'Hierarchical Organization', in *Music in the Social and Behavioral Sciences: An Encyclopedia*, ed. William Forde Thompson (London: Sage, 2014), 551–3.
14. Johnson, *Who Needs Classical Music?*, 76.
15. Adam Krims, 'Marxism, Urban Geography and Classical Recording: An Alternative to Cultural Studies', *Music Analysis*, 20/3 (October 2001), 355.
16. Krims, 'Marxism, Urban Geography and Classical Recording', 351.

17. Ruth Levitt and Ruth Rennie, *Classical Music and Social Result* (London: Office for Public Management, 1999), 7.
18. See, for example: the work of the Chineke! Foundation (f. 2015) to increase representation of black and minority ethnic classical musicians; Christina Scharff's pioneering work on *Equality and Diversity in the Classical Music Profession* (Economic and Social Research Council and King's College London, 2015), http://blogs.kcl.ac.uk/young-female-and-entrepreneurial/files/2014/02/Equality-and-Diversity-in-the-Classical-Music-Profession.pdf; and Natalie Bleicher, *New Music Commissioning in the UK: Equality and Diversity in New Music Commissioning* (British Academy of Songwriters, Composers & Authors, 2016), https://basca.org.uk/newsletter/BASCA_Music-Commissioning.pdf.
19. See Lucy K. Dearn and Stephanie E. Pitts, '(Un)popular Music and Young Audiences: Exploring the Classical Chamber Music Concert From the Perspective of Young Adult Listeners', *Journal of Popular Music Education*, 1/1 (March 2017), 43–62.
20. Dearn and Pitts, '(Un)popular Music and Young Audiences', 52; emphasis added.
21. See Elizabeth Hellmuth Margulis, 'When Program Notes Don't Help: Music Descriptions and Enjoyment', *Psychology of Music*, 38/3 (July 2010), 295.
22. Hellmuth Margulis, 'When Program Notes Don't Help', 295.
23. Tim Lihoreau, *The Classic FM Musical Treasury: A Curious Collection of New Meanings for Old Worlds* (London: Elliott & Thompson, 2017), 217.
24. William Haley, writing in the Radio Times (27 September 1946), and quoted in Caroline High, *For the Love of Classical Music* (Chichester: Summersdale, 2015), 179.
25. See John Reith, *Broadcast Over Britain* (London: Hodder & Stoughton, 1924), 174.
26. Paul Driver, 'The Dying of the Light: Paul Driver Casts a Vote of No-Confidence in Contemporary Culture', *Musical Times*, 134/1805 (July 1993), 380.
27. See Luke B. Howard, 'Motherhood, Billboard, and the Holocaust: Perceptions and Receptions of Górecki's Symphony No. 3', *Musical Quarterly*, 82/1 (Spring, 1998), 131–59.
28. Howard, 'Motherhood, Billboard, and the Holocaust, '148.
29. In a modern sense, crossover classical can be traced back at least as far as Wendy Carlos's debut album *Switched-On Bach* (1968, released as Walter Carlos). In the written history of the genre, literally hundreds of subsequent examples would follow, but in a similar vein to Carlos we might pick out Sam Fonteyn's song 'Pop Looks Bach' (1976, better known as the theme tune to the BBC's *Ski Sunday*) and the eponymous albums of English/Australian instrumental rock group Sky (f. 1978), spearheaded by guitarist John Williams. The difficulty for anyone looking to codify crossover classical is that the runaway success of Nigel Kennedy's 1989 recording of Antonio Vivaldi's *Le quattro stagioni* (*The Four Seasons*) and The Three Tenors' football-affiliated *Carreras Domingo Pavarotti in Concert* (1990) made them the genre's best-known releases by far, yet they are so different to earlier blueprints, where musical hybridity and popularity coincide. Moreover, the fact that later examples, such as Tony Britten's *Zadok the Priest*-aping *Champions League* (1992), owe a cultural and musical debt to The Three Tenors shows how polysemous the term "classical crossover" has become.
30. Richard Barbrook, 'Melodies or Rhythms? The Competition for the Greater London FM Radio Licence', *Popular Music*, 9/2 (April 1990), 209.
31. Arnold Schoenberg, 'The Radio: Reply to a Questionnaire [1930]', in *Style and Idea: Selected Writings of Arnold Schoenberg*, trans. Leo Black, ed. Leonard

Stein (London, Faber: 1984), 147. Schoenberg's warning itself resonates with a broader tradition epitomised by Theodor W. Adorno, who was highly critical of the supposed ill effects of the industrialisation of musical and cultural production. See, for example, Theodor W. Adorno, 'A Social Critique of Radio Music', *The Kenyon Review*, 7/2 (Spring, 1945), 208–17.

32. Michael Chanan, 'Television's Problem With (Classical) Music', *Popular Music*, 21/3, "Music and Television" (October 2002), 373.

33. Chanan, 'Television's Problem with (Classical) Music', 373.

34. 'Smoothness', it should be noted, is not exclusive to classical music. In recent history, it has been used to codify jazz (as a subgenre), then classical, and more generically still to include certain types of "middle of the road" (MOR), soul, and R&B music. Global, who own Classic FM, also own Smooth Radio.

35. Darren Henley, *Everything You Ever Wanted to Know About Classical Music* (London: Elliott & Thompson, 2015), 182.

36. Henley, *Everything You Ever Wanted to Know About Classical Music*, ix.

37. Alexandra Wilson, 'Killing Time: Contemporary Representations of Opera in British Culture', *Cambridge Opera Journal*, 19/3 (November 2007), 258.

38. As a *Musical Times* editorial once thundered: 'The problem now, as Classic FM has roundly demonstrated . . . is that, elevated by the market and technology, muzak has become a powerful source of cultural corruption. Blame for this must lie partly with the listener.' 'Editorial: Music or Muzak?', *The Musical Times*, 141/1870 (Spring, 2000), 2.

39. Driver, 'The Dying of the Light', 381.

40. Morley, 'An Outsider at the RPS Awards'.

41. Morley's view is (ironically) crowd-pleasing, at least in certain circles.

42. Driver, 'The Dying of the Light', 381.

43. See, for example, Nicholas de Jongh, 'Radio 3: Low-Brow, Lightweight and Losing Its Way?', *The Independent* (10 January 2011), www.independent.co.uk/arts-entertainment/tv/features/radio-3-low-brow-lightweight-and-losing-its-way-2180201.html (accessed 3 March 2017).

44. See House of Commons, 'Culture, Media and Sport Committee—Future of the BBC: Fourth Report of Session, 2014/15' (February 2015), https://publications.parliament.uk/pa/cm201415/cmselect/cmcumeds/315/315.pdf (accessed 3 March 2017).

45. Voting begins every January; a #300 to #1 countdown begins at Easter, revealing that year's "Hall of Fame" (www.classicfm.com/radio/hall-of-fame).

46. Wilson, 'Killing Time', 258.

47. "Chromatic" derives from "colour" (specifically, the Greek *krōhmat-*) but their respective technical and general use is typically dissimilar.

48. While this category is therefore difficult to quantity, it was possible to identity 18 separate occasions on which Radio 3 presenters talked at length (that is, for more than a few seconds) on historical, topical or analytical themes, and 9 occasions on which Classic FM presenters did likewise.

49. Johnson, *Who Needs Classical Music?*, 75.

50. Henley, *Everything You Ever Wanted to Know About Classical Music*, 246.

51. Driver, 'The Dying of the Light', 380.

52. Charles Henry Purday, Letter to Musical World (11 November 1836), quoted in Basil Hogarth, 'The Programme Note: A Plea for Reform', *Musical Times*, 75/1099 (September 1934), 795.

53. Two recent events have explored the theme: 'The Past, Present and Future of Public Musicology', 30 January–1 February 2015, organised by Eric Hung, Westminster Choir College of Rider University, Princeton, United States; and 'Public Musicology: An International Symposium', organised by the Society

for Musicology in Ireland, The National Concert Hall, Dublin, Ireland, 26 April 2017. See also Alexandra Wilson, 'Public Musicology Today' (13 February 2017), https://obertobrookes.com/2017/02/13/public-musicology-today-by-dr-alexandra-wilson/ (accessed 17 December 2017).

54. Classical music bloggers such as Jessica Duchen, Alex Ross ('The Rest Is Noise'), and Frances Wilson (a.k.a. The Cross-Eyed Pianist) were pioneering voices, and continue to share and host news, reviews, and debates. See: https://jessicamusic.blogspot.co.uk/; www.therestisnoise.com/; https://crosseyedpianist.com/ (each accessed 26 April 2017).

55. For example, the Multi-Story Orchestra's "Living Programme Notes", discussed by Julia Haferkorn in Chapter 11 of this volume, 'Dancing to Another Tune: Classical Music in Nightclubs and Other Non-Traditional Venues'.

56. Applied musicology is an uncommon and therefore ill-defined moniker, ranging from exploration of how specific industry sectors and musicology relate, to scholars identifying as applied ethnomusicologists and seeking to bridge the gap between research and action.

57. For example, the National Council on Public History (f. 1980); see http://ncph.org/what-is-public-history/about-the-field (accessed 16 June 2017).

58. See Numberphile, www.youtube.com/user/numberphile and www.numberphile.com (accessed 16 June 2017).

59. Composer Jonathan Harvey once made a similar suggestion, describing how open rehearsals might serve listeners by acting as a wordless programme note. See Jonathan Harvey, 'Sounding Out the Inner Self: Jonathan Harvey's Quest for the Spiritual Core of New Music', *Musical Times*, 133/1798 (December 1992), 614.

60. Spotify made waves at the end of 2017 by curating a 382-"song" playlist entitled The Sound of Serialism (https://open.spotify.com/user/thesoundsofspotify/playlist/6L5r0Dapop0UDxN5ple8pT), which they chose alongside nine other 'biggest emerging[!] genres', including such dubious neologisms as trap latino, gamecore, chaotic black metal, chillhop, and vintage swoon. Unfortunately, Spotify's public-musicological act of endorsement was undermined by its inclusion of just three pieces by Schoenberg (*Verklärte Nacht*, the first of the *Drei Klavierstücke*, and an early tonal *Presto* string-quartet movement), of which none were actually conceived serially.

Bibliography

Adorno, Theodor W. 'A Social Critique of Radio Music', *The Kenyon Review*, 7/2 (Spring 1945), 208–17.

Alink-Argerich Foundation. *Piano Competitions Worldwide: 2017–2018–2019*, www.alink-argerich.org/books/detail/id/23.

Allen, Kim, Jocey Quinn, Sumi Hollingworth and Anthea Rose. 'Becoming Employable Students and "Ideal" Creative Workers: Exclusion and Inequality in Higher Education Work Placements', *British Journal of Sociology of Education*, 34 (2013), 431–52.

Allen, Paul. *Artist Management for the Music Business* (3rd edn; Oxford: Focal Press, 2014).

Anderson, Terri. *Giving Music Its Due* (London: MCPS-PRS Alliance, 2004).

Andrewes, Thom and Dimitri Djuric. *We Break Strings: The Alternative Classical Scene in London* (London: Hackney Classical Press, 2014).

Archer, Louise, Sumi Hollingworth and Anna Halsall. ' "University's Not for Me—I'm a Nike Person": Urban, Working-Class Young People's Negotiations of "Style", Identity and Educational Engagement', *Sociology*, 41 (2007), 219–37.

Arthur, Michael B., Svetlana N. Khapova and Celeste P. Wilderom. 'Career Success in a Boundaryless Career World', *Journal of Organizational Behavior*, 26/2 (March 2005), 177–202.

Arts Council England. *Great Art and Culture for Everyone: 10-Year Strategic Framework, 2010–2020* (2nd edn; Arts Council England, 2013), www.artscouncil.org.uk/sites/default/files/download-file/Great_art_and_culture_for_everyone.pdf and www.artscouncil.org.uk/sites/default/files/download-file/Great-art-and-culture-for-everyone_Much-done-many-challenges-remain_15–2–16.pdf.

Arts Council England. *Equality and Diversity Within the Arts and Cultural Sector in England* (2014), www.artscouncil.org.uk/media/uploads/Equality_and_diversity_within_the_arts_and_cultural_sector_in_England.pdf.

Ashley, Louise, Jo Duberley, Hilary Sommerlad and Dora Scholarios. *Non-Educational Barriers to the Elite Profession Evaluation* (Social Mobility & Child Poverty Commission, 2015), www.gov.uk/government/news/study-into-non-educational-barriers-to-top-jobs-published.

Augustin, Sally. *Place Advantage: Applied Psychology for Interior Architecture* (Chichester: Wiley, 2009).

Bain, Alison L. 'Female Artistic Identity in Place: The Studio', *Social & Cultural Geography*, 5/2 (2004), 171–93.

Baker, Geoffrey. *El Sistema: Orchestrating Venezuela's Youth* (New York: Oxford University Press, 2014).

Ball, Stephen J. and Carol Vincent. '"I Heard It on the Grapevine": "Hot" Knowledge and School Choice', *British Journal of Sociology of Education*, 19/3 (1998), 377–400.

Baltes, Paul B. 'On the Incomplete Architecture of Human Ontogeny: Selection, Optimization, and Compensation as Foundation of Developmental Theory', *American Psychologist*, 52/4 (April 1997), 366–80.

Baltes, Paul B. and Margaret M. Baltes (eds.). *Successful Aging: Perspectives From the Behavioral Sciences* (New York: Cambridge University Press, 1990).

Baltes, Boris B. and Marcus W. Dickson. 'Using Life-Span Models in Industrial-Organizational Psychology: The Theory of Selective Optimization with Compensation', *Applied Developmental Science*, 5/1 (June 2001), 51–62.

Banks, Mark and David Hesmondhalgh. 'Looking for Work in Creative Industries Policy', *International Journal of Cultural Policy*, 15/4 (November 2009), 415–30.

Banks, Mark and Kate Oakley. 'The Dance Goes on Forever? Art Schools, Class and UK Higher Education', *International Journal of Cultural Policy*, 22 (2015), 1–17.

Baltes, Paul B., Ursula M. Staudinger and Ulman Lindenberger. 'Lifespan Psychology: Theory and Application to Intellectual Functioning', *Annual Review of Psychology*, 50/1 (February 1999), 471–507.

Barbrook, Richard. 'Melodies or Rhythms? The Competition for the Greater London FM Radio Licence', *Popular Music*, 9/2 (April 1990), 203–19.

Barfe, Louis. *Where Have All the Good Times Gone?* (London: Atlantic, 2004).

Baricco, Alessandro. *The Barbarians: An Essay on the Mutation of Culture* [2006], trans. Stephen Sartarelli (New York: Rizzoli, 2014).

Barlow, James, Peter Dickens, Tony Fielding and Mike Savage. *Property, Bureaucracy and Culture: Middle Class Formation in Contemporary Britain* (London: Routledge, 1995).

Barron, Anne. 'Harmony or Dissonance? Copyright Concepts and Musical Practice', *Social and Legal Studies*, 15/1 (March 2006), 25–51.

Bartleet, Brydie-Leigh. 'Women Conductors on the Orchestral Podium: Pedagogical and Professional Implications', *College Music Symposium*, 48 (2008), 31–51.

Baruch, Yehuda. 'Transforming Careers: From Linear to Multidirectional Career Paths: Organizational and Individual Perspectives', *Career Development International*, 9/1 (2004), 58–73.

Beech, Nic, Charlotte Gilmore, Paul Hibbert and Sierk Ybema. 'Identity-in-the-Work and Musicians' Struggles: The Production of Self-Questioning Identity Work', *Work, Employment and Society*, 30/3 (June 2016), 506–22.

Belina-Johnson, Anastasia and Scott Derek B. (eds.). *The Business of Opera* (Farnham: Ashgate, 2015).

Bennet, Lucy. 'Texting and Tweeting at Live Music Concerts: Flow, Fandom and Connecting With Other Audiences Through Mobile Phone Technology', in *Coughing and Clapping: Investigating Audience Experience*, ed. Karen Burland and Stephanie Pitts (Aldershot: Ashgate, 2014), 89–99.

Bennett, Dawn. 'Developing Employability in Higher Education Music', *Arts and Humanities in Higher Education*, 15/3–4 (July 2016), 386–413.

Bennett, Dawn. *Understanding the Classical Music Profession: The Past, the Present and Strategies for the Future* (Abingdon: Ashgate, 2008).

Bennett, Dawn and Pamela Burnard. 'Human Capital Career Creativities for Creative Industries Work: Lessons Underpinned by Bourdieu's Tools for Thinking', in

Higher Education and the Creative Economy: Beyond the Campus, ed. Roberta Comunian and Abigail Gilmore (London: Routledge, 2016), 123–42.

Bennett, Dawn, Jane Coffey, Scott Fitzgerald, Peter Petocz and Al Rainnie. 'Beyond the Creative: Understanding the Intersection of Specialist and Embedded Work for Creatives in Metropolitan Perth', in *Creative Work Beyond the Creative Industries: Innovation, Employment, and Education*, ed. Greg Hearn, Ruth Bridgstock, Ben Goldsmith and Jess Rodgers (Cheltenham: Edward Elgar, 2014), 158–74.

Bennett, Tony, Mike Savage, Elizabeth Bortolaia Silva, Alan Warde, Modesto Gayo-Cal and David Wright. *Culture, Class, Distinction* (New York: Routledge, 2009).

Berlotti Buitoni Trust. 'Is the Concert Hall the Only Place?' (2015), www.youtube.com/watch?v=FefcZzAIGLA.

Bettig, Ronald. *Copyrighting Culture: The Political Economy of Intellectual Property* (Westview: Avalon, 1996).

Bleicher, Natalie. *New Music Commissioning in the UK: Equality and Diversity in New Music Commissioning* (British Academy of Songwriters, Composers & Authors, 2016), https://basca.org.uk/newsletter/BASCA_Music-Commissioning.pdf.

Bols, Ingrid. *Programming Choices and National Culture: The Case of French and British Symphony Orchestras* (Ph.D. diss.; University of Glasgow, forthcoming).

Bomberger, E. Douglas. 'The Thalberg Effect: Playing the Violin on the Piano', *Musical Quarterly*, 75/2 (Summer 1991), 198–208.

Bonds, Mark Evan. 'Aesthetic Amputations: Absolute Music and the Deleted Endings of Hanslick's *Vom Musikalisch-Schönen*', *19th-Century Music*, 36/1 (2012), 3–23.

Born, Georgina and Kyle Devine, 'Music Technology, Gender, and Class: Digitization, Educational and Social Change in Britain', *Twentieth-Century Music*, 12/2 (2015), 135–72.

Botstein, Leon. 'Music of a Century: Museum Culture and the Politics of Subsidy', in *The Cambridge History of Twentieth Century Music*, ed. Nicholas Cook and Anthony Pople (Cambridge: Cambridge University Press, 2004), 40–68.

Botstein, Leon. 'Music in Times of Economic Distress', *Musical Quarterly*, 90/2 (Summer 2007), 167–75.

Bouckaert, Thierry. *Elisabeth's Dream—A Musical Offering: Fifty Years of the Queen Elisabeth Competition*, trans. Peter King and Sara Montgomery (Brussels: Complexe, 2001).

Bourdieu, Pierre. *Distinction: A Social Critique of the Judgement of Taste*, trans. Richard Nice (Cambridge, MA: Harvard University Press, 1984).

Bourdieu, Pierre. 'The Forms of Capital', in *Handbook of Theory of Research for the Sociology of Education*, ed. John Richardson (New York: Greenwood Press, 1986), 241–58.

Boyd, Denise and Helen Bee. *Lifespan Development* (7th edn; London: Pearson, 2015).

British Phonographic Industry. *All About the Music 2017—Recorded Music in the UK: Fact, Figures and Analysis* (London: BPI, 2017), 38.

Brown, Alan. 'Smart Concerts: Orchestras in the Age of Edutainment' (12 January 2004), https://knightfoundation.org/reports/magic-music-issues-brief-5-smart-concerts-orchestr.

Bull, Anna. 'El Sistema as a Bourgeois Social Project: Class, Gender, and Victorian Values', *Action, Criticism & Theory for Music Education*, 15/1 (January 2016a), 120–53.

Bull, Anna. 'Gendering the Middle Classes: The Construction of Conductors' Authority in Youth Classical Music Groups', *The Sociological Review*, 64/4 (2016b), 855–71.

Bull, Anna. *The Musical Body: How Gender and Class Are Reproduced Among Young People Playing Classical Music in England* (Ph.D. diss.; Goldsmiths, University of London, 2015).

Bull, Anna and Christina Scharff, ' "McDonalds Music" Versus "Serious Music": How Production and Consumption Practices Help to Reproduce Class Inequality in the Classical Music Profession', *Cultural Sociology*, 11/3 (2017), 283–301.

Burke, Penny Jane and Jackie McManus. ' "Art for a Few": Exclusion and Misrecognition in Art and Design Higher Education Admissions', *National Arts Learning Network* (2009), http://blueprintfiles.s3.amazonaws.com/1321362562-AFAF_finalcopy.pdf.

Buyens, Dirk, Jans van Dijk, Thomas Dewilde and Ans de Vos. 'The Aging Workforce: Perceptions of Career Ending', *Journal of Managerial Psychology*, 24/2 (2009), 102–17.

Cabrera, Elizabeth F. 'Opting Out and Opting In: Understanding the Complexities of Women's Career Transitions', *Career Development International*, 12/3 (2007), 218–37.

Cannadine, David. *Class in Britain* (3rd edn; London: Penguin, 2000).

Carboni, Marius. 'The Classical Music Business', in *The Music Industry Handbook*, ed. Paul Rutter (Abingdon: Routledge, 2011), 195–223.

Chanan, Michael. 'Television's Problem with (Classical) Music', *Popular Music*, 21/3, 'Music and Television' (October 2002), 367–74.

Church, Michael. (ed.). *The Other Classical Musics: Fifteen Great Traditions* (Woodbridge: Boydell Press, 2015).

Cleave, Shirley and Karen Dust. *A Sound Start: The Schools' Instrumental Music Service* (Windsor: NFER-Nelson, 1989).

Colwell, Richard and Hildegard Froehlich. *Sociology for Music Teachers: Perspectives for Practice* (London: Pearson Education, 2007).

Connell, John and Chris Gibson. *Sound Tracks: Popular Music Identity and Place* (London: Routledge, 2003).

Conor, Bridget. *Screenwriting: Creative Labour and Professional Practice* (London: Routledge, 2014).

Conor, Bridget, Rosalind Gill and Stephanie Taylor. (eds.). *Gender and Creative Labour* (Chichester: Wiley, 2015).

Cook, Nicholas. *Beyond the Score: Music as Performance* (Oxford: Oxford University Press, 2013).

Cook, Nicholas. *Music: A Very Short Introduction* (Oxford: Oxford University Press, 1998).

Cooper, Martin. 'Competitions' [*Daily Telegraph*, 20 January 1980], in *Judgements of Value: Selected Writings*, ed. Dominic Cooper (Oxford: Oxford University Press, 1988), 151–3.

Costas, Jana and Peter Fleming. 'Beyond Dis-Identification: A Discursive Approach to Self-Alienation in Contemporary Organizations', *Human Relations*, 62/3 (March 2009), 353–78.

Cottrell, Stephen. *Professional Music-Making in London: Ethnography and Experience* (Aldershot: Ashgate, 2004).

Coulangeon, Philippe, Hyacinthe Ravet and Ionela Roharik. 'Gender Differentiated Effect of Time in Performing Arts Professions: Musicians, Actors and Dancers in Contemporary France', *Poetics*, 33/5 (2005), 369–87.

Christensen, Clayton M. *The Innovator's Dilemma, When New Technologies Cause Great Firms to Fail* (Boston: Harvard Business School, 1997).

Christensen, Clayton M. and Joseph L. Bower, 'Disruptive Technologies Catching the Wave', *Harvard Business Review*, 73/1 (January—February 1995), 43–53.

Crawford, Garry, Victoria Gosling, Gaynor Bagnall and Ben Light, 'An Orchestral Audience: Classical Music and Continued Patterns of Distinction', *Cultural Sociology*, 8/4 (2014), 483–500.

Crompton, Rosemary. *Class and Stratification* (3rd edn; Cambridge: Polity, 2015).

Culture Hive. *Case Study—The Night Shift: Orchestra of the Age of Enlightenment* (2013), http://culturehive.co.uk/wp-content/uploads/2013/05/Case-study-OAE-The-Night-Shift.pdf.

Cummins-Russell, Thomas. A. and Norma M. Rantisi. 'Networks and Place in Montreal's Independent Music Industry', *The Canadian Geographer*, 56/1 (February 2012), 80–97.

Daubney, Ally and Duncan Mackrill. *Changes in Secondary Music Curriculum Provision Over Time 2012–16* (11 November 2016), www.ism.org/images/files/Changes-in-Secondary-Music-Curriculum-Provision-Over-Time-Music-Mark-Conference.pdf and www.ism.org/professional-development/webinars/changes-in-secondary-music-provision.

Davey, Alan. 'Don't Apologise for Classical Music's Complexity—That's Its Strength', *The Guardian* (8 May 2017), www.theguardian.com/music/2017/may/08/dont-apologise-for-classical-music-complexity-alan-davey-radio-3.

Davies, Peter Maxwell. 'Royal Philharmonic Society Lecture: Will Serious Music Become Extinct? (24 April 2005), https://royalphilharmonicsociety.org.uk//images/files/RPS_Lecture_2005_PMD.pdf.

Dearn, Lucy K. and Stephanie E. Pitts. '(Un)popular Music and Young Audiences: Exploring the Classical Chamber Music Concert from the Perspective of Young Adult Listeners', *Journal of Popular Music Education*, 1/1 (March 2017), 43–62.

Deazley, Ronan. 'Commentary on *Copyright Amendment Act* 1842', in *Primary Sources on Copyright (1450–1900)*, ed. Lionel Bently and Martin Kretschmer (2008), www.copyrighthistory.org.

Delbert, Raymond M., June Hart Romeo and Karoline V. Kumke. 'A Pilot Study of Occupational Injury and Illness Experienced By Classical Musicians', *Workplace Health and Safety*, 60/1 (January 2012), 19–24.

Demers, Joanna. *Steal this Music: How Intellectual Property Law Affects Musical Creativity* (Atlanta: University of Georgia Press, 2006).

Demonet, Giles. *Les marchés de la musique vivante: La représentation musicale au XXIe siècle* (Paris: Presses de l'université Paris-Sorbonne, 2015).

Dempster, Douglas. 'Wither the Audience for Classical Music?', *Harmony: Forum of the Symphony Orchestra Institute*, 11 (October 2000), www.polyphonic.org/wp-content/uploads/2012/03/Audience_Music.Dempster.pdf.

Department for Business, Innovation and Skills, 'Pupils on Free School Meals Attending Music Colleges. A Freedom of Information Request to Department for Business, Innovation and Skills' (31 July 2013), www.whatdotheyknow.com/request/pupils_on_free_school_meals_atte#incoming-414358.

DiMaggio, Paul J. 'Cultural Entrepreneurship in Nineteenth-Century Boston', in *Nonprofit Enterprise in the Arts: Studies in Mission and Constraint*, ed. Paul J. DiMaggio (New York: Oxford University Press, 1986), 41–61.

Dobson, Melissa C. 'New Audiences for Classical Music: The Experiences of Non-Attenders at Live Orchestral Concerts', *Journal of New Music Research*, 39/3 (2010), 111–24.

Dries, Nicky, Roland Pepermans and Olivier Carlier. 'Career Success: Constructing a Multidimensional Model', *Journal of Vocational Behavior*, 73/2 (October 2008), 254–67.

Driver, Paul. 'The Dying of the Light: Paul Driver Casts a Vote of No-Confidence in Contemporary Culture', *Musical Times*, 134/1805 (July 1993), 380–83.

Dromey, Christopher. 'Competitions: Classical and Popular', in *Music in the Social and Behavioral Sciences: An Encyclopedia*, ed. William Forde Thompson (London: Sage, 2014a), 207–9.

Dromey, Christopher. 'Hierarchical Organization', in *Music in the Social and Behavioral Sciences*, ed. William Forde Thompson (London: Sage, 2014b), 551–3.

Dromey, Christopher. *The Pierrot Ensembles: Chronicle and Catalogue, 1912–2012* (London: Plumbago, 2013).

Duchen, Jessica. 'The Cellist Who Wants to Shake Up London With a Classical Mystery Tour', *The Independent* (21 January 2011), www.independent.co.uk/arts-entertainment/classical/features/the-cellist-who-wants-to-shake-up-london-with-a-classical-mystery-tour-2190095.html.

Duchen, Jessica. 'Gabriel Prokofiev on the BBC's Ten Pieces, Nonclassical, and a New Carnival of the Animals', *The Independent* (24 June 2015), www.independent.co.uk/arts-entertainment/classical/features/gabriel-prokofiev-on-the-bbcs-ten-pieces-nonclassical-and-a-new-carnival-of-the-animals-10340546.html.

Duerksen, George L. 'Some Effects of Expectation on Evaluation of Recorded Musical Performance', *Journal of Research in Music Education*, 20/2 (Summer 1972) 268–72.

Eby, Lillian T., Marcus Butts and Angie Lockwood. 'Predictors of Success in the Era of the Boundaryless Career', *Journal of Organizational Behavior*, 24/6 (August 2003), 689–708.

Ehrlich, Cyril. *Harmonious Alliance: A History of the Performing Right Society* (Oxford: Oxford University Press, 1989).

Eikhof, Doris R. and Chris Warhurst. 'The Promised Land? Why Social Inequalities are Systemic in the Creative Industries', *Employee Relations*, 35/5 (2013), 495–508.

European Commission, *Public Consultation on the Review of the EU Copyright Rules* (2013–14), http://ec.europa.eu/internal_market/consultations/2013/copyright-rules/index_en.htm.

Evans, Paul and Gary McPherson. 'Identity and Practice: The Motivational Benefits of a Long-Term Musical Identity', *Psychology of Music*, 43/3 (January 2015), 407–22.

Faggian, Alessandra, Roberta Comunian, Sarah Jewell and Ursula Kelly, 'Bohemian Graduates in the UK: Disciplines and Location Determinants of Creative Careers', *Regional Studies*, 47/2 (April 2013), 183–200.

Faultless, Maggie. 'Purcell and a Pint: Welcome to a New Kind of Classical Concert', *The Guardian* (6 February 2012), www.theguardian.com/music/musicblog/2012/feb/06/classical-music-in-a-pub.

Feeny, Antony. *Notes and Coins: The Financial Sustainability of Opera and Orchestral Music* (Ph.D. diss.; Royal Holloway, University of London, 2018).

Feldman, Daniel C. and Mark C. Bolino. 'Career Patterns of the Self-Employed: Career Motivations and Career Outcomes', *Journal of Small Business Management*, 38/3 (July 2000), 53–67.

Fifield, Christopher. *Ibbs and Tillett: The Rise and Fall of a Musical Empire* (Aldershot: Ashgate, 2005).

Fineberg, Joshua. *Classical Music, Why Bother? Hearing the World of Contemporary Culture Through a Composer's Ears* (New York: Routledge, 2006).

Fiske, Harold E. *The Effect of a Training Procedure in Music Performance Evaluation on Judge Reliability* (Ontario Educational Research Council Report, 1978).

Flôres, Renato and Victor Ginsburgh. 'The Queen Elisabeth Musical Competition: How Fair Is the Final Ranking?', *The Statistician*, 45/1 (1996), 97–104.

Francis, Becky, Barbara Read and Christine Skelton, *The Identities and Practices of High Achieving Pupils: Negotiating Achievement and Peer Cultures* (London: Bloomsbury, 2012).

Freeman, Robert. *The Crisis of Classical Music in America: Lessons From a Life in the Education of Musicians* (Lanham: Rowman & Littlefield, 2014).

Friedland, Roger and Robert R. Alford, 'Bringing Society Back In: Symbols, Practices, and Institutional Contradiction', in *The New Institutionalism in Organisational Analysis*, ed. Walter W. Powell and Paul. J. DiMaggio (Chicago: University of Chicago Press, 1991), 232–66.

Friedman, Sam, 'Habitus Clivé and the Emotional Imprint of Social Mobility', *The Sociological Review*, 64/1 (February 2016), 129–47.

Frith, Simon. 'Music and Morality', in *Music and Copyright*, ed. Simon Frith and Lee Marshall (1st edn; Edinburgh: Edinburgh University Press, 1993), 1–21.

Gill, Rosalind. 'Cool, Creative and Egalitarian? Exploring Gender in Project-Based New Media Work in Europe', *Information, Communication & Society*, 5/1 (2002), 70–89.

Gill, Rosalind. 'Unspeakable Inequalities: Post Feminism, Entrepreneurial Subjectivity, and the Repudiation of Sexism among Cultural Workers', *Social Politics: International Studies in Gender, State and Society*, 21/4 (2014), 509–28.

Glynn, Mary Ann and Michael Lounsbury. 'From the Critics' Corner: Logic Blending, Discursive Change and Authenticity in a Cultural Production System', *Journal of Management Studies*, 42/5 (2005) 1031–55.

Goehr, Lydia. *The Imaginary Museum of Musical Works: An Essay in the Philosophy of Music* (2nd edn; Oxford: Oxford University Press, 2007).

Gotsi, Manto, Constantine Andriopoulos, Marianne W. Lewis and Amy E. Ingram. 'Managing Creatives: Paradoxical Approaches to Identity Regulation', *Human Relations*, 63/6 (February 2010), 781–805.

Gould, Glenn. 'The Prospects of Recording', *High Fidelity*, 16/4 (April 1966), 46–63, www.collectionscanada.gc.ca/glenngould/028010-4020.01-e.html.

Greenwood, Royston and Roy Suddaby. 'Institutional Entrepreneurship in Mature Fields: The Big Five Accounting Firms', *Academy of Management Journal*, 49/1 (2006), 27–48.

Grugulis, Irena and Dimitrinka Stoyanova. 'Social Capital and Networks in Film and TV: Jobs for the Boys?', *Organization Studies*, 33/10 (2012), 1311–31.

Haferkorn, Julia. *The Composer's Toolkit* (Sound and Music, 2013a), www.sound andmusic.org/create/toolkit.

Haferkorn, Julia. *The Producer's Toolkit* (Sound and Music, 2013b), www.soundand music.org/create/producerstoolkit.

Hall, Clare. *Voices of Distinction: Choirboys' Narratives of Music, Masculinity and the Middle-Class* (Ph.D. diss; Monash University, 2011).

Hallam, Susan, Andrea Creech, Ioulia Papageorgi and Lynne Rogers. *Local Authority Music Services Provision (2007) for Key Stages 1 and 2* (London: Institute of Education, 2007).

Hallam, Susan and Vanessa Prince. *Research into Instrumental Music Services* (London: Institute of Education, 2000).

Hargreaves, Ian. *Digital Opportunity: A Review of Intellectual Property and Growth* (Department for Business, Innovation and Skills, 2011), www.gov.uk/government/ publications/digital-opportunity-review-of-intellectual-property-and-growth.

Harper, Beatrice. 'Health and Safety in the Classical Music Industry in the UK and Germany', *Cultural Trends*, 11/41 (January 2001), 43–91.

Harvey, Fiona. *Youth Ensembles Survey Report* (Association of British Orchestras, 2014), www.abo.org.uk/media/33505/ABO-Youth-Ensemble-Survey-Report-App. pdf.

Hellmuth Margulis, Elizabeth. 'When Program Notes Don't Help: Music Descriptions and Enjoyment', *Psychology of Music*, 38/3 (July 2010), 285–302.

Henley, Darren. *Everything You Ever Wanted to Know About Classical Music* (London: Elliott & Thompson, 2015).

Hennekam, Sophie. 'Challenges of Older Self-Employed Workers in Creative Industries: The Case of the Netherlands', *Management Decision*, 53/4 (2015), 876–91.

Hennekam, Sophie. 'Dealing With Multiple Incompatible Work-Related Identities: The Case of Artists', *Personnel Review*, 46/5 (2017), 970–87.

Hennekam, Sophie and Dawn Bennett. 'Involuntary Career Transition and Identity Within the Artist Population', *Personnel Review*, 45/6 (2016), 1114–31.

Hennekam, Sophie and Olivier Herrbach. 'HRM Practices and Low Occupational Status Older Workers', *Employee Relations*, 35/3 (2013), 339–55.

Hennion, Antoine. 'Music Lovers: Taste as Performance', *Theory, Culture & Society*, 18/5 (October 2001), 1–22.

Hesmondhalgh, David and Sarah Baker. 'Sex, Gender and Work Segregation in the Cultural Industries', in *Gender and Creative Labour*, ed. Bridget Conor, Rosalind Gill and Sarah Taylor (Chichester: Wiley, 2015), 23–36.

Hewett, Ivan. 'Music Education: A Middle-Class Preserve?', *The Telegraph* (11 June 2014), www.telegraph.co.uk/culture/music/music-news/10891882/Music-education-a-middle-class-preserve.html.

High, Caroline. *For The Love of Classical Music* (Chichester: Summersdale, 2015).

Hodge, Tom. 'Musical Places in Unusual Spaces', *Huffington Post* (29 September 2014), www.huffingtonpost.co.uk/tom-hodge/classical-music-venues_b_5875526. html.

Hogarth, Basil. 'The Programme Note: A Plea for Reform', *Musical Times*, 75/1099 (September 1934), 795–98.

House of Commons, 'Culture, Media and Sport Committee—The Performing Right Society and the Abolition of The Classical Music Subsidy' (1999), www.publica tions.parliament.uk/pa/cm199899/cmselect/cmcumeds/468/46803.htm.

House of Commons, 'Culture, Media and Sport Committee—Future of the BBC: Fourth Report of Session, 2014/15' (February 2015), https://publications.parlia ment.uk/pa/cm201415/cmselect/cmcumeds/315/315.pdf.

Howard, Luke B. 'Motherhood, *Billboard*, and the Holocaust: Perceptions and Receptions of Górecki's Symphony No. 3', *Musical Quarterly* 82/1 (Spring 1998), 131–59.

Hume, Simon and Emma Wells. *ABRSM: Making Music* (London: Associated Board of the Royal Schools of Music, 2014), http://gb.abrsm.org/de/making-music/#.

Idema, Johan. *Present! Rethinking Live Classical Music* (Amsterdam: Muziek Centrum Nederland, 2012).

Irwin, Sarah and Sharon Elley. 'Concerted Cultivation? Parenting Values, Education and Class Diversity', *Sociology*, 45/3 (June 2011), 480–95.

Isacoff, Stuart. 'Competition Judging: Keeping Evil Out of the Jury Room', *Musical America* (3 February 2015), www.musicalamerica.com/news/newsstory.cfm?story ID=33290&categoryID=7.

Johnson, Julian. *Who Needs Classical Music? Cultural Choice and Musical Value* (Oxford: Oxford University Press, 2002).

Jones, Rhian. 'Classic FM and Decca Launch Streaming Service', *Music Week* (11 November 2014), www.musicweek.com/news/read/classic-fm-and-decca-launch-classical-music-streaming-service/060090.

Kanfer, Ruth and Phillip L. Ackerman. 'Aging, Adult Development, and Work Motivation', *Academy of Management Review*, 29/3 (July 2004), 440–58.

Kawohl, Friedemann. 'Commentary on the Prussian Copyright Act (1837)', in *Primary Sources on Copyright (1450–1900)*, ed. Lionel Bently and Martin Kretschmer (2008), www.copyrighthistory.org.

Kellersmann, Christian. 'Der Frack ist bitte an der Garderobe abzugeben' (19 August 2013), http://christiankellersmann.de/der-frack-ist-bitte-an-der-garderobe-abzugeben.

Kingsbury, Henry. *Music, Talent, and Performance: A Conservatory Cultural System* (Philadelphia: Temple University Press, 1988).

Kirby, Phillip. *Leading People 2016* (The Sutton Trust, 2016), www.suttontrust.com/researcharchive/leading-people-2016.

Kok, Roe-Min. 'Music for a Postcolonial Child: Theorizing Malaysian Memories', in *Musical Childhoods and the Cultures of Youth*, ed. Susan Boynton and Roe-Min Kok (Connecticut: Wesleyan University Press, 2006), 89–104.

Kolb, Bonita M. 'The Effect of Generational Change on Classical Music Concert Attendance and Orchestras' Responses in the UK and US', *Cultural Trends*, 11/41 (2001), 1–35.

Kolb, Bonita M. *Marketing for Cultural Organizations: New Strategies for Attracting Audiences* (3rd edn; Abingdon: Routledge, 2013).

Kramer, Lawrence. *Why Classical Music Still Matters* (Berkeley: University of California Press, 2009).

Krims, Adam. 'Marxism, Urban Geography and Classical Recording: An Alternative to Cultural Studies', *Music Analysis*, 20/3 (October 2001), 347–63.

Kusek, David and Gerd Leonhard. *The Future of Music: Manifesto for the Digital Music Revolution* (Boston: Berkley Press, 2005).

Lamb, Roberta. 'The Possibilities of/for Feminist Music Criticism in Music Education', *British Journal of Music Education*, 10/3 (November 1993), 169–80.

Lamont, Alexandra, David J. Hargreaves, Nigel A. Marshall and Mark Tarrant, 'Young People's Music In and Out of School', *British Journal of Music Education*, 20/3 (2003), 229–41.

Lamont, Michèle. *Money, Morals and Manners: The Culture of the French and American Upper-Middle Class* (Chicago: University of Chicago Press, 1992).

Lebrecht, Norman. *When the Music Stops: Managers, Maestros and the Corporate Murder of Classical Music* (London: Simon & Schuster, 1996).

Lee, Annabelle. *#Classical: An Analysis of Social Media Marketing in the Classical Music Industry* (Ph.D. diss., Royal Holloway, University of London, 2017).

Leech-Wilkinson, Daniel. 'Classical Music as Enforced Utopia', *Arts and Humanities in Higher Education*, 15/3–4 (July 2016), 325–36.

Leppänen, Taru. 'The West and the Rest of Classical Music: Asian Musicians in the Finnish Media Coverage of the 1995 Jean Sibelius Violin Competition', *European Journal of Cultural Studies*, 18/1 (2014), 19–34.

Lessig, Lawrence. *Free Culture: How Big Media Uses Technology and the Law to Lock Down Culture and Control Creativity* (New York: Penguin, 2004); www. free-culture.cc/freeculture.pdf.

Lessig, Lawrence. *Remix: Making Art and Commerce Thrive in the Hybrid Economy* (London: Bloomsbury, 2008).

Levitt, Ruth and Rennie, Ruth. *Classical Music and Social Result* (London: Office for Public Management, 1999).

Lihoreau, Tim. *The Classic FM Musical Treasury: A Curious Collection of New Meanings for Old Worlds* (London: Elliott & Thompson, 2017).

Lockwood, David, 'Introduction: Marking Out the Middle Class(es)', in *Social Change and the Middle Classes*, ed. Tim Butler and Michael Savage (London: UCL Press, 1995), 1–14.

McAndrew, Siobhan and Martin Everett. 'Symbolic Versus Commercial Success Among British Female Composers', in *Social Networks and Music Worlds*, ed. Nick Crossley, Siobhan McAndrew and Paul Widdop (Abingdon: Routledge, 2015), 61–88.

McCormick, Lisa. 'Higher, Faster, Louder: Representations of the International Music Competition', *Cultural Sociology*, 3/1 (2009), 5–30.

McCormick, Lisa. *Performing Civility: International Competitions in Classical Music* (Cambridge: Cambridge University Press, 2015).

McRobbie, Angela. *Be Creative: Making a Living in the New Culture Industries* (Cambridge: Polity Press, 2015).

Madird, Alejandro L. 'Diversity, Tokenism, Non-Canonical Musics, and the Crisis of the Humanities in U.S. Academia, *Journal of Music History Pedagogy*, 7/2 (2017), 124–9.

Marshall, Lee. *Bootlegging: Romanticism and Copyright in the Music Industry* (Thousand Oaks: Sage, 2005).

Maxwell, Claire and Peter Aggleton. 'Agentic Practice and Privileging Orientations Among Privately Educated Young Women', *The Sociological Review*, 62/4 (August 2014), 800–20.

Meier, Leslie M. 'Popular Music Making and Promotional Work Inside the "New" Music Industry', in *The Routledge Companion to the Cultural Industries*, ed. Kate Oakley and Justin O'Connor (Abingdon: Routledge, 2015), 402–12.

Mietzner, Dana and Martin Kamprath. 'A Competence Portfolio for Professionals in the Creative Industries', *Creativity and Innovation Management*, 22/3 (March 2013), 280–94.

Mills, Janet. 'Working in Music: Becoming a Performer-Teacher', *Music Education Research*, 6/3 (2004), 245–61.

Molteni, Luca and Andrea Ordanini. 'Consumption Patterns, Digital Technology and Music Downloading', *Long Range Planning*, 36 (2003), 389–406.

Monopolies and Mergers Commission. *Performing Rights: A Report on the Supply in the UK of the Services of Administering Performing Rights and Film Synchronisation Rights* (February 1996), http://webarchive.nationalarchives. gov.uk/20111202195250/http:/competition-commission.org.uk/rep_pub/ reports/1996/378performing.htm.

Montgomery, Robert and Threlfall, Robert. *Music and Copyright: The Case of Delius and His Publishers* (Aldershot: Ashgate, 2007).

Moore, Gillian. 'Concert Etiquette: The New Rules' (16 September 2015), http:// freyahellier.com/gillian-moore.

Moore, Ro. *Basil Bernstein: The Thinker and the Field* (New York: Routledge, 2013).

Morley, Paul. 'An Outsider at the RPS Awards', *Sinfini Music* (24 May 2013), www. sinfinimusic.com/uk/features/series/paul-morley/paul-morley-on-the-rps-awards#.

Mortier, Gerard. *Dramaturgie van een passie*, trans. Jan Vandenhouwe (Antwerp: De Bezige Bij, 2014).

Moss, Stephen. 'Used Notes Only', *The Guardian* (11 January 2001), www.the-guardian.com/culture/2001/jan/11/artsfeatures.

Moy, Ron. *Authorship Roles in Popular Music: Issues and Debates* (New York: Routledge, 2015).

Musgrave, Michael. *Brahms: A German Requiem* (Cambridge: Cambridge University Press, 1996).

Musicians' Union. *The Working Musician* (2012), www.musiciansunion.org.uk/ Files/Reports/Industry/The-Working-Musician-report.aspx.

Ng, Thomas W.H., Lillian T. Eby, Kelly L. Sorensen and Daniel C. Feldman. 'Predictors of Objective and Subjective Career Success: A Meta-Analysis', *Personnel Psychology*, 58/2 (May 2005), 367–408.

Noonan, Caitriona. 'Professional Mobilities in the Creative Industries: The Role of "Place" for Young People Aspiring for a Creative Career', *Cultural Trends*, 24/4 (September 2015), 299–309.

Oakley, Kate and Dave O'Brien. 'Learning to Labour Unequally: Understanding the Relationship between Cultural Production, Cultural Consumption and Inequality', *Social Identities*, 22/5 (2016), 471–86.

O'Brien, Dave, Daniel Laurison, Andrew Miles and Sam Friedman. 'Are the Creative Industries Meritocratic? An Analysis of the 2014 British Labour Force Survey', *Cultural Trends*, 25 (2016), 116–31.

Osborne, William and Abbie Conant. *A Survey of Women Orchestral Players in Major UK Orchestras as of March 1, 2010* (2010), www.osborne-conant.org/ orch-uk.htm.

Oyserman, Daphna and Leah James. 'Possible Identities', in *Handbook of Identity Theory and Research*, ed. Seth J. Schwartz, Koen Luyckx and Vivian Vignoles (New York: Springer, 2011), 117–45.

Pace, Ian. 'Response to Charlotte C. Gill Article on Music and Notation' (30 March 2017), https://ianpace.wordpress.com/2017/03/30/response-to-charlotte-c-gill-article-on-music-and-notation-full-list-of-signatories.

Parkes, Kelly A. and Brett D. Jones. 'Motivational Constructs Influencing Undergraduate Students' Choices to Become Classroom Music Teachers or Music Performers', *Journal of Research in Music Education*, 60/1 (February 2012), 101–23.

Patmore, David. 'The Marketing of Orchestras and Symphony Concerts', in *The Routledge Companion to Arts Marketing*, ed. Daragh O'Reilly, Ruth Rentschler and Theresa A. Kirchner (London: Routledge, 2013), 384–92.

Peacock, Alan and Ronald Weir. *The Composer in the Market Place* (London: Faber, 1975).

Performing Right Society, *PRS News*, 33–55 (Autumn 1991–August 1999).

Performing Right Society, *PRS Yearbooks* (1978–91).

Performing Right Society, *M: PRS Members' Music Magazine*, 7–12 (2003–04).

Peterson, Richard A. 'Understanding Audience Segmentation: From Elite and Mass to Omnivore and Univore', *Poetics*, 21/4 (1992), 243–58.

Pickett, Kate and Richard Wilkinson. *The Spirit Level: Why Equality Is Better for Everyone* (London: Penguin, 2010).

Pitts, Stephanie E. 'What Makes an Audience? Investigating the Roles and Experiences of Listeners at a Chamber Music Festival', *Music & Letters*, 86/2 (May 2005), 257–69.

Pohlman, Lisa. 'Creativity, Gender and the Family: A Study of Creative Writers', *The Journal of Creative Behavior*, 30/18 (1996), 1–24.

Price, Sarah M. *Risk and Reward in Classical Music Concert Attendance: Investigating the Engagement of 'Art' and 'Entertainment' Audiences with a Regional Symphony Orchestra in the UK* (Ph.D. diss.; University of Sheffield, 2017).

Proctor-Thomson, Sarah. 'Feminist Futures of Cultural Work: Creativity, Gender and Diversity in the Digital Media Sector', in *Theorizing Cultural Work: Labour, Continuity and Change in the Creative Industries*, ed. Mark Banks, Stephanie Taylor and Rosalind Gill (London: Routledge, 2013), 137–48.

Rabkin, Nick. 'Teaching Artists: A Century of Tradition and a Commitment to Change', *Work and Occupations*, 40/4 (October 2013), 506–13.

Randle, Keith, Cynthia Forson and Moira Calveley. 'Towards a Bourdieusian Analysis of the Social Composition of the UK Film and Television Workforce', *Work, Employment & Society*, 29/4 (2015), 590–606.

Ranson, Phil. *"By Any Other Name": A Guide to the Popular Names and Nicknames of Classical Music, and to Theme Music in Films, Radio, Television and Broadcast Advertisements* (5th edn; Newcastle: Northern Library System, 1984).

Raykoff, Ivan and Robert Deam Tobin (eds.). *A Song for Europe: Popular Music and Politics in the Eurovision Song Contest* (Aldershot: Ashgate, 2007).

Reay, Diane, Gill Crozier and John Clayton, ' "Fitting In" or "Standing Out": Working-Class Students in UK Higher Education', *British Educational Research Journal*, 36/1 (February 2010), 107–24.

Reay, Diane, Gill Crozier and David James, *White Middle Class Identities and Urban Schooling* (Basingstoke: Palgrave Macmillan, 2011).

Reith, John. *Broadcast Over Britain* (London: Hodder & Stoughton, 1924).

Richens, Frances. 'Classical Music Becoming Middle Class, Committee Hears', *Arts Professional* (9 September 2016), www.artsprofessional.co.uk/news/classical-music-becoming-middle-class-committee-hears.

Rivera, Lauren A. *Pedigree: How Elite Students Get Elite Jobs* (rev. edn; Princeton: Princeton University Press, 2016).

Robinson, Sarah May. *Chamber Music in Alternative Venues in the 21st Century U.S.: Investigating the Effect of New Venues on Concert Culture, Programming and the Business of Classical Music* (DMus diss.; University of South Carolina, 2013).

Rodgers, Sarah, David Bedford and Patrick Rackow. 'Tackling the Pirates', *Classical Music* (4 July 2009), 69.

Rogers, Lynne and Susan Hallam, 'Music Services', in *Music Education in the 21st Century in the United Kingdom: Achievements, Analysis and Aspirations*, ed. Susan Hallam and Andrea Creech (London: Institute of Education, 2010), 279–94.

Rollock, Nicola, David Gillborn, Carol Vincent and Stephen J. Ball. *The Colour of Class: The Educational Strategies of the Black Middle Classes* (London: Routledge, 2015).

Sallis, Friedemann. *Music Sketches* (Cambridge: Cambridge University Press, 2015).

Sandow, Greg. 'A Young, Hip, Classical Crowd', *The Wall Street Journal* (28 March 2009), www.wsj.com/articles/SB123819267920260779.

Savage, Mike. 'The Musical Field', *Cultural Trends*, 15/2–3 (2006), 159–74.

Scales, Amanda. '*Sola, Perduta, Abbandonata*: Are the Copyright Act and Performing Rights Organizations Killing Classical Music?', *Vanderbilt Journal of Entertainment Law and Practice*, 7/2 (Spring 2005), 281–99.

Scharff, Christina. 'Blowing Your Own Trumpet: Exploring the Gendered Dynamics of Self-Promotion in the Classical Music Profession', *The Sociological Review*, 63 (May 2015a), 97–112.

Scharff, Christina. *Equality and Diversity in the Classical Music Profession* (Economic and Social Research Council and King's College London, 2015b), http://blogs.kcl.ac.uk/young-female-and-entrepreneurial/files/2014/02/Equality-and-Diversity-in-the-Classical-Music-Profession.pdf.

Scharff, Christina. 'The Psychic Life of Neoliberalism: Mapping the Contours of Entrepreneurial Subjectivity', *Theory, Culture and Society*, 33/6 (July 2015c), 107–22.

Scharff, Christina. *Gender, Subjectivity, and Cultural Work: The Classical Music Profession* (London: Routledge, 2018).

Schmid, Hans Ulrich. *Aber spielen müssen Sie selber: Aus den Erinnerungen eines Impresarios*, ed. Astrid Becker and Cornelia Schmid (Hildesheim: Georg Olms Verlag, 2013).

Schmidt, Margaret and Jelani Canser. 'Clearing the Fog: Constructing Shared Stories of a Novice Teacher's Journey', *Research Studies in Music Education*, 27/2 (December 2006), 55–68.

Schoenberg, Arnold. 'The Radio: Reply To A Questionnaire [1930]', in *Style and Idea: Selected Writings of Arnold Schoenberg*, trans. Leo Black, ed. Leonard Stein (London: Faber, 1984), 147–8.

Silver, Jeremy. 'Blockchain or the Chaingang? Challenges, Opportunities and Hype: The Music Industry and Blockchain Technologies' (Centre for Copyright and New Business Models in the Creative Economy (CREATe), 2016), https://zenodo.org/record/51326/files/CREATe-Working-Paper-2016-05.pdf.

Skeggs, Beverley. 'Class, Culture and Morality: Legacies and Logics in the Space for Identification', in *The SAGE Handbook of Identities*, ed. Margaret Wetherell and Chandra Talpade Mohanty (London: Sage, 2010), 339–59.

Skeggs, Beverley. *Class, Self, Culture* (London: Routledge, 2003).

Skeggs, Beverley. *Formations of Class and Gender: Becoming Respectable* (London: Sage, 1997).

Skillset. *Women in the Creative Media Industries* (2010), www.ewawomen.com/uploads/files/surveyskillset.pdf.

Small, Christopher. *Musicking: The Meanings of Performing and Listening* (Middletown: Wesleyan University Press, 1998).

Smithuijsen, Cas. *Stilte! Het ontstaan van concertetiquette* (Amsterdam: Podium, 2001).

Spaan, Masa. *Hier komen de Barbaren! Innovations in Concert Practices* (MA diss.; ArtEZ University of the Arts, Arnhem, 2013).

Steele, Claude M. 'The Psychology of Self-Affirmation: Sustaining the Integrity of the Self', *Advances in Experimental Social Psychology*, 21 (1988), 261–302.

Stewart, Andrew. 'PRS under Fire from Classical Music Pressure Group', *Classical Music* (6 March 1999), 5.

Svejenova, Silviya. '"The Path with the Heart": Creating the Authentic Career', *Journal of Management Studies*, 42/5 (July 2005), 947–74.

Taylor, Stephanie. 'Negotiating Oppositions and Uncertainties: Gendered Conflicts in Creative Identity Work', *Feminism & Psychology*, 21/3 (2011), 354–71.

Taylor, Stephanie and Karen Littleton. *Contemporary Identities of Creativity and Creative Work* (Farnham: Ashgate, 2012).

Thanki, Ashika and Steve Jefferys. 'Who Are the Fairest? Ethnic Segmentation in London's Media Production', *Work Organisation, Labour & Globalisation*, 1/1 (2007), 108–18.

Thornton, Patricia H. and William Ocasio. 'Institutional Logics and the Historical Contingency of Power in Organisations: Executive Succession in the Higher Education Publishing Industry, 1958–1990', *The American Journal of Sociology*, 105/3 (1999), 801–43.

Thorpe, Vanessa, 'Ed Vaizey: "No Excuse" for Lack of Diversity in British Orchestras', *The Guardian* (23 January 2016), www.theguardian.com/music/2016/jan/23/ed-vaizey-no-excuse-for-lack-of-diversity-in-british-orchestras.

Toronyi-Lalic, Igor. 'Imagined Occasions', *The Arts Desk* (28 May 2013), www.lcorchestra.co.uk/reviews/imagined-occasions-3/.

Toynbee, Jason. 'Musicians', in *Music and Copyright*, ed. Simon Frith and Lee Marshall (2nd edn; Edinburgh: Edinburgh University Press, 2004), 123–38.

Tschmuck, Peter. *The Economics of Music* (Newcastle upon Tyne: Agenda, 2017).

Turino, Thomas. *Music as Social Life: The Politics of Participation* (Chicago: University of Chicago Press, 2008).

Vaidyanathan, Siva. *Copyrights and Copywrongs: The Rise of Intellectual Property and How It Threatens Creativity* (New York: New York University Press, 2001).

Van Dijk, Jan. *The Network Society* (3rd edn; London: Sage, 2012).

Vincent, Carol, Nicola Rollock, Stephen Ball and David Gillborn. 'Raising Middle-Class Black Children: Parenting Priorities, Actions and Strategies', *Sociology*, 47 (2012), 427–42.

Wakeling, Paul and Mike Savage. 'Entry to Elite Positions and the Stratification of Higher Education in Britain', *The Sociological Review*, 63/2 (2015), 290–320.

Walkerdine, Valerie, Helen Lucey and June Melody. *Growing Up Girl: Psychosocial Explorations of Gender and Class* (New York: New York University Press, 2001).

Wallace, Helen. *Boosey & Hawkes: The Publishing Story* (London: Boosey & Hawkes, 2007).

Wang, Grace. 'Interlopers in the Realm of High Culture: "Music Moms" and the Performance of Asian and Asian American Identities', *American Quarterly*, 61/4 (2009), 881–903.

Warwick Commission. *Enriching Britain: Culture, Creativity and Growth* (University of Warwick, 2015), https://www2.warwick.ac.uk/research/warwickcommission/futureculture/finalreport/warwick_commission_report_2015.pdf.

Waterman, Fanny and Wendy Thompson. *Piano Competition: The Story of the Leeds* (London: Faber, 1990).

Weber, Robert P. *Basic Content Analysis* (Newbury Park: Sage, 1990).

Whitley, Kate and Christopher Stark. 'Orchestral Manoeuvres in the Car Park', *The Guardian* (20 June 2014), www.theguardian.com/music/musicblog/2014/jun/20/peckham-car-park-multi-story-orchestra-sibelius.

Wikström, Patrik. *The Music Industry: Music in the Cloud* (2nd edn, Cambridge: Polity, 2013).

Wilkinson, Ray. 'Changing Interactional Behaviour: Using Conversation Analysis Intervention Programmes for Aphasic Conversation', in *Applied Conversation Analysis: Changing Institutional Practices*, ed. Charles Antaki (Basingstoke: Palgrave Macmillan, 2011), 32–53.

Wilson, Alexandra. 'Killing Time: Contemporary Representations of Opera in British Culture', *Cambridge Opera Journal*, 19/3 (November 2007), 249–70.

Wing-Fai, Leung, Rosalind Gill and Keith Randle. 'Getting In, Getting On, Getting Out? Women as Career Scramblers in the UK Film and Television Industries', in *Gender and Creative Labour*, ed. Bridget Conor, Rosalind Gill and Stephanie Taylor (Chichester: Wiley, 2015), 50–65.

Witt, Stephen. *How Music Got Free: What Happens When an Entire Generation Commits the Same Crime?* (London: Bodley Head, 2015).

Witts, Dick. 'Stockhausen Meets the Technocrats', *The Wire*, 141 (November 1995), 33–5.

Wolff, Konrad (ed.). *Robert Schumann on Music and Musicians*, trans. Paul Rosenfeld (New York: Pantheon, 1946).

Women in Music. *BBC Proms Survey* (2016). www.womeninmusic.org.uk/proms-survey.htm.

Wreyford, Natalie. *The Gendered Contexts of Screenwriting Work: Socialized Recruitment and Judgments of Taste and Talent in the UK Film Industry* (Ph.D. diss.; King's College London, 2015).

Wright, David. *The Associated Board of the Royal Schools of Music: A Social and Cultural History* (Woodbridge: Boydell & Brewer, 2013).

Wright, Katy. 'Teachers Blame EBacc for Decline in Music Student Numbers', *Music Teacher* (10 March 2017), www.rhinegold.co.uk/music_teacher/teachers-blame-ebacc-decline-music-student-numbers.

Yang, Mina. 'East Meets West in the Concert Hall: Asians and Classical Music in the Century of Imperialism, Post-colonialism, and Multiculturalism', *Asian Music*, 38/1 (2007), 1–30.

Yoshihara, Mari. *Musicians from a Different Shore: Asians and Asian Americans in Classical Music* (Philadelphia: Temple University Press, 2008).

Zacher, Hannes, Felicia Chan, Arnold B. Bakker and Evangelia Demerouti. 'Selection, Optimization, and Compensation Strategies: Interactive Effects on Daily Work Engagement', *Journal of Vocational Behavior*, 87 (April 2015), 101–7.

Index